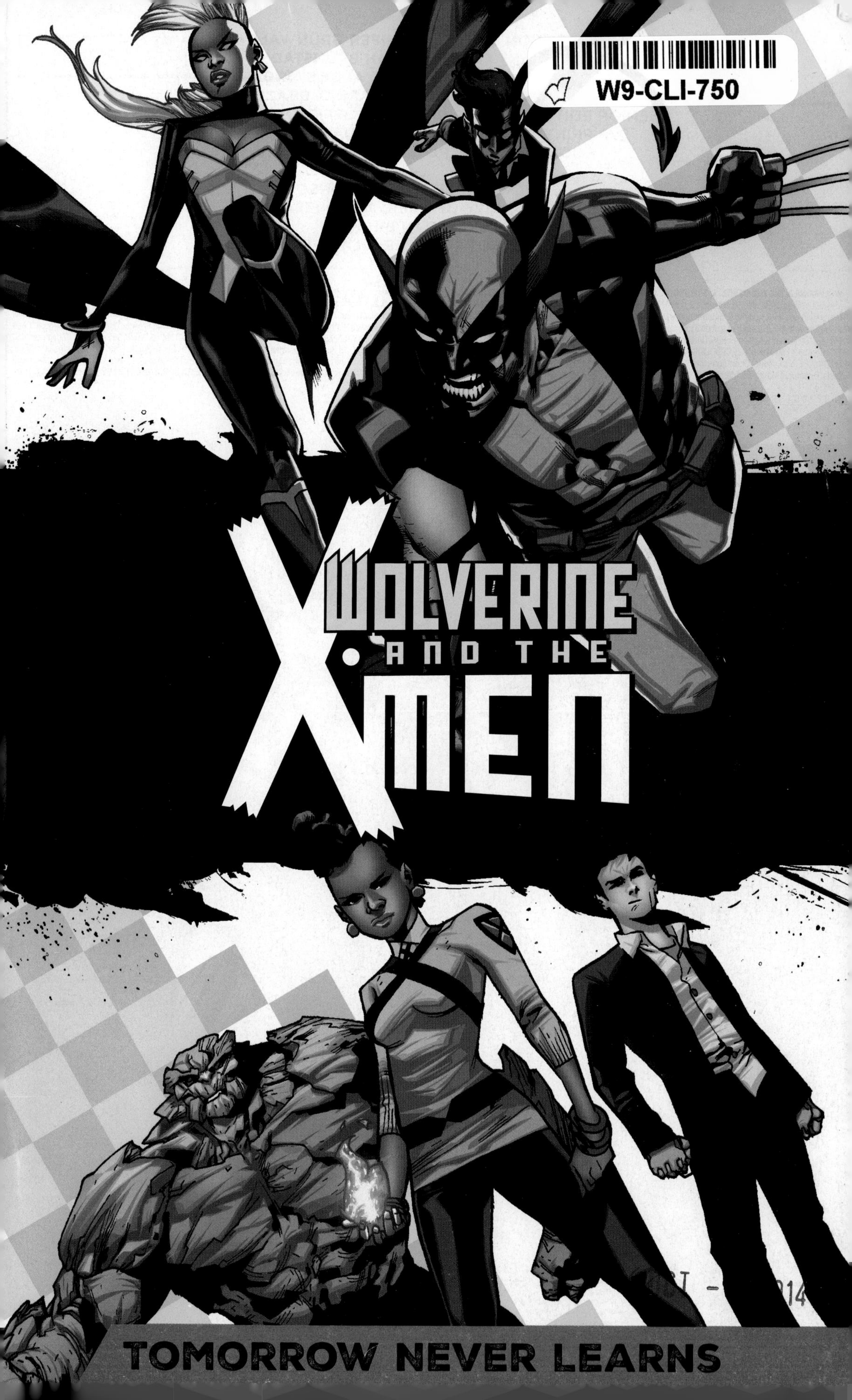
WOLVERINE
AND THE
X-MEN
TOMORROW NEVER LEARNS

COLLECTION EDITOR: **JENNIFER GRÜNWALD**
ASSISTANT EDITOR: **SARAH BRUNSTAD**
ASSOCIATE MANAGING EDITOR: **ALEX STARBUCK**
EDITOR, SPECIAL PROJECTS: **MARK D. BEAZLEY**
SENIOR EDITOR, SPECIAL PROJECTS: **JEFF YOUNGQUIST**
SVP PRINT, SALES & MARKETING: **DAVID GABRIEL**
BOOK DESIGNER: **RODOLFO MURAGUCHI**

EDITOR IN CHIEF: **AXEL ALONSO**
CHIEF CREATIVE OFFICER: **JOE QUESADA**
PUBLISHER: **DAN BUCKLEY**
EXECUTIVE PRODUCER: **ALAN FINE**

WOLVERINE & THE X-MEN VOL. 1: TOMORROW NEVER LEARNS. Contains material originally published in magazine form as WOLVERINE & THE X-MEN #1-6. First printing 2014. ISBN# 978-0-7851-8992-3. Published by MARVEL WORLDWIDE, INC., a subsidiary of MARVEL ENTERTAINMENT, LLC. OFFICE OF PUBLICATION: 135 West 50th Street, New York, NY 10020. **Printed in the U.S.A.** ALAN FINE, EVP - Office of the President, Marvel Worldwide, Inc. and EVP & CMO Marvel Characters B.V.; DAN BUCKLEY, Publisher & President - Print, Animation & Digital Divisions; JOE QUESADA, Chief Creative Officer; TOM BREVOORT, SVP of Publishing; DAVID BOGART, SVP of Operations & Procurement, Publishing; C.B. CEBULSKI, SVP of Creator & Content Development; DAVID GABRIEL, SVP Print, Sales & Marketing; JIM O'KEEFE, VP of Operations & Logistics; DAN CARR, Executive Director of Publishing Technology; SUSAN CRESPI, Editorial Operations Manager; ALEX MORALES, Publishing Operations Manager; STAN LEE, Chairman Emeritus. For information regarding advertising in Marvel Comics or on Marvel.com, please contact Niza Disla, Director of Marvel Partnerships, at ndisla@marvel.com. For Marvel subscription inquiries, please call 800-217-9158. **Manufactured between 9/5/2014 and 10/13/2014 by R.R. DONNELLEY, INC., SALEM, VA, USA.**

10 9 8 7 6 5 4 3 2 1

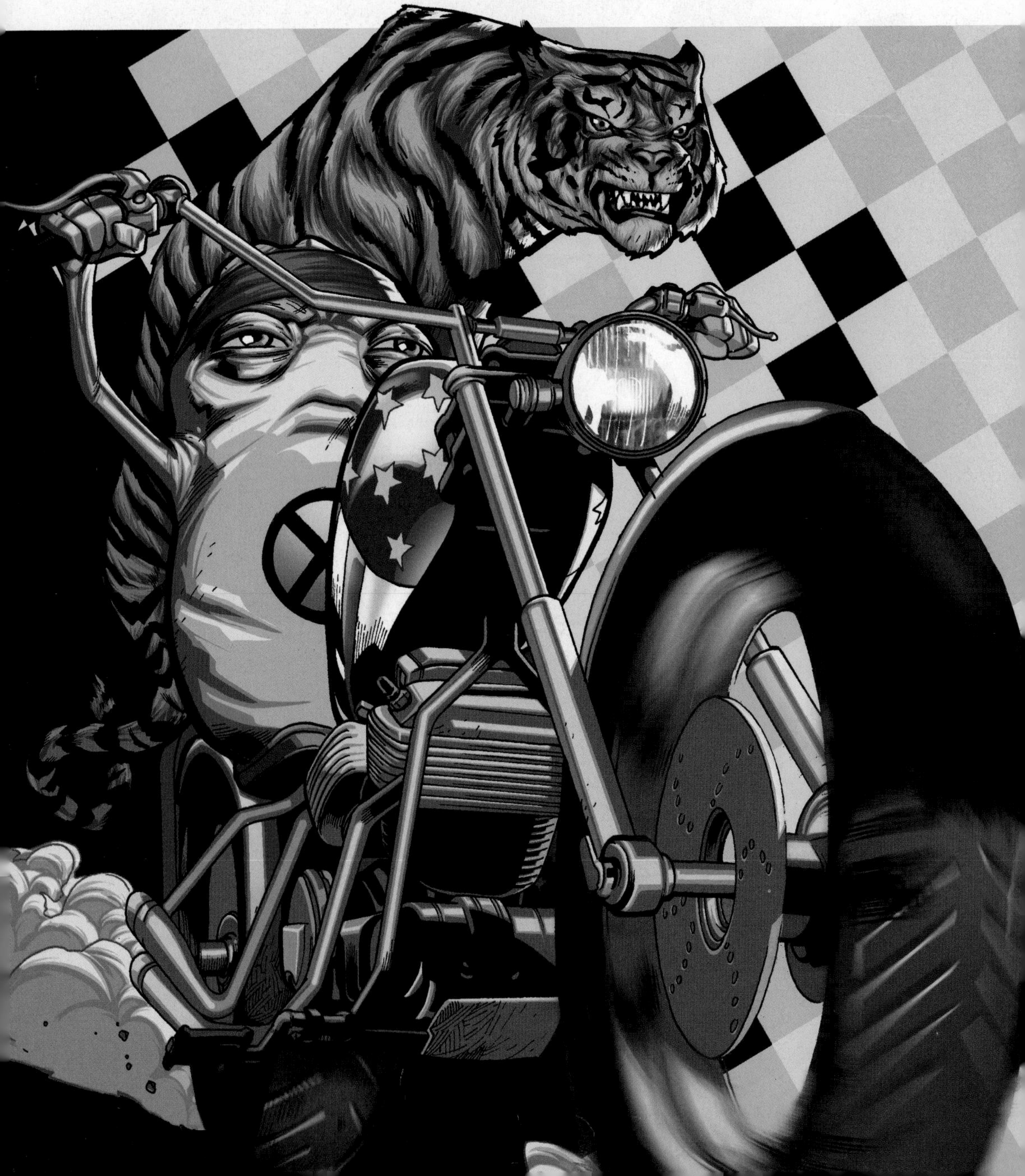

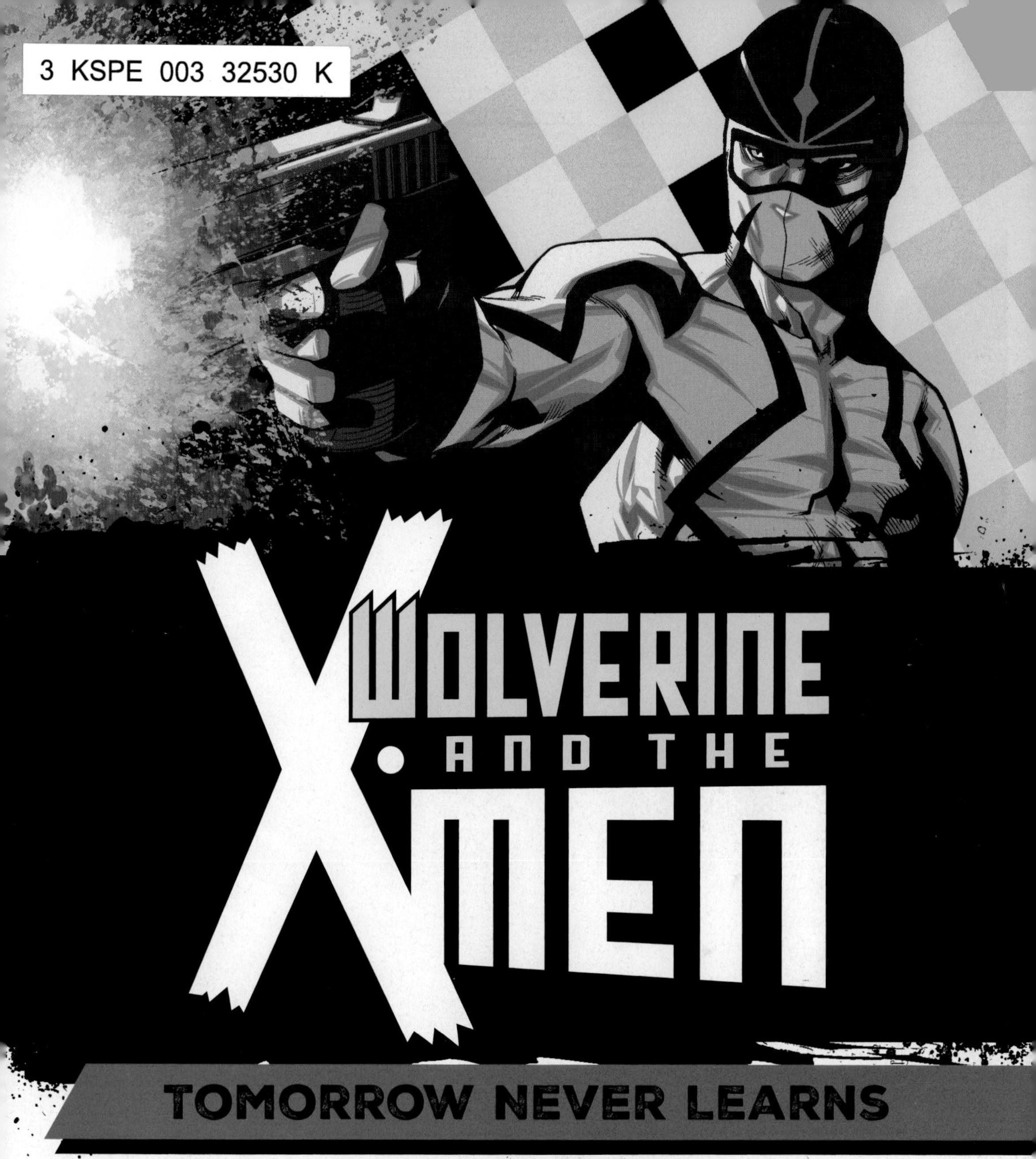

WOLVERINE AND THE X-MEN

TOMORROW NEVER LEARNS

writer:
JASON LATOUR

artist:
MAHMUD ASRAR with
MATTEO LOLLI (#5),
PEPE LARRAZ (#6),
DAVID MESSINA (#6),
MASSIMILIANO VELTRI (#6)
& **MARC DEERING** (#6)

color artist:
ISRAEL SILVA

letterer:
VC'S CLAYTON COWLES

cover:
MAHMUD ASRAR & MARTE GRACIA

assistant editor: **FRANKIE JOHNSON**
editors: **TOM BRENNAN, JEANINE SCHAEFER & KATIE KUBERT**
group editors: **MIKE MARTS & NICK LOWE**

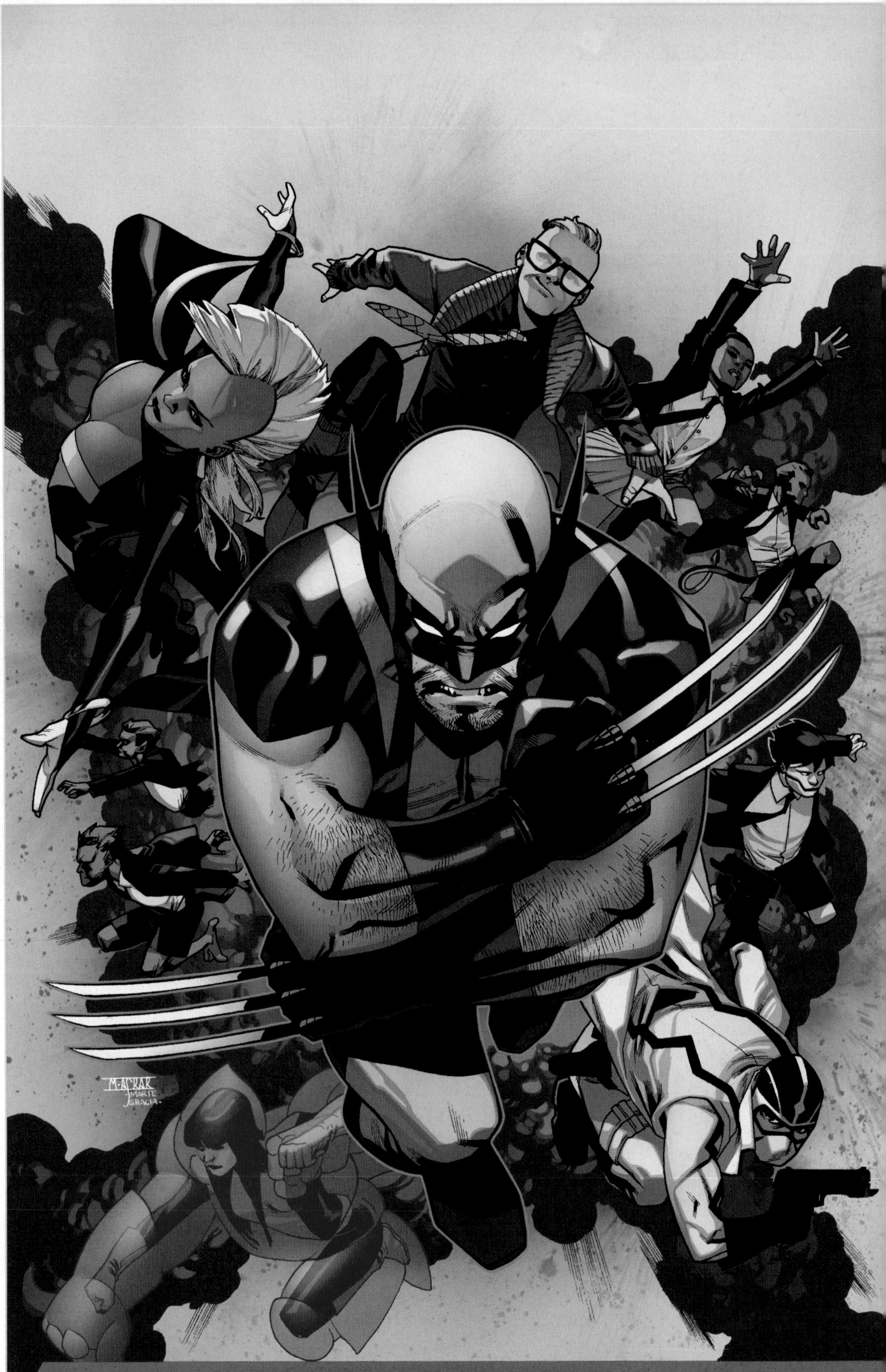

1

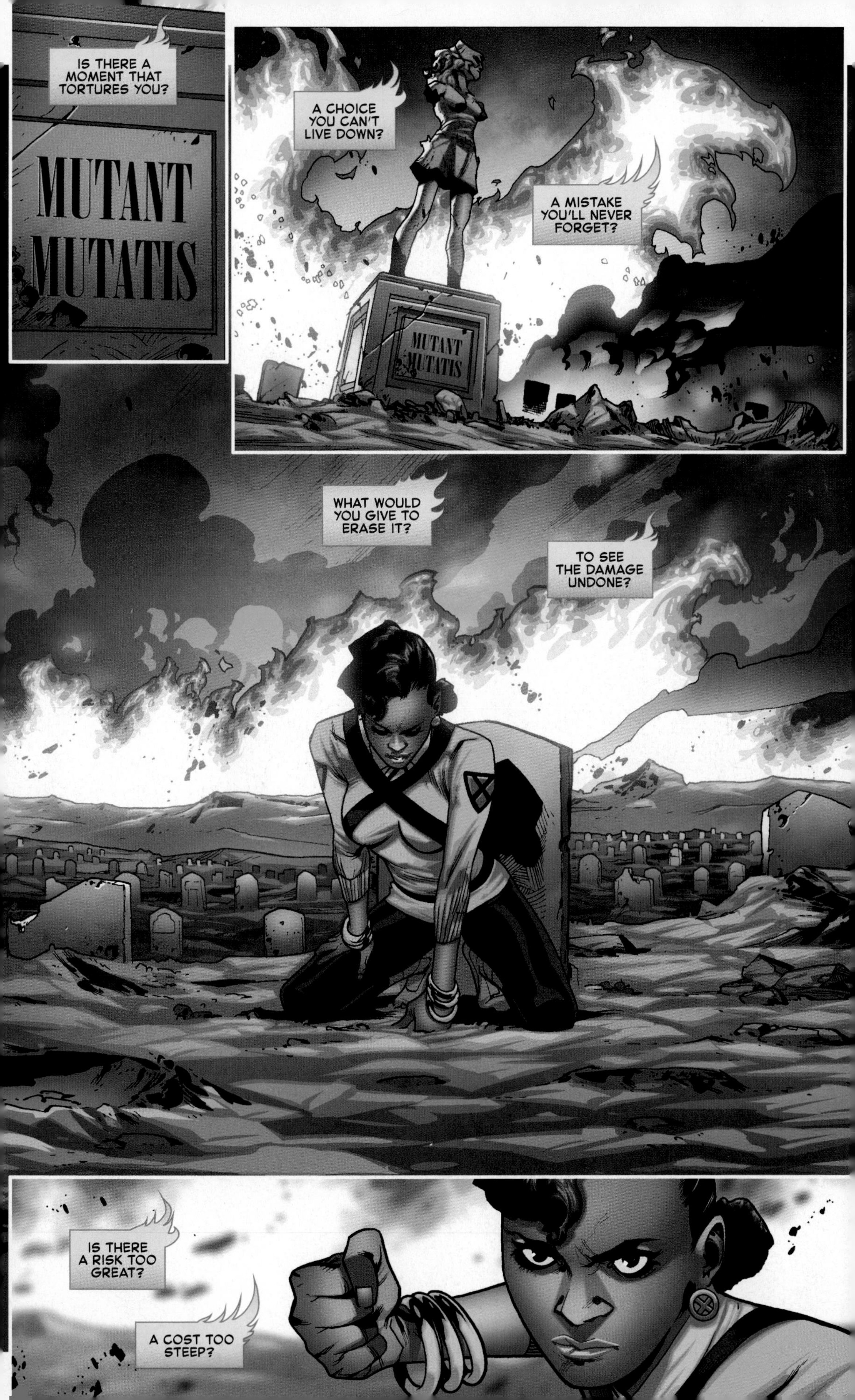
IS THERE A MOMENT THAT TORTURES YOU?
MUTANT MUTATIS
A CHOICE YOU CAN'T LIVE DOWN?
A MISTAKE YOU'LL NEVER FORGET?
MUTANT MUTATIS
WHAT WOULD YOU GIVE TO ERASE IT?
TO SEE THE DAMAGE UNDONE?
IS THERE A RISK TOO GREAT?
A COST TOO STEEP?

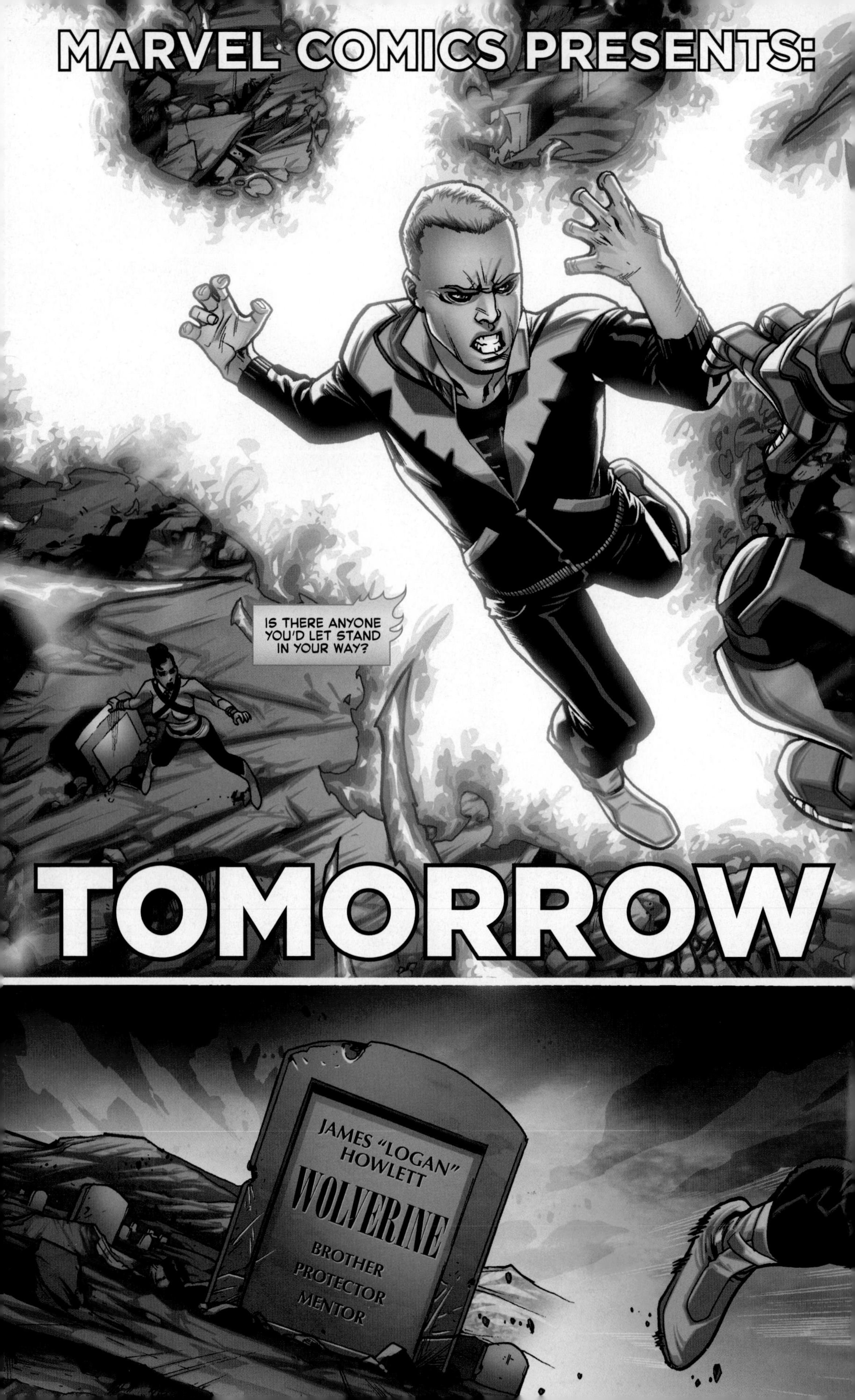
MARVEL COMICS PRESENTS:
IS THERE ANYONE YOU'D LET STAND IN YOUR WAY?
TOMORROW
JAMES "LOGAN" HOWLETT
WOLVERINE
BROTHER
PROTECTOR
MENTOR

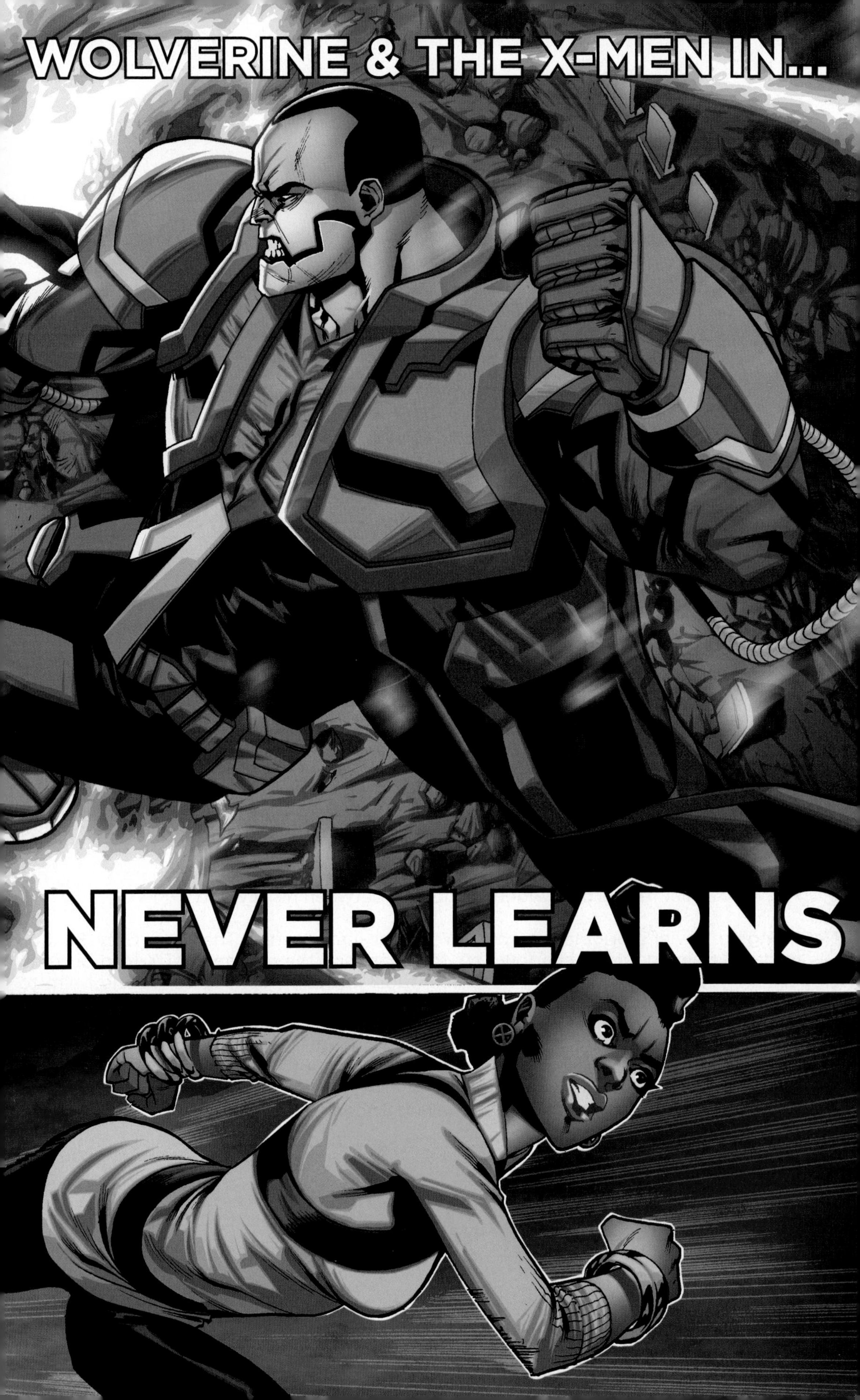
WOLVERINE & THE X-MEN IN...
NEVER LEARNS

"NO MORE PHOENIX..."

With those words the powerful cosmic entity known as The Phoenix was seemingly erased from existence, and war between the X-Men and Avengers ended.

But the conflict was not without cost. Claiming the life of Professor Charles Xavier, the conflict has further widened the gap between his divided X-Men.

Returning to Xavier's original campus, Wolverine has opened The Jean Grey School. His students train under the shadow of X-Men past and the guidance of X-Men present. But school years end and Wolverine's recent loss of his healing factor has led him to contemplate the future of his school...and who will protect the legacy after he dies.

Among the students in Wolverine's charge was Quentin Quire, a troubled young man who gave Wolverine and his staff no end of challenges. But Quentin recently made some changes in his life and graduated from school. He is also destined to someday wield a mysteriously renewed Phoenix Force

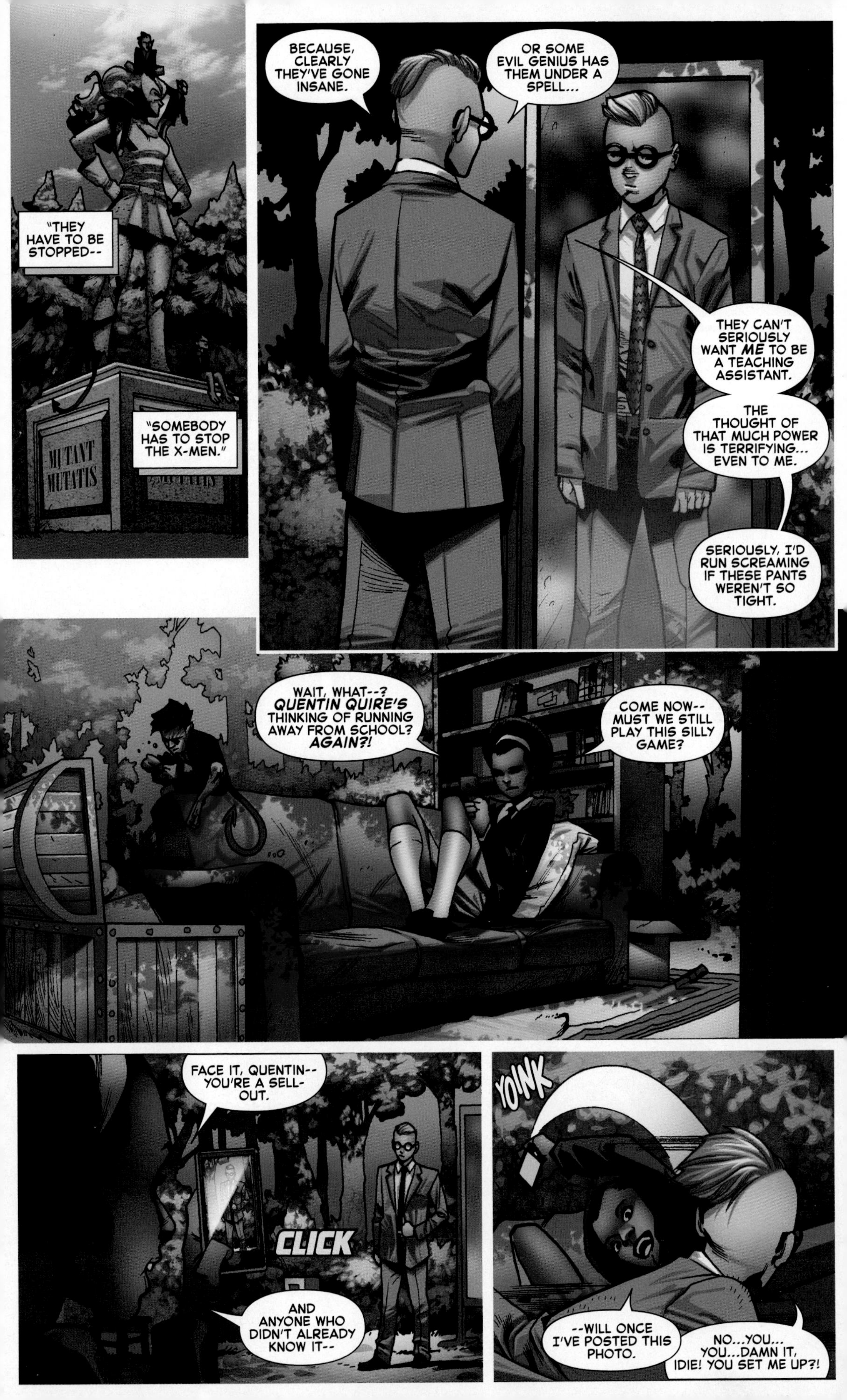
"THEY HAVE TO BE STOPPED--
"SOMEBODY HAS TO STOP THE X-MEN."
MUTANT MUTATIS
BECAUSE, CLEARLY THEY'VE GONE INSANE.
OR SOME EVIL GENIUS HAS THEM UNDER A SPELL...
THEY CAN'T SERIOUSLY WANT *ME* TO BE A TEACHING ASSISTANT.
THE THOUGHT OF THAT MUCH POWER IS TERRIFYING... EVEN TO ME.
SERIOUSLY, I'D RUN SCREAMING IF THESE PANTS WEREN'T SO TIGHT.
WAIT, WHAT--? *QUENTIN QUIRE'S* THINKING OF RUNNING AWAY FROM SCHOOL? *AGAIN?!*
COME NOW-- MUST WE STILL PLAY THIS SILLY GAME?
FACE IT, QUENTIN-- YOU'RE A SELL-OUT.
CLICK
AND ANYONE WHO DIDN'T ALREADY KNOW IT--
YOINK
--WILL ONCE I'VE POSTED THIS PHOTO.
NO...YOU... YOU...DAMN IT, IDIE! YOU SET ME UP?!

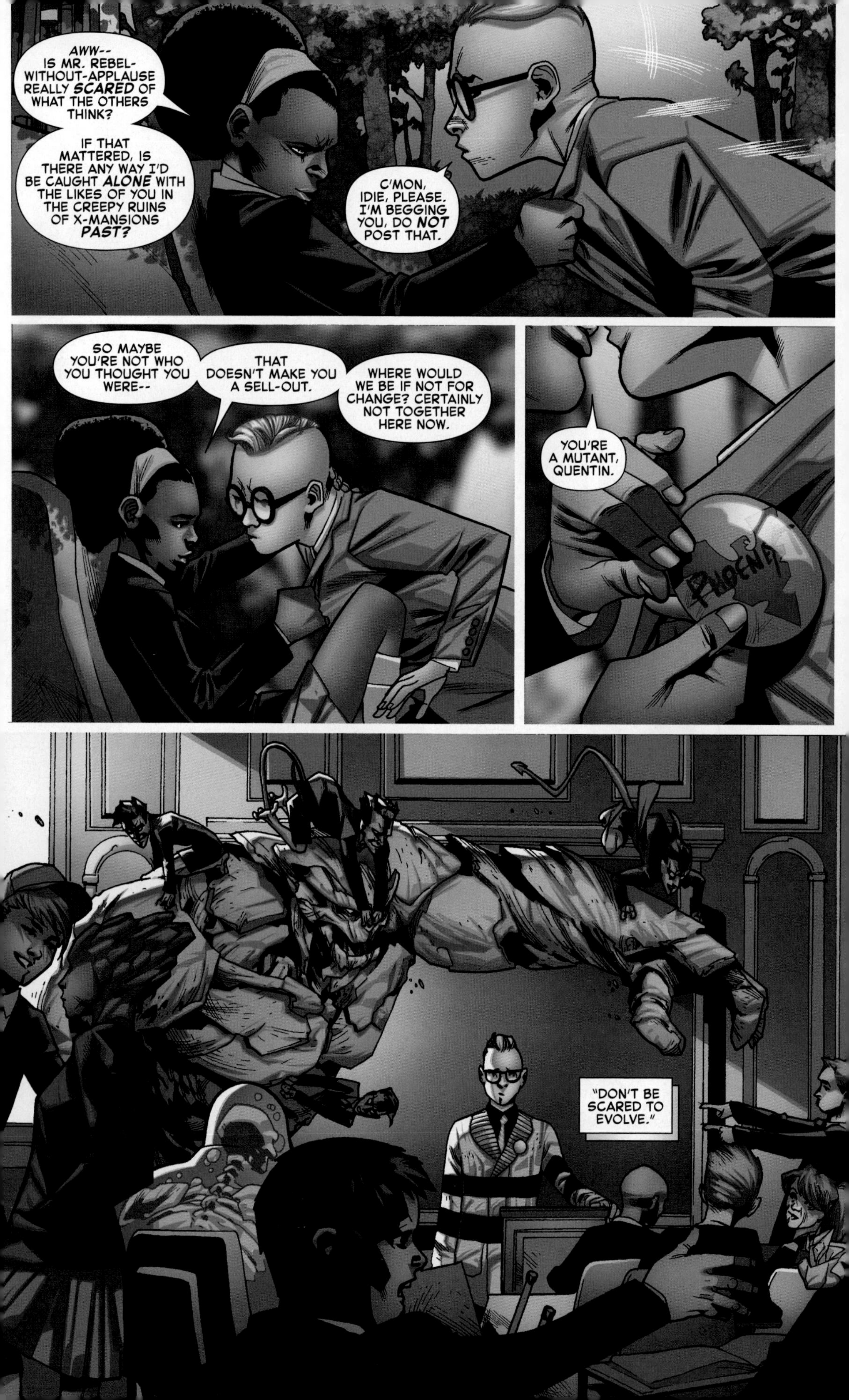
AWW-- IS MR. REBEL-WITHOUT-APPLAUSE REALLY SCARED OF WHAT THE OTHERS THINK?
IF THAT MATTERED, IS THERE ANY WAY I'D BE CAUGHT ALONE WITH THE LIKES OF YOU IN THE CREEPY RUINS OF X-MANSIONS PAST?
C'MON, IDIE, PLEASE. I'M BEGGING YOU, DO NOT POST THAT.
SO MAYBE YOU'RE NOT WHO YOU THOUGHT YOU WERE--
THAT DOESN'T MAKE YOU A SELL-OUT.
WHERE WOULD WE BE IF NOT FOR CHANGE? CERTAINLY NOT TOGETHER HERE NOW.
YOU'RE A MUTANT, QUENTIN.
"DON'T BE SCARED TO EVOLVE."

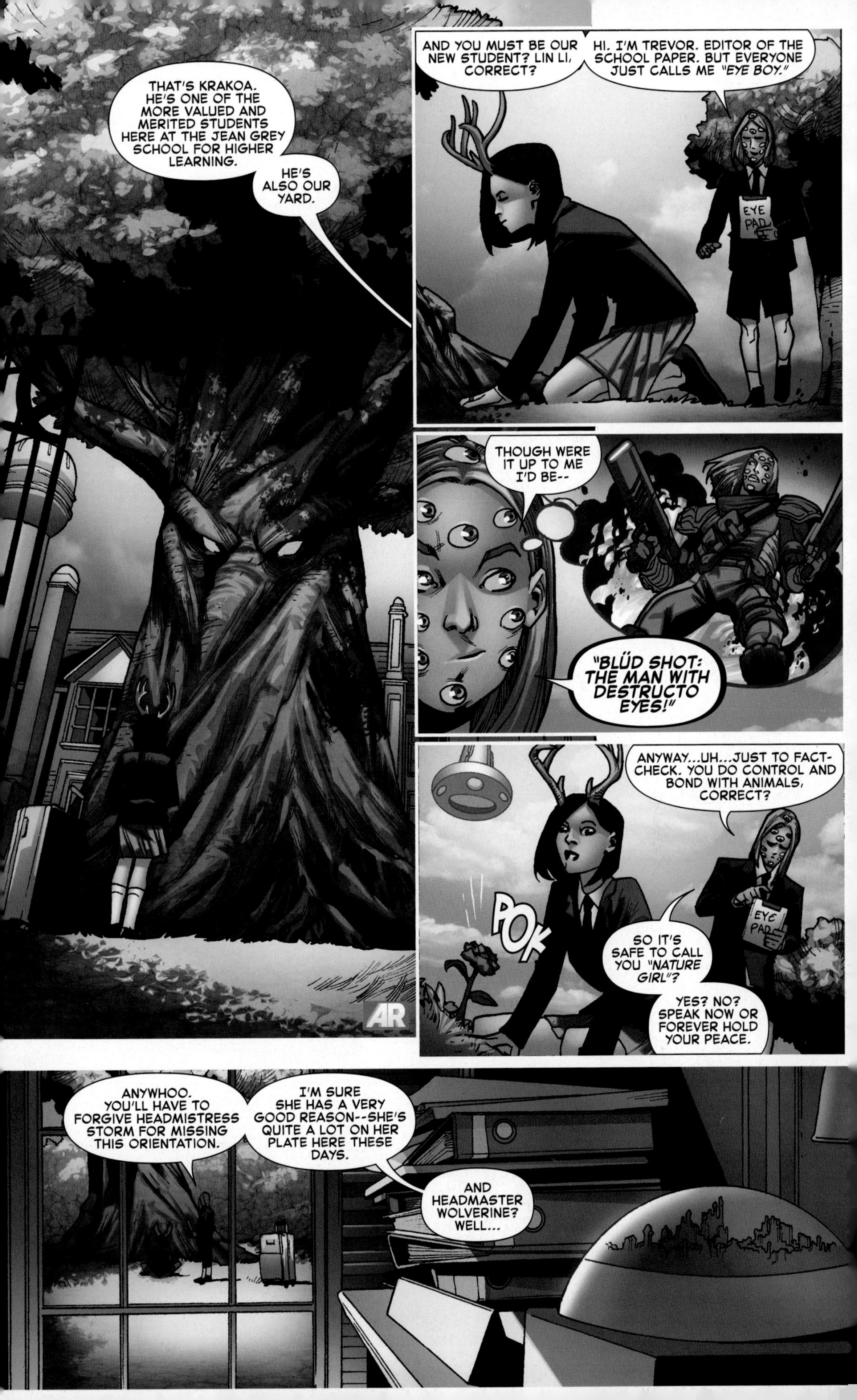
THAT'S KRAKOA. HE'S ONE OF THE MORE VALUED AND MERITED STUDENTS HERE AT THE JEAN GREY SCHOOL FOR HIGHER LEARNING.
HE'S ALSO OUR YARD.
AND YOU MUST BE OUR NEW STUDENT? LIN LI, CORRECT?
HI. I'M TREVOR. EDITOR OF THE SCHOOL PAPER. BUT EVERYONE JUST CALLS ME "EYE BOY."
EYE PAD
THOUGH WERE IT UP TO ME I'D BE--
"BLÜD SHOT: THE MAN WITH DESTRUCTO EYES!"
ANYWAY...UH...JUST TO FACT-CHECK. YOU DO CONTROL AND BOND WITH ANIMALS, CORRECT?
POK
SO IT'S SAFE TO CALL YOU "NATURE GIRL"?
YES? NO? SPEAK NOW OR FOREVER HOLD YOUR PEACE.
EYE PAD
AR
ANYWHOO. YOU'LL HAVE TO FORGIVE HEADMISTRESS STORM FOR MISSING THIS ORIENTATION.
I'M SURE SHE HAS A VERY GOOD REASON--SHE'S QUITE A LOT ON HER PLATE HERE THESE DAYS.
AND HEADMASTER WOLVERINE? WELL...

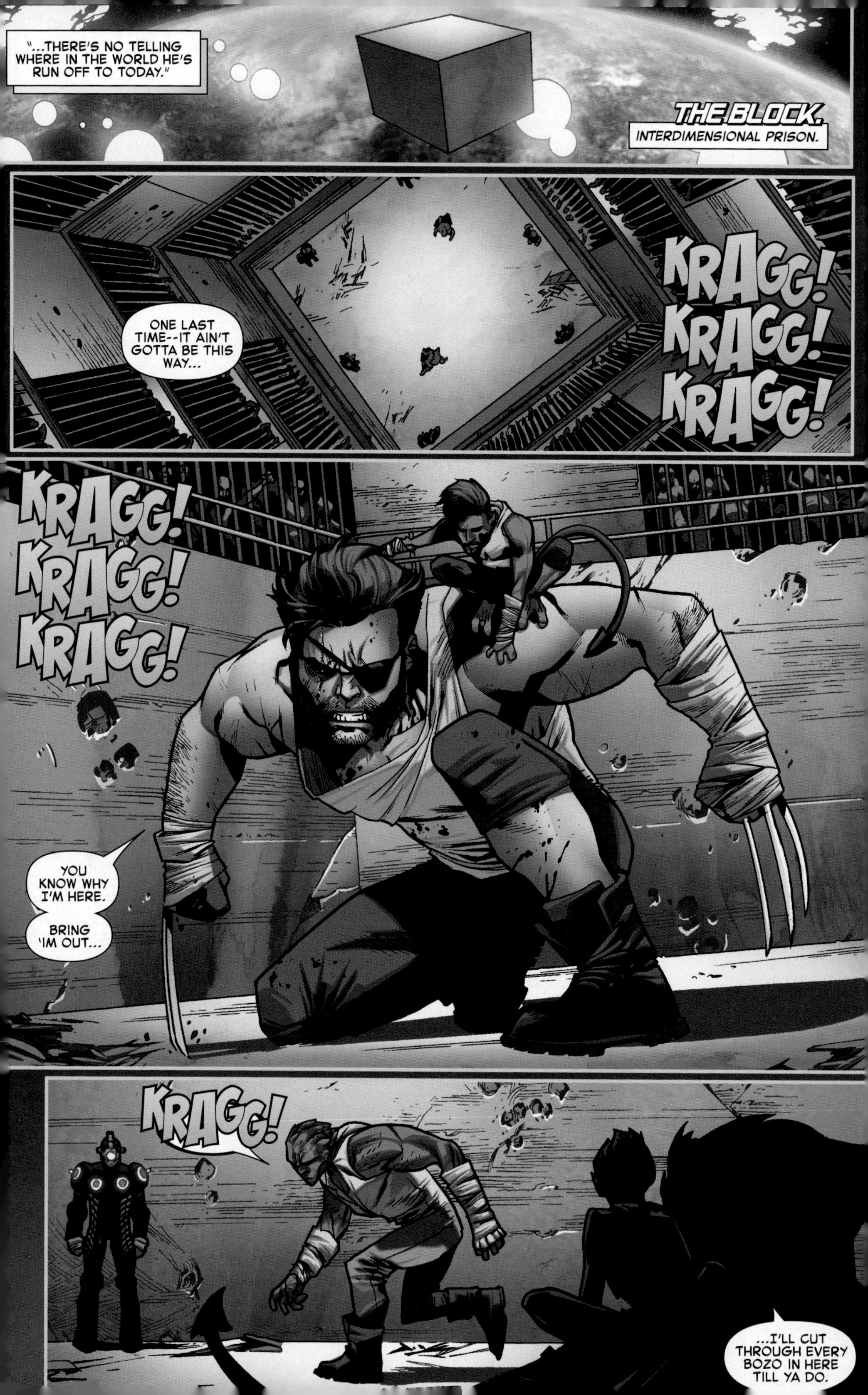
"...THERE'S NO TELLING WHERE IN THE WORLD HE'S RUN OFF TO TODAY."
THE BLOCK.
INTERDIMENSIONAL PRISON.
ONE LAST TIME--IT AIN'T GOTTA BE THIS WAY...
KRAGG! KRAGG! KRAGG!
KRAGG! KRAGG! KRAGG!
YOU KNOW WHY I'M HERE.
BRING 'IM OUT...
KRAGG!
...I'LL CUT THROUGH EVERY BOZO IN HERE TILL YA DO.

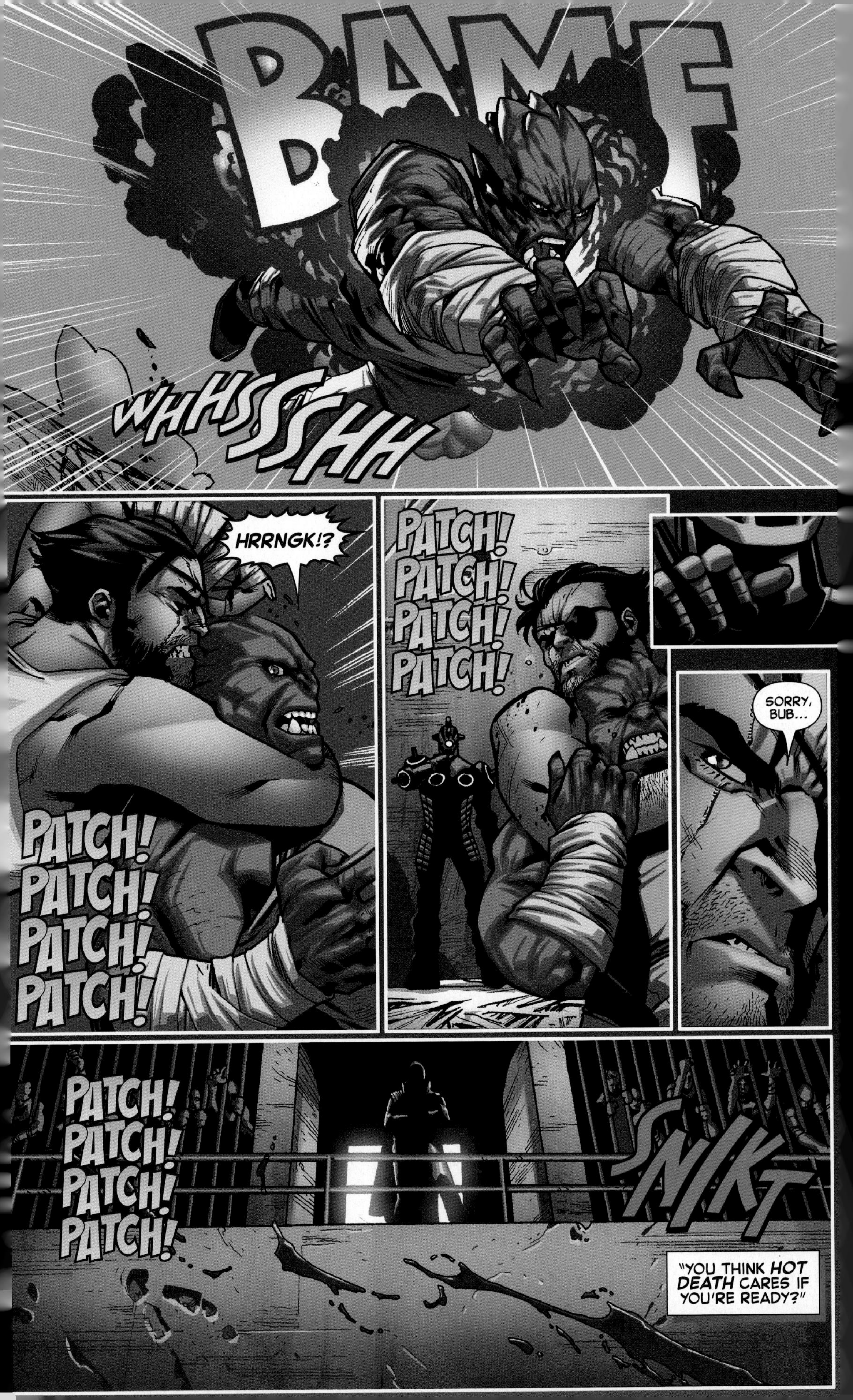
BAMF
WHHSSSHH
HRRNGK!?
PATCH! PATCH! PATCH! PATCH!
PATCH! PATCH! PATCH! PATCH!
SORRY, BUB...
PATCH! PATCH! PATCH! PATCH!
SNIKT
"YOU THINK HOT DEATH CARES IF YOU'RE READY?"

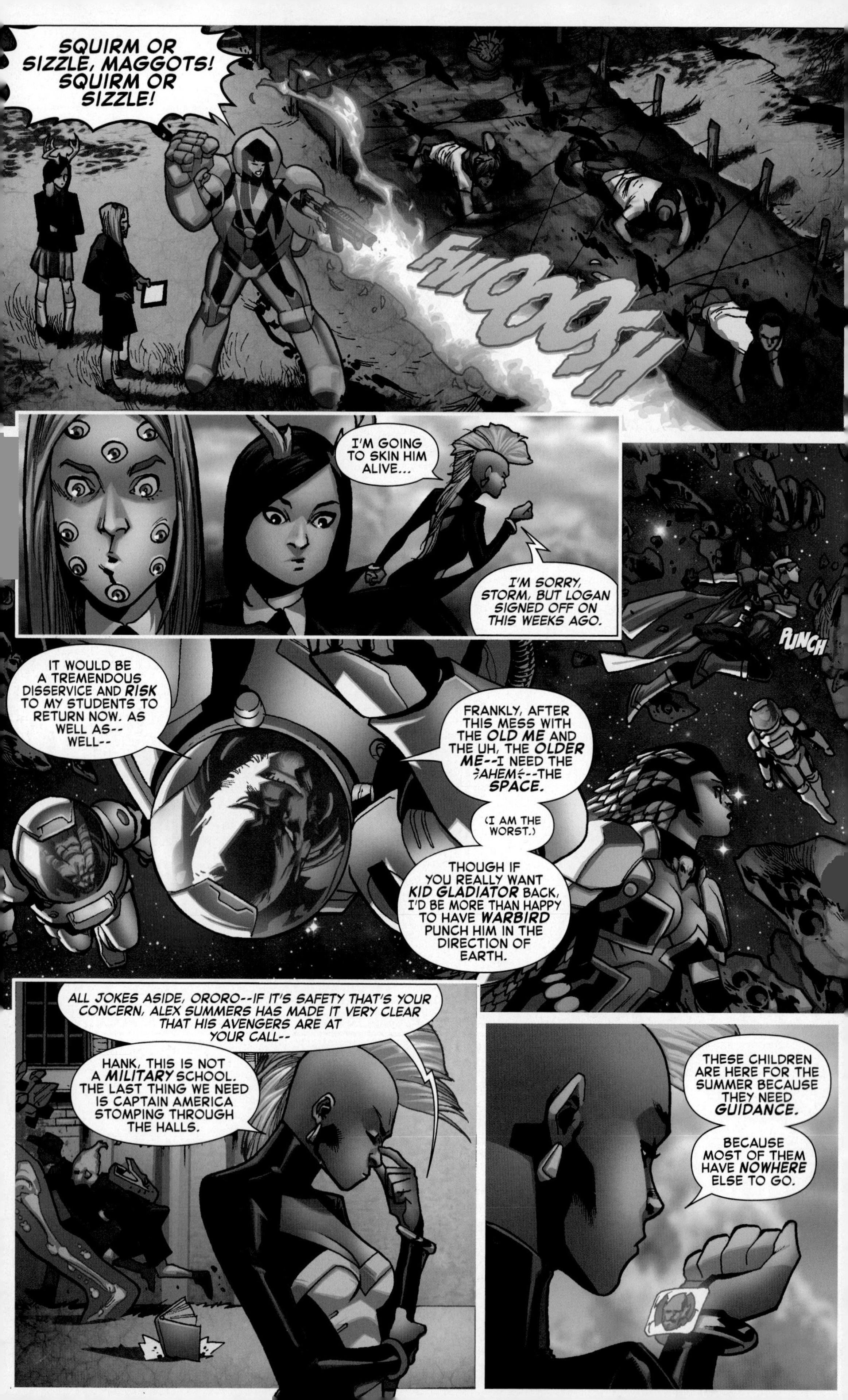

SQUIRM OR SIZZLE, MAGGOTS! SQUIRM OR SIZZLE!
FWOOOSH
I'M GOING TO SKIN HIM ALIVE...
I'M SORRY, STORM, BUT LOGAN SIGNED OFF ON THIS WEEKS AGO.
PUNCH
IT WOULD BE A TREMENDOUS DISSERVICE AND RISK TO MY STUDENTS TO RETURN NOW. AS WELL AS-- WELL--
FRANKLY, AFTER THIS MESS WITH THE OLD ME AND THE UH, THE OLDER ME--I NEED THE *AHEM*--THE SPACE.
(I AM THE WORST.)
THOUGH IF YOU REALLY WANT KID GLADIATOR BACK, I'D BE MORE THAN HAPPY TO HAVE WARBIRD PUNCH HIM IN THE DIRECTION OF EARTH.
ALL JOKES ASIDE, ORORO--IF IT'S SAFETY THAT'S YOUR CONCERN, ALEX SUMMERS HAS MADE IT VERY CLEAR THAT HIS AVENGERS ARE AT YOUR CALL--
HANK, THIS IS NOT A MILITARY SCHOOL. THE LAST THING WE NEED IS CAPTAIN AMERICA STOMPING THROUGH THE HALLS.
THESE CHILDREN ARE HERE FOR THE SUMMER BECAUSE THEY NEED GUIDANCE.
BECAUSE MOST OF THEM HAVE NOWHERE ELSE TO GO.

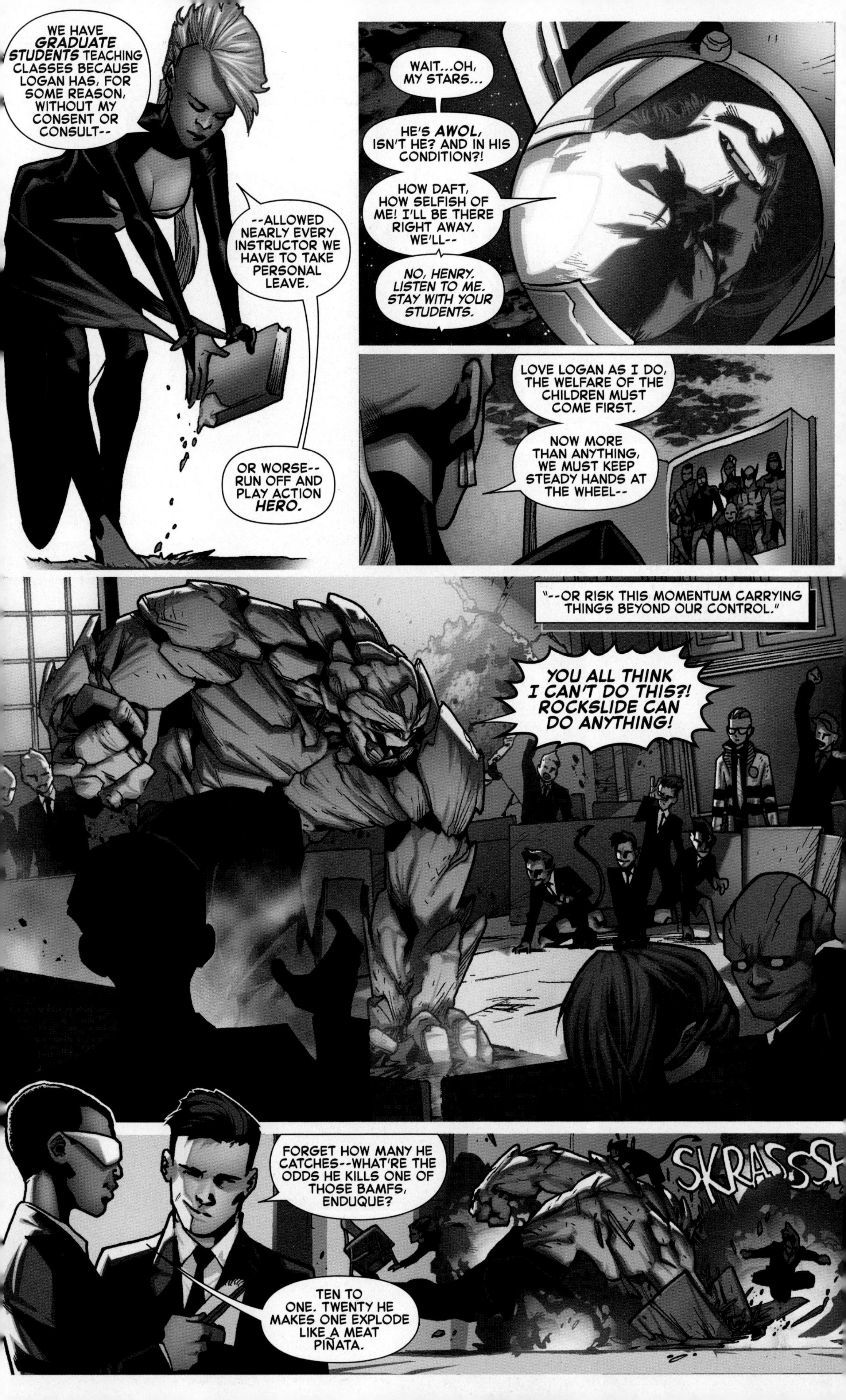
WE HAVE GRADUATE STUDENTS TEACHING CLASSES BECAUSE LOGAN HAS, FOR SOME REASON, WITHOUT MY CONSENT OR CONSULT--
--ALLOWED NEARLY EVERY INSTRUCTOR WE HAVE TO TAKE PERSONAL LEAVE.
OR WORSE--RUN OFF AND PLAY ACTION HERO.
WAIT...OH, MY STARS...
HE'S AWOL, ISN'T HE? AND IN HIS CONDITION?!
HOW DAFT, HOW SELFISH OF ME! I'LL BE THERE RIGHT AWAY. WE'LL--
NO, HENRY. LISTEN TO ME. STAY WITH YOUR STUDENTS.
LOVE LOGAN AS I DO, THE WELFARE OF THE CHILDREN MUST COME FIRST.
NOW MORE THAN ANYTHING, WE MUST KEEP STEADY HANDS AT THE WHEEL--
"--OR RISK THIS MOMENTUM CARRYING THINGS BEYOND OUR CONTROL."
YOU ALL THINK I CAN'T DO THIS?! ROCKSLIDE CAN DO ANYTHING!
FORGET HOW MANY HE CATCHES--WHAT'RE THE ODDS HE KILLS ONE OF THOSE BAMFS, ENDUQUE?
SKRASSSH
TEN TO ONE. TWENTY HE MAKES ONE EXPLODE LIKE A MEAT PIÑATA.

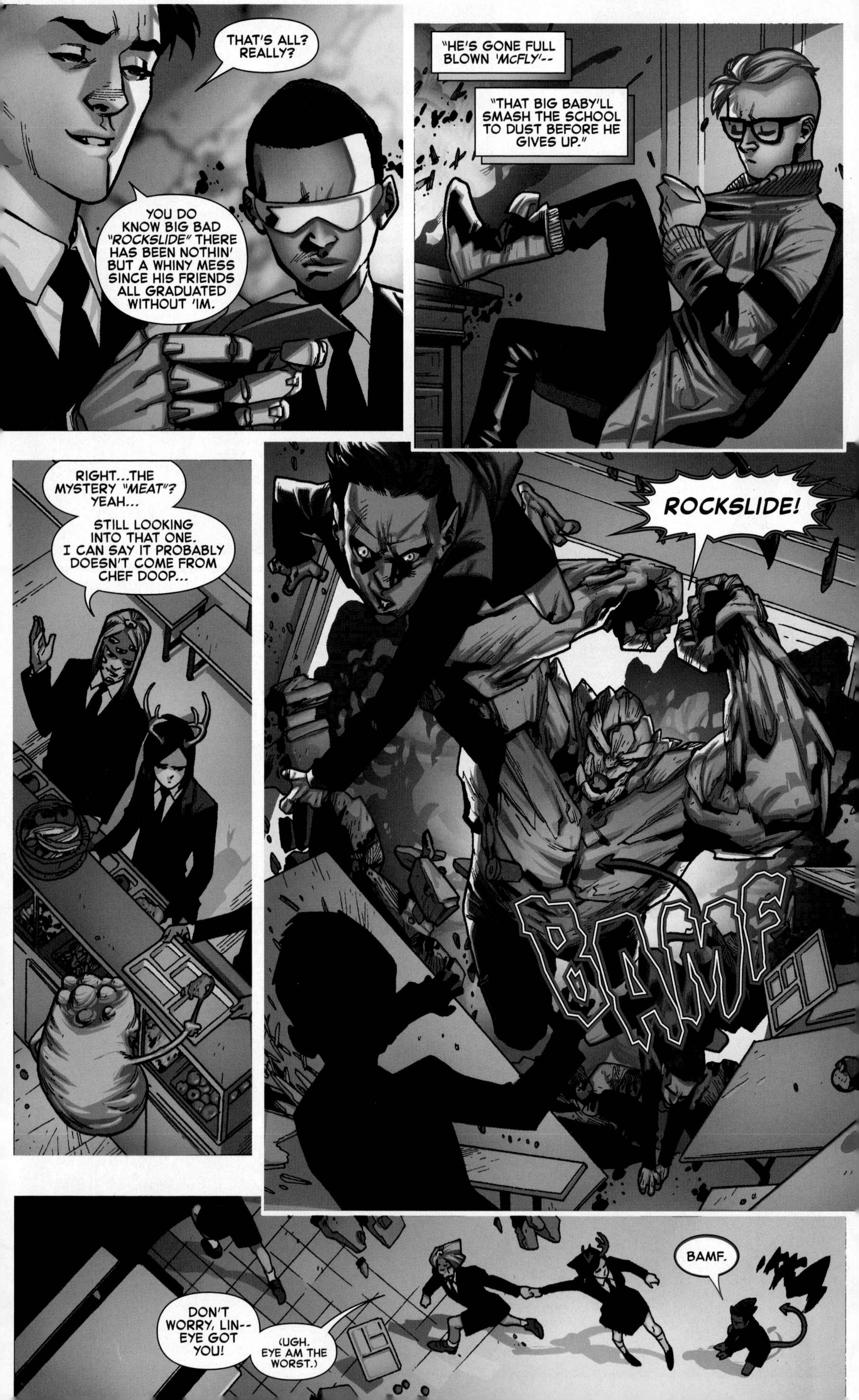
THAT'S ALL? REALLY?
YOU DO KNOW BIG BAD "ROCKSLIDE" THERE HAS BEEN NOTHIN' BUT A WHINY MESS SINCE HIS FRIENDS ALL GRADUATED WITHOUT 'IM.
"HE'S GONE FULL BLOWN 'MCFLY'--
"THAT BIG BABY'LL SMASH THE SCHOOL TO DUST BEFORE HE GIVES UP."
RIGHT...THE MYSTERY "MEAT"? YEAH...
STILL LOOKING INTO THAT ONE. I CAN SAY IT PROBABLY DOESN'T COME FROM CHEF DOOP...
ROCKSLIDE!
BAMF
DON'T WORRY, LIN-- EYE GOT YOU!
(UGH. EYE AM THE WORST.)
BAMF.

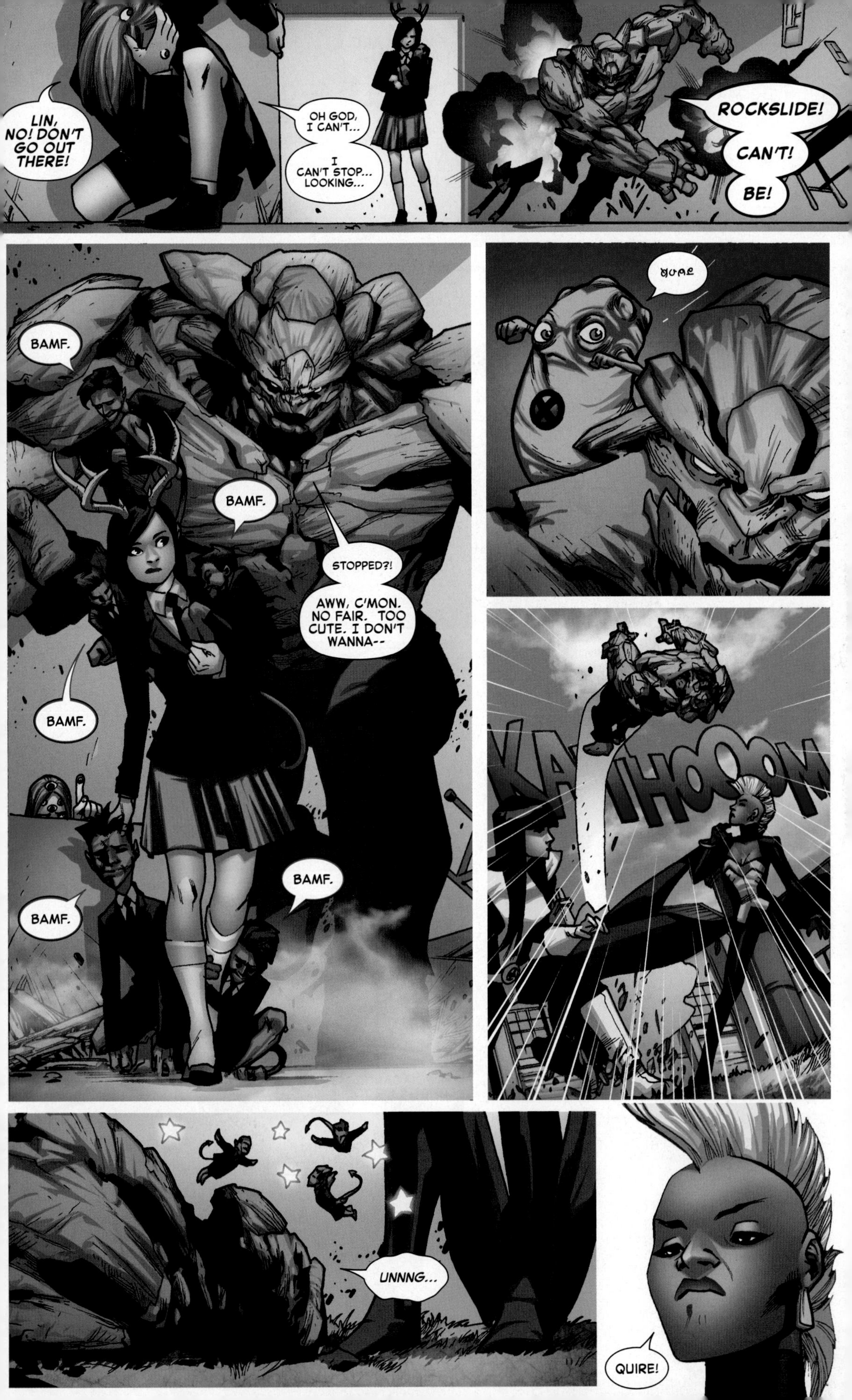
LIN, NO! DON'T GO OUT THERE!
OH GOD, I CAN'T...
I CAN'T STOP... LOOKING...
ROCKSLIDE!
CAN'T!
BE!
BAMF.
BAMF.
STOPPED?!
AWW, C'MON. NO FAIR. TOO CUTE. I DON'T WANNA--
BAMF.
BAMF.
BAMF.
KATHOOOM
UNNNG...
QUIRE!

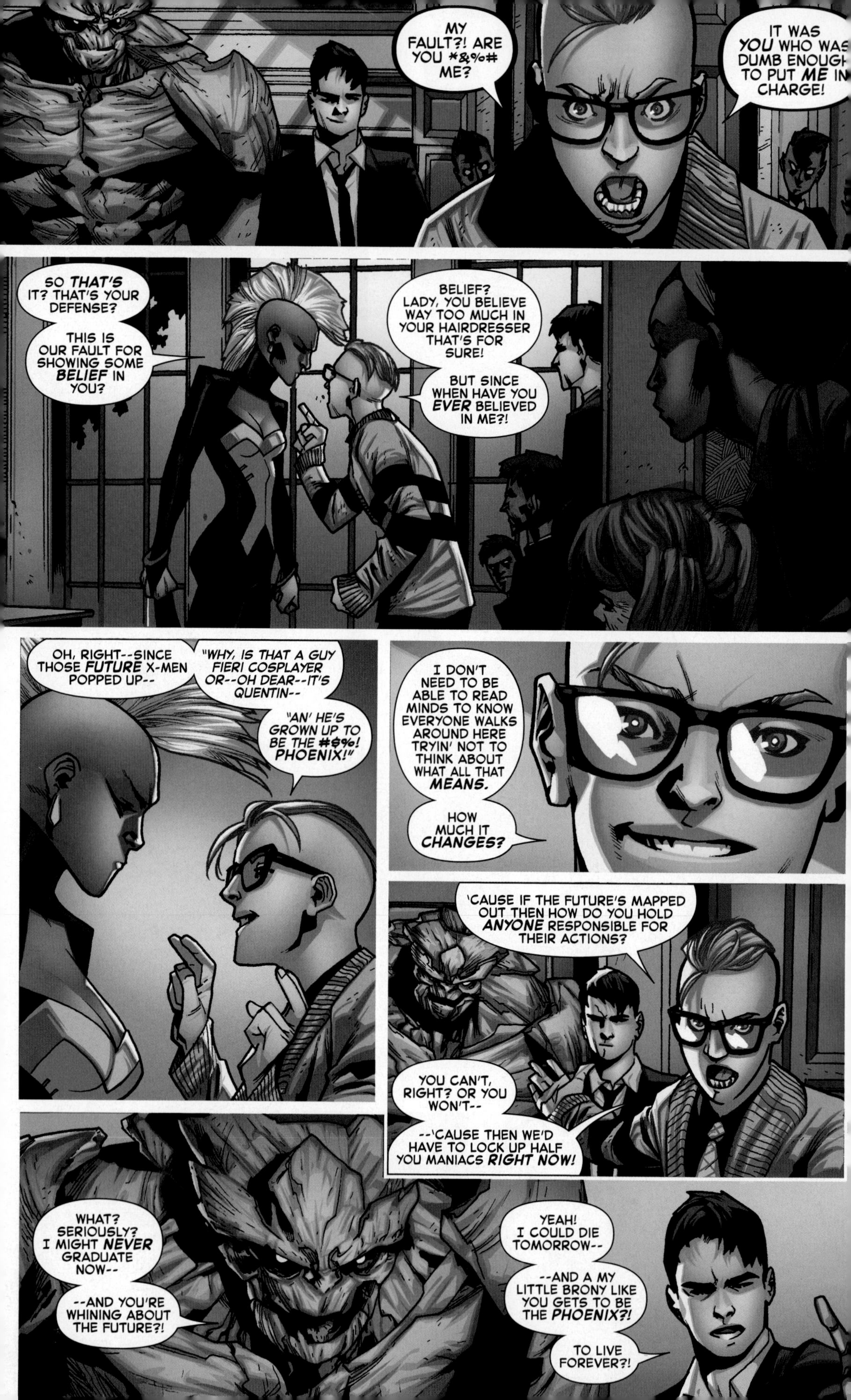
MY FAULT?! ARE YOU *&%# ME?
IT WAS YOU WHO WAS DUMB ENOUGH TO PUT ME IN CHARGE!
SO THAT'S IT? THAT'S YOUR DEFENSE?
THIS IS OUR FAULT FOR SHOWING SOME BELIEF IN YOU?
BELIEF? LADY, YOU BELIEVE WAY TOO MUCH IN YOUR HAIRDRESSER THAT'S FOR SURE!
BUT SINCE WHEN HAVE YOU EVER BELIEVED IN ME?!
OH, RIGHT--SINCE THOSE FUTURE X-MEN POPPED UP--
"WHY, IS THAT A GUY FIERI COSPLAYER OR--OH DEAR--IT'S QUENTIN--
"AN' HE'S GROWN UP TO BE THE #$%! PHOENIX!"
I DON'T NEED TO BE ABLE TO READ MINDS TO KNOW EVERYONE WALKS AROUND HERE TRYIN' NOT TO THINK ABOUT WHAT ALL THAT MEANS.
HOW MUCH IT CHANGES?
'CAUSE IF THE FUTURE'S MAPPED OUT THEN HOW DO YOU HOLD ANYONE RESPONSIBLE FOR THEIR ACTIONS?
YOU CAN'T, RIGHT? OR YOU WON'T--
--'CAUSE THEN WE'D HAVE TO LOCK UP HALF YOU MANIACS RIGHT NOW!
WHAT? SERIOUSLY? I MIGHT NEVER GRADUATE NOW--
--AND YOU'RE WHINING ABOUT THE FUTURE?!
YEAH! I COULD DIE TOMORROW--
--AND A MY LITTLE BRONY LIKE YOU GETS TO BE THE PHOENIX?!
TO LIVE FOREVER?!

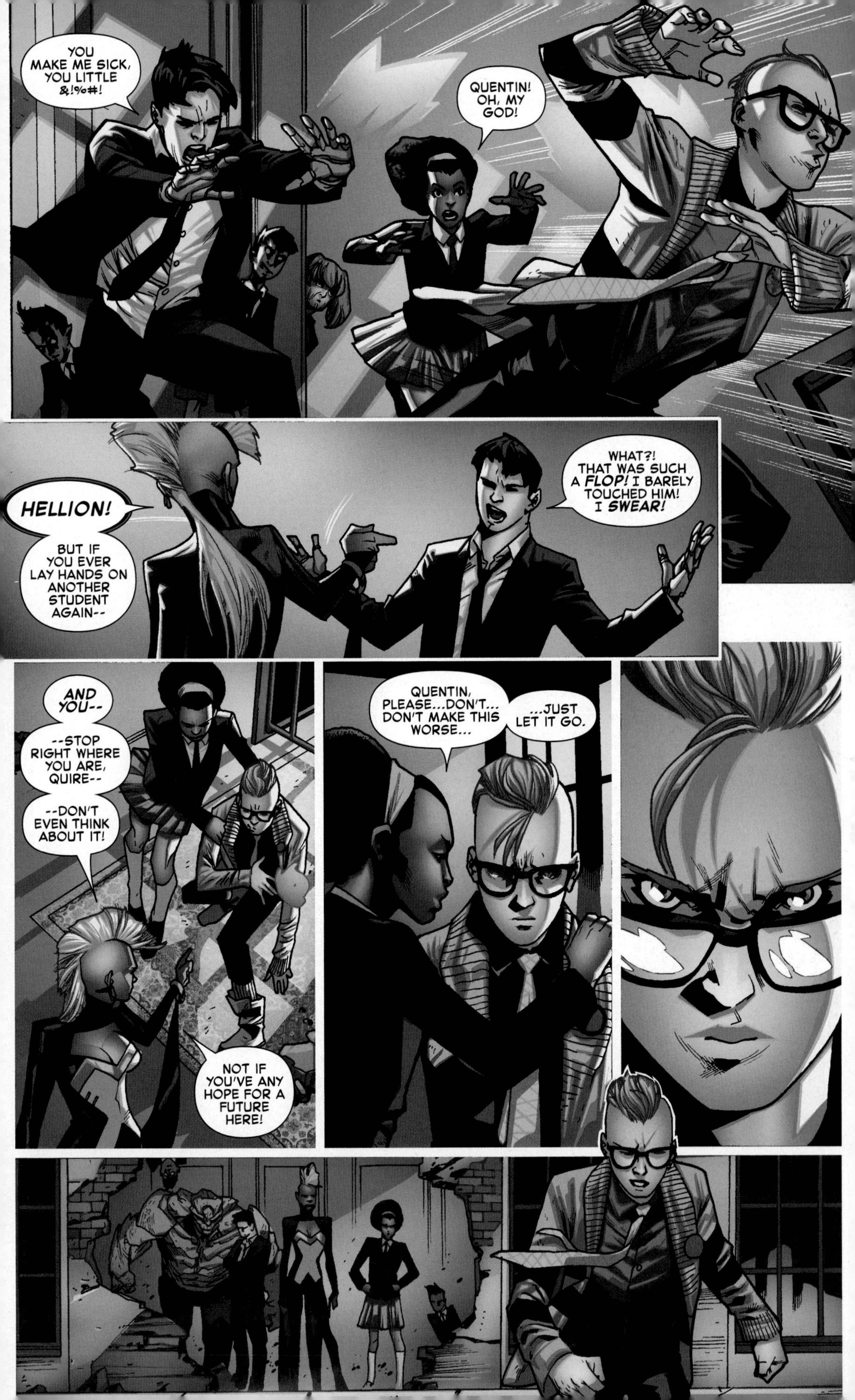

YOU MAKE ME SICK, YOU LITTLE &!%#!
QUENTIN! OH, MY GOD!
HELLION!
WHAT?! THAT WAS SUCH A FLOP! I BARELY TOUCHED HIM! I SWEAR!
BUT IF YOU EVER LAY HANDS ON ANOTHER STUDENT AGAIN--
AND YOU--
--STOP RIGHT WHERE YOU ARE, QUIRE--
--DON'T EVEN THINK ABOUT IT!
NOT IF YOU'VE ANY HOPE FOR A FUTURE HERE!
QUENTIN, PLEASE...DON'T... DON'T MAKE THIS WORSE...
...JUST LET IT GO.

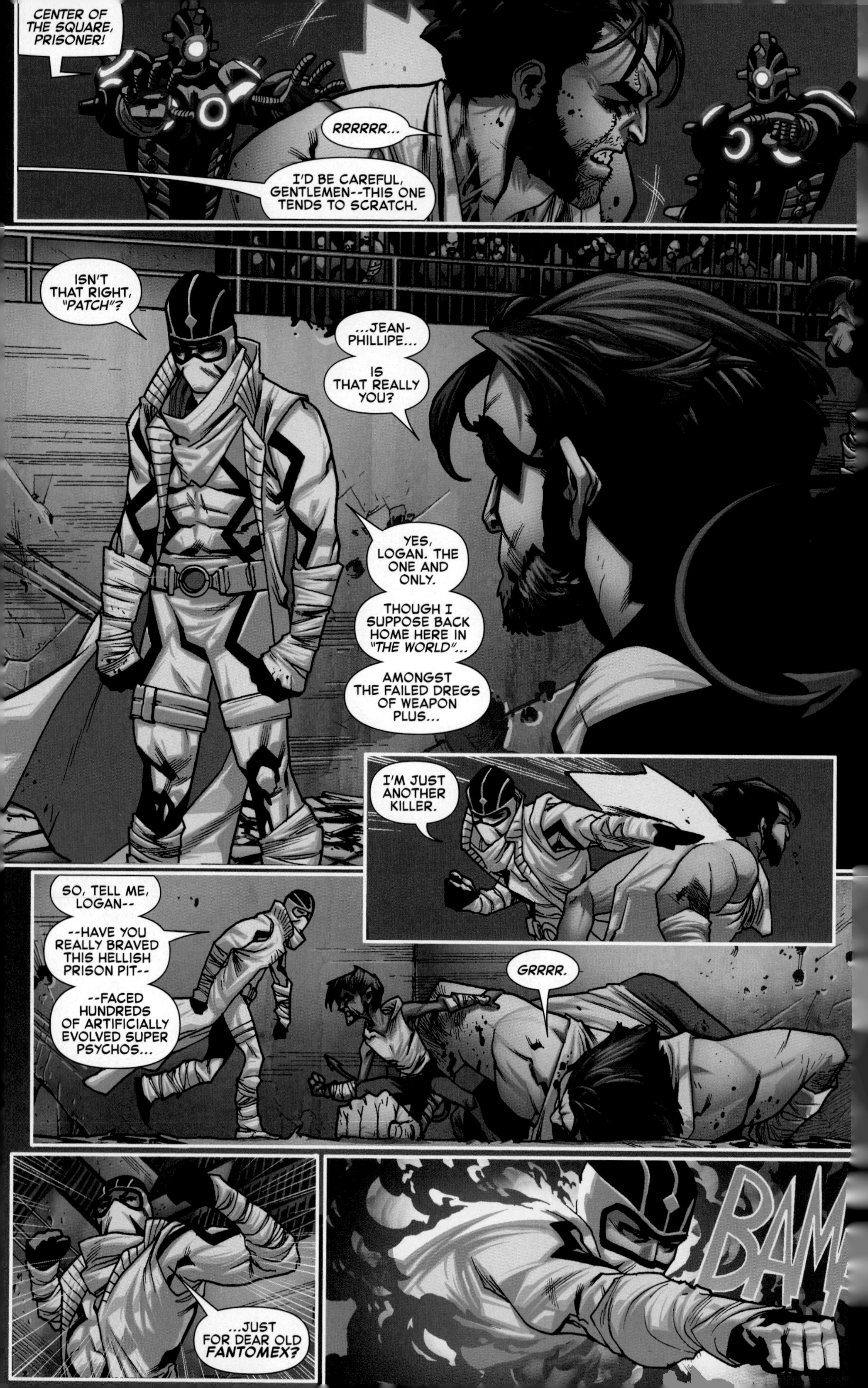
CENTER OF THE SQUARE, PRISONER!
RRRRRR...
I'D BE CAREFUL, GENTLEMEN--THIS ONE TENDS TO SCRATCH.
ISN'T THAT RIGHT, "PATCH"?
...JEAN-PHILLIPE...
IS THAT REALLY YOU?
YES, LOGAN. THE ONE AND ONLY.
THOUGH I SUPPOSE BACK HOME HERE IN "THE WORLD"...
AMONGST THE FAILED DREGS OF WEAPON PLUS...
I'M JUST ANOTHER KILLER.
SO, TELL ME, LOGAN--
--HAVE YOU REALLY BRAVED THIS HELLISH PRISON PIT--
--FACED HUNDREDS OF ARTIFICIALLY EVOLVED SUPER PSYCHOS...
GRRRR.
...JUST FOR DEAR OLD FANTOMEX?
BAM

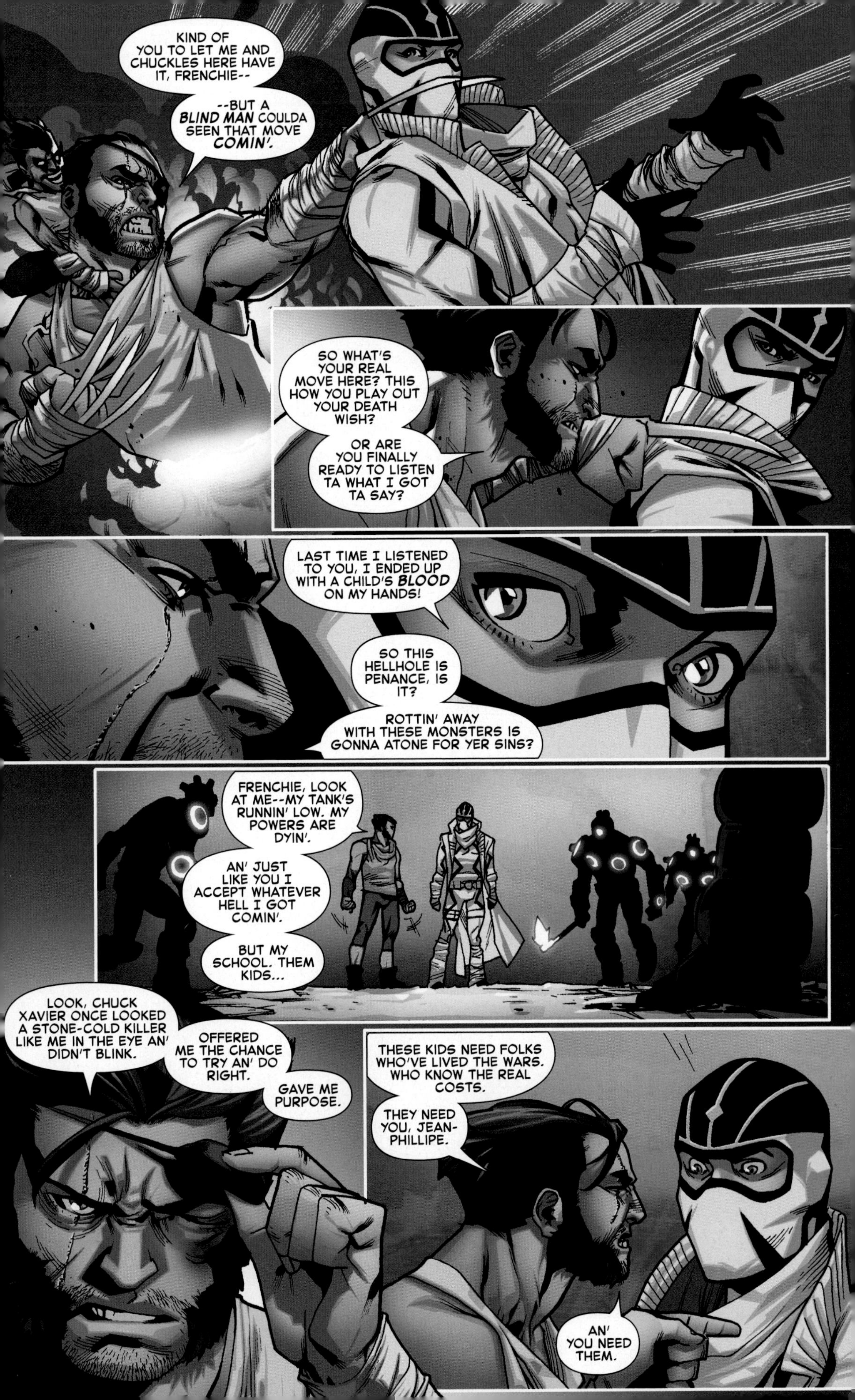
KIND OF YOU TO LET ME AND CHUCKLES HERE HAVE IT, FRENCHIE--
--BUT A *BLIND MAN* COULDA SEEN THAT MOVE *COMIN'*.
SO WHAT'S YOUR REAL MOVE HERE? THIS HOW YOU PLAY OUT YOUR DEATH WISH?
OR ARE YOU FINALLY READY TO LISTEN TA WHAT I GOT TA SAY?
LAST TIME I LISTENED TO YOU, I ENDED UP WITH A CHILD'S *BLOOD* ON MY HANDS!
SO THIS HELLHOLE IS PENANCE, IS IT?
ROTTIN' AWAY WITH THESE MONSTERS IS GONNA ATONE FOR YER SINS?
FRENCHIE, LOOK AT ME--MY TANK'S RUNNIN' LOW. MY POWERS ARE DYIN'.
AN' JUST LIKE YOU I ACCEPT WHATEVER HELL I GOT COMIN'.
BUT MY SCHOOL. THEM KIDS...
LOOK, CHUCK XAVIER ONCE LOOKED A STONE-COLD KILLER LIKE ME IN THE EYE AN' DIDN'T BLINK.
OFFERED ME THE CHANCE TO TRY AN' DO RIGHT.
GAVE ME PURPOSE.
THESE KIDS NEED FOLKS WHO'VE LIVED THE WARS. WHO KNOW THE REAL COSTS.
THEY NEED YOU, JEAN-PHILLIPE.
AN' YOU NEED THEM.

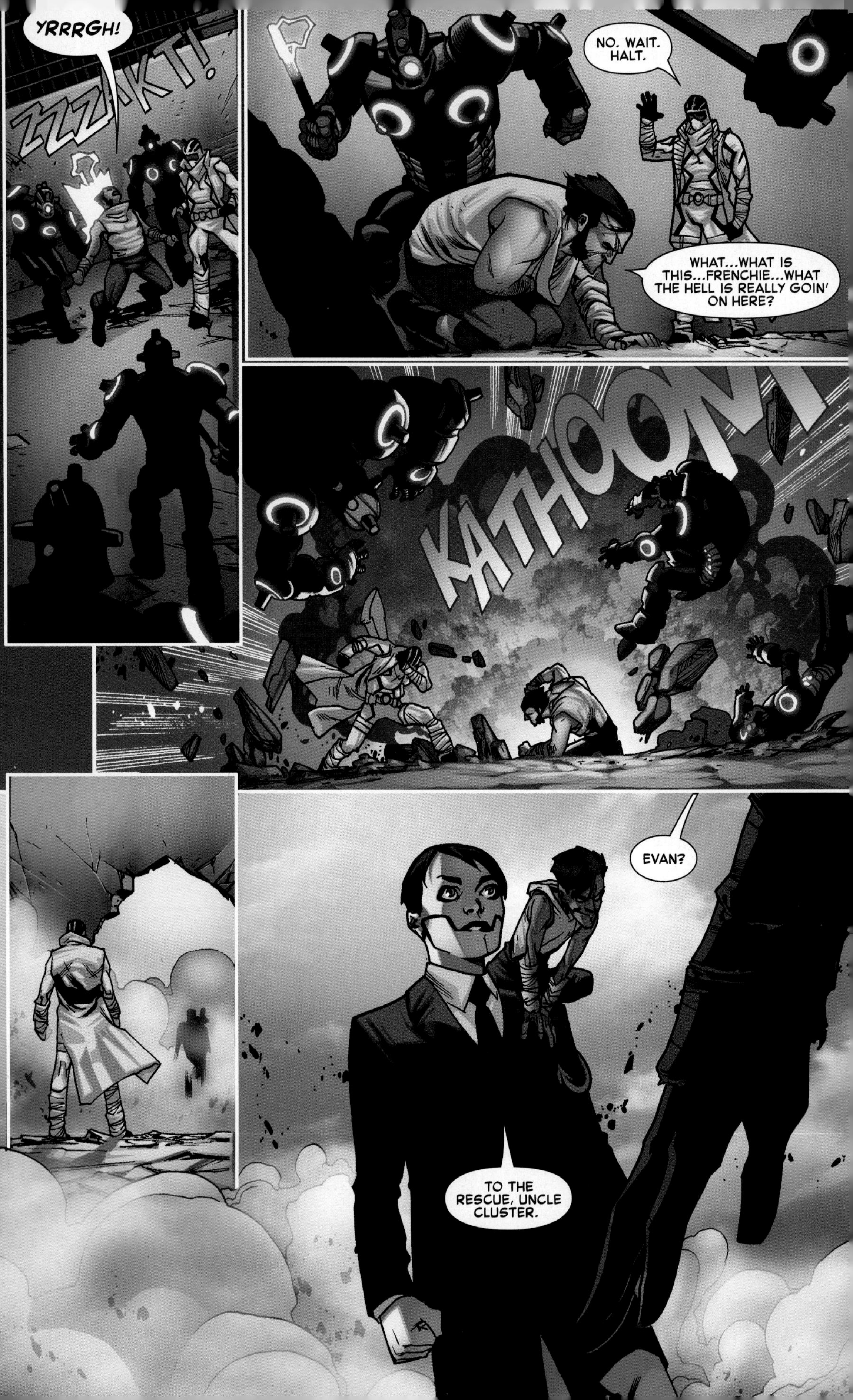
YRRRGH!
ZZZAKT!
NO. WAIT. HALT.
WHAT...WHAT IS THIS...FRENCHIE...WHAT THE HELL IS REALLY GOIN' ON HERE?
KATHOOM!
EVAN?
TO THE RESCUE, UNCLE CLUSTER.

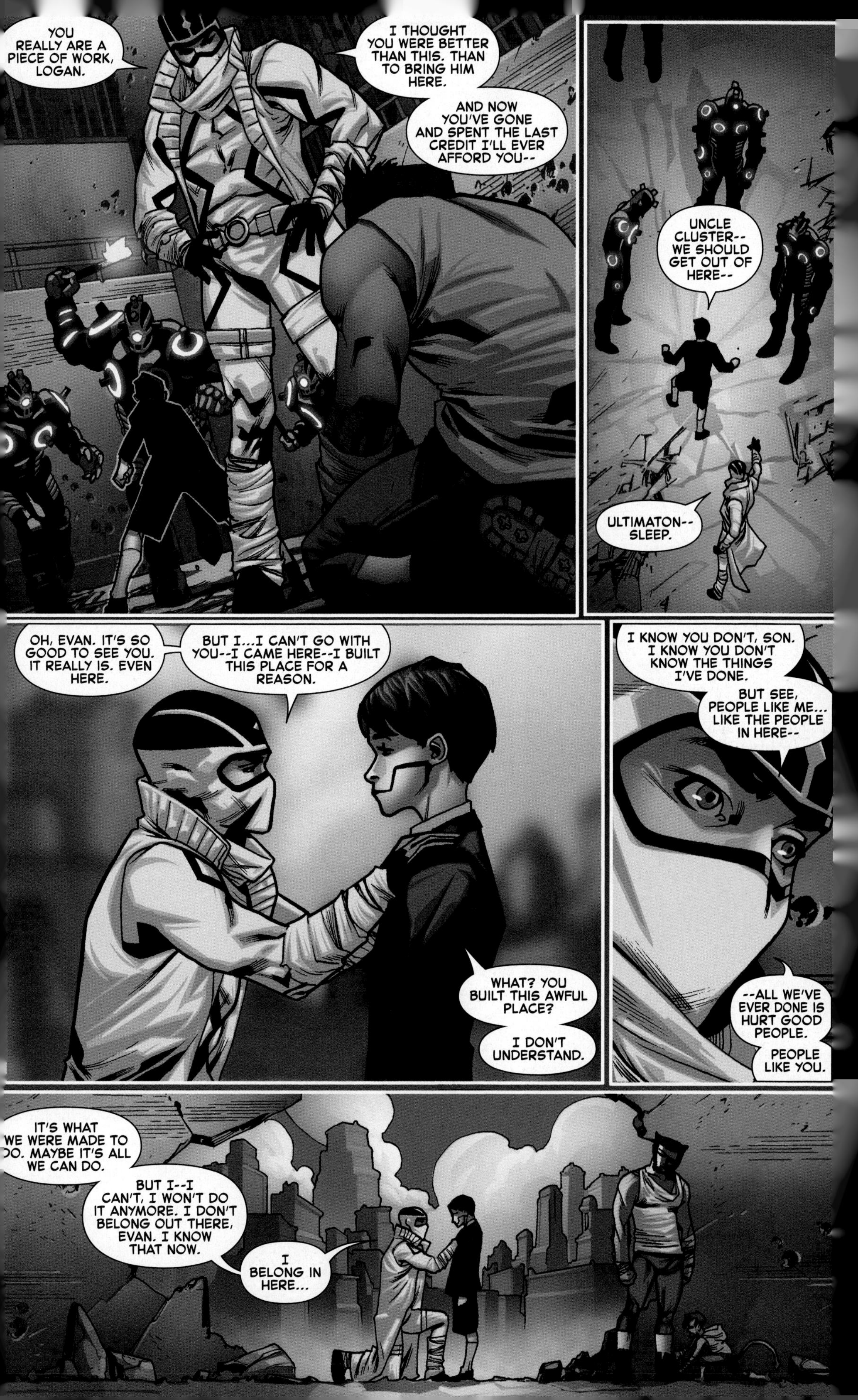

YOU REALLY ARE A PIECE OF WORK, LOGAN.
I THOUGHT YOU WERE BETTER THAN THIS. THAN TO BRING HIM HERE.
AND NOW YOU'VE GONE AND SPENT THE LAST CREDIT I'LL EVER AFFORD YOU--
UNCLE CLUSTER-- WE SHOULD GET OUT OF HERE--
ULTIMATON-- SLEEP.
OH, EVAN. IT'S SO GOOD TO SEE YOU. IT REALLY IS. EVEN HERE.
BUT I...I CAN'T GO WITH YOU--I CAME HERE--I BUILT THIS PLACE FOR A REASON.
WHAT? YOU BUILT THIS AWFUL PLACE?
I DON'T UNDERSTAND.
I KNOW YOU DON'T, SON. I KNOW YOU DON'T KNOW THE THINGS I'VE DONE.
BUT SEE, PEOPLE LIKE ME... LIKE THE PEOPLE IN HERE--
--ALL WE'VE EVER DONE IS HURT GOOD PEOPLE.
PEOPLE LIKE YOU.
IT'S WHAT WE WERE MADE TO DO. MAYBE IT'S ALL WE CAN DO.
BUT I--I CAN'T, I WON'T DO IT ANYMORE. I DON'T BELONG OUT THERE, EVAN. I KNOW THAT NOW.
I BELONG IN HERE...

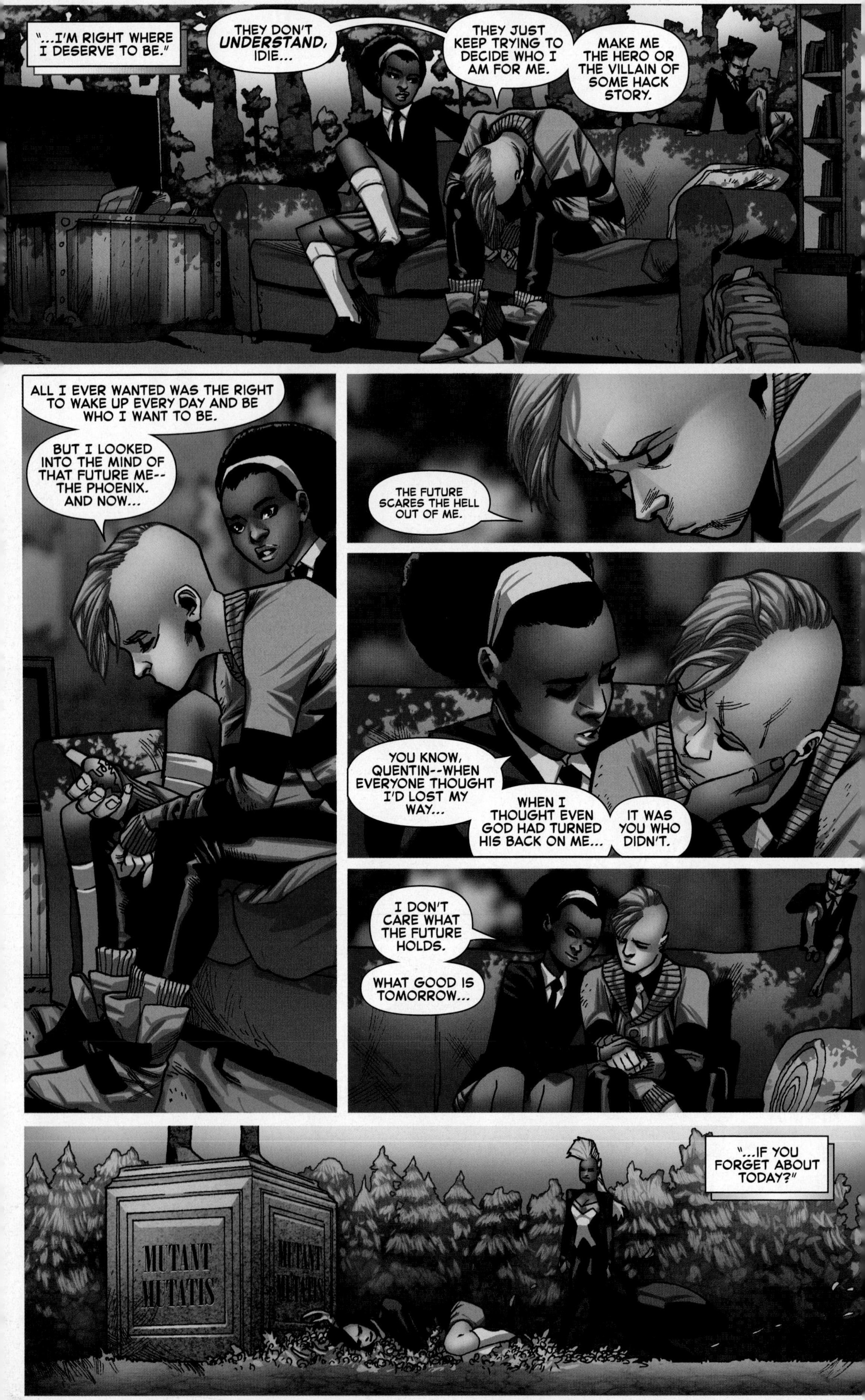
"...I'M RIGHT WHERE I DESERVE TO BE."
THEY DON'T *UNDERSTAND,* IDIE...
THEY JUST KEEP TRYING TO DECIDE WHO I AM FOR ME.
MAKE ME THE HERO OR THE VILLAIN OF SOME HACK STORY.
ALL I EVER WANTED WAS THE RIGHT TO WAKE UP EVERY DAY AND BE WHO I WANT TO BE.
BUT I LOOKED INTO THE MIND OF THAT FUTURE ME-- THE PHOENIX. AND NOW...
THE FUTURE SCARES THE HELL OUT OF ME.
YOU KNOW, QUENTIN--WHEN EVERYONE THOUGHT I'D LOST MY WAY...
WHEN I THOUGHT EVEN GOD HAD TURNED HIS BACK ON ME...
IT WAS YOU WHO DIDN'T.
I DON'T CARE WHAT THE FUTURE HOLDS.
WHAT GOOD IS TOMORROW...
MUTANT MUTATIS
MUTANT MUTATIS
"...IF YOU FORGET ABOUT TODAY?"

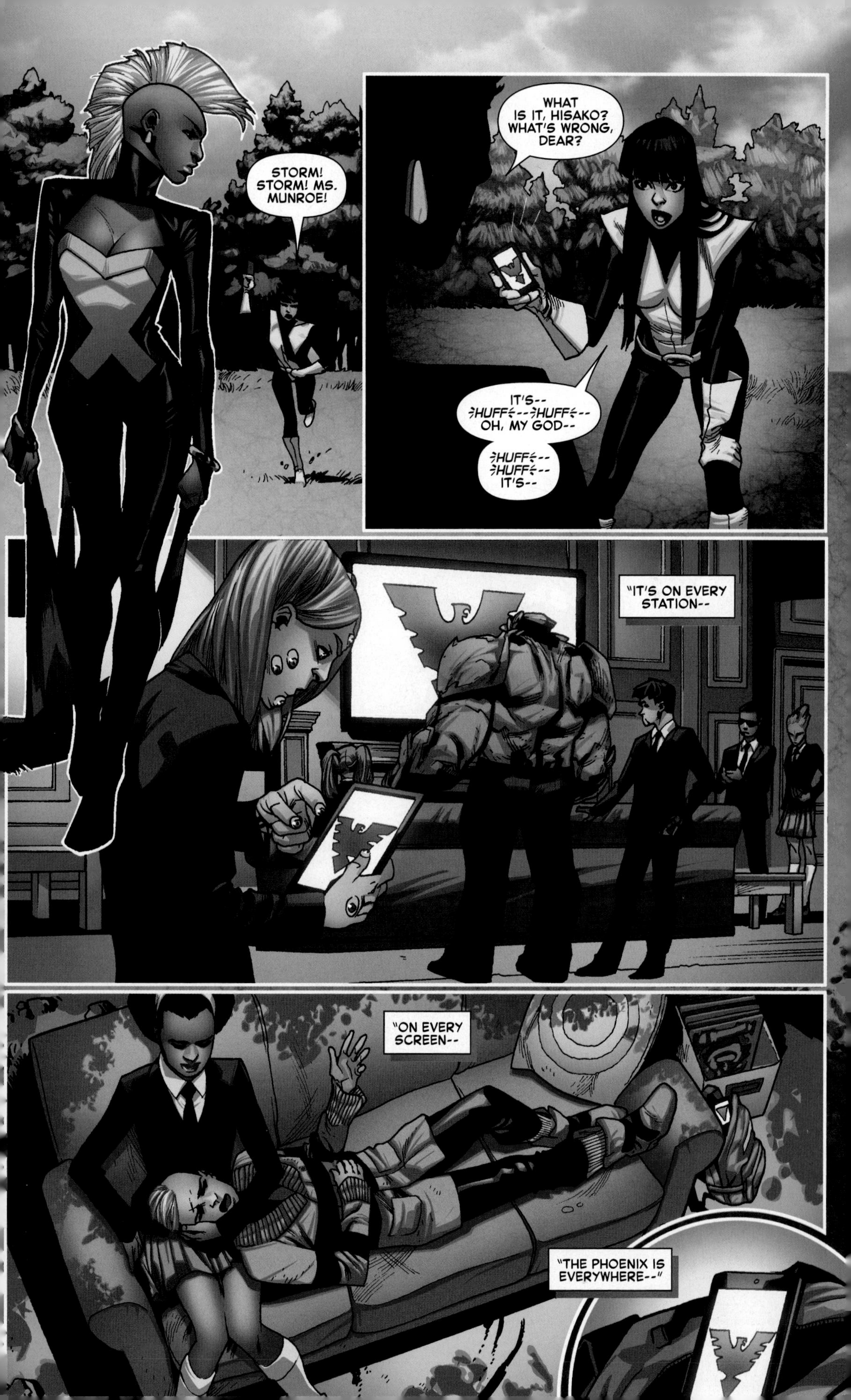
STORM! STORM! MS. MUNROE!
WHAT IS IT, HISAKO? WHAT'S WRONG, DEAR?
IT'S-- *HUFF*-- *HUFF*-- OH, MY GOD--
HUFF-- *HUFF*-- IT'S--
"IT'S ON EVERY STATION--
"ON EVERY SCREEN--
"THE PHOENIX IS EVERYWHERE--"

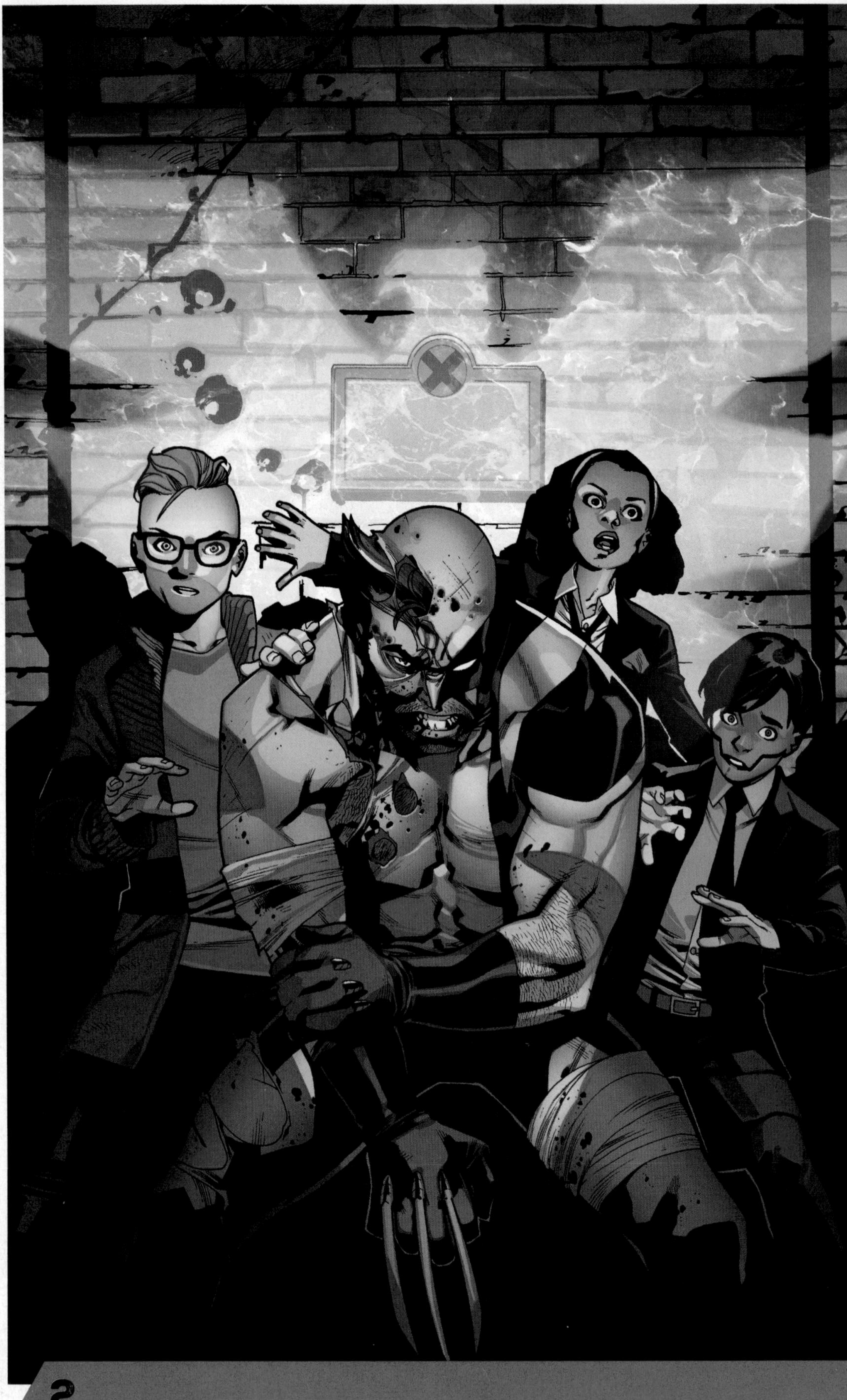

2

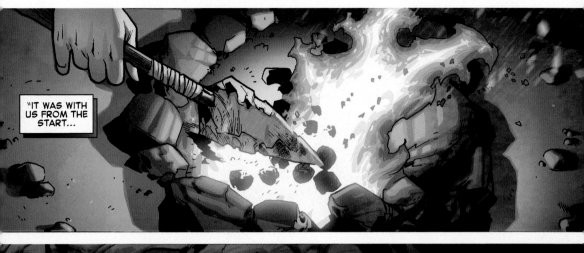

"IT WAS WITH US FROM THE START...

"OUR CURIOSITY.

"OUR INGENUITY.

"OUR PASSION.

"THE FIRE BURNING WITHIN.

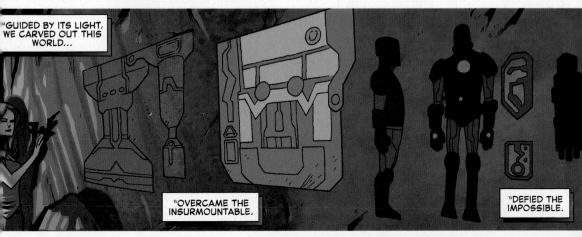

"GUIDED BY ITS LIGHT, WE CARVED OUT THIS WORLD...

"OVERCAME THE INSURMOUNTABLE.

"DEFIED THE IMPOSSIBLE.

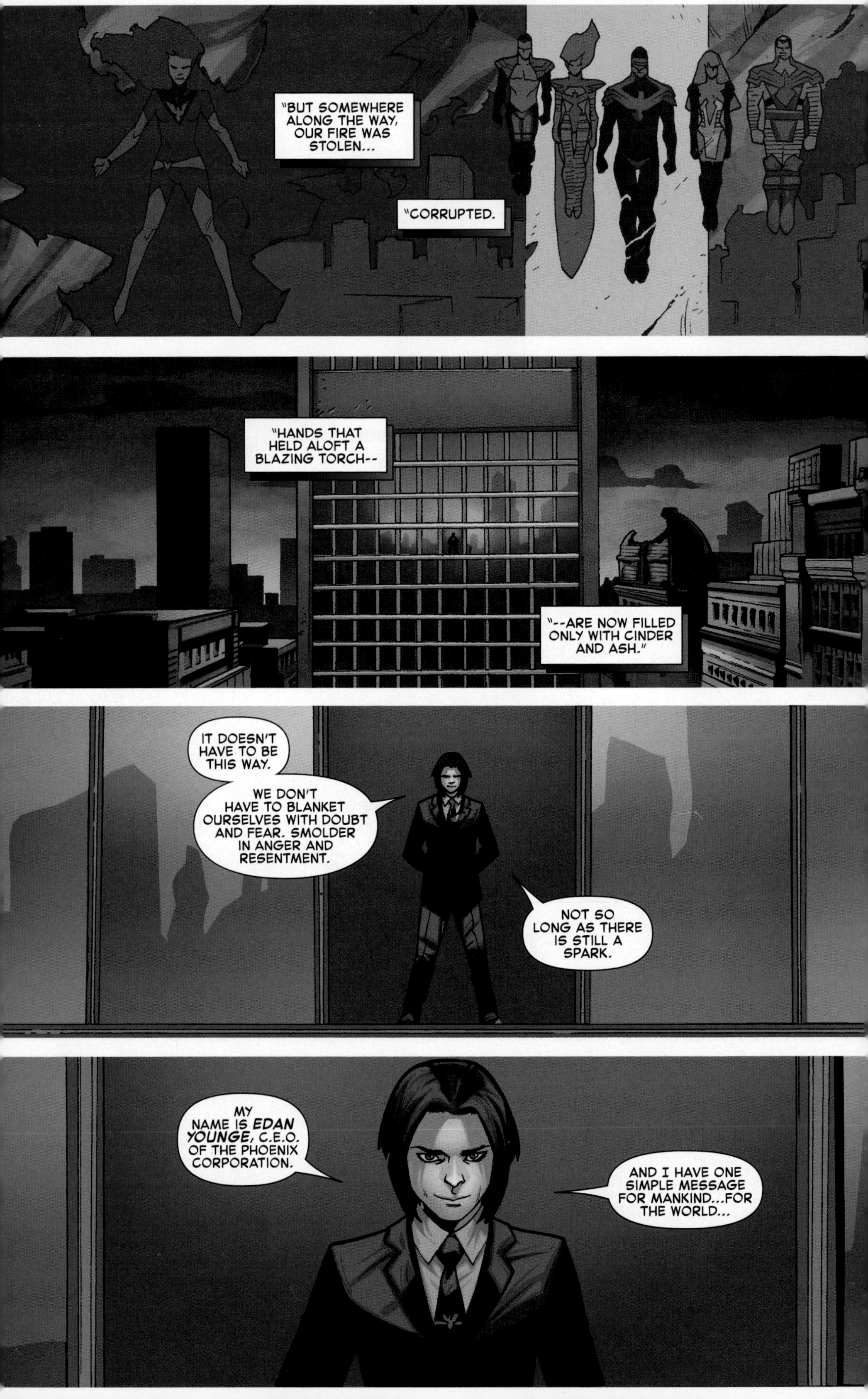
"BUT SOMEWHERE ALONG THE WAY, OUR FIRE WAS STOLEN...
"CORRUPTED.
"HANDS THAT HELD ALOFT A BLAZING TORCH--
"--ARE NOW FILLED ONLY WITH CINDER AND ASH."
IT DOESN'T HAVE TO BE THIS WAY.
WE DON'T HAVE TO BLANKET OURSELVES WITH DOUBT AND FEAR. SMOLDER IN ANGER AND RESENTMENT.
NOT SO LONG AS THERE IS STILL A SPARK.
MY NAME IS ***EDAN YOUNGE***, C.E.O. OF THE PHOENIX CORPORATION.
AND I HAVE ONE SIMPLE MESSAGE FOR MANKIND...FOR THE WORLD...

RISE

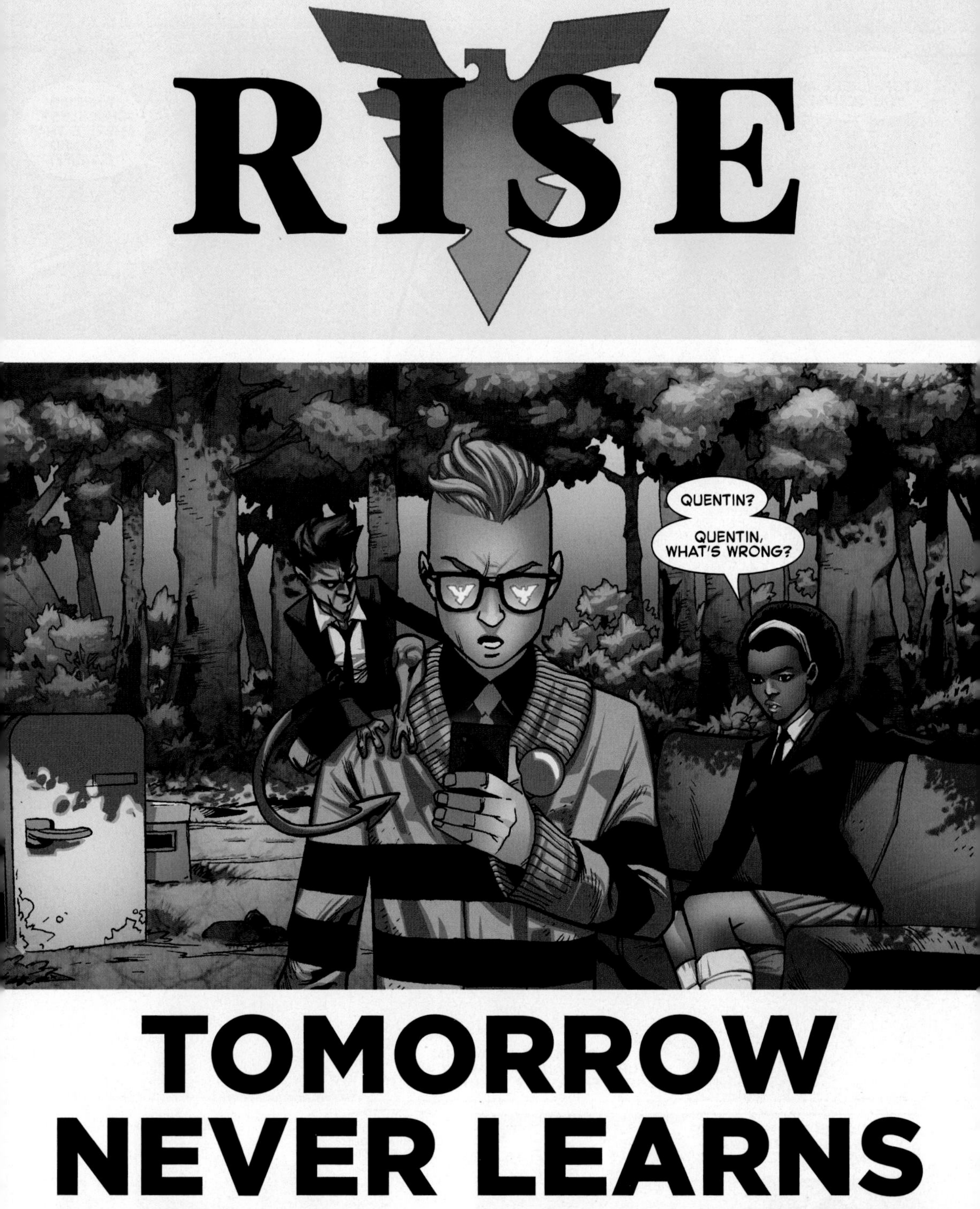
QUENTIN?
QUENTIN, WHAT'S WRONG?

TOMORROW NEVER LEARNS

CHAPTER 2: STORM CHASERS

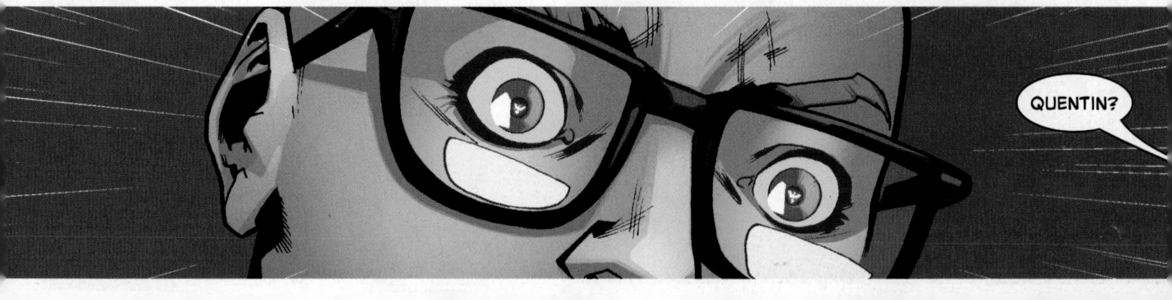
QUENTIN?

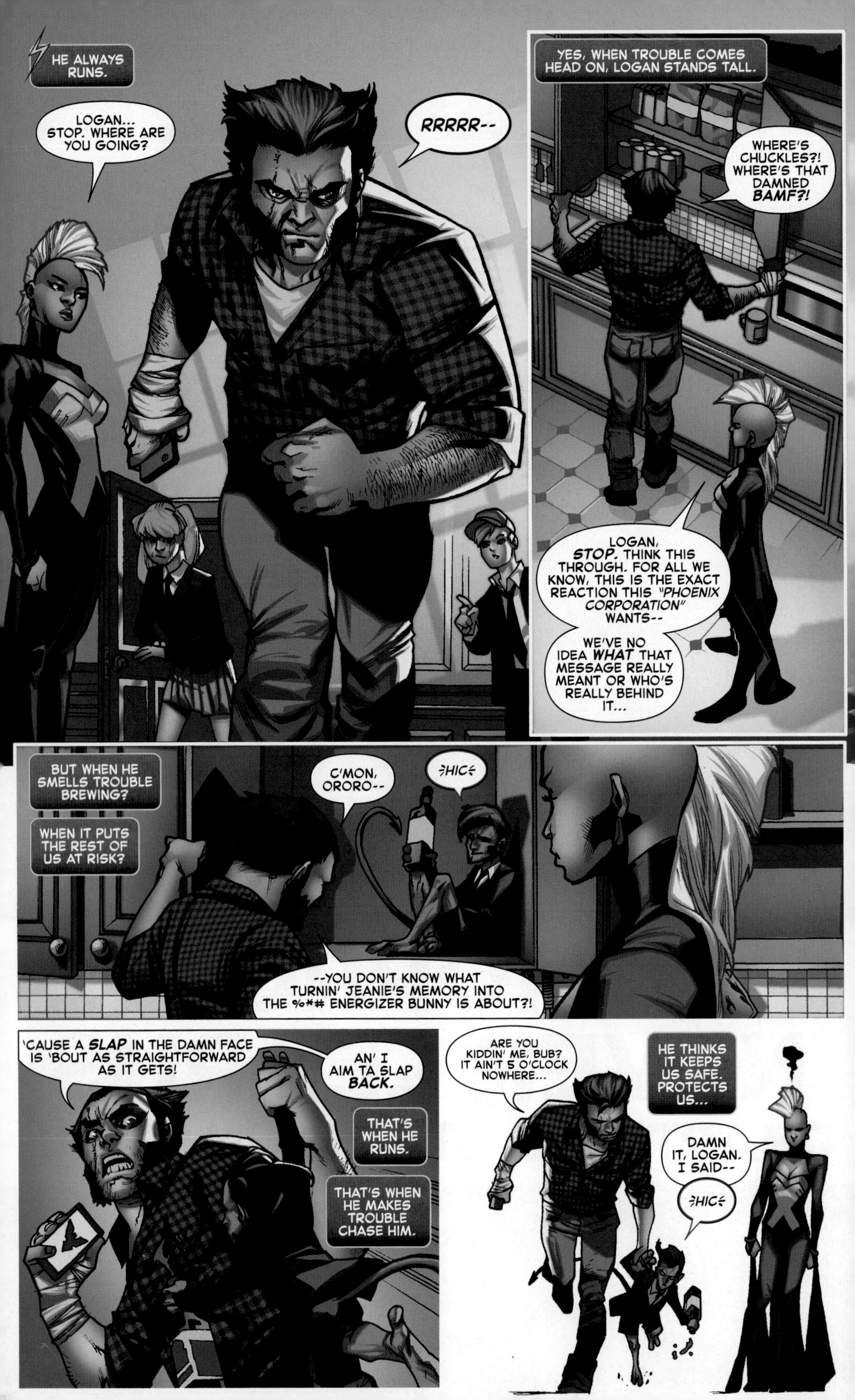

HE ALWAYS RUNS.
LOGAN... STOP. WHERE ARE YOU GOING?
RRRRR--
YES, WHEN TROUBLE COMES HEAD ON, LOGAN STANDS TALL.
WHERE'S CHUCKLES?! WHERE'S THAT DAMNED BAMF?!
LOGAN, STOP. THINK THIS THROUGH. FOR ALL WE KNOW, THIS IS THE EXACT REACTION THIS "PHOENIX CORPORATION" WANTS--
WE'VE NO IDEA WHAT THAT MESSAGE REALLY MEANT OR WHO'S REALLY BEHIND IT...
BUT WHEN HE SMELLS TROUBLE BREWING?
WHEN IT PUTS THE REST OF US AT RISK?
C'MON, ORORO--
HIC
--YOU DON'T KNOW WHAT TURNIN' JEANIE'S MEMORY INTO THE %*# ENERGIZER BUNNY IS ABOUT?!
'CAUSE A SLAP IN THE DAMN FACE IS 'BOUT AS STRAIGHTFORWARD AS IT GETS!
AN' I AIM TA SLAP BACK.
THAT'S WHEN HE RUNS.
THAT'S WHEN HE MAKES TROUBLE CHASE HIM.
ARE YOU KIDDIN' ME, BUB? IT AIN'T 5 O'CLOCK NOWHERE...
HE THINKS IT KEEPS US SAFE. PROTECTS US...
DAMN IT, LOGAN. I SAID--
HIC

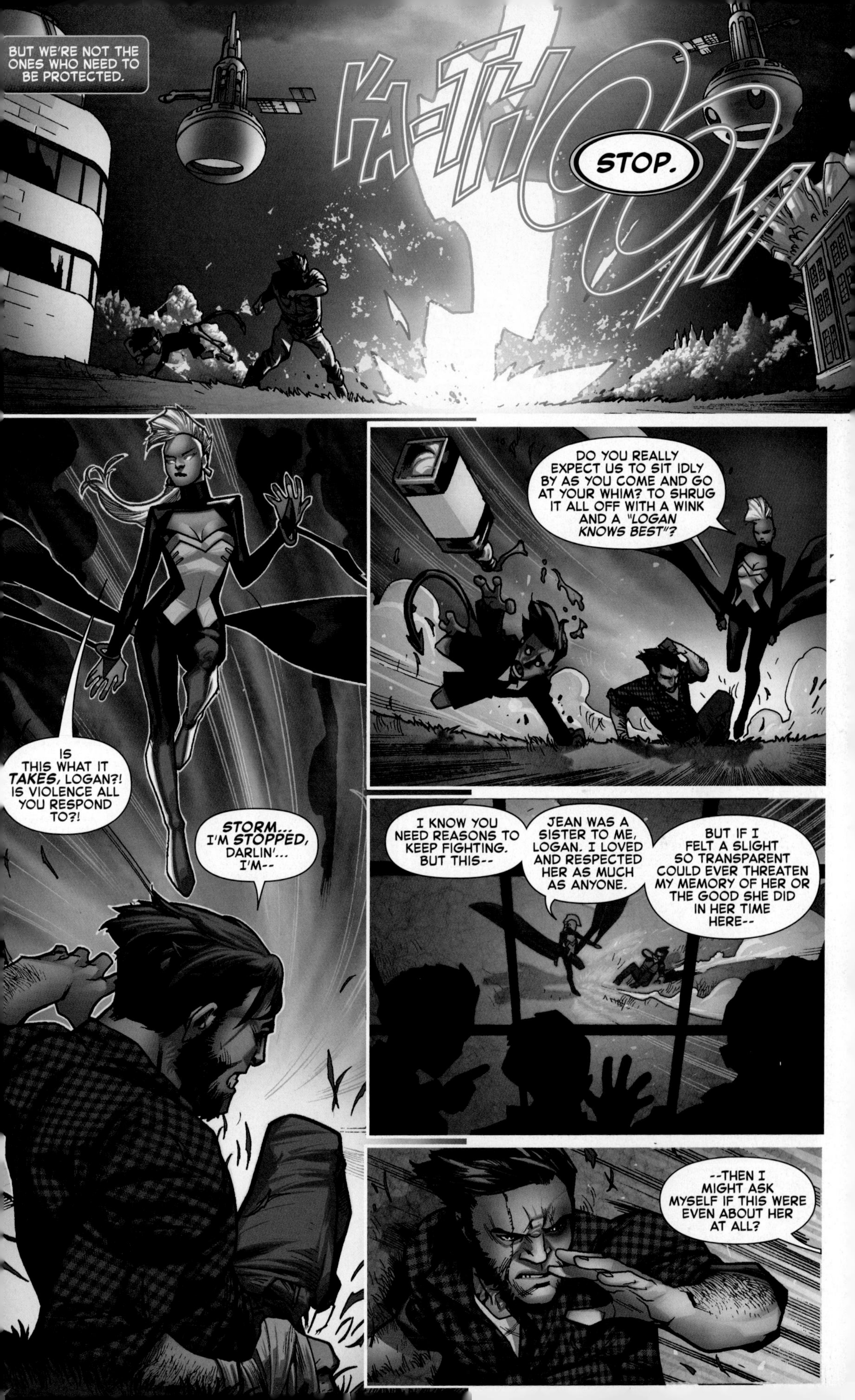

BUT WE'RE NOT THE ONES WHO NEED TO BE PROTECTED.
KA-THOOOM
STOP.
IS THIS WHAT IT TAKES, LOGAN?! IS VIOLENCE ALL YOU RESPOND TO?!
STORM... I'M STOPPED, DARLIN'... I'M--
DO YOU REALLY EXPECT US TO SIT IDLY BY AS YOU COME AND GO AT YOUR WHIM? TO SHRUG IT ALL OFF WITH A WINK AND A "LOGAN KNOWS BEST"?
I KNOW YOU NEED REASONS TO KEEP FIGHTING. BUT THIS--
JEAN WAS A SISTER TO ME, LOGAN. I LOVED AND RESPECTED HER AS MUCH AS ANYONE.
BUT IF I FELT A SLIGHT SO TRANSPARENT COULD EVER THREATEN MY MEMORY OF HER OR THE GOOD SHE DID IN HER TIME HERE--
--THEN I MIGHT ASK MYSELF IF THIS WERE EVEN ABOUT HER AT ALL?

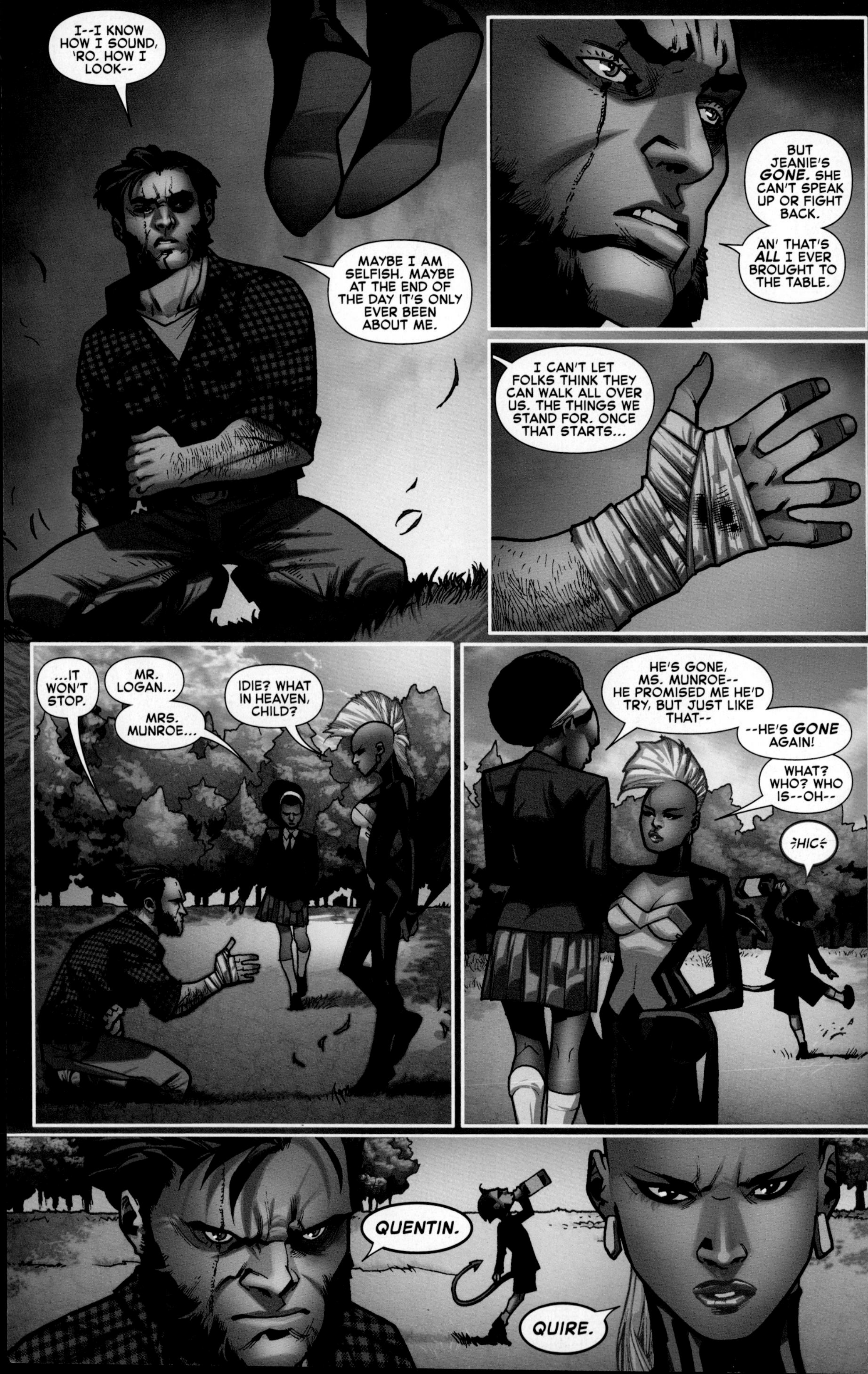

I--I KNOW HOW I SOUND, 'RO. HOW I LOOK--
MAYBE I AM SELFISH. MAYBE AT THE END OF THE DAY IT'S ONLY EVER BEEN ABOUT ME.
BUT JEANIE'S GONE. SHE CAN'T SPEAK UP OR FIGHT BACK.
AN' THAT'S ALL I EVER BROUGHT TO THE TABLE.
I CAN'T LET FOLKS THINK THEY CAN WALK ALL OVER US. THE THINGS WE STAND FOR. ONCE THAT STARTS...
...IT WON'T STOP.
MR. LOGAN...
MRS. MUNROE...
IDIE? WHAT IN HEAVEN, CHILD?
HE'S GONE, MS. MUNROE-- HE PROMISED ME HE'D TRY, BUT JUST LIKE THAT--
--HE'S GONE AGAIN!
WHAT? WHO? WHO IS--OH--
HIC
QUENTIN.
QUIRE.

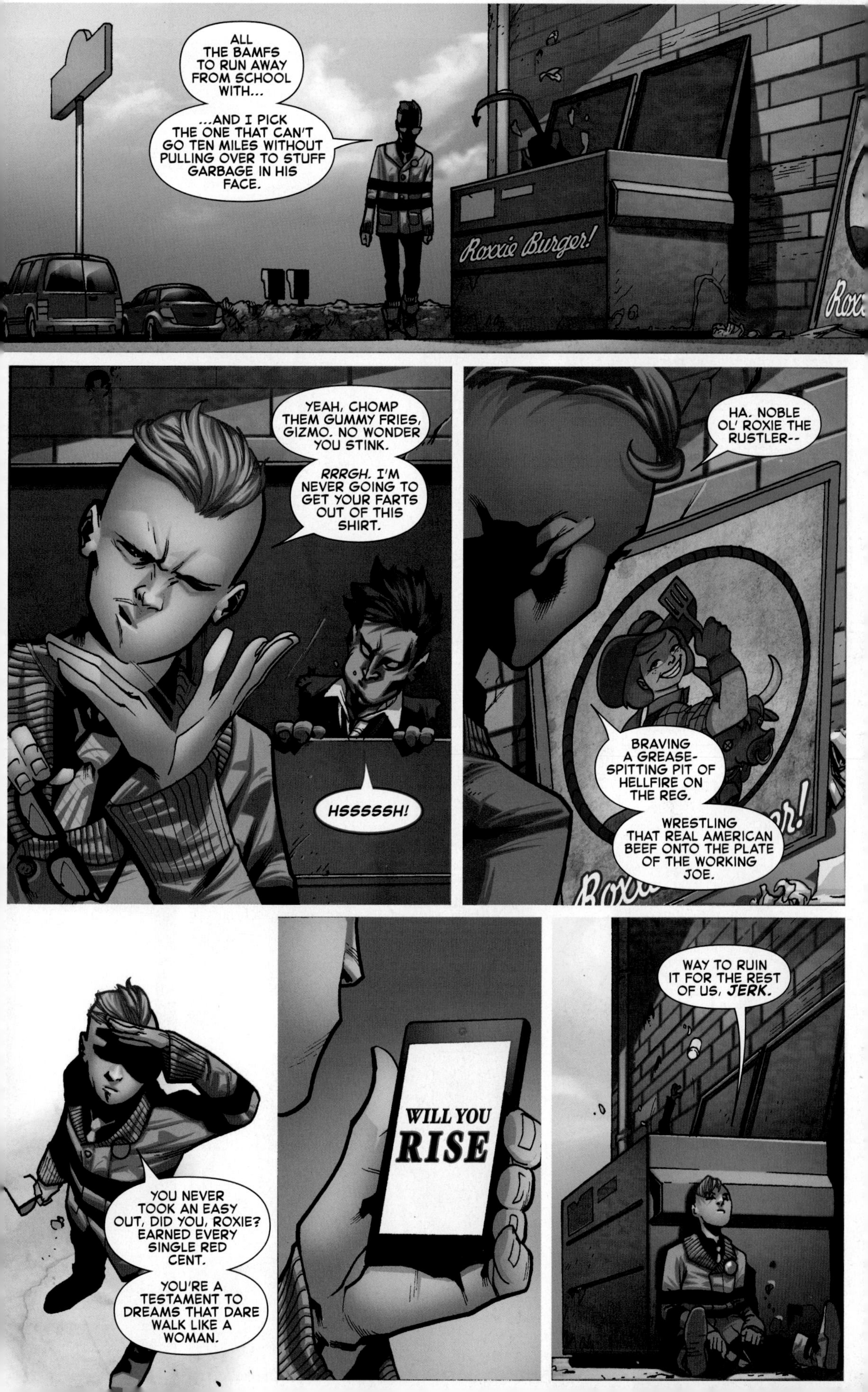
ALL THE BAMFS TO RUN AWAY FROM SCHOOL WITH...
...AND I PICK THE ONE THAT CAN'T GO TEN MILES WITHOUT PULLING OVER TO STUFF GARBAGE IN HIS FACE.
Roxxie Burger!
YEAH, CHOMP THEM GUMMY FRIES, GIZMO. NO WONDER YOU STINK.
RRRGH. I'M NEVER GOING TO GET YOUR FARTS OUT OF THIS SHIRT.
HSSSSSH!
HA. NOBLE OL' ROXIE THE RUSTLER--
BRAVING A GREASE-SPITTING PIT OF HELLFIRE ON THE REG.
WRESTLING THAT REAL AMERICAN BEEF ONTO THE PLATE OF THE WORKING JOE.
YOU NEVER TOOK AN EASY OUT, DID YOU, ROXIE? EARNED EVERY SINGLE RED CENT.
YOU'RE A TESTAMENT TO DREAMS THAT DARE WALK LIKE A WOMAN.
WILL YOU RISE
WAY TO RUIN IT FOR THE REST OF US, JERK.

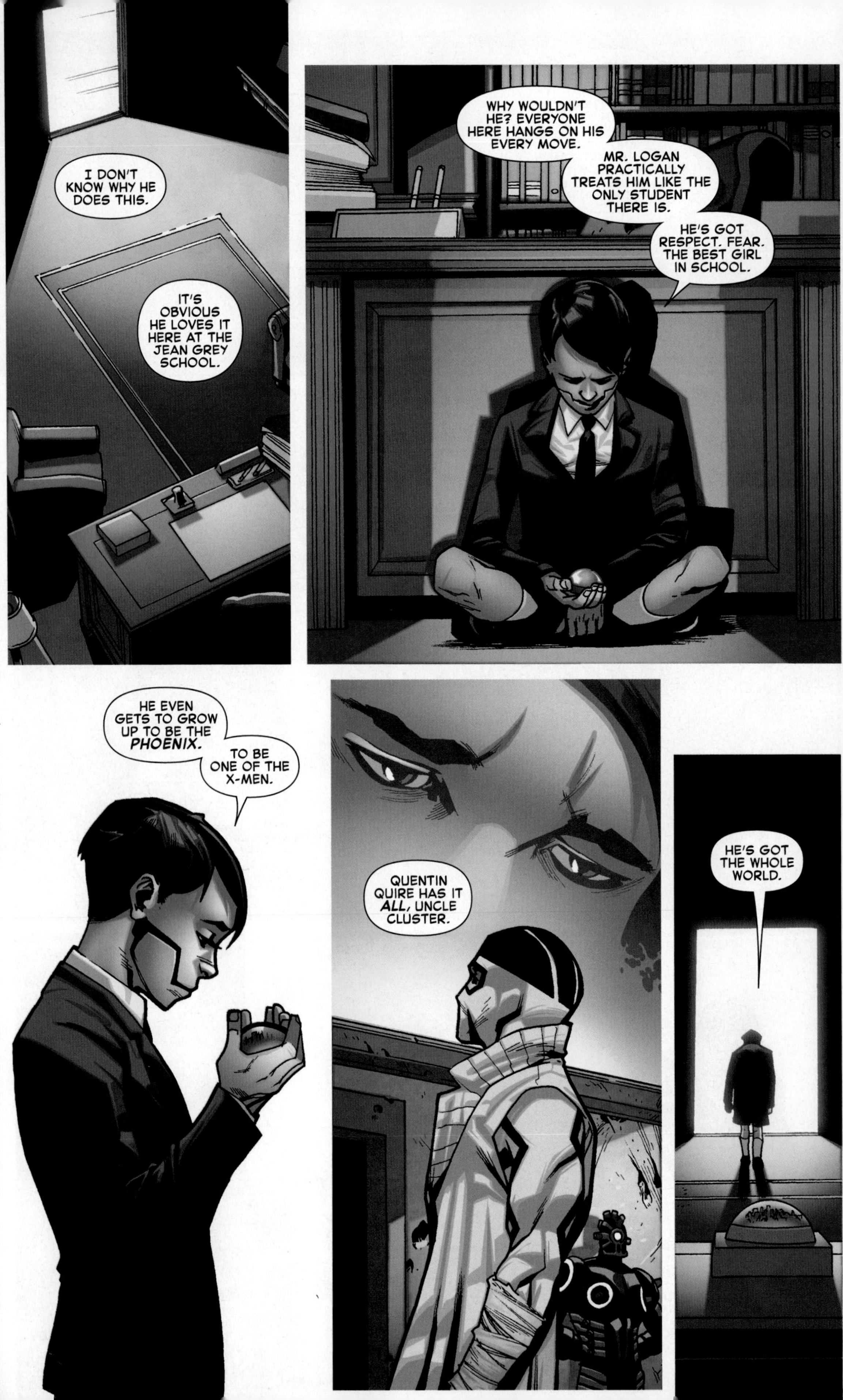
I DON'T KNOW WHY HE DOES THIS.
IT'S OBVIOUS HE LOVES IT HERE AT THE JEAN GREY SCHOOL.
WHY WOULDN'T HE? EVERYONE HERE HANGS ON HIS EVERY MOVE.
MR. LOGAN PRACTICALLY TREATS HIM LIKE THE ONLY STUDENT THERE IS.
HE'S GOT RESPECT. FEAR. THE BEST GIRL IN SCHOOL.
HE EVEN GETS TO GROW UP TO BE THE *PHOENIX.*
TO BE ONE OF THE X-MEN.
QUENTIN QUIRE HAS IT *ALL,* UNCLE CLUSTER.
HE'S GOT THE WHOLE WORLD.

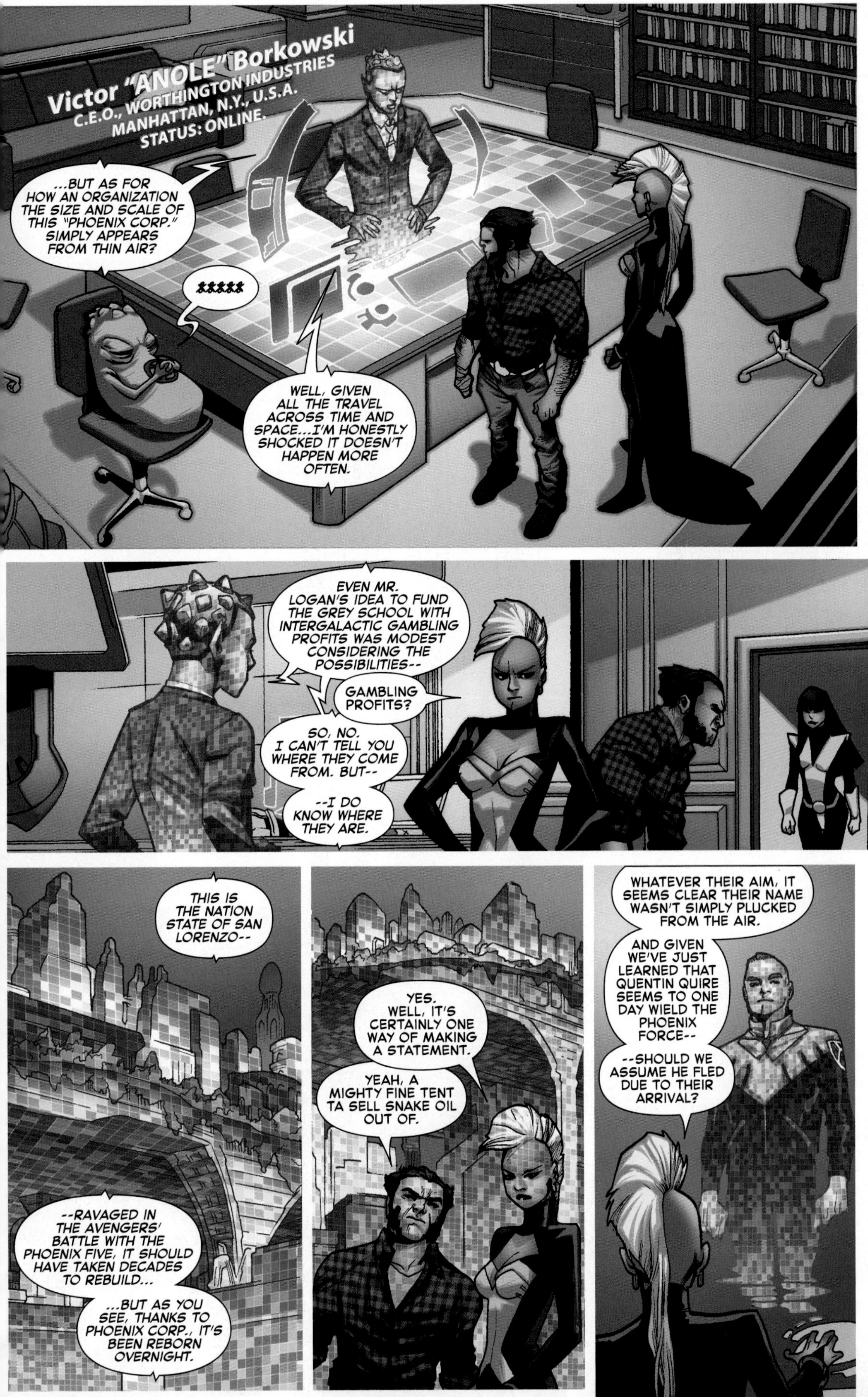

Victor "ANOLE" Borkowski
C.E.O., WORTHINGTON INDUSTRIES
MANHATTAN, N.Y., U.S.A.
STATUS: ONLINE.
...BUT AS FOR HOW AN ORGANIZATION THE SIZE AND SCALE OF THIS "PHOENIX CORP." SIMPLY APPEARS FROM THIN AIR?
*****
WELL, GIVEN ALL THE TRAVEL ACROSS TIME AND SPACE...I'M HONESTLY SHOCKED IT DOESN'T HAPPEN MORE OFTEN.
EVEN MR. LOGAN'S IDEA TO FUND THE GREY SCHOOL WITH INTERGALACTIC GAMBLING PROFITS WAS MODEST CONSIDERING THE POSSIBILITIES--
GAMBLING PROFITS?
SO, NO. I CAN'T TELL YOU WHERE THEY COME FROM. BUT--
--I DO KNOW WHERE THEY ARE.
THIS IS THE NATION STATE OF SAN LORENZO--
--RAVAGED IN THE AVENGERS' BATTLE WITH THE PHOENIX FIVE, IT SHOULD HAVE TAKEN DECADES TO REBUILD...
...BUT AS YOU SEE, THANKS TO PHOENIX CORP., IT'S BEEN REBORN OVERNIGHT.
YES. WELL, IT'S CERTAINLY ONE WAY OF MAKING A STATEMENT.
YEAH, A MIGHTY FINE TENT TA SELL SNAKE OIL OUT OF.
WHATEVER THEIR AIM, IT SEEMS CLEAR THEIR NAME WASN'T SIMPLY PLUCKED FROM THE AIR.
AND GIVEN WE'VE JUST LEARNED THAT QUENTIN QUIRE SEEMS TO ONE DAY WIELD THE PHOENIX FORCE--
--SHOULD WE ASSUME HE FLED DUE TO THEIR ARRIVAL?

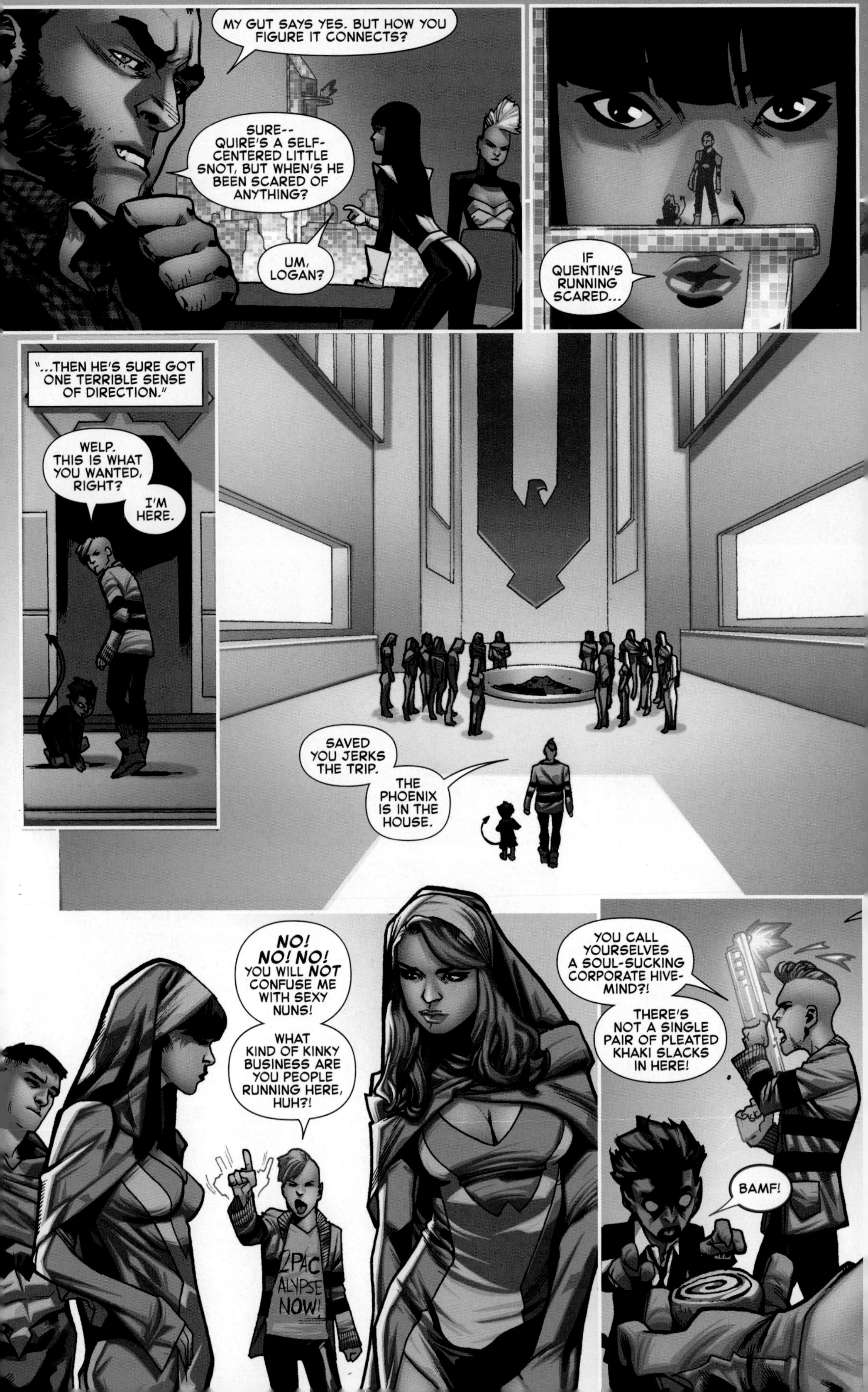

MY GUT SAYS YES. BUT HOW YOU FIGURE IT CONNECTS?
SURE-- QUIRE'S A SELF-CENTERED LITTLE SNOT, BUT WHEN'S HE BEEN SCARED OF ANYTHING?
UM, LOGAN?
IF QUENTIN'S RUNNING SCARED...
"...THEN HE'S SURE GOT ONE TERRIBLE SENSE OF DIRECTION."
WELP. THIS IS WHAT YOU WANTED, RIGHT?
I'M HERE.
SAVED YOU JERKS THE TRIP.
THE PHOENIX IS IN THE HOUSE.
NO! NO! NO! YOU WILL NOT CONFUSE ME WITH SEXY NUNS!
WHAT KIND OF KINKY BUSINESS ARE YOU PEOPLE RUNNING HERE, HUH?!
2PAC ALYPSE NOW!
YOU CALL YOURSELVES A SOUL-SUCKING CORPORATE HIVE-MIND?!
THERE'S NOT A SINGLE PAIR OF PLEATED KHAKI SLACKS IN HERE!
BAMF!

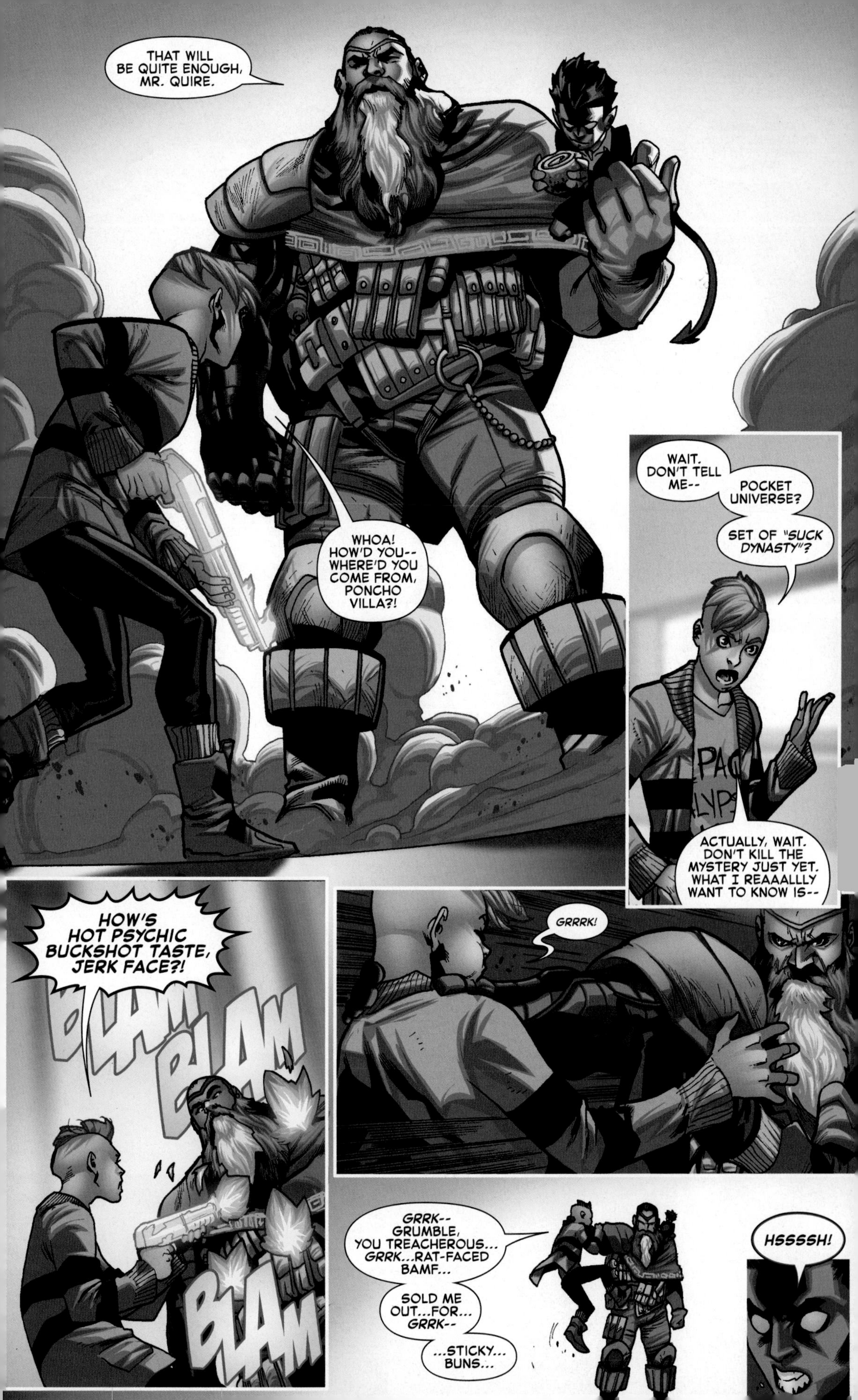

THAT WILL BE QUITE ENOUGH, MR. QUIRE.
WHOA! HOW'D YOU-- WHERE'D YOU COME FROM, PONCHO VILLA?!
WAIT. DON'T TELL ME--
POCKET UNIVERSE?
SET OF "SUCK DYNASTY"?
ACTUALLY, WAIT. DON'T KILL THE MYSTERY JUST YET. WHAT I REAAALLLY WANT TO KNOW IS--
HOW'S HOT PSYCHIC BUCKSHOT TASTE, JERK FACE?!
BLAM
BLAM
BLAM
GRRRK!
GRRK-- GRUMBLE, YOU TREACHEROUS... GRRK...RAT-FACED BAMF...
SOLD ME OUT...FOR... GRRK--
...STICKY... BUNS...
HSSSSH!

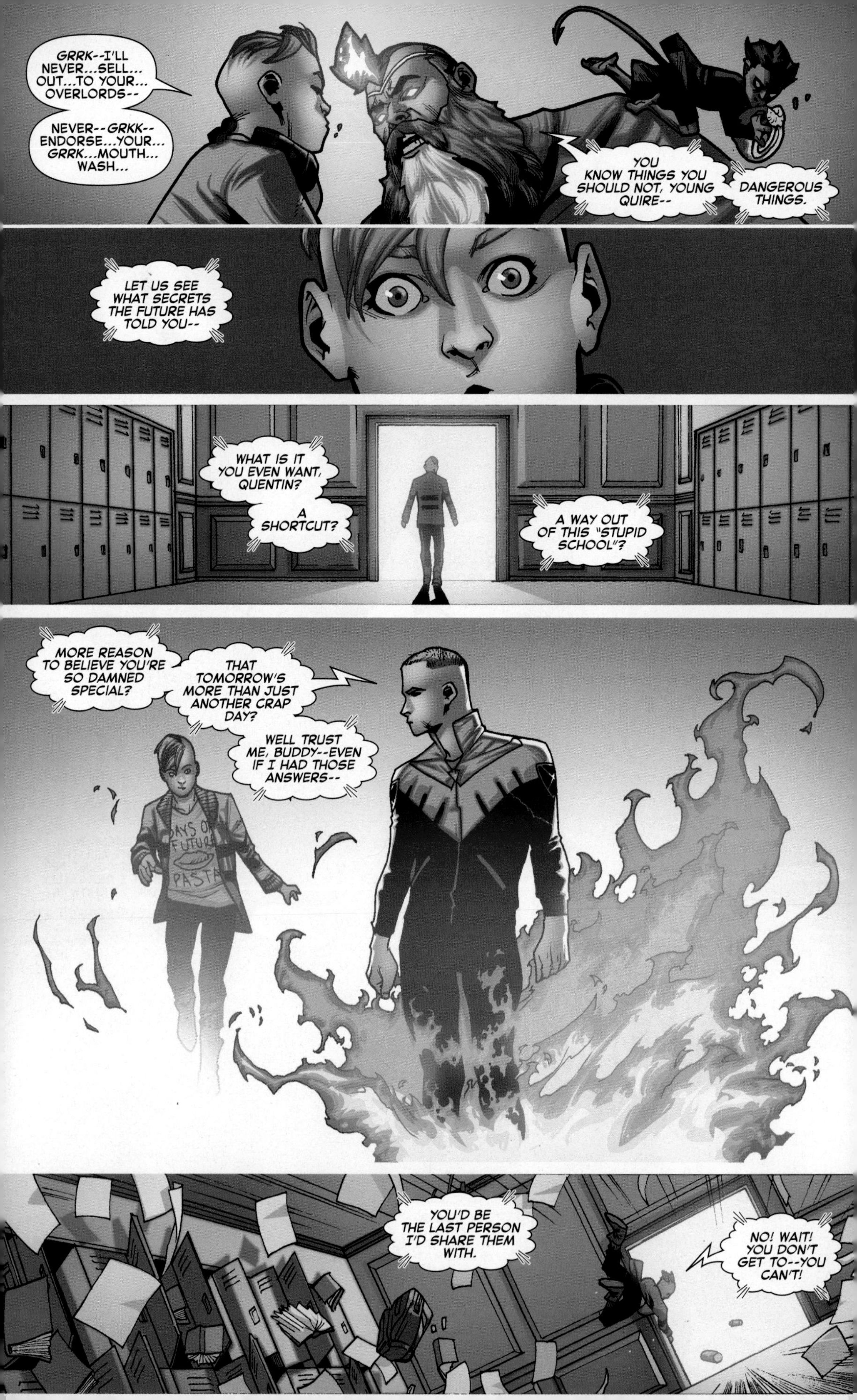
GRRK--I'LL NEVER...SELL... OUT...TO YOUR... OVERLORDS--
NEVER--GRKK-- ENDORSE...YOUR... GRRK...MOUTH... WASH...
YOU KNOW THINGS YOU SHOULD NOT, YOUNG QUIRE--
DANGEROUS THINGS.
LET US SEE WHAT SECRETS THE FUTURE HAS TOLD YOU--
WHAT IS IT YOU EVEN WANT, QUENTIN?
A SHORTCUT?
A WAY OUT OF THIS "STUPID SCHOOL"?
MORE REASON TO BELIEVE YOU'RE SO DAMNED SPECIAL?
THAT TOMORROW'S MORE THAN JUST ANOTHER CRAP DAY?
WELL TRUST ME, BUDDY--EVEN IF I HAD THOSE ANSWERS--
DAYS OF FUTURE PASTA
YOU'D BE THE LAST PERSON I'D SHARE THEM WITH.
NO! WAIT! YOU DON'T GET TO--YOU CAN'T!

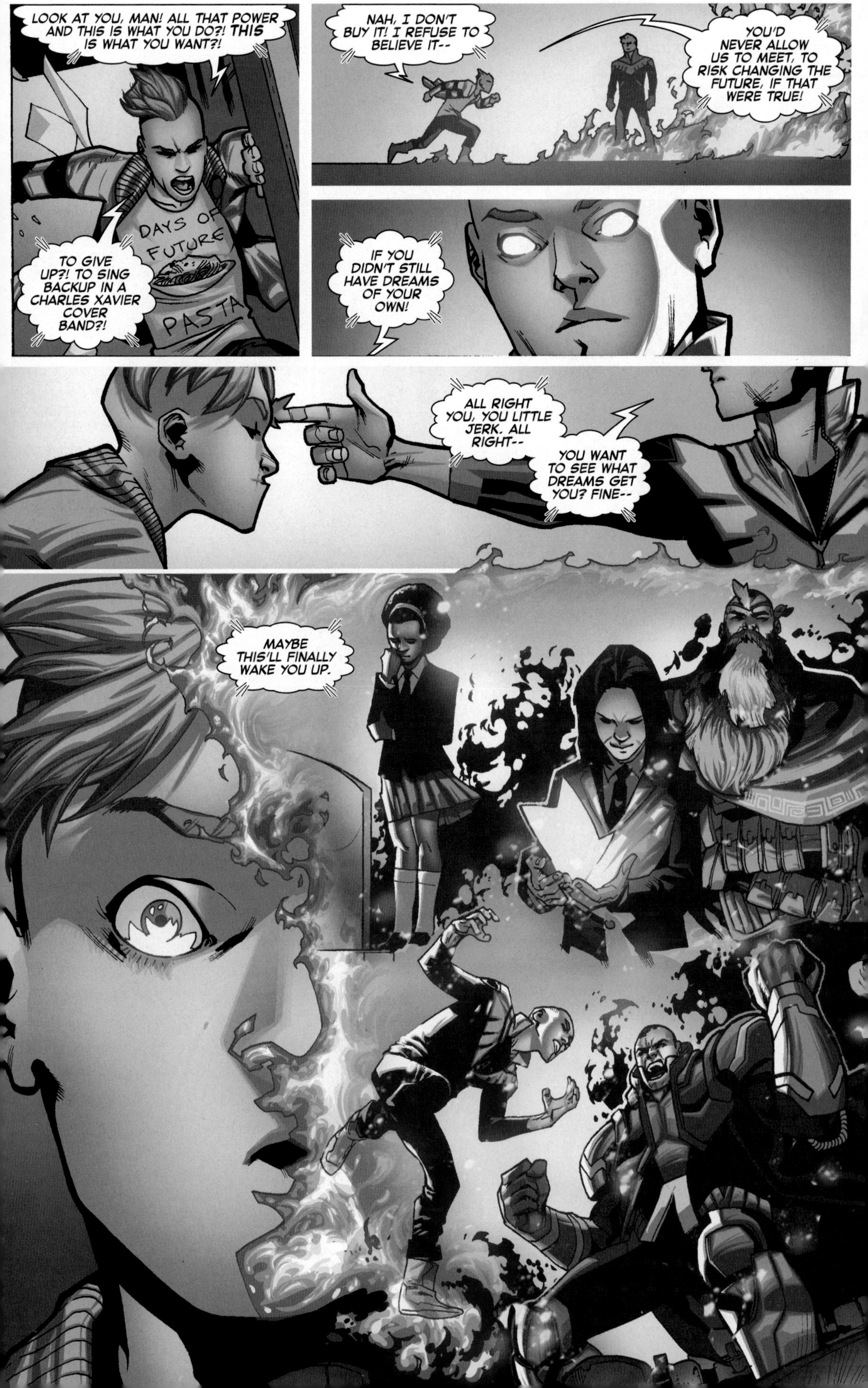
LOOK AT YOU, MAN! ALL THAT POWER AND THIS IS WHAT YOU DO?! THIS IS WHAT YOU WANT?!
DAYS OF FUTURE PASTA
TO GIVE UP?! TO SING BACKUP IN A CHARLES XAVIER COVER BAND?!
NAH, I DON'T BUY IT! I REFUSE TO BELIEVE IT--
YOU'D NEVER ALLOW US TO MEET, TO RISK CHANGING THE FUTURE, IF THAT WERE TRUE!
IF YOU DIDN'T STILL HAVE DREAMS OF YOUR OWN!
ALL RIGHT YOU, YOU LITTLE JERK. ALL RIGHT--
YOU WANT TO SEE WHAT DREAMS GET YOU? FINE--
MAYBE THIS'LL FINALLY WAKE YOU UP.

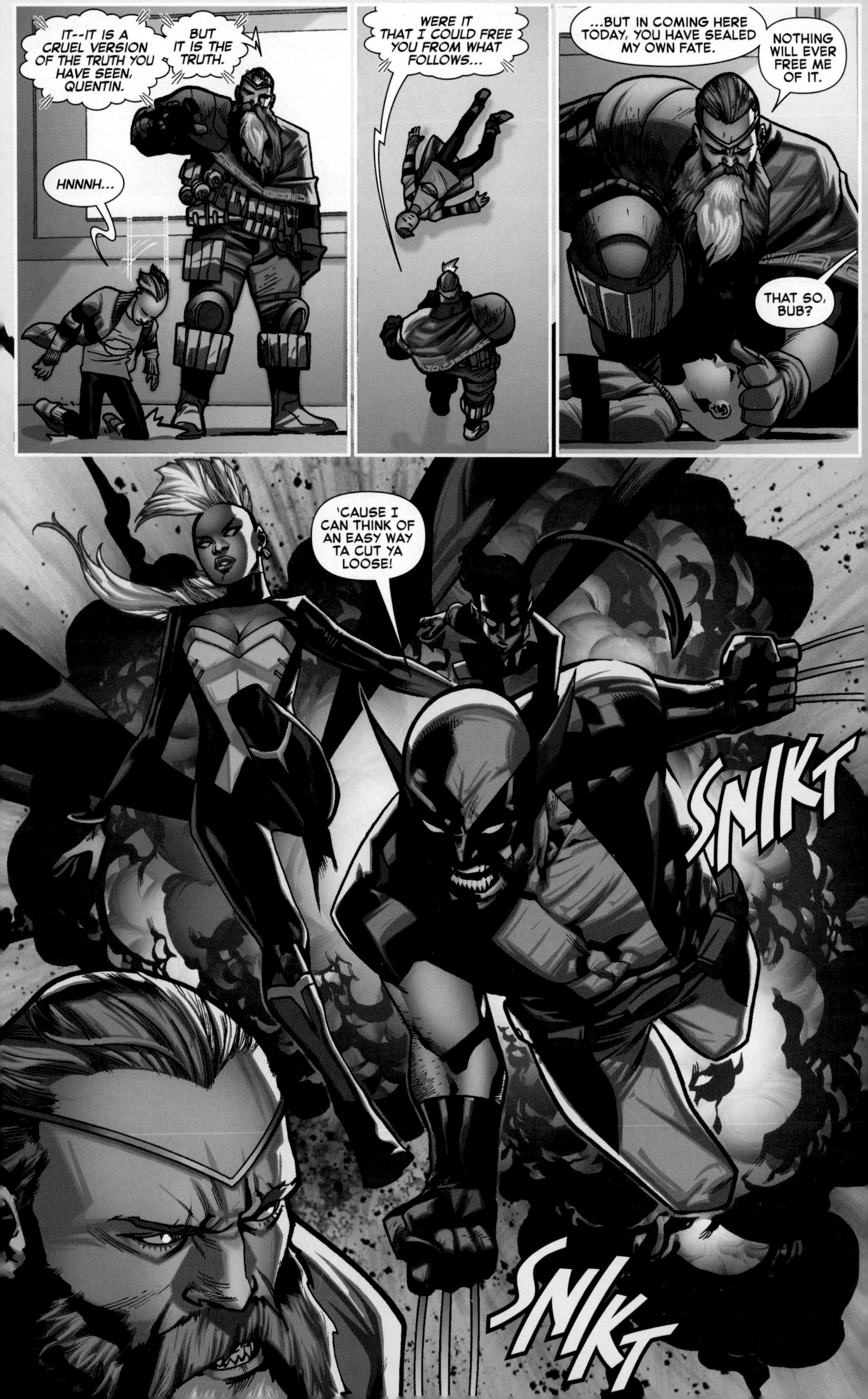
IT--IT IS A CRUEL VERSION OF THE TRUTH YOU HAVE SEEN, QUENTIN.
BUT IT IS THE TRUTH.
HNNNH...
WERE IT THAT I COULD FREE YOU FROM WHAT FOLLOWS...
...BUT IN COMING HERE TODAY, YOU HAVE SEALED MY OWN FATE.
NOTHING WILL EVER FREE ME OF IT.
THAT SO, BUB?
'CAUSE I CAN THINK OF AN EASY WAY TA CUT YA LOOSE!
SNIKT
SNIKT

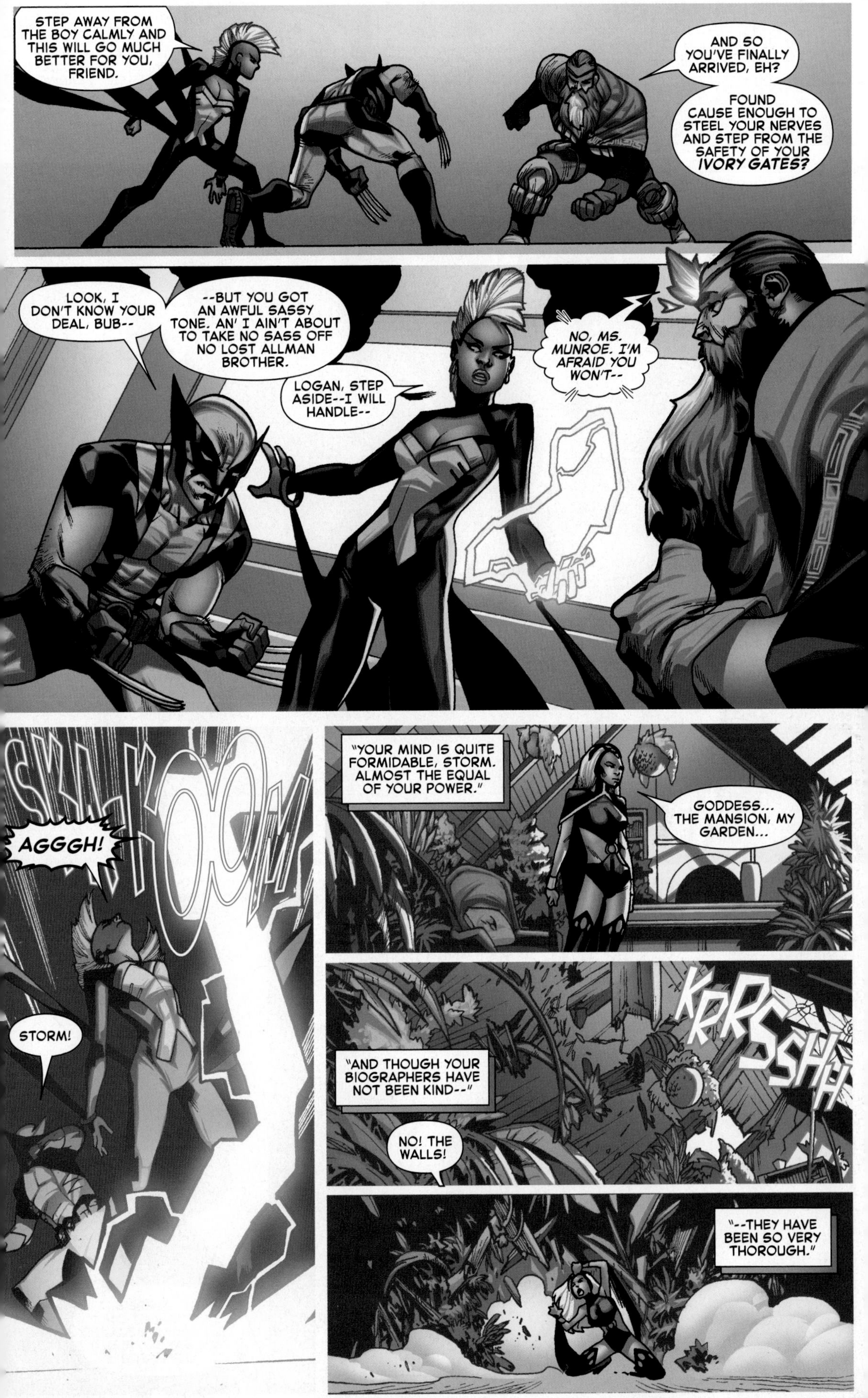
STEP AWAY FROM THE BOY CALMLY AND THIS WILL GO MUCH BETTER FOR YOU, FRIEND.
AND SO YOU'VE FINALLY ARRIVED, EH?
FOUND CAUSE ENOUGH TO STEEL YOUR NERVES AND STEP FROM THE SAFETY OF YOUR *IVORY GATES?*
LOOK, I DON'T KNOW YOUR DEAL, BUB--
--BUT YOU GOT AN AWFUL SASSY TONE. AN' I AIN'T ABOUT TO TAKE NO SASS OFF NO LOST ALLMAN BROTHER.
LOGAN, STEP ASIDE--I WILL HANDLE--
NO, MS. MUNROE. I'M AFRAID YOU WON'T--
SKA-KOOM
AGGGH!
STORM!
"YOUR MIND IS QUITE FORMIDABLE, STORM. ALMOST THE EQUAL OF YOUR POWER."
GODDESS... THE MANSION, MY GARDEN...
KRRSSHH
"AND THOUGH YOUR BIOGRAPHERS HAVE NOT BEEN KIND--"
NO! THE WALLS!
"--THEY HAVE BEEN SO VERY THOROUGH."

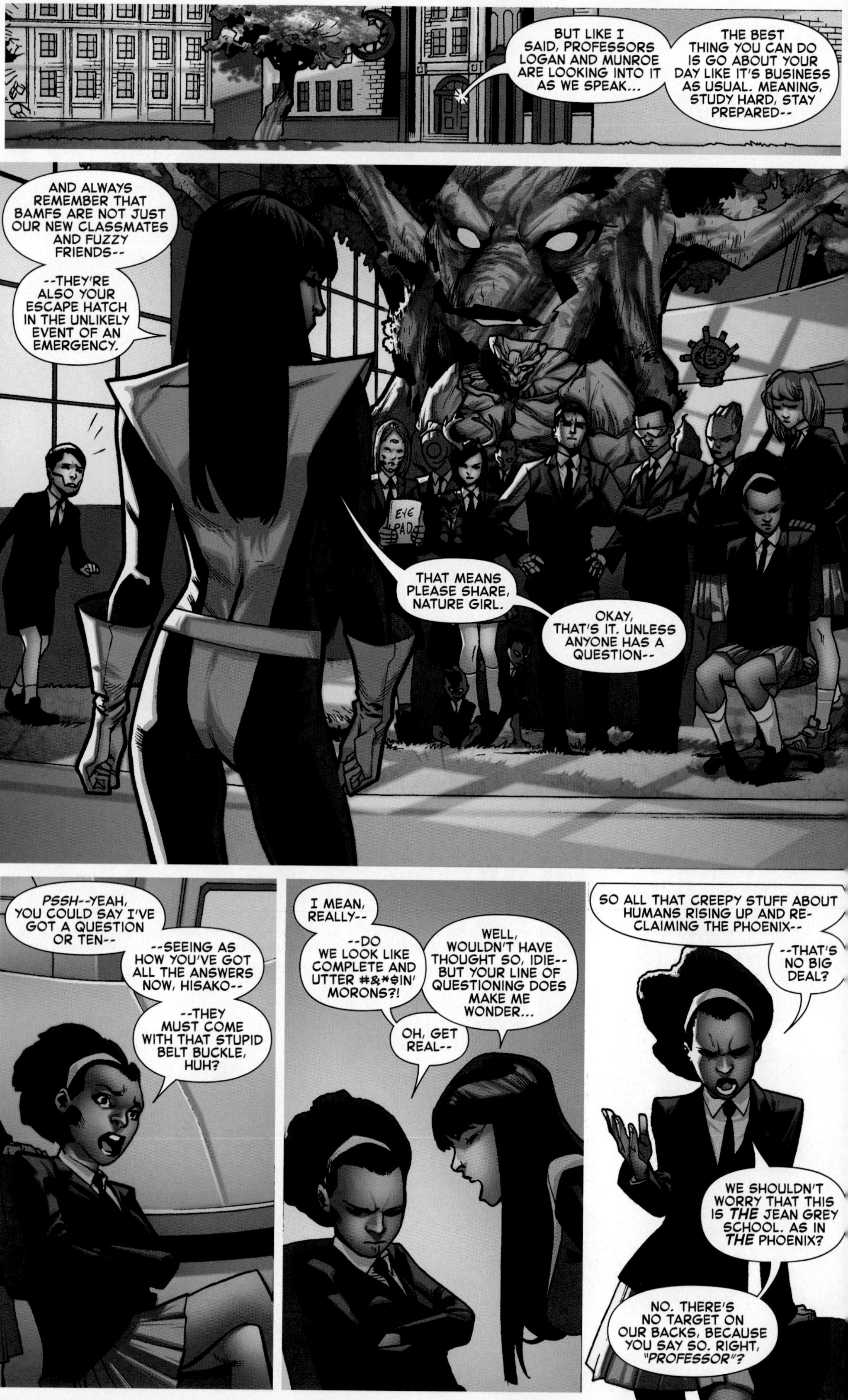
BUT LIKE I SAID, PROFESSORS LOGAN AND MUNROE ARE LOOKING INTO IT AS WE SPEAK...
THE BEST THING YOU CAN DO IS GO ABOUT YOUR DAY LIKE IT'S BUSINESS AS USUAL. MEANING, STUDY HARD, STAY PREPARED--
AND ALWAYS REMEMBER THAT BAMFS ARE NOT JUST OUR NEW CLASSMATES AND FUZZY FRIENDS--
--THEY'RE ALSO YOUR ESCAPE HATCH IN THE UNLIKELY EVENT OF AN EMERGENCY.
EYE PAD
THAT MEANS PLEASE SHARE, NATURE GIRL.
OKAY, THAT'S IT. UNLESS ANYONE HAS A QUESTION--
PSSH--YEAH, YOU COULD SAY I'VE GOT A QUESTION OR TEN--
--SEEING AS HOW YOU'VE GOT ALL THE ANSWERS NOW, HISAKO--
--THEY MUST COME WITH THAT STUPID BELT BUCKLE, HUH?
I MEAN, REALLY--
--DO WE LOOK LIKE COMPLETE AND UTTER #&*$IN' MORONS?!
WELL, WOULDN'T HAVE THOUGHT SO, IDIE--BUT YOUR LINE OF QUESTIONING DOES MAKE ME WONDER...
OH, GET REAL--
SO ALL THAT CREEPY STUFF ABOUT HUMANS RISING UP AND RE-CLAIMING THE PHOENIX--
--THAT'S NO BIG DEAL?
WE SHOULDN'T WORRY THAT THIS IS *THE* JEAN GREY SCHOOL. AS IN *THE* PHOENIX?
NO. THERE'S NO TARGET ON OUR BACKS, BECAUSE YOU SAY SO. RIGHT, "*PROFESSOR*"?

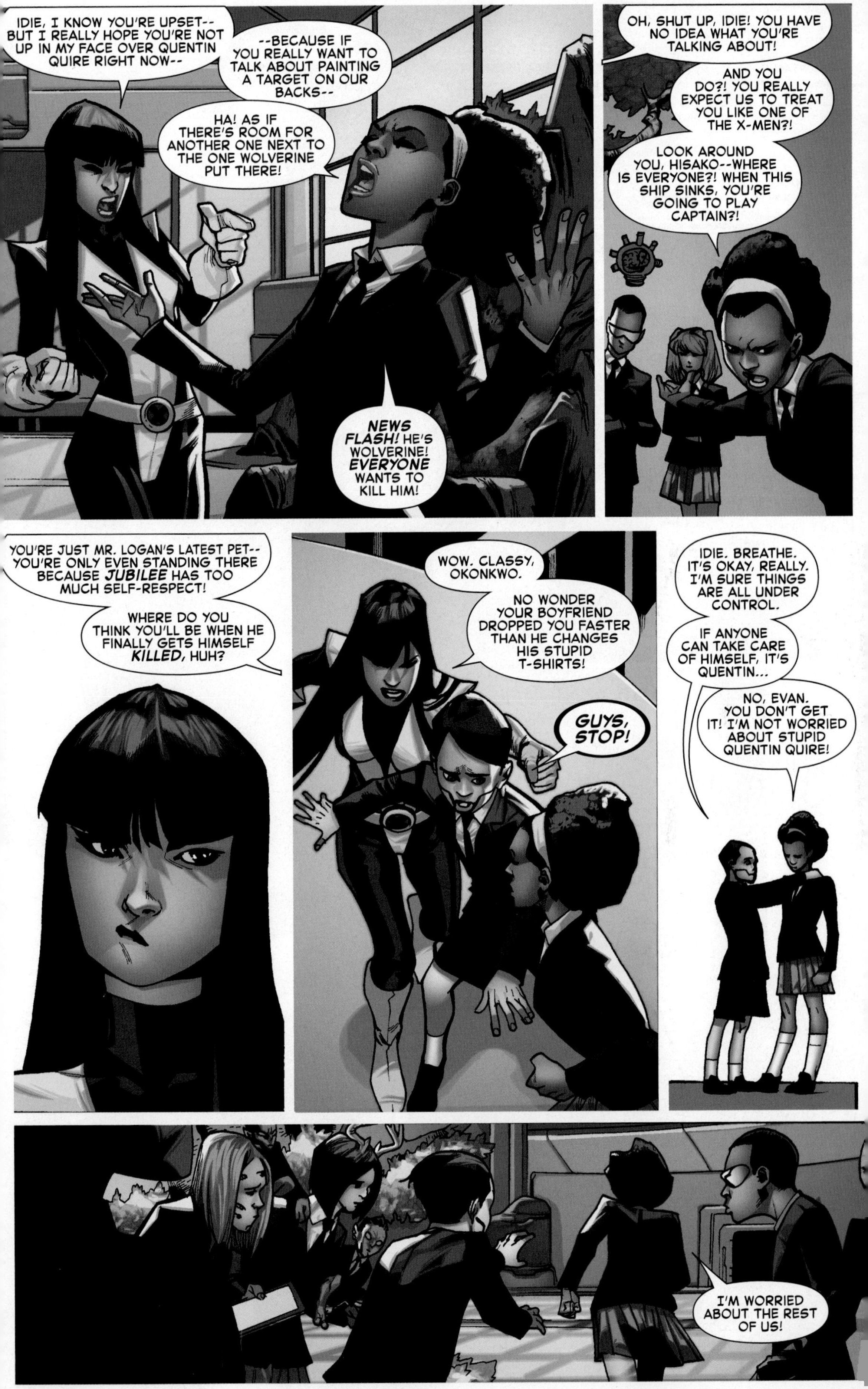

IDIE, I KNOW YOU'RE UPSET-- BUT I REALLY HOPE YOU'RE NOT UP IN MY FACE OVER QUENTIN QUIRE RIGHT NOW--
--BECAUSE IF YOU REALLY WANT TO TALK ABOUT PAINTING A TARGET ON OUR BACKS--
HA! AS IF THERE'S ROOM FOR ANOTHER ONE NEXT TO THE ONE WOLVERINE PUT THERE!
NEWS FLASH! HE'S WOLVERINE! EVERYONE WANTS TO KILL HIM!
OH, SHUT UP, IDIE! YOU HAVE NO IDEA WHAT YOU'RE TALKING ABOUT!
AND YOU DO?! YOU REALLY EXPECT US TO TREAT YOU LIKE ONE OF THE X-MEN?!
LOOK AROUND YOU, HISAKO--WHERE IS EVERYONE?! WHEN THIS SHIP SINKS, YOU'RE GOING TO PLAY CAPTAIN?!
YOU'RE JUST MR. LOGAN'S LATEST PET-- YOU'RE ONLY EVEN STANDING THERE BECAUSE JUBILEE HAS TOO MUCH SELF-RESPECT!
WHERE DO YOU THINK YOU'LL BE WHEN HE FINALLY GETS HIMSELF KILLED, HUH?
WOW. CLASSY, OKONKWO.
NO WONDER YOUR BOYFRIEND DROPPED YOU FASTER THAN HE CHANGES HIS STUPID T-SHIRTS!
GUYS, STOP!
IDIE. BREATHE. IT'S OKAY, REALLY. I'M SURE THINGS ARE ALL UNDER CONTROL.
IF ANYONE CAN TAKE CARE OF HIMSELF, IT'S QUENTIN...
NO, EVAN. YOU DON'T GET IT! I'M NOT WORRIED ABOUT STUPID QUENTIN QUIRE!
I'M WORRIED ABOUT THE REST OF US!

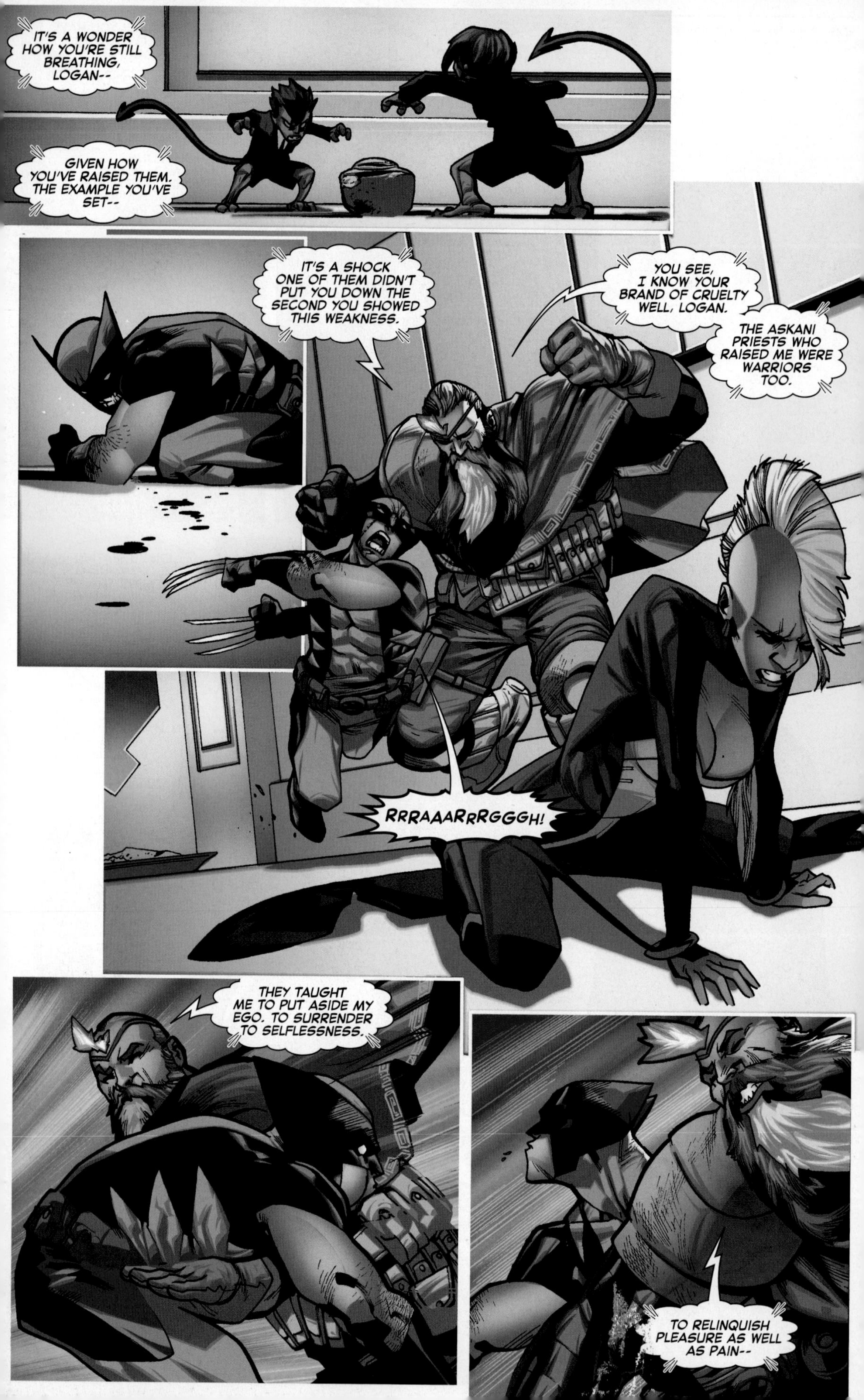
IT'S A WONDER HOW YOU'RE STILL BREATHING, LOGAN--
GIVEN HOW YOU'VE RAISED THEM. THE EXAMPLE YOU'VE SET--
IT'S A SHOCK ONE OF THEM DIDN'T PUT YOU DOWN THE SECOND YOU SHOWED THIS WEAKNESS.
YOU SEE, I KNOW YOUR BRAND OF CRUELTY WELL, LOGAN.
THE ASKANI PRIESTS WHO RAISED ME WERE WARRIORS TOO.
RRRAAARRRGGGH!
THEY TAUGHT ME TO PUT ASIDE MY EGO. TO SURRENDER TO SELFLESSNESS.
TO RELINQUISH PLEASURE AS WELL AS PAIN--

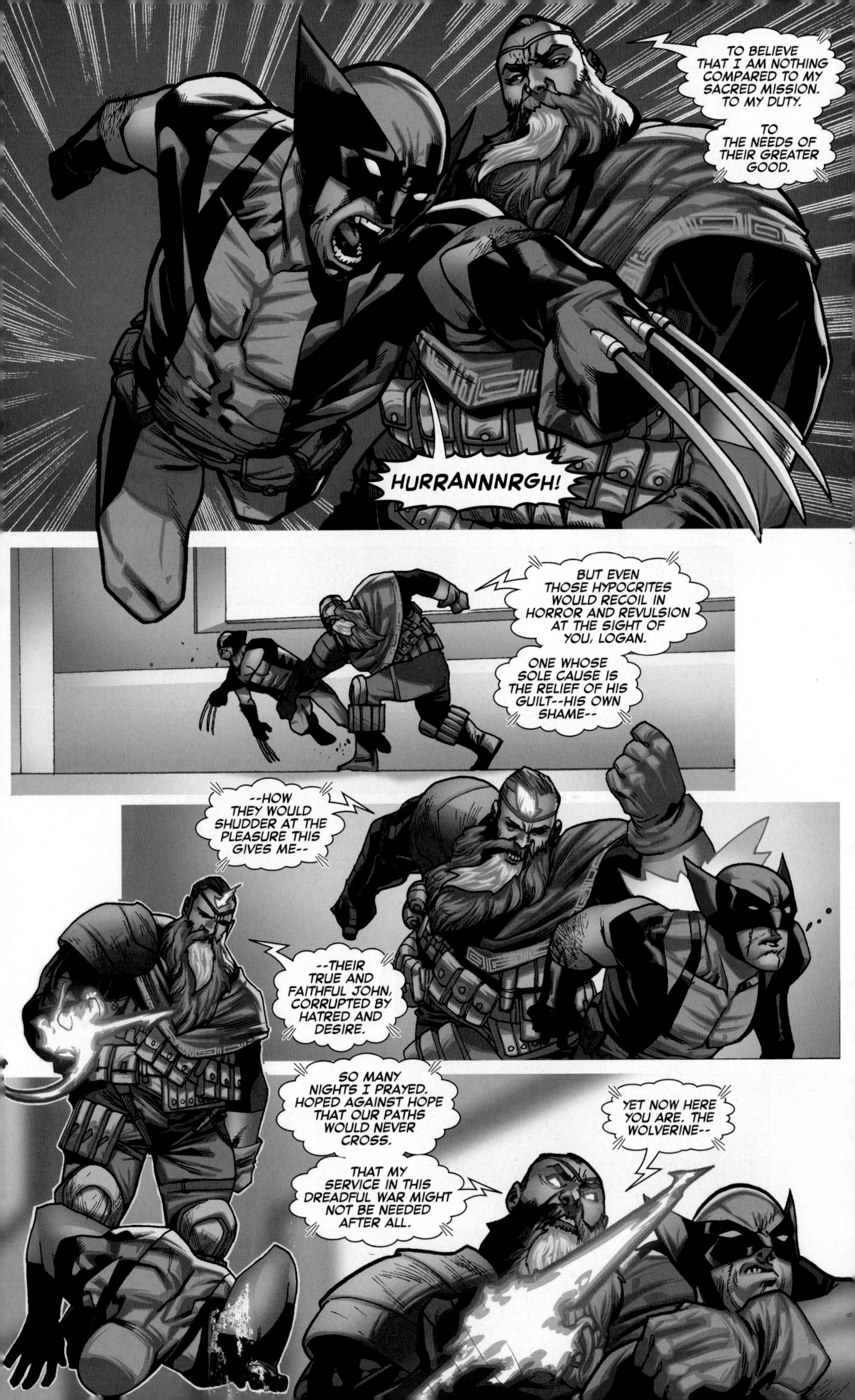
TO BELIEVE THAT I AM NOTHING COMPARED TO MY SACRED MISSION. TO MY DUTY.
TO THE NEEDS OF THEIR GREATER GOOD.
HURRANNNRGH!
BUT EVEN THOSE HYPOCRITES WOULD RECOIL IN HORROR AND REVULSION AT THE SIGHT OF YOU, LOGAN.
ONE WHOSE SOLE CAUSE IS THE RELIEF OF HIS GUILT--HIS OWN SHAME--
--HOW THEY WOULD SHUDDER AT THE PLEASURE THIS GIVES ME--
--THEIR TRUE AND FAITHFUL JOHN, CORRUPTED BY HATRED AND DESIRE.
SO MANY NIGHTS I PRAYED. HOPED AGAINST HOPE THAT OUR PATHS WOULD NEVER CROSS.
THAT MY SERVICE IN THIS DREADFUL WAR MIGHT NOT BE NEEDED AFTER ALL.
YET NOW HERE YOU ARE. THE WOLVERINE--

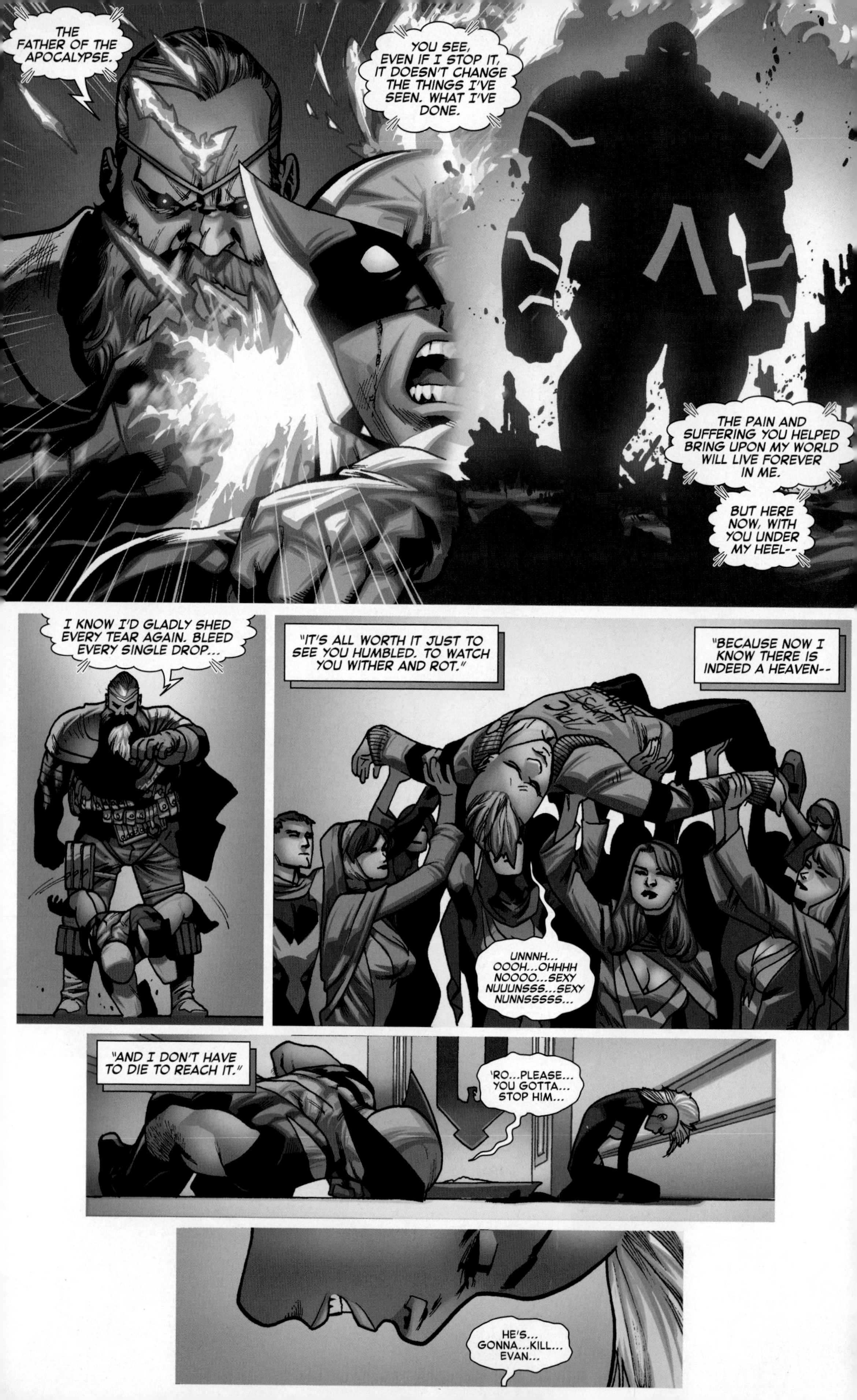
THE FATHER OF THE APOCALYPSE.
YOU SEE, EVEN IF I STOP IT, IT DOESN'T CHANGE THE THINGS I'VE SEEN. WHAT I'VE DONE.
THE PAIN AND SUFFERING YOU HELPED BRING UPON MY WORLD WILL LIVE FOREVER IN ME.
BUT HERE NOW, WITH YOU UNDER MY HEEL--
I KNOW I'D GLADLY SHED EVERY TEAR AGAIN. BLEED EVERY SINGLE DROP...
"IT'S ALL WORTH IT JUST TO SEE YOU HUMBLED. TO WATCH YOU WITHER AND ROT."
"BECAUSE NOW I KNOW THERE IS INDEED A HEAVEN--
UNNNH... OOOH...OHHHH NOOOO...SEXY NUUUNSSS...SEXY NUNNSSSSS...
"AND I DON'T HAVE TO DIE TO REACH IT."
'RO...PLEASE... YOU GOTTA... STOP HIM...
HE'S... GONNA...KILL... EVAN...

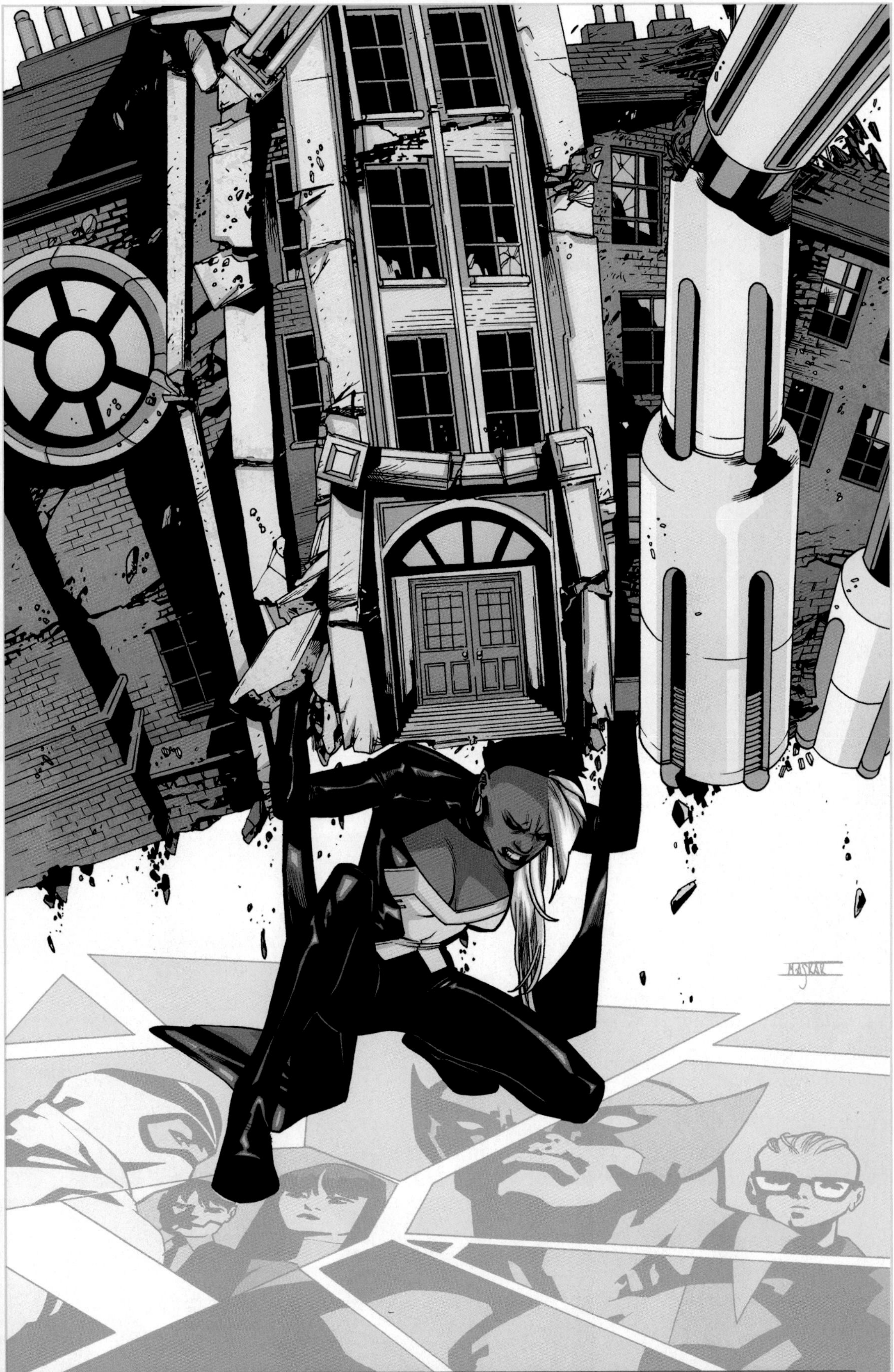

3

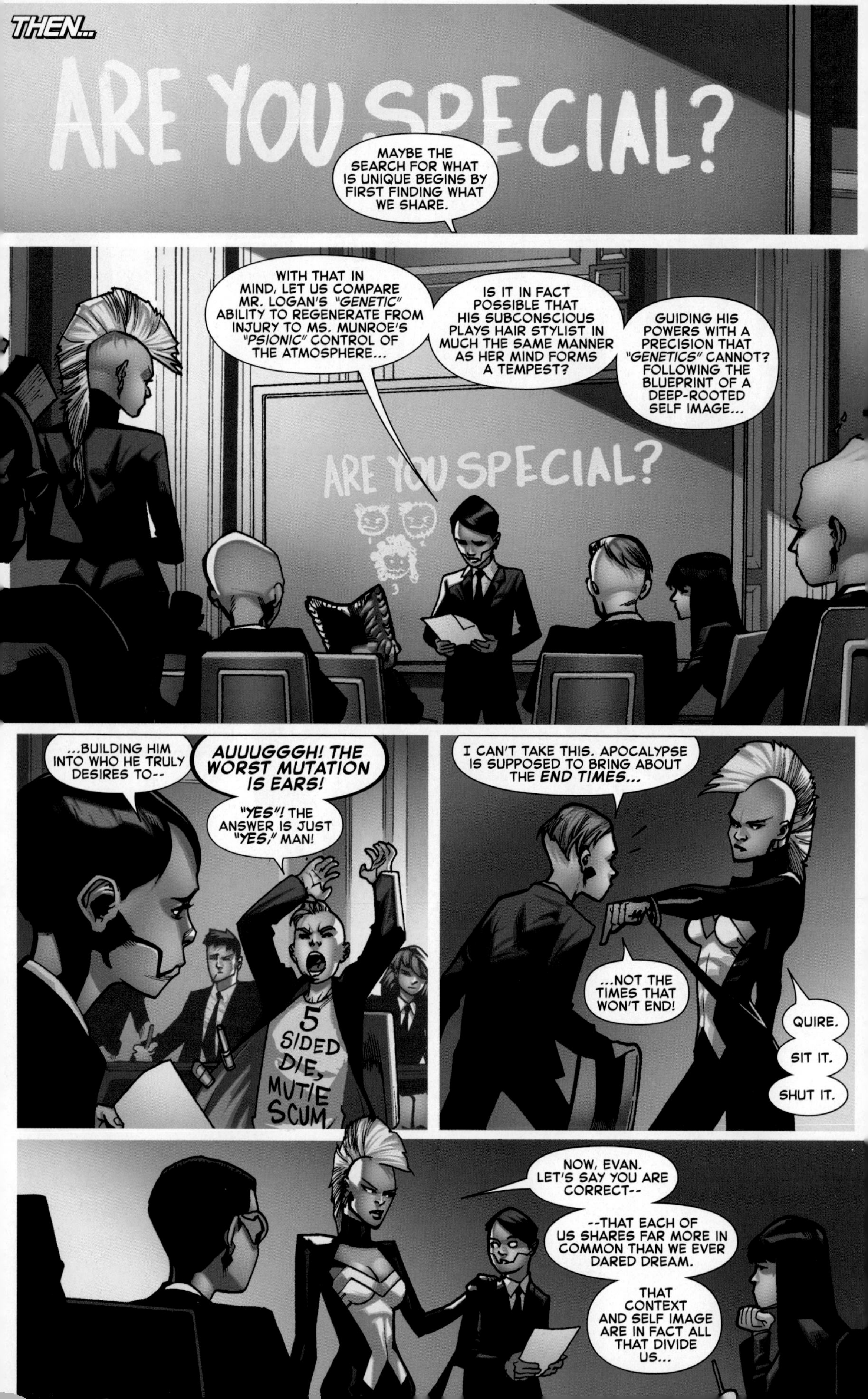
THEN...
ARE YOU SPECIAL?
MAYBE THE SEARCH FOR WHAT IS UNIQUE BEGINS BY FIRST FINDING WHAT WE SHARE.
WITH THAT IN MIND, LET US COMPARE MR. LOGAN'S "GENETIC" ABILITY TO REGENERATE FROM INJURY TO MS. MUNROE'S "PSIONIC" CONTROL OF THE ATMOSPHERE...
IS IT IN FACT POSSIBLE THAT HIS SUBCONSCIOUS PLAYS HAIR STYLIST IN MUCH THE SAME MANNER AS HER MIND FORMS A TEMPEST?
GUIDING HIS POWERS WITH A PRECISION THAT "GENETICS" CANNOT? FOLLOWING THE BLUEPRINT OF A DEEP-ROOTED SELF IMAGE...
ARE YOU SPECIAL?
...BUILDING HIM INTO WHO HE TRULY DESIRES TO--
AUUUGGGH! THE WORST MUTATION IS EARS!
"YES"! THE ANSWER IS JUST "YES," MAN!
5 SIDED DIE, MUTIE SCUM
I CAN'T TAKE THIS. APOCALYPSE IS SUPPOSED TO BRING ABOUT THE END TIMES...
...NOT THE TIMES THAT WON'T END!
QUIRE.
SIT IT.
SHUT IT.
NOW, EVAN. LET'S SAY YOU ARE CORRECT--
--THAT EACH OF US SHARES FAR MORE IN COMMON THAN WE EVER DARED DREAM.
THAT CONTEXT AND SELF IMAGE ARE IN FACT ALL THAT DIVIDE US...

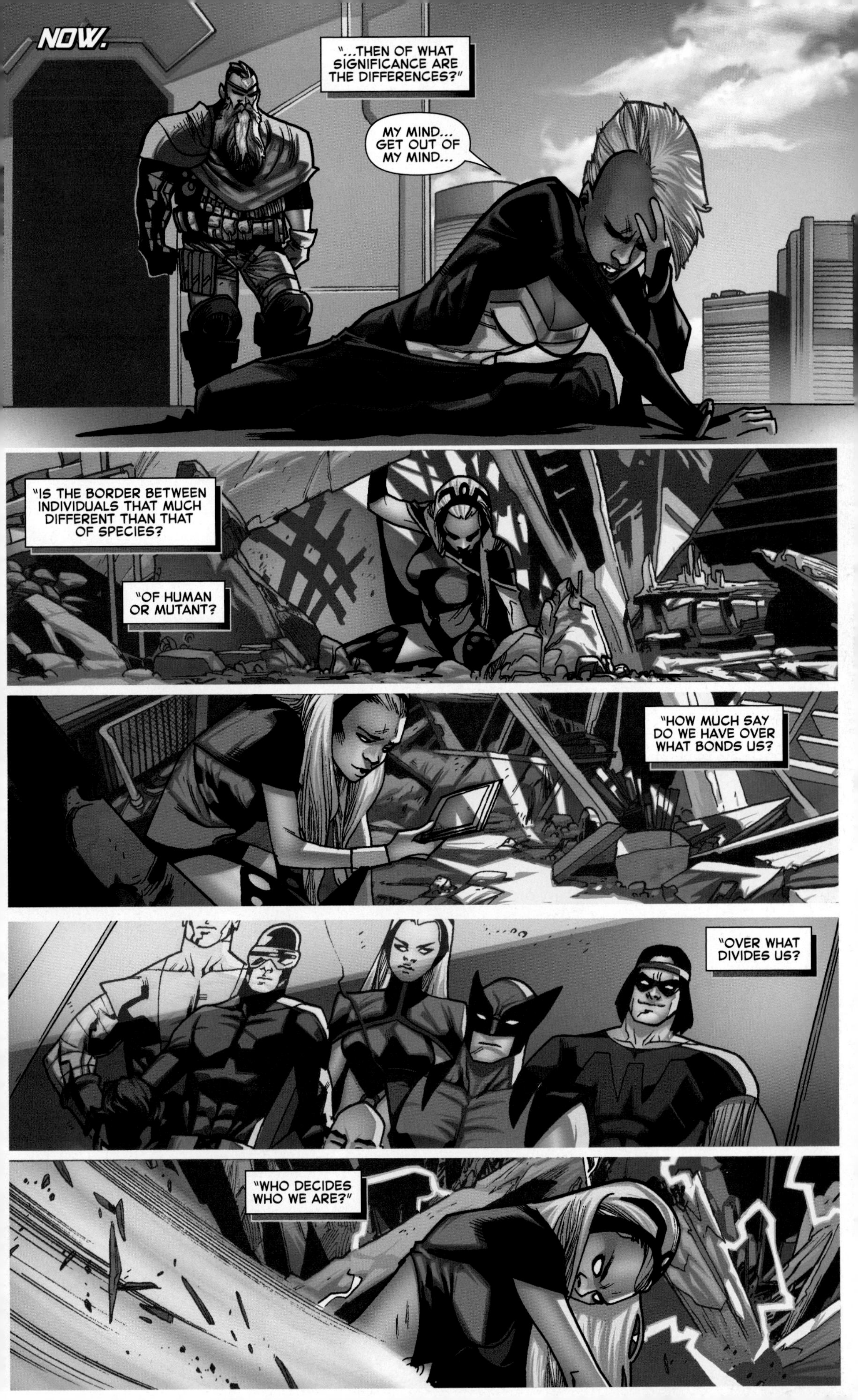
NOW.
"...THEN OF WHAT SIGNIFICANCE ARE THE DIFFERENCES?"
MY MIND... GET OUT OF MY MIND...
"IS THE BORDER BETWEEN INDIVIDUALS THAT MUCH DIFFERENT THAN THAT OF SPECIES?
"OF HUMAN OR MUTANT?
"HOW MUCH SAY DO WE HAVE OVER WHAT BONDS US?
"OVER WHAT DIVIDES US?
"WHO DECIDES WHO WE ARE?"

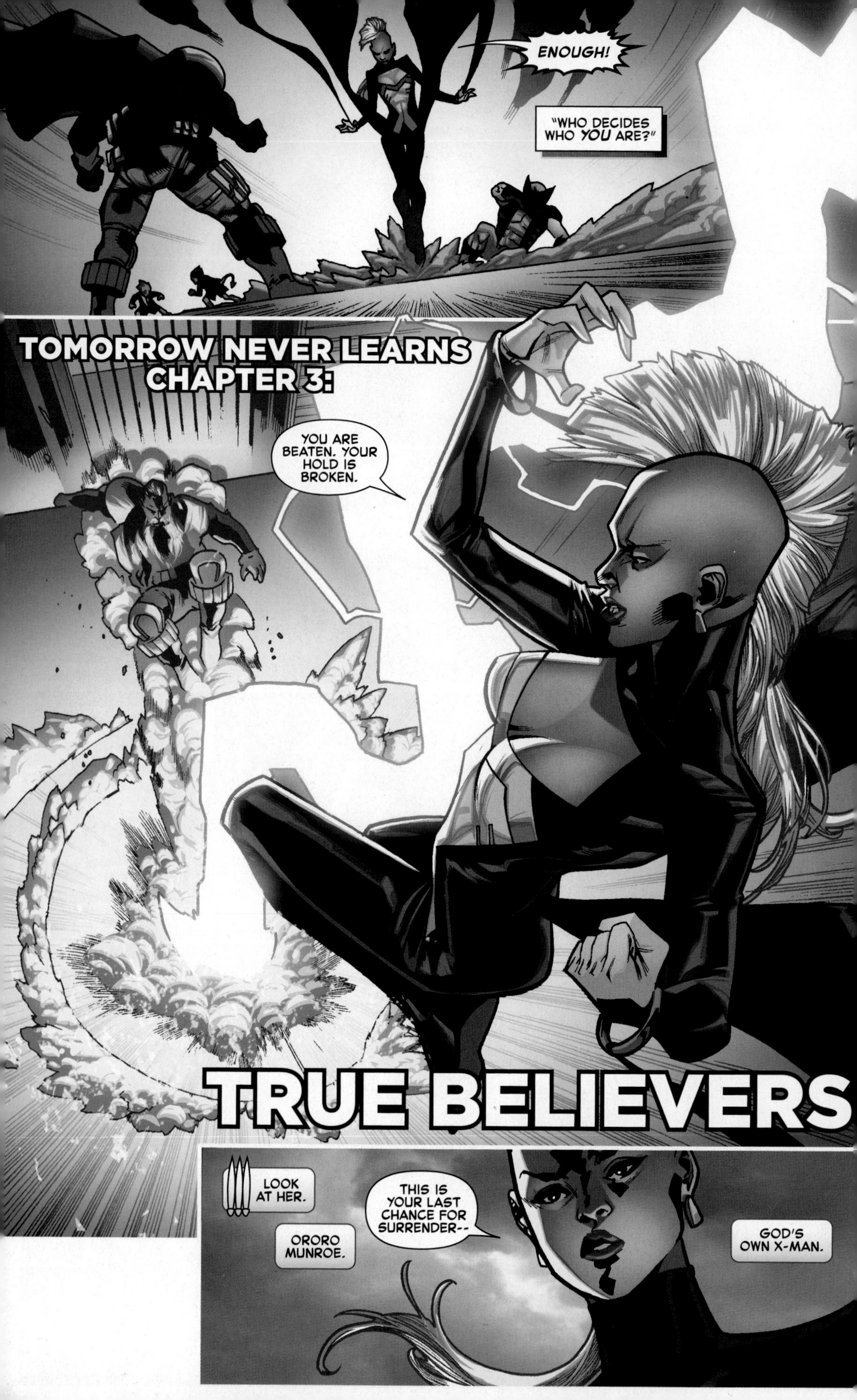
ENOUGH!
"WHO DECIDES WHO YOU ARE?"
TOMORROW NEVER LEARNS CHAPTER 3:
YOU ARE BEATEN. YOUR HOLD IS BROKEN.
TRUE BELIEVERS
LOOK AT HER.
ORORO MUNROE.
THIS IS YOUR LAST CHANCE FOR SURRENDER--
GOD'S OWN X-MAN.

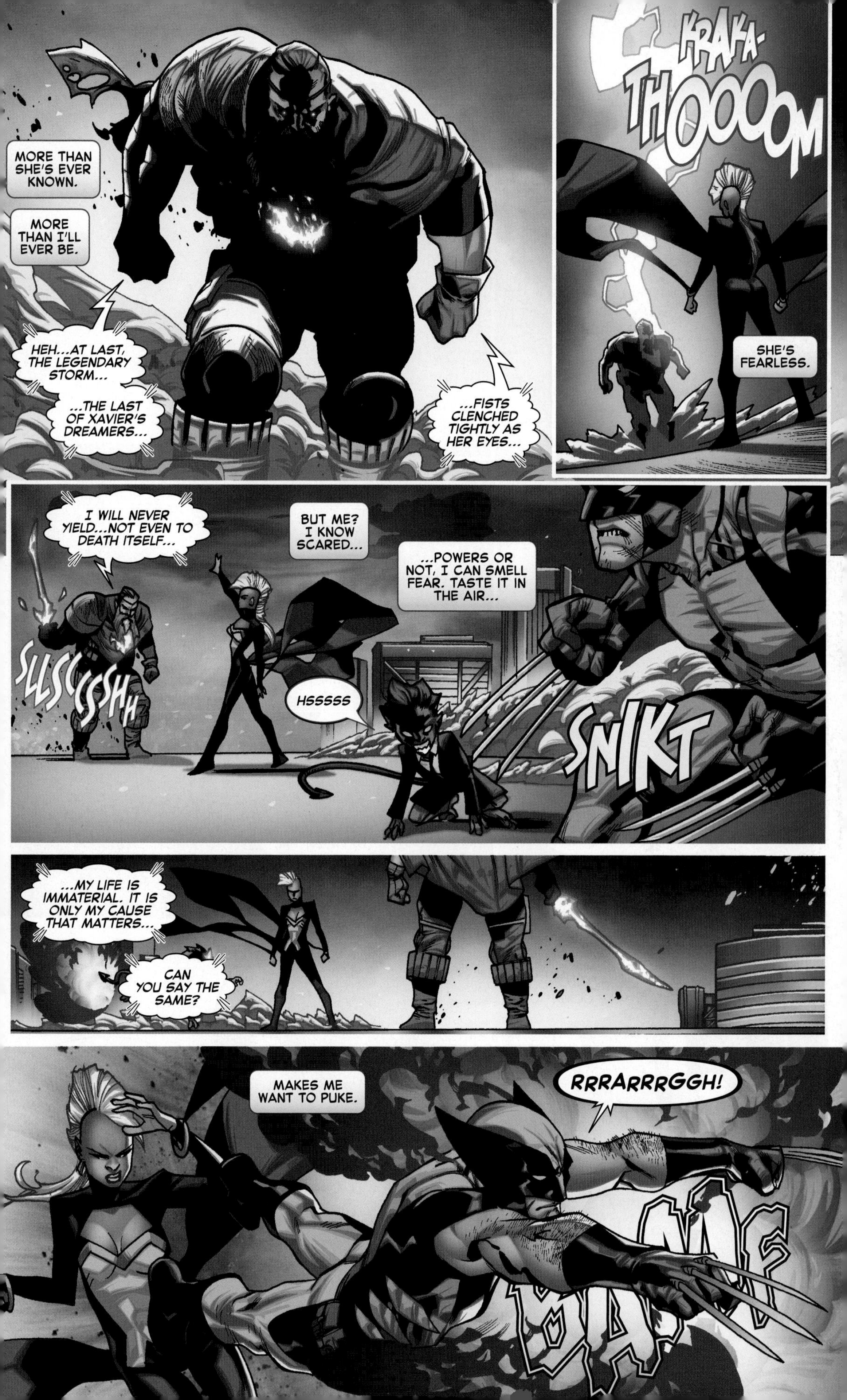
MORE THAN SHE'S EVER KNOWN.
MORE THAN I'LL EVER BE.
HEH...AT LAST, THE LEGENDARY STORM...
...THE LAST OF XAVIER'S DREAMERS...
...FISTS CLENCHED TIGHTLY AS HER EYES...
KRAKA-THOOOOM
SHE'S FEARLESS.
I WILL NEVER YIELD...NOT EVEN TO DEATH ITSELF...
SLLSCSSHH
BUT ME? I KNOW SCARED...
...POWERS OR NOT, I CAN SMELL FEAR. TASTE IT IN THE AIR...
HSSSSS
SNIKT
...MY LIFE IS IMMATERIAL. IT IS ONLY MY CAUSE THAT MATTERS...
CAN YOU SAY THE SAME?
MAKES ME WANT TO PUKE.
RRRARRRGGH!

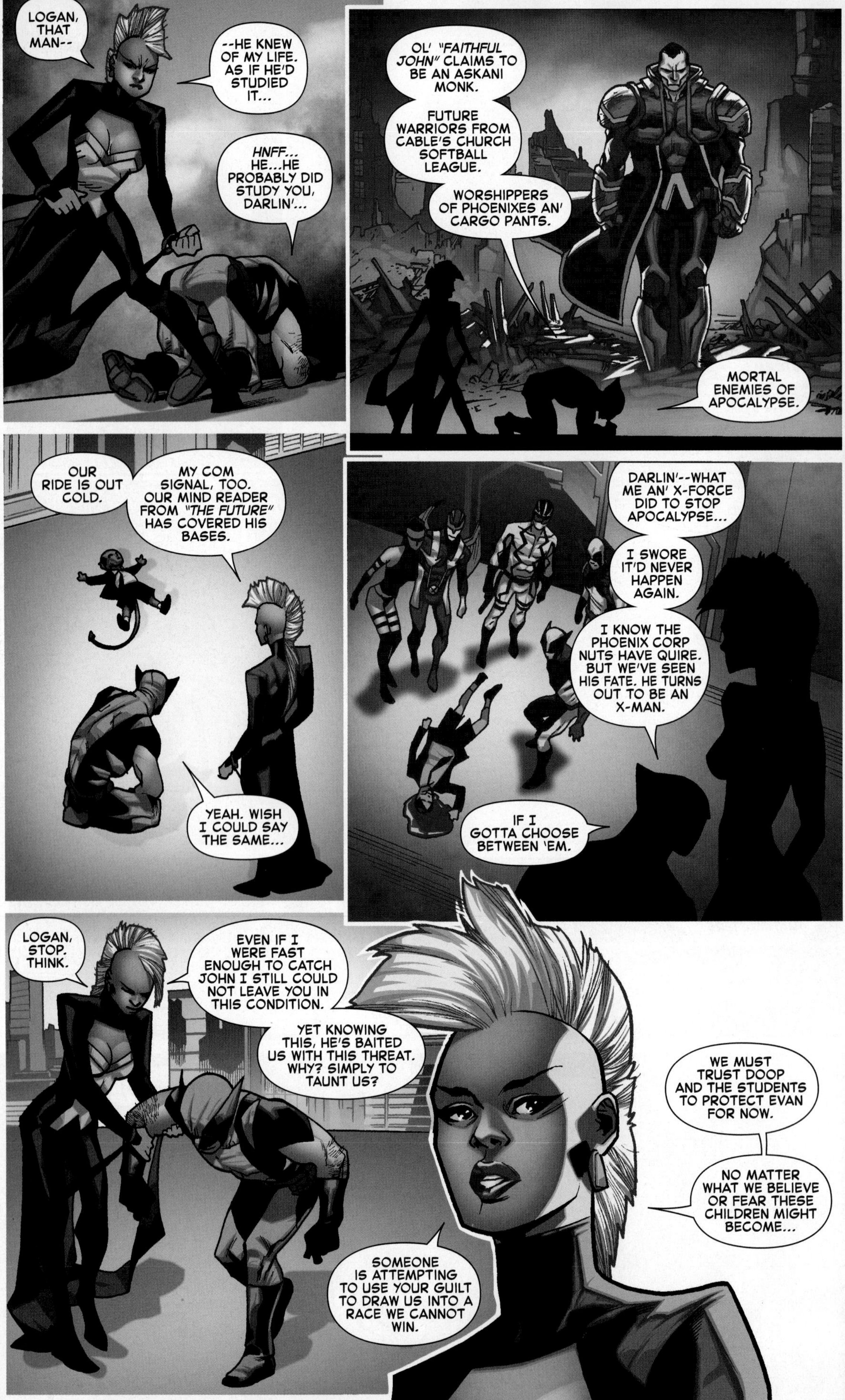
LOGAN, THAT MAN--
--HE KNEW OF MY LIFE. AS IF HE'D STUDIED IT...
HNFF... HE...HE PROBABLY DID STUDY YOU, DARLIN'...
OL' "FAITHFUL JOHN" CLAIMS TO BE AN ASKANI MONK.
FUTURE WARRIORS FROM CABLE'S CHURCH SOFTBALL LEAGUE.
WORSHIPPERS OF PHOENIXES AN' CARGO PANTS.
MORTAL ENEMIES OF APOCALYPSE.
OUR RIDE IS OUT COLD.
MY COM SIGNAL, TOO. OUR MIND READER FROM "THE FUTURE" HAS COVERED HIS BASES.
YEAH. WISH I COULD SAY THE SAME...
DARLIN'--WHAT ME AN' X-FORCE DID TO STOP APOCALYPSE...
I SWORE IT'D NEVER HAPPEN AGAIN.
I KNOW THE PHOENIX CORP NUTS HAVE QUIRE. BUT WE'VE SEEN HIS FATE. HE TURNS OUT TO BE AN X-MAN.
IF I GOTTA CHOOSE BETWEEN 'EM.
LOGAN, STOP. THINK.
EVEN IF I WERE FAST ENOUGH TO CATCH JOHN I STILL COULD NOT LEAVE YOU IN THIS CONDITION.
YET KNOWING THIS, HE'S BAITED US WITH THIS THREAT. WHY? SIMPLY TO TAUNT US?
SOMEONE IS ATTEMPTING TO USE YOUR GUILT TO DRAW US INTO A RACE WE CANNOT WIN.
WE MUST TRUST DOOP AND THE STUDENTS TO PROTECT EVAN FOR NOW.
NO MATTER WHAT WE BELIEVE OR FEAR THESE CHILDREN MIGHT BECOME...

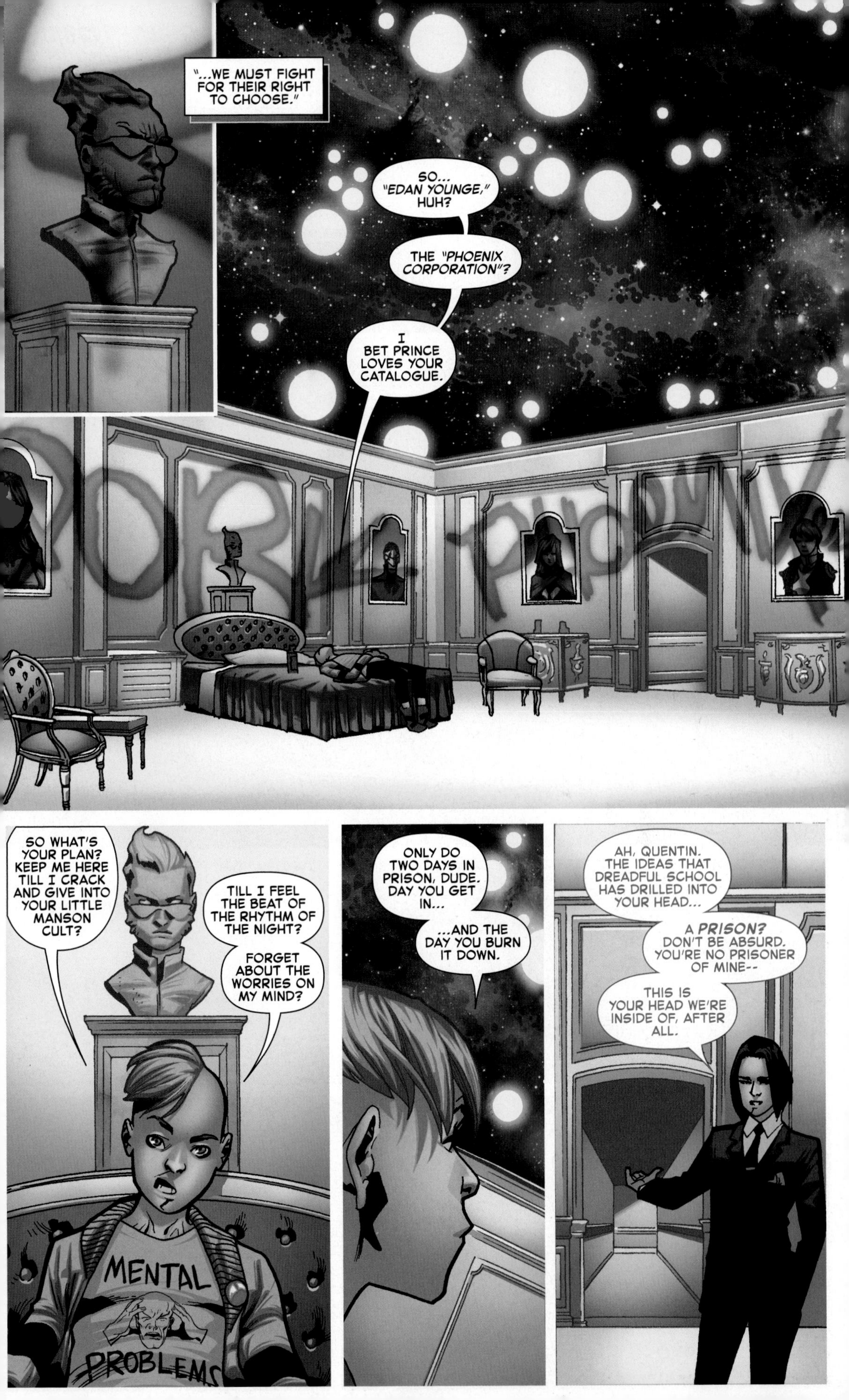
"...WE MUST FIGHT FOR THEIR RIGHT TO CHOOSE."
SO... "EDAN YOUNGE," HUH?
THE "PHOENIX CORPORATION"?
I BET PRINCE LOVES YOUR CATALOGUE.
SO WHAT'S YOUR PLAN? KEEP ME HERE TILL I CRACK AND GIVE INTO YOUR LITTLE MANSON CULT?
TILL I FEEL THE BEAT OF THE RHYTHM OF THE NIGHT?
FORGET ABOUT THE WORRIES ON MY MIND?
MENTAL
PROBLEMS
ONLY DO TWO DAYS IN PRISON, DUDE. DAY YOU GET IN...
...AND THE DAY YOU BURN IT DOWN.
AH, QUENTIN. THE IDEAS THAT DREADFUL SCHOOL HAS DRILLED INTO YOUR HEAD...
A *PRISON?* DON'T BE ABSURD. YOU'RE NO PRISONER OF MINE--
THIS IS YOUR HEAD WE'RE INSIDE OF, AFTER ALL.

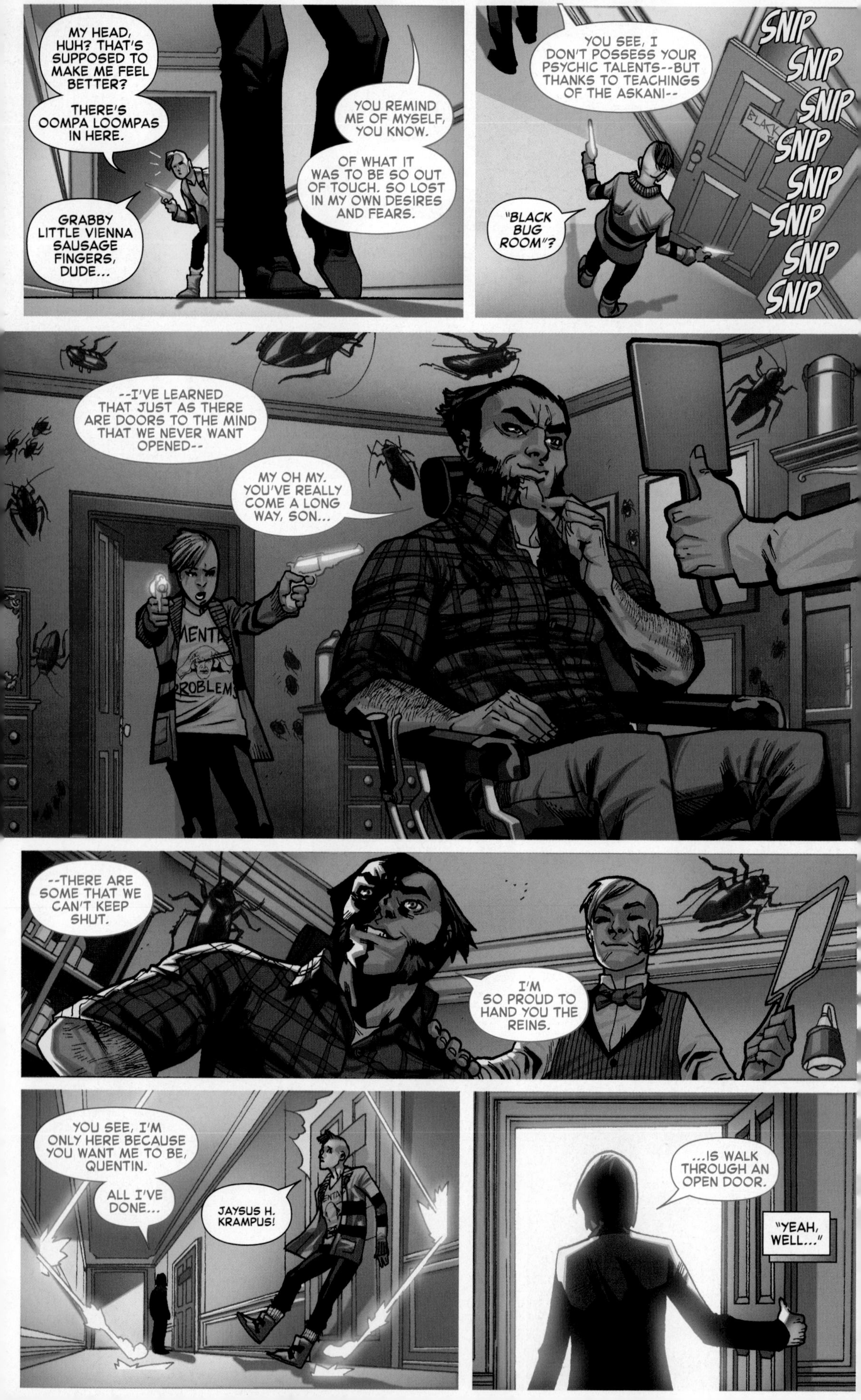

MY HEAD, HUH? THAT'S SUPPOSED TO MAKE ME FEEL BETTER?
THERE'S OOMPA LOOMPAS IN HERE.
GRABBY LITTLE VIENNA SAUSAGE FINGERS, DUDE...
YOU REMIND ME OF MYSELF, YOU KNOW.
OF WHAT IT WAS TO BE SO OUT OF TOUCH. SO LOST IN MY OWN DESIRES AND FEARS.
YOU SEE, I DON'T POSSESS YOUR PSYCHIC TALENTS--BUT THANKS TO TEACHINGS OF THE ASKANI--
"BLACK BUG ROOM"?
SNIP SNIP SNIP SNIP SNIP SNIP SNIP SNIP
--I'VE LEARNED THAT JUST AS THERE ARE DOORS TO THE MIND THAT WE NEVER WANT OPENED--
MY OH MY. YOU'VE REALLY COME A LONG WAY, SON...
MENTAL PROBLEMS
--THERE ARE SOME THAT WE CAN'T KEEP SHUT.
I'M SO PROUD TO HAND YOU THE REINS.
YOU SEE, I'M ONLY HERE BECAUSE YOU WANT ME TO BE, QUENTIN.
ALL I'VE DONE...
JAYSUS H. KRAMPUS!
...IS WALK THROUGH AN OPEN DOOR.
"YEAH, WELL..."

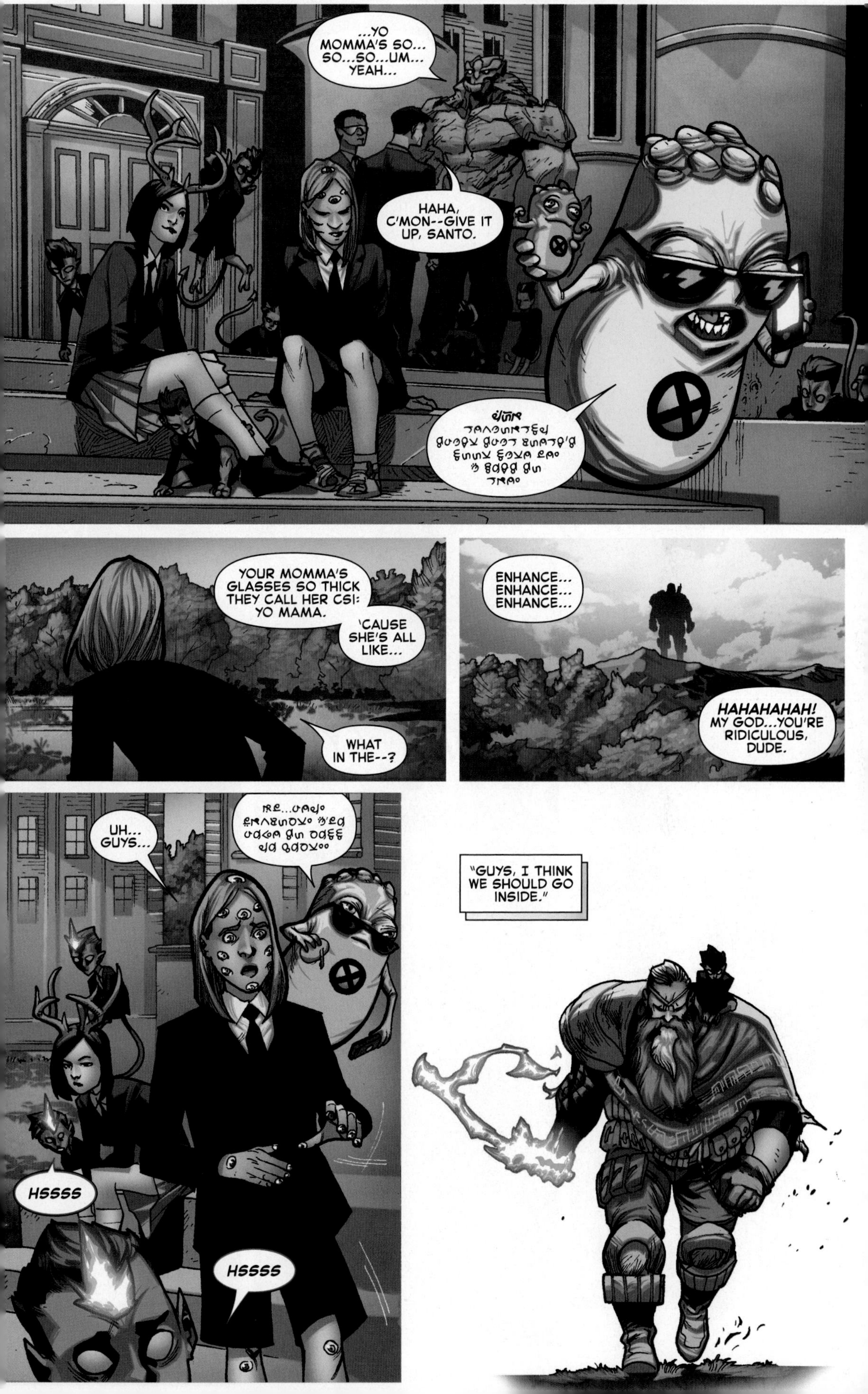
...YO MOMMA'S SO... SO...SO...UM... YEAH...
HAHA, C'MON--GIVE IT UP, SANTO.
YOUR MOMMA'S GLASSES SO THICK THEY CALL HER CSI: YO MAMA.
'CAUSE SHE'S ALL LIKE...
WHAT IN THE--?
ENHANCE... ENHANCE... ENHANCE...
HAHAHAHAH! MY GOD...YOU'RE RIDICULOUS, DUDE.
UH... GUYS...
HSSSS
HSSSS
"GUYS, I THINK WE SHOULD GO INSIDE."

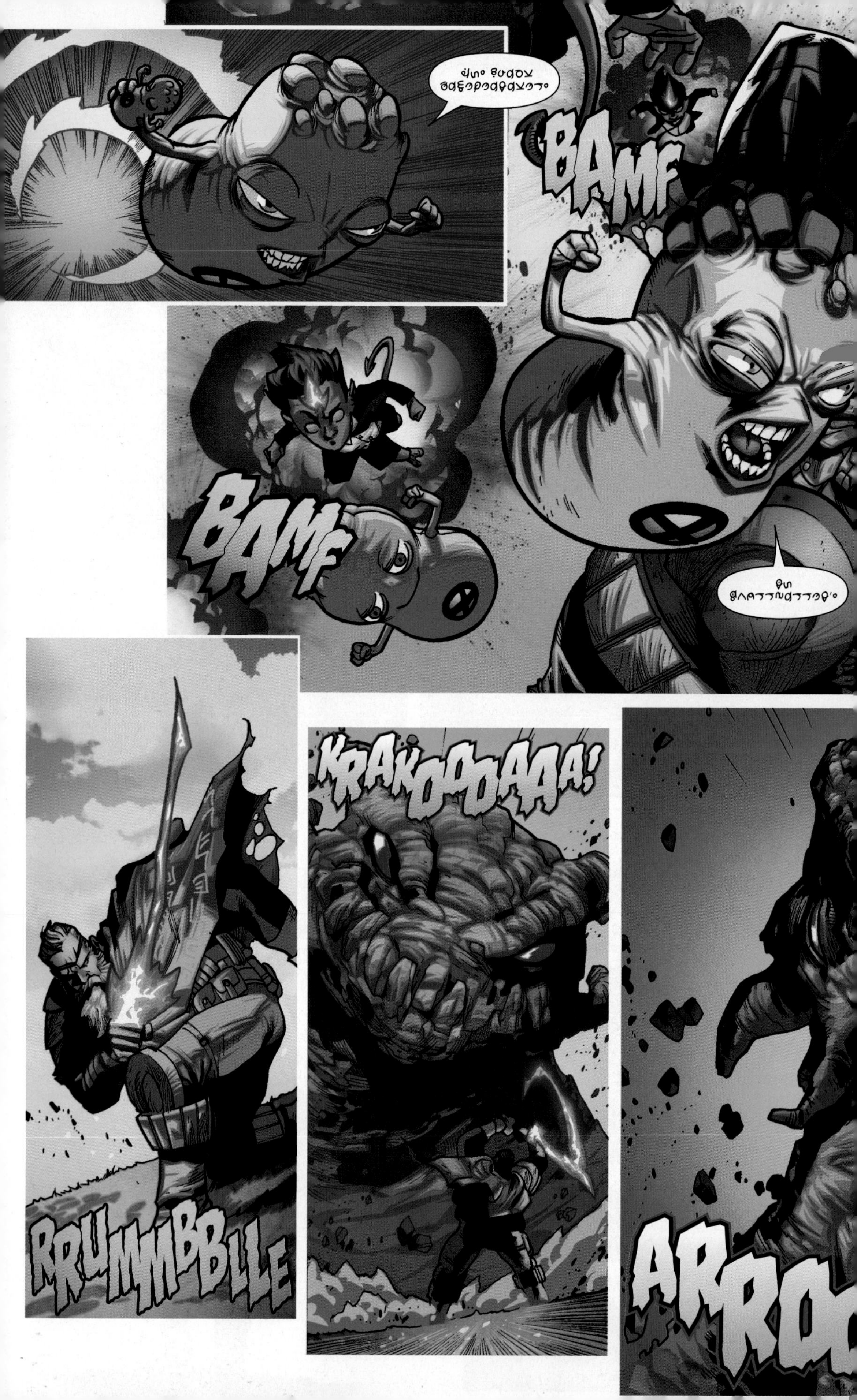
BAMF
BAMF
RRUMMBBLE
KRAKOOOAAA!
ARRO

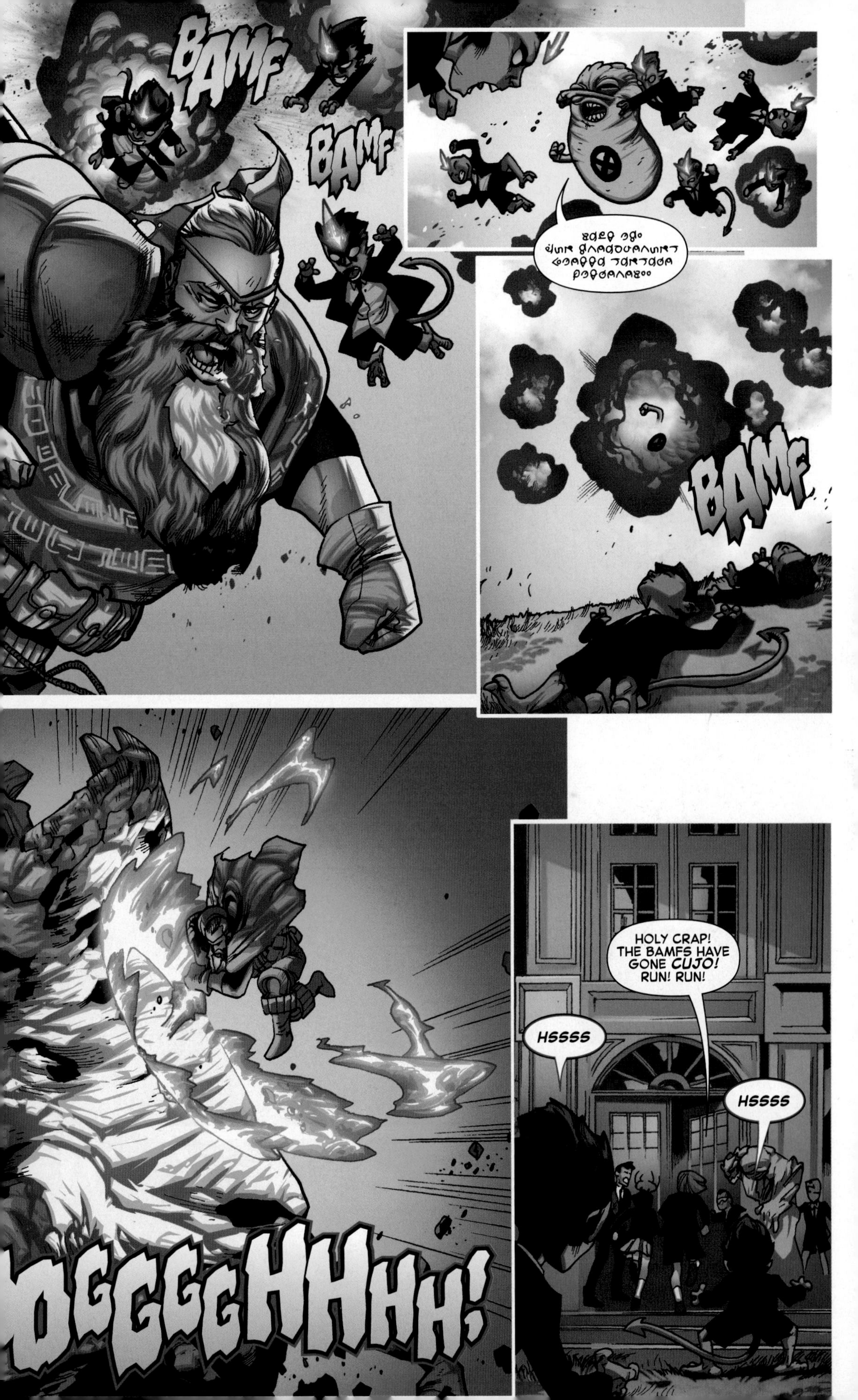
BAMF
BAMF
BAMF
HOLY CRAP! THE BAMFS HAVE GONE *CUJO*! RUN! RUN!
HSSSS
HSSSS
OGGGHHHH!

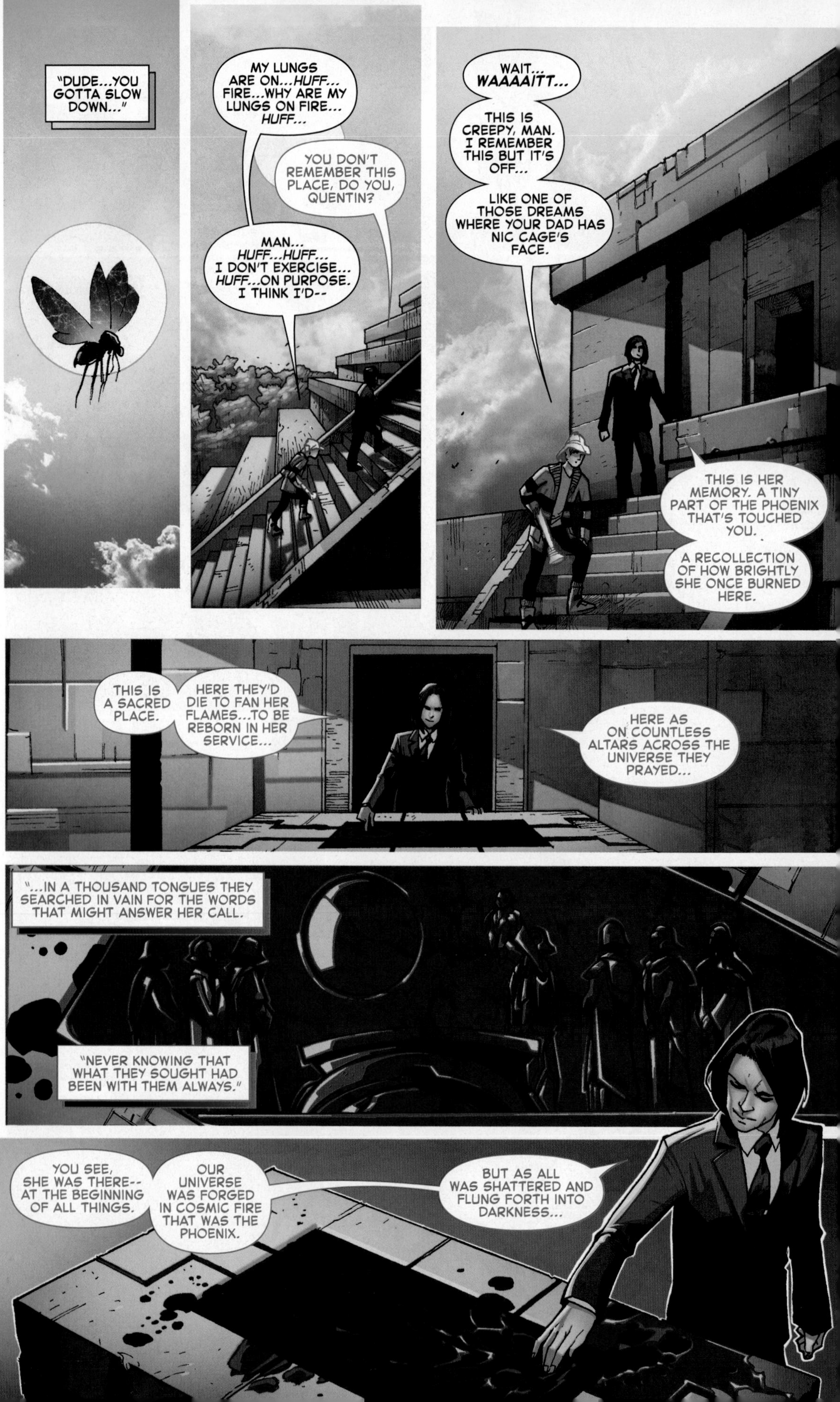
"DUDE...YOU GOTTA SLOW DOWN..."
MY LUNGS ARE ON...HUFF... FIRE...WHY ARE MY LUNGS ON FIRE... HUFF...
YOU DON'T REMEMBER THIS PLACE, DO YOU, QUENTIN?
MAN... HUFF...HUFF... I DON'T EXERCISE... HUFF...ON PURPOSE. I THINK I'D--
WAIT... WAAAAITT...
THIS IS CREEPY, MAN. I REMEMBER THIS BUT IT'S OFF...
LIKE ONE OF THOSE DREAMS WHERE YOUR DAD HAS NIC CAGE'S FACE.
THIS IS HER MEMORY. A TINY PART OF THE PHOENIX THAT'S TOUCHED YOU.
A RECOLLECTION OF HOW BRIGHTLY SHE ONCE BURNED HERE.
THIS IS A SACRED PLACE.
HERE THEY'D DIE TO FAN HER FLAMES...TO BE REBORN IN HER SERVICE...
HERE AS ON COUNTLESS ALTARS ACROSS THE UNIVERSE THEY PRAYED...
"...IN A THOUSAND TONGUES THEY SEARCHED IN VAIN FOR THE WORDS THAT MIGHT ANSWER HER CALL.
"NEVER KNOWING THAT WHAT THEY SOUGHT HAD BEEN WITH THEM ALWAYS."
YOU SEE, SHE WAS THERE-- AT THE BEGINNING OF ALL THINGS.
OUR UNIVERSE WAS FORGED IN COSMIC FIRE THAT WAS THE PHOENIX.
BUT AS ALL WAS SHATTERED AND FLUNG FORTH INTO DARKNESS...

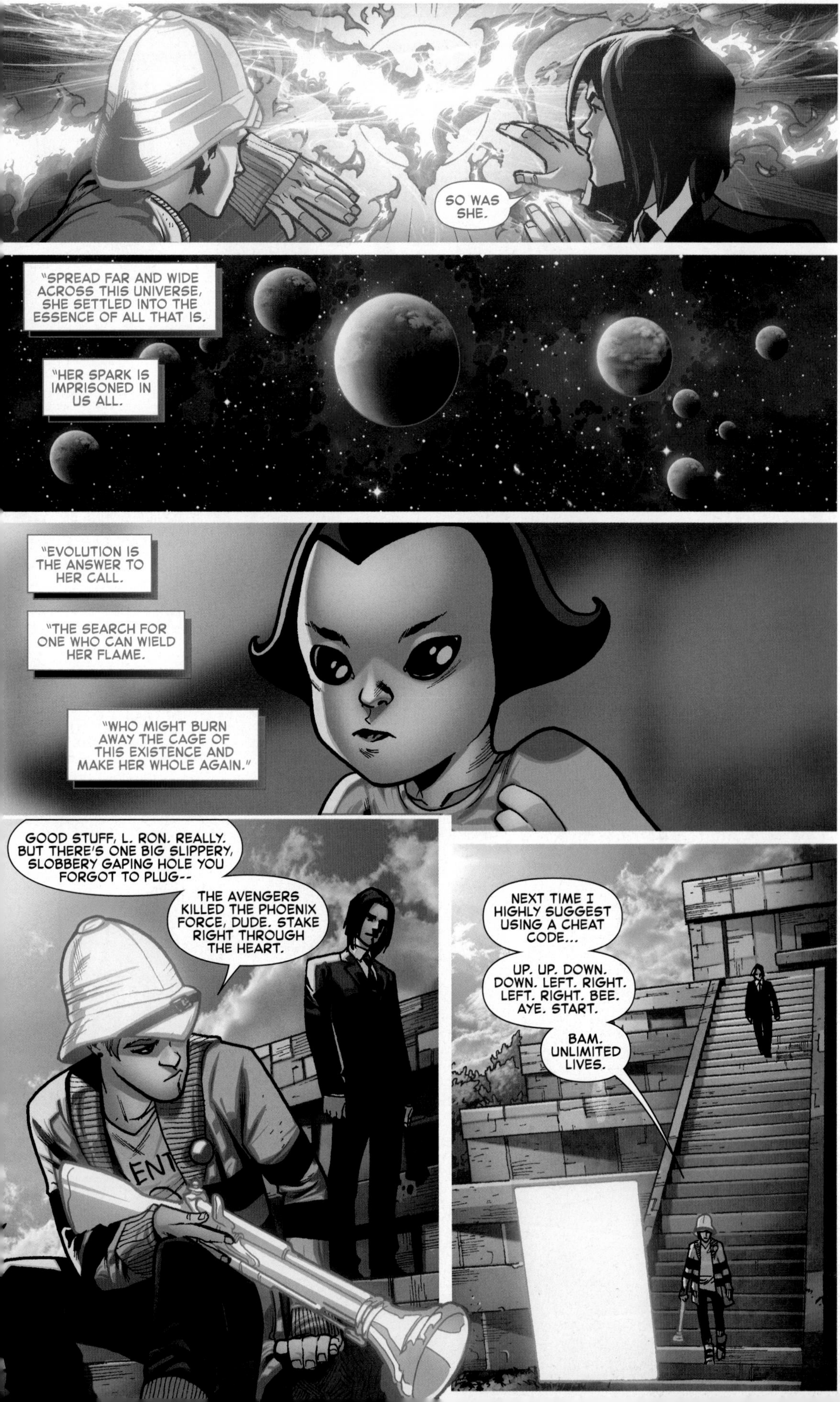

SO WAS SHE.
"SPREAD FAR AND WIDE ACROSS THIS UNIVERSE, SHE SETTLED INTO THE ESSENCE OF ALL THAT IS.
"HER SPARK IS IMPRISONED IN US ALL.
"EVOLUTION IS THE ANSWER TO HER CALL.
"THE SEARCH FOR ONE WHO CAN WIELD HER FLAME.
"WHO MIGHT BURN AWAY THE CAGE OF THIS EXISTENCE AND MAKE HER WHOLE AGAIN."
GOOD STUFF, L. RON. REALLY. BUT THERE'S ONE BIG SLIPPERY, SLOBBERY GAPING HOLE YOU FORGOT TO PLUG--
THE AVENGERS KILLED THE PHOENIX FORCE, DUDE. STAKE RIGHT THROUGH THE HEART.
NEXT TIME I HIGHLY SUGGEST USING A CHEAT CODE...
UP. UP. DOWN. DOWN. LEFT. RIGHT. LEFT. RIGHT. BEE. AYE. START.
BAM. UNLIMITED LIVES.

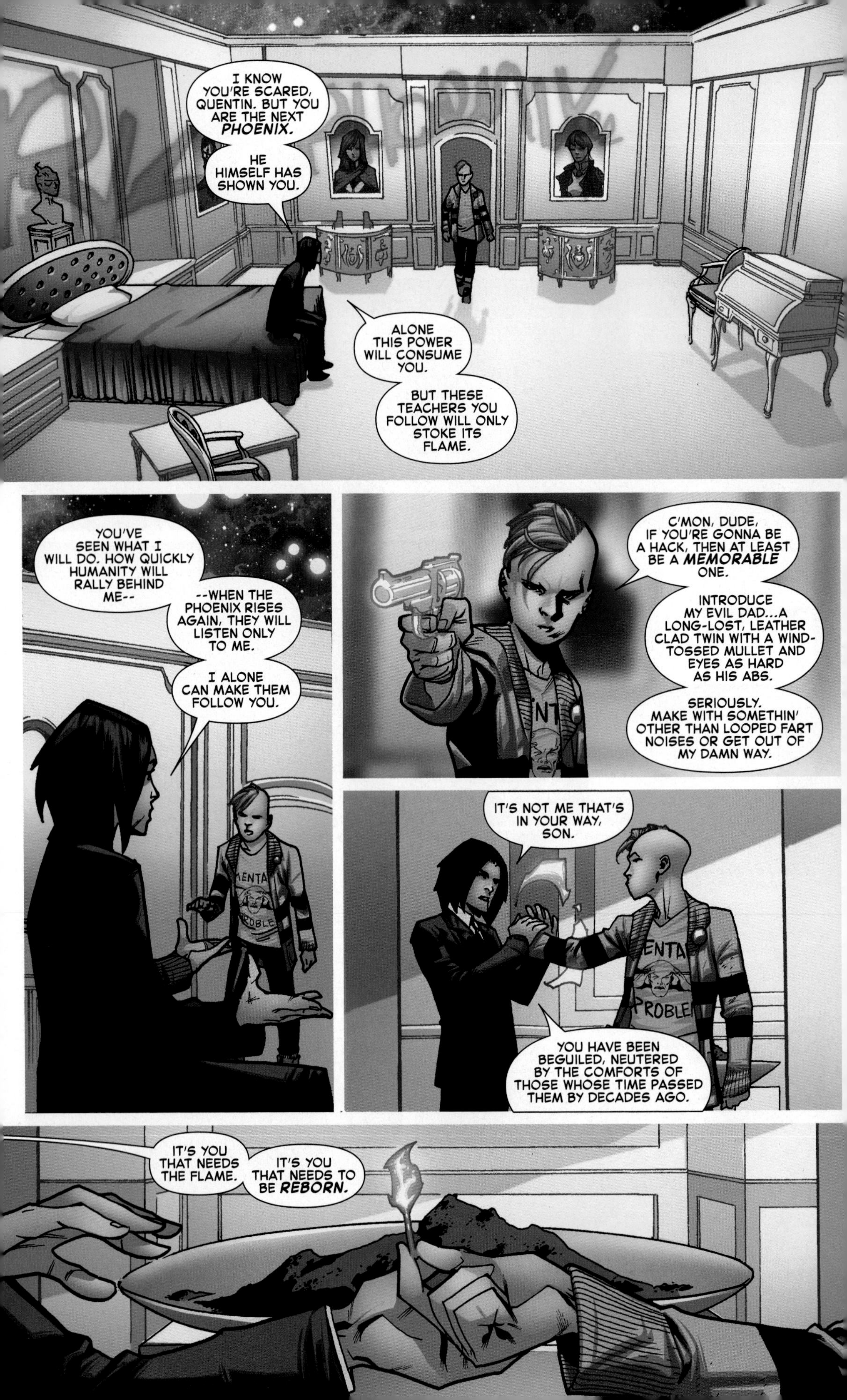
I KNOW YOU'RE SCARED, QUENTIN. BUT YOU ARE THE NEXT PHOENIX.
HE HIMSELF HAS SHOWN YOU.
ALONE THIS POWER WILL CONSUME YOU.
BUT THESE TEACHERS YOU FOLLOW WILL ONLY STOKE ITS FLAME.
YOU'VE SEEN WHAT I WILL DO. HOW QUICKLY HUMANITY WILL RALLY BEHIND ME--
--WHEN THE PHOENIX RISES AGAIN, THEY WILL LISTEN ONLY TO ME.
I ALONE CAN MAKE THEM FOLLOW YOU.
C'MON, DUDE, IF YOU'RE GONNA BE A HACK, THEN AT LEAST BE A MEMORABLE ONE.
INTRODUCE MY EVIL DAD...A LONG-LOST, LEATHER CLAD TWIN WITH A WIND-TOSSED MULLET AND EYES AS HARD AS HIS ABS.
SERIOUSLY. MAKE WITH SOMETHIN' OTHER THAN LOOPED FART NOISES OR GET OUT OF MY DAMN WAY.
IT'S NOT ME THAT'S IN YOUR WAY, SON.
YOU HAVE BEEN BEGUILED, NEUTERED BY THE COMFORTS OF THOSE WHOSE TIME PASSED THEM BY DECADES AGO.
IT'S YOU THAT NEEDS THE FLAME.
IT'S YOU THAT NEEDS TO BE REBORN.

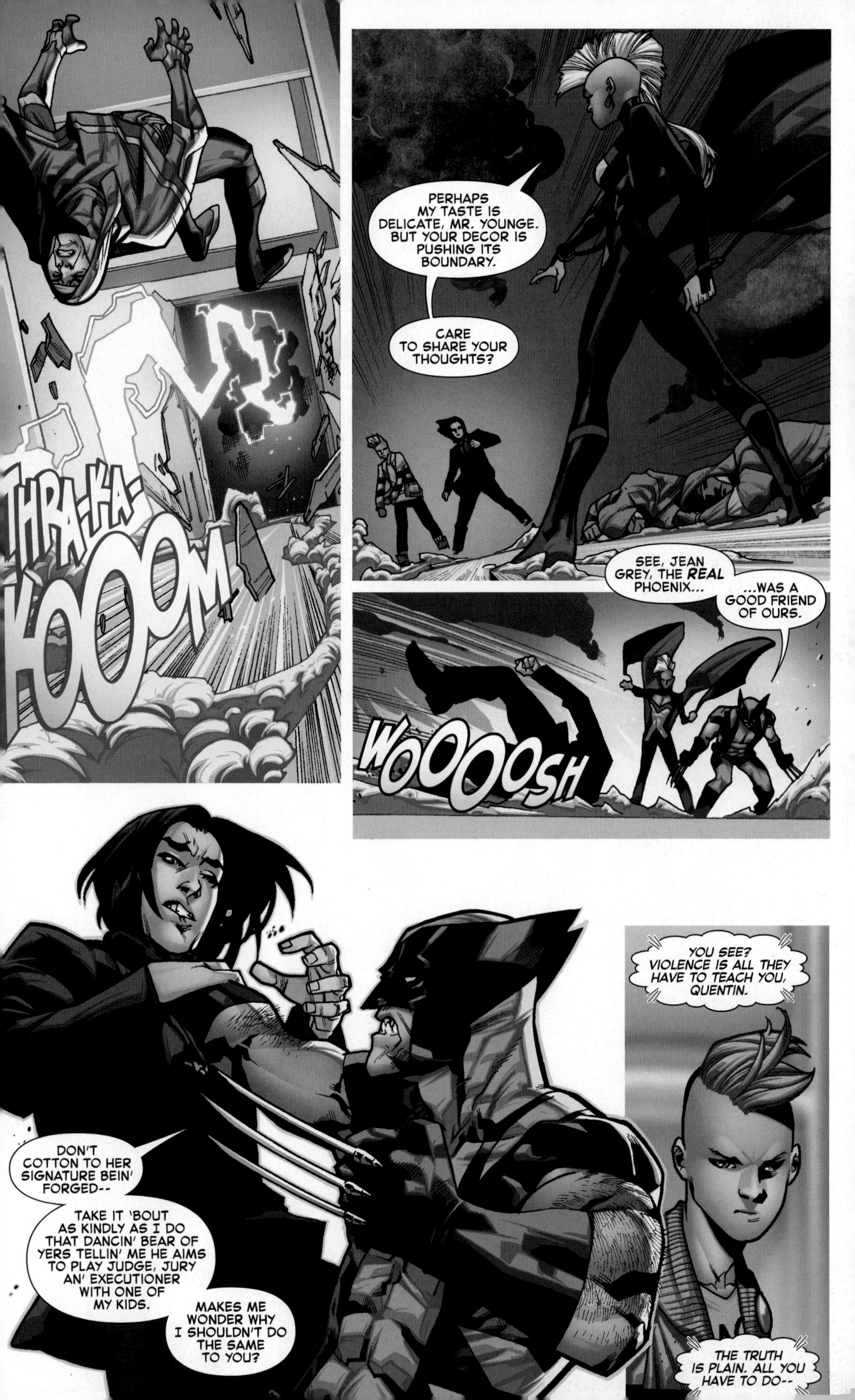
THRA-KA-KOOOM
PERHAPS MY TASTE IS DELICATE, MR. YOUNGE. BUT YOUR DECOR IS PUSHING ITS BOUNDARY.
CARE TO SHARE YOUR THOUGHTS?
SEE, JEAN GREY, THE REAL PHOENIX...
...WAS A GOOD FRIEND OF OURS.
WOOOOSH
DON'T COTTON TO HER SIGNATURE BEIN' FORGED--
TAKE IT 'BOUT AS KINDLY AS I DO THAT DANCIN' BEAR OF YERS TELLIN' ME HE AIMS TO PLAY JUDGE, JURY AN' EXECUTIONER WITH ONE OF MY KIDS.
MAKES ME WONDER WHY I SHOULDN'T DO THE SAME TO YOU?
YOU SEE? VIOLENCE IS ALL THEY HAVE TO TEACH YOU, QUENTIN.
THE TRUTH IS PLAIN. ALL YOU HAVE TO DO--

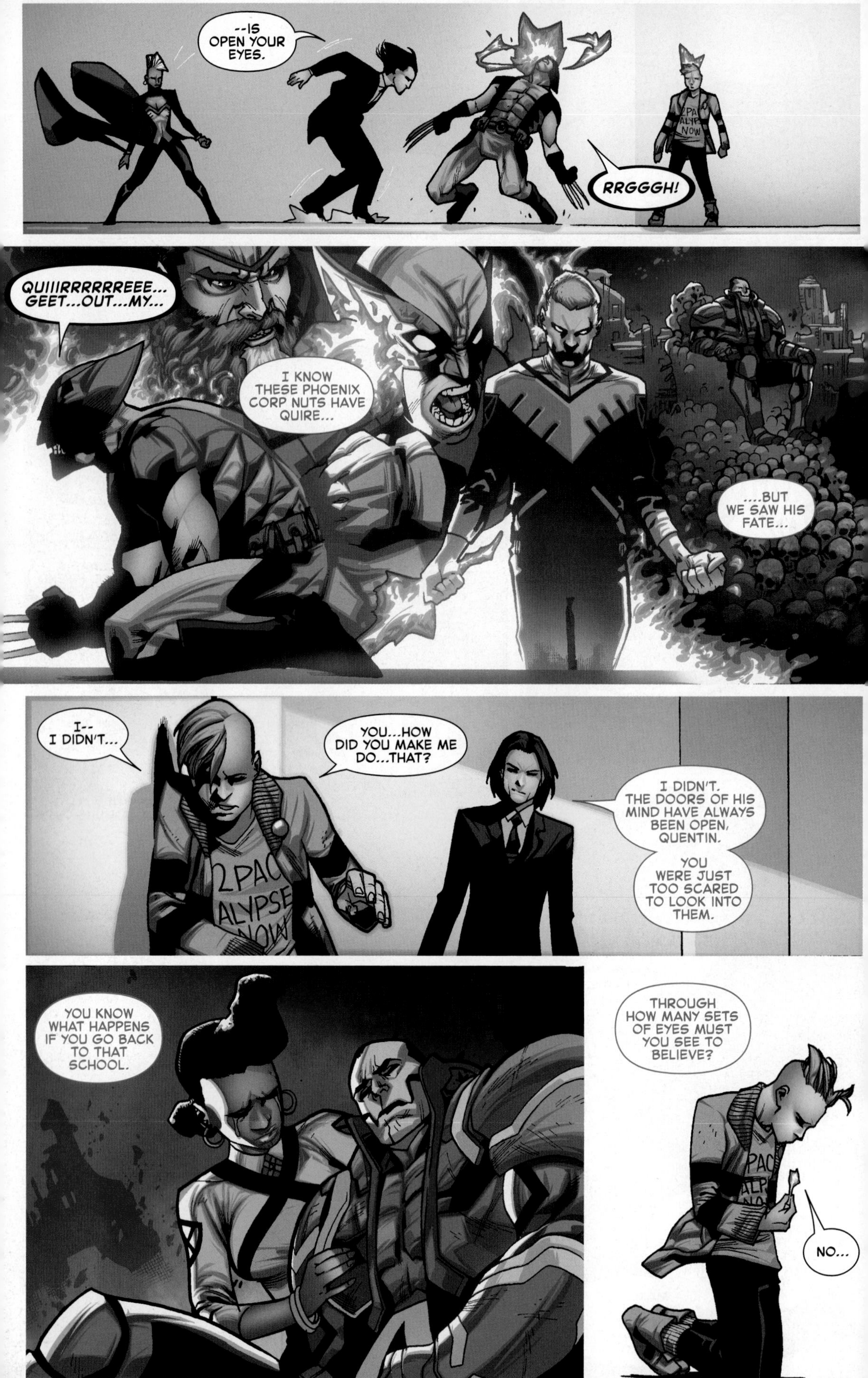
--IS OPEN YOUR EYES.
RRGGGH!
2PAC ALYP NOW
QUIIIRRRRRREEE... GEET...OUT...MY...
I KNOW THESE PHOENIX CORP NUTS HAVE QUIRE...
....BUT WE SAW HIS FATE...
I-- I DIDN'T...
YOU...HOW DID YOU MAKE ME DO...THAT?
I DIDN'T. THE DOORS OF HIS MIND HAVE ALWAYS BEEN OPEN, QUENTIN.
YOU WERE JUST TOO SCARED TO LOOK INTO THEM.
2PAC ALYPSE NOW
YOU KNOW WHAT HAPPENS IF YOU GO BACK TO THAT SCHOOL.
THROUGH HOW MANY SETS OF EYES MUST YOU SEE TO BELIEVE?
NO...

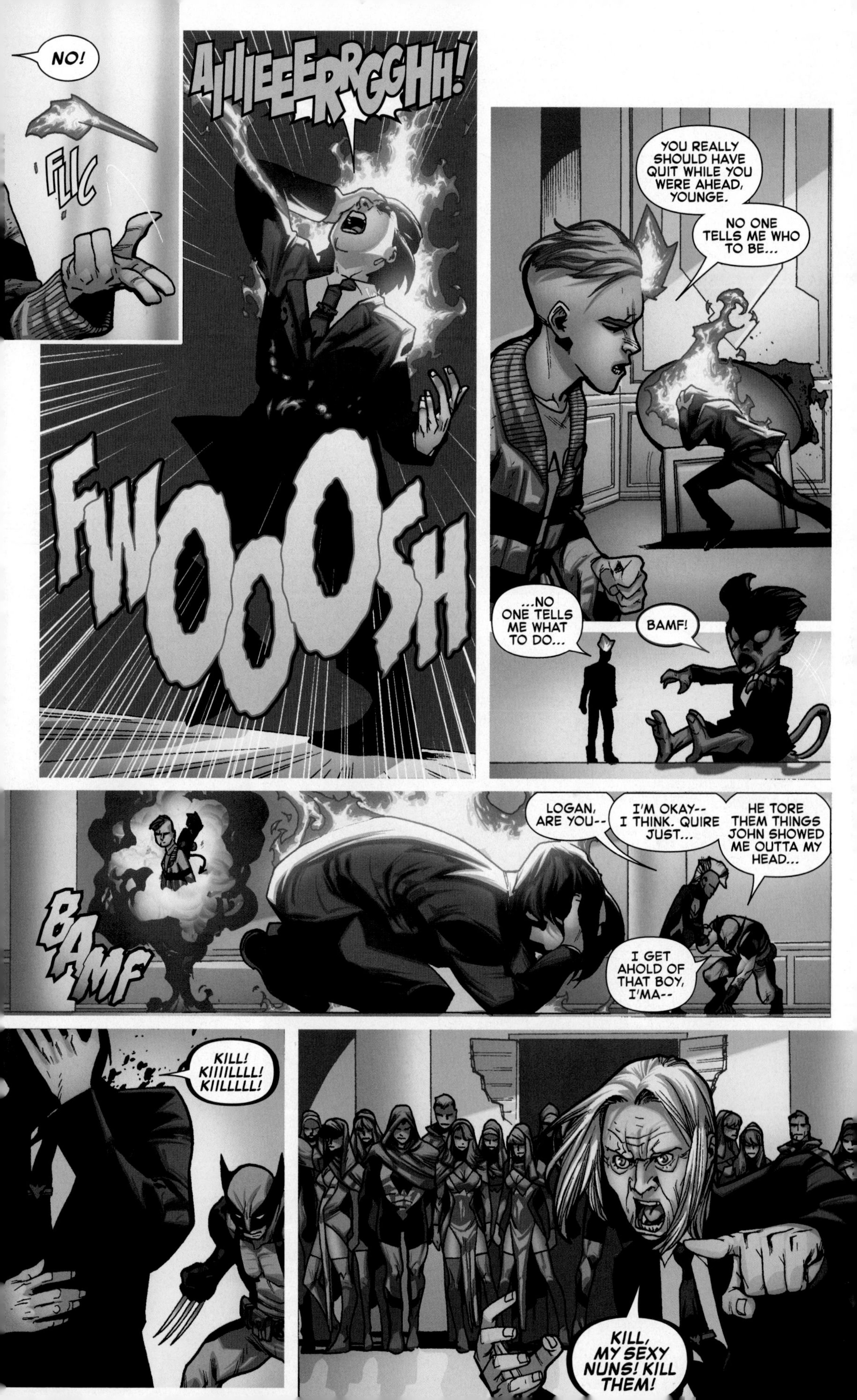
NO!
FLIC
AIIIIEEEERRGGHH!
FWOOOSH
YOU REALLY SHOULD HAVE QUIT WHILE YOU WERE AHEAD, YOUNGE.
NO ONE TELLS ME WHO TO BE...
...NO ONE TELLS ME WHAT TO DO...
BAMF!
BAMF
LOGAN, ARE YOU--
I'M OKAY-- I THINK. QUIRE JUST...
HE TORE THEM THINGS JOHN SHOWED ME OUTTA MY HEAD...
I GET AHOLD OF THAT BOY, I'MA--
KILL! KIIIILLLL! KIILLLLL!
KILL, MY SEXY NUNS! KILL THEM!

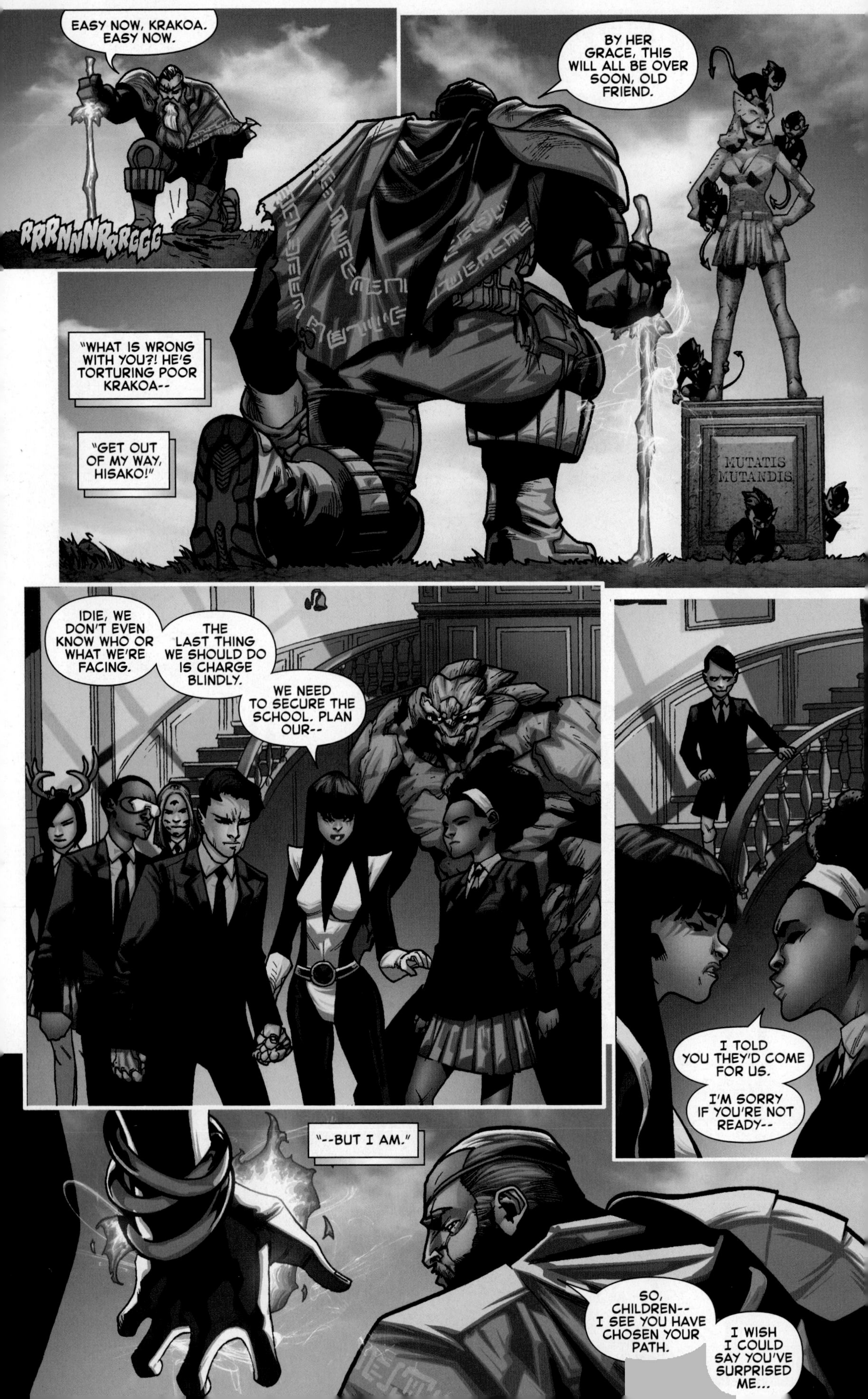
EASY NOW, KRAKOA. EASY NOW.
RRRNNNRRRGGG
BY HER GRACE, THIS WILL ALL BE OVER SOON, OLD FRIEND.
"WHAT IS WRONG WITH YOU?! HE'S TORTURING POOR KRAKOA--
"GET OUT OF MY WAY, HISAKO!"
MUTATIS MUTANDIS
IDIE, WE DON'T EVEN KNOW WHO OR WHAT WE'RE FACING.
THE LAST THING WE SHOULD DO IS CHARGE BLINDLY.
WE NEED TO SECURE THE SCHOOL. PLAN OUR--
I TOLD YOU THEY'D COME FOR US.
I'M SORRY IF YOU'RE NOT READY--
"--BUT I AM."
SO, CHILDREN-- I SEE YOU HAVE CHOSEN YOUR PATH.
I WISH I COULD SAY YOU'VE SURPRISED ME...

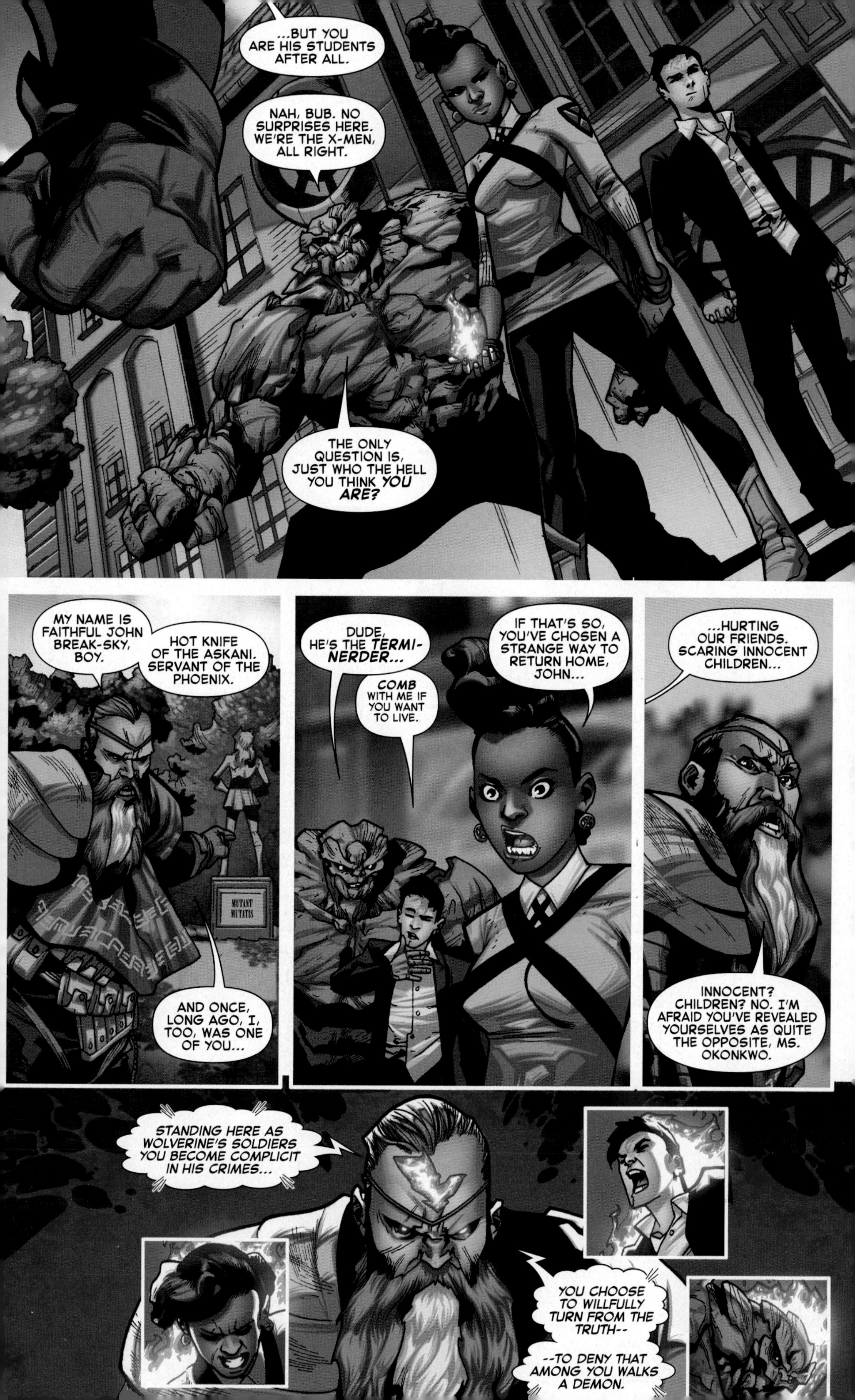
...BUT YOU ARE HIS STUDENTS AFTER ALL.
NAH, BUB. NO SURPRISES HERE. WE'RE THE X-MEN, ALL RIGHT.
THE ONLY QUESTION IS, JUST WHO THE HELL YOU THINK YOU ARE?
MY NAME IS FAITHFUL JOHN BREAK-SKY, BOY.
HOT KNIFE OF THE ASKANI. SERVANT OF THE PHOENIX.
MUTANT MUTATIS
AND ONCE, LONG AGO, I, TOO, WAS ONE OF YOU...
DUDE, HE'S THE TERMI-NERDER...
COMB WITH ME IF YOU WANT TO LIVE.
IF THAT'S SO, YOU'VE CHOSEN A STRANGE WAY TO RETURN HOME, JOHN...
...HURTING OUR FRIENDS. SCARING INNOCENT CHILDREN...
INNOCENT? CHILDREN? NO. I'M AFRAID YOU'VE REVEALED YOURSELVES AS QUITE THE OPPOSITE, MS. OKONKWO.
STANDING HERE AS WOLVERINE'S SOLDIERS YOU BECOME COMPLICIT IN HIS CRIMES...
YOU CHOOSE TO WILLFULLY TURN FROM THE TRUTH--
--TO DENY THAT AMONG YOU WALKS A DEMON.

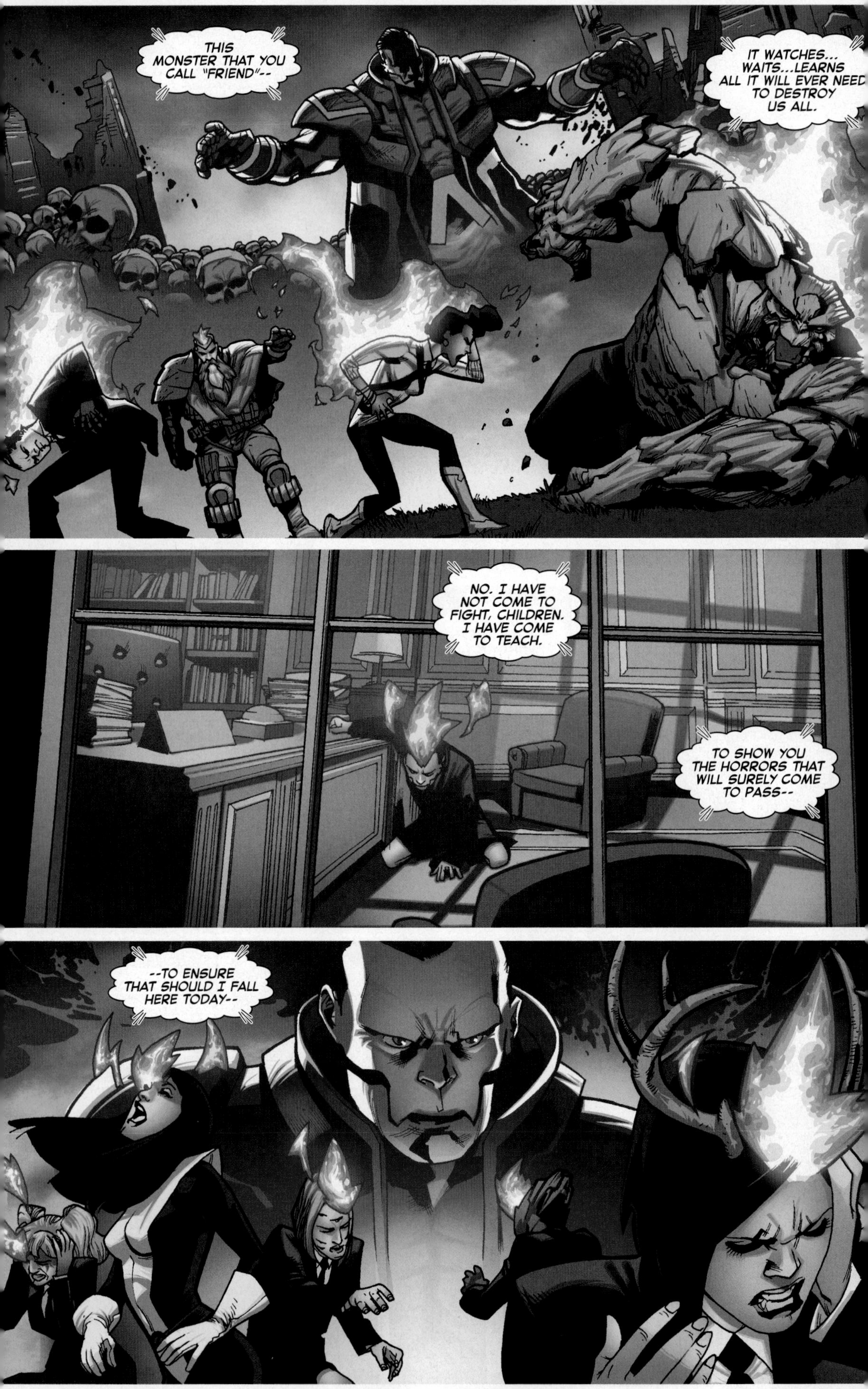
THIS MONSTER THAT YOU CALL "FRIEND"--
IT WATCHES... WAITS...LEARNS ALL IT WILL EVER NEED TO DESTROY US ALL.
NO. I HAVE NOT COME TO FIGHT, CHILDREN. I HAVE COME TO TEACH.
TO SHOW YOU THE HORRORS THAT WILL SURELY COME TO PASS--
--TO ENSURE THAT SHOULD I FALL HERE TODAY--

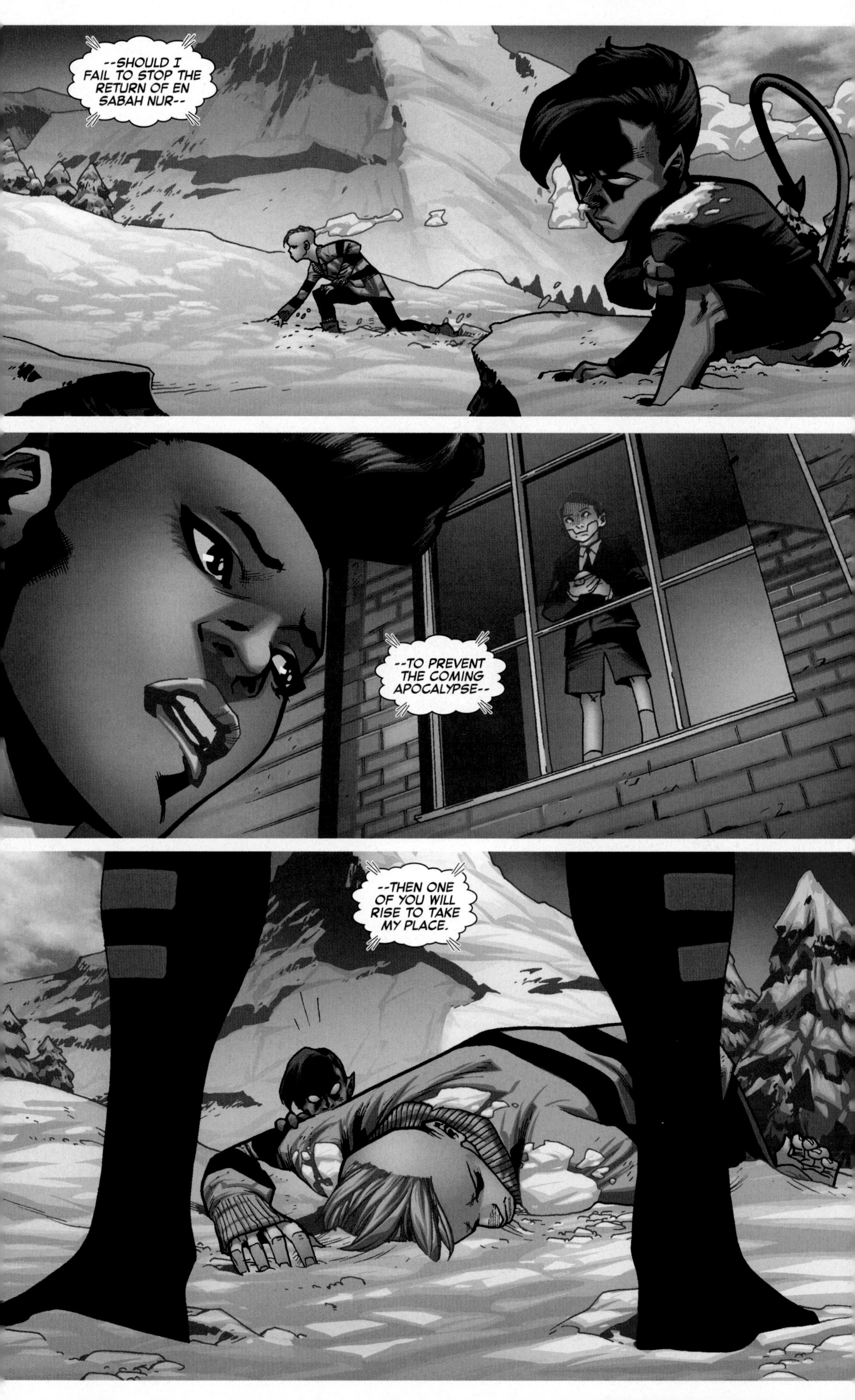
--SHOULD I FAIL TO STOP THE RETURN OF EN SABAH NUR--
--TO PREVENT THE COMING APOCALYPSE--
--THEN ONE OF YOU WILL RISE TO TAKE MY PLACE.

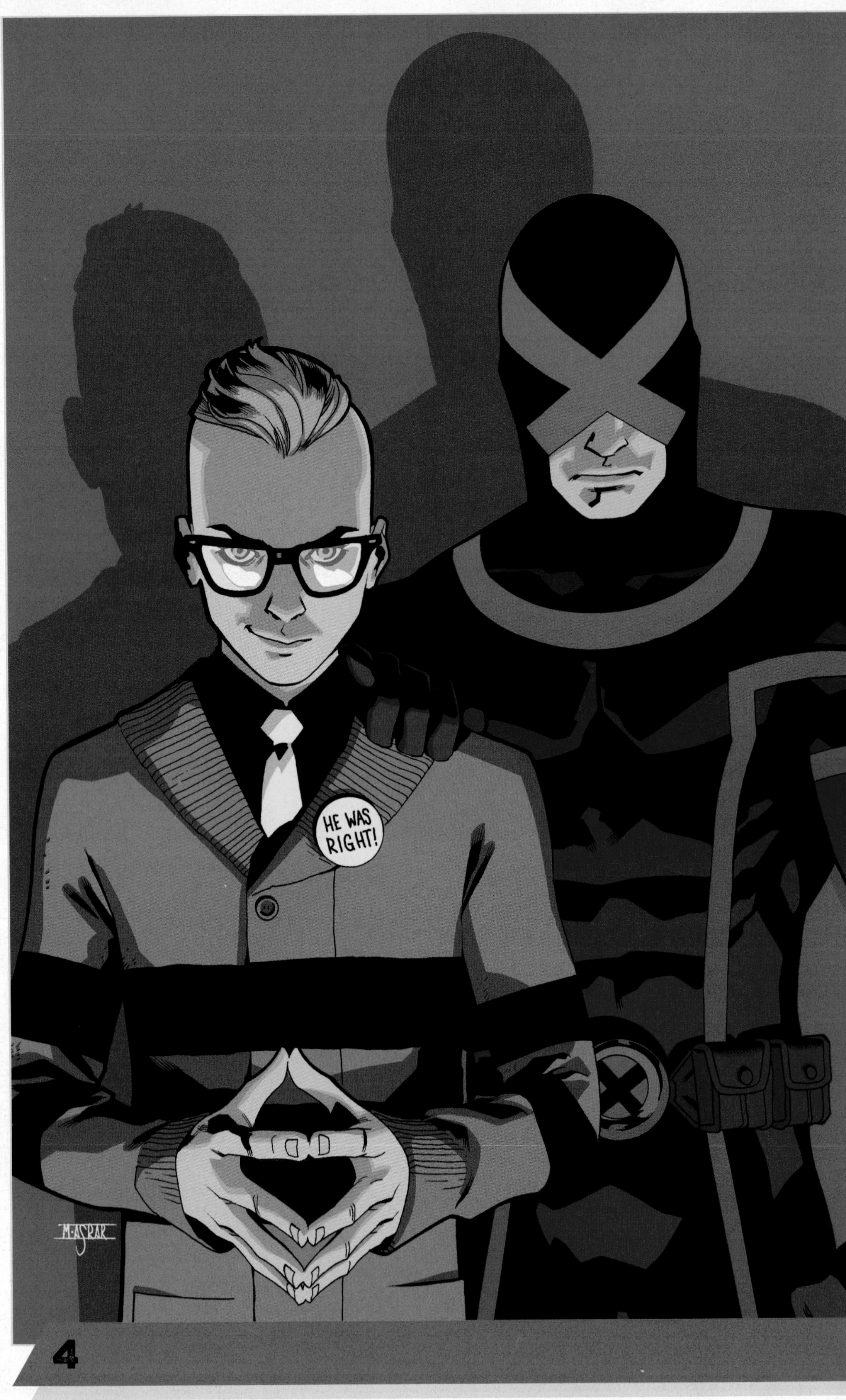
HE WAS RIGHT!
M-ASRAR
4

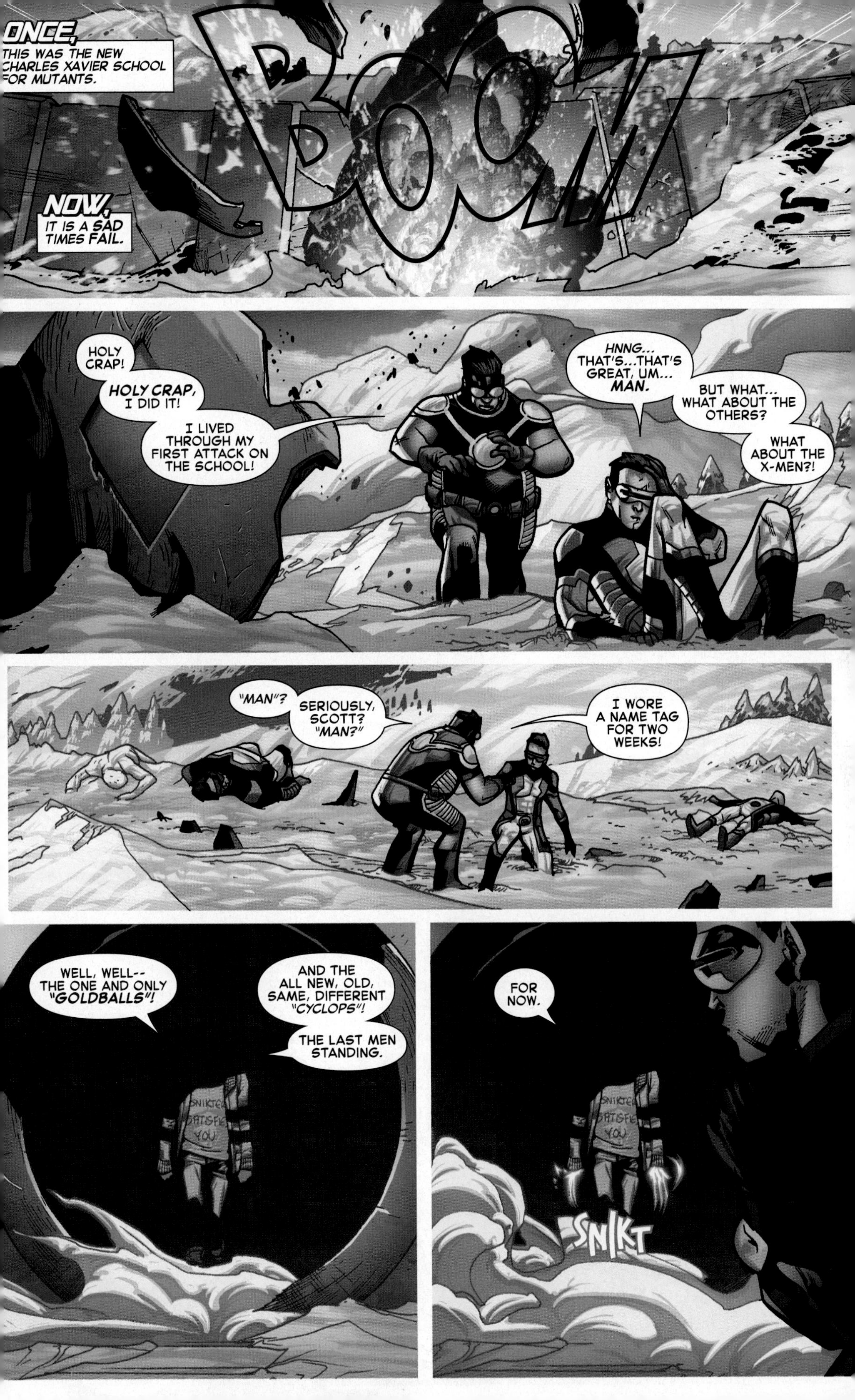
ONCE, THIS WAS THE NEW CHARLES XAVIER SCHOOL FOR MUTANTS.
BOOM
NOW, IT IS A SAD TIMES FAIL.
HOLY CRAP!
HOLY CRAP, I DID IT!
I LIVED THROUGH MY FIRST ATTACK ON THE SCHOOL!
HNNG... THAT'S...THAT'S GREAT, UM... MAN.
BUT WHAT... WHAT ABOUT THE OTHERS?
WHAT ABOUT THE X-MEN?!
"MAN"?
SERIOUSLY, SCOTT? "MAN?"
I WORE A NAME TAG FOR TWO WEEKS!
WELL, WELL-- THE ONE AND ONLY "GOLDBALLS"!
AND THE ALL NEW, OLD, SAME, DIFFERENT "CYCLOPS"!
THE LAST MEN STANDING.
FOR NOW.
SNIKT

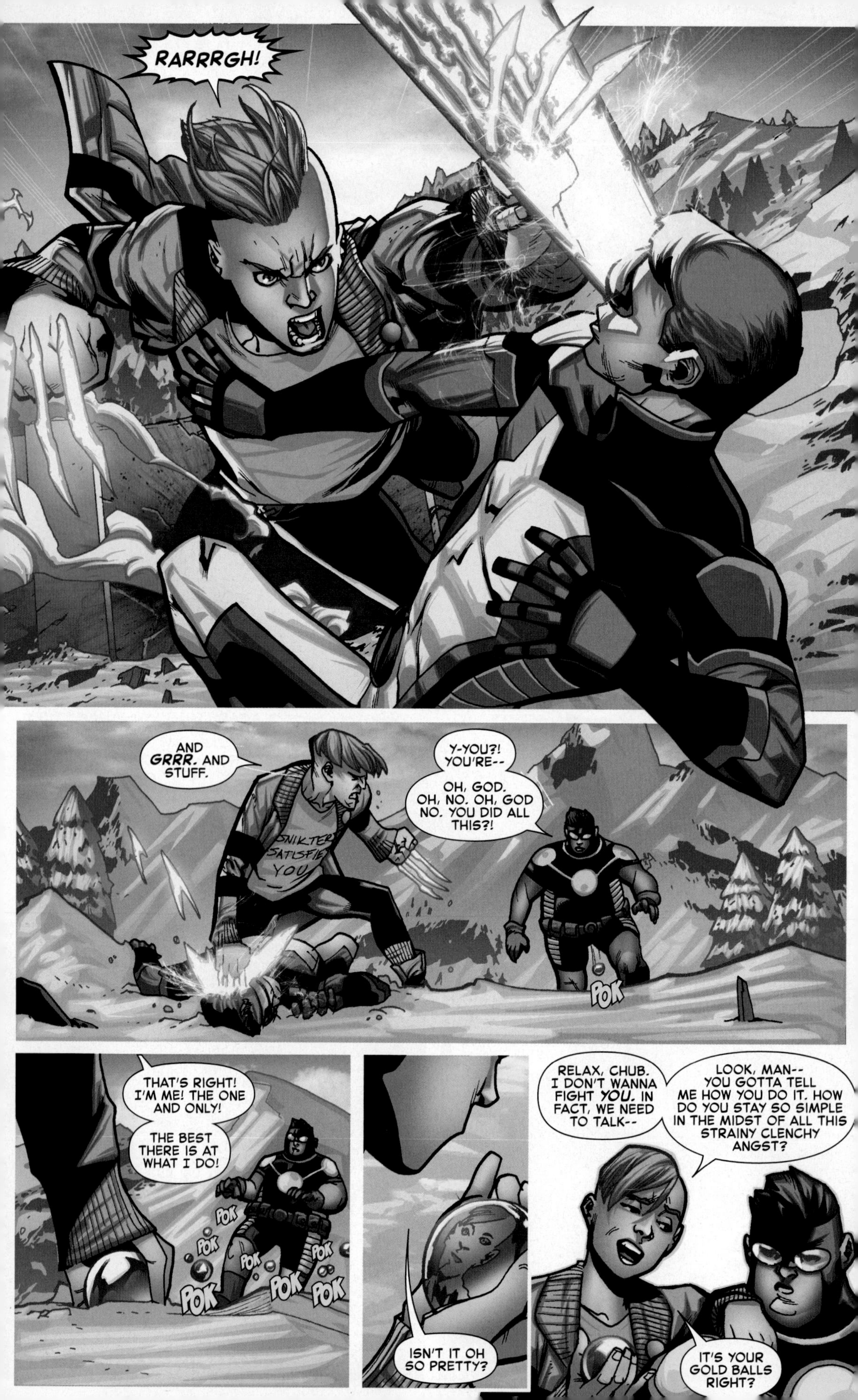
RARRRGH!
AND GRRR. AND STUFF.
Y-YOU?! YOU'RE--
OH, GOD. OH, NO. OH, GOD NO. YOU DID ALL THIS?!
SNIKTER SATISFIES YOU
POK
THAT'S RIGHT! I'M ME! THE ONE AND ONLY!
THE BEST THERE IS AT WHAT I DO!
POK
POK
POK
POK
POK
POK
POK
ISN'T IT OH SO PRETTY?
RELAX, CHUB. I DON'T WANNA FIGHT YOU. IN FACT, WE NEED TO TALK--
LOOK, MAN-- YOU GOTTA TELL ME HOW YOU DO IT. HOW DO YOU STAY SO SIMPLE IN THE MIDST OF ALL THIS STRAINY CLENCHY ANGST?
IT'S YOUR GOLD BALLS RIGHT?

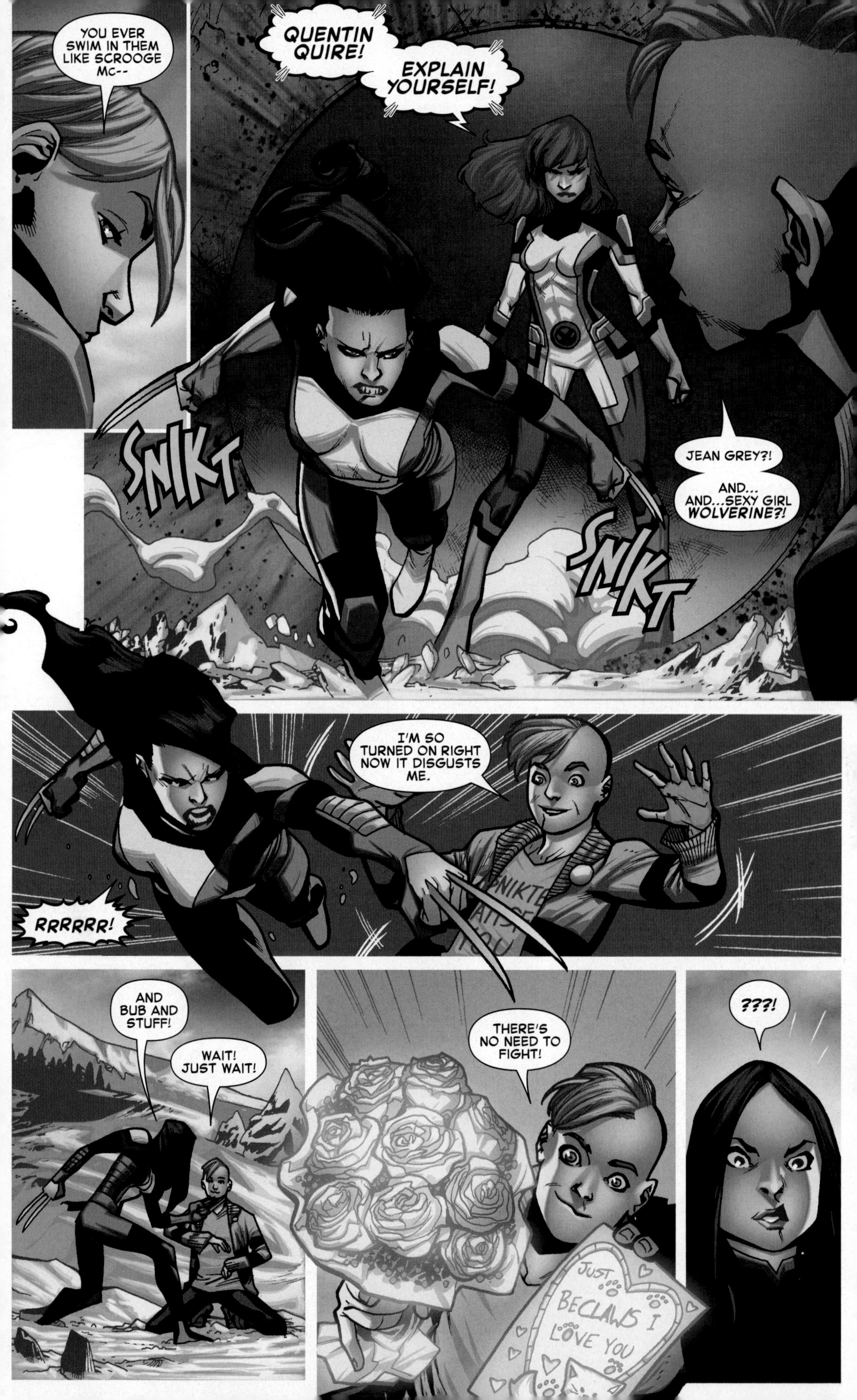

YOU EVER SWIM IN THEM LIKE SCROOGE MC--
QUENTIN QUIRE!
EXPLAIN YOURSELF!
SNIKT
SNIKT
JEAN GREY?!
AND... AND...SEXY GIRL WOLVERINE?!
I'M SO TURNED ON RIGHT NOW IT DISGUSTS ME.
RRRRRR!
AND BUB AND STUFF!
WAIT! JUST WAIT!
THERE'S NO NEED TO FIGHT!
???!
JUST BECLAWS I LOVE YOU

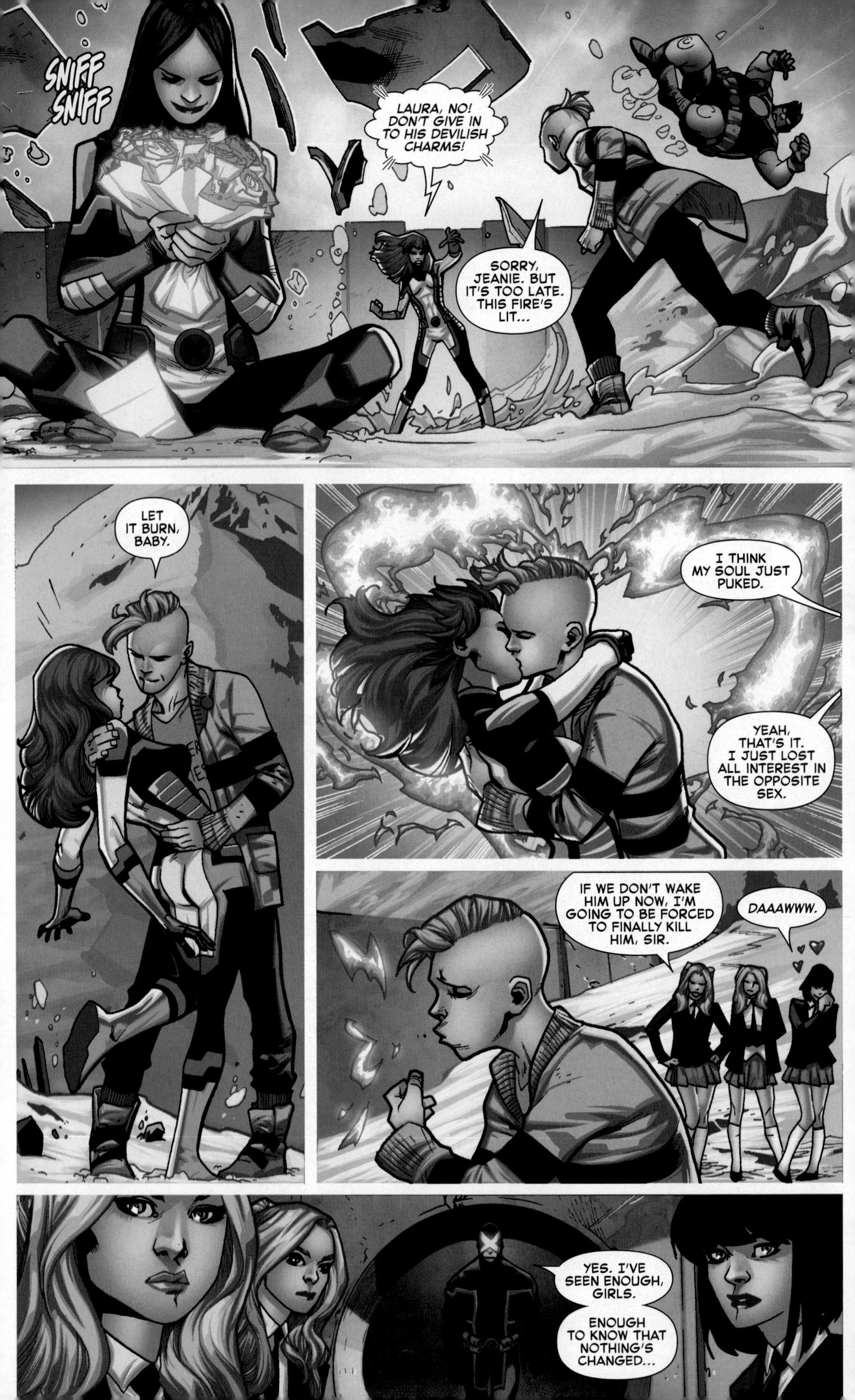
SNIFF SNIFF
LAURA, NO! DON'T GIVE IN TO HIS DEVILISH CHARMS!
SORRY, JEANIE. BUT IT'S TOO LATE. THIS FIRE'S LIT...
LET IT BURN, BABY.
I THINK MY SOUL JUST PUKED.
YEAH, THAT'S IT. I JUST LOST ALL INTEREST IN THE OPPOSITE SEX.
IF WE DON'T WAKE HIM UP NOW, I'M GOING TO BE FORCED TO FINALLY KILL HIM, SIR.
DAAAWWW.
YES. I'VE SEEN ENOUGH, GIRLS.
ENOUGH TO KNOW THAT NOTHING'S CHANGED...

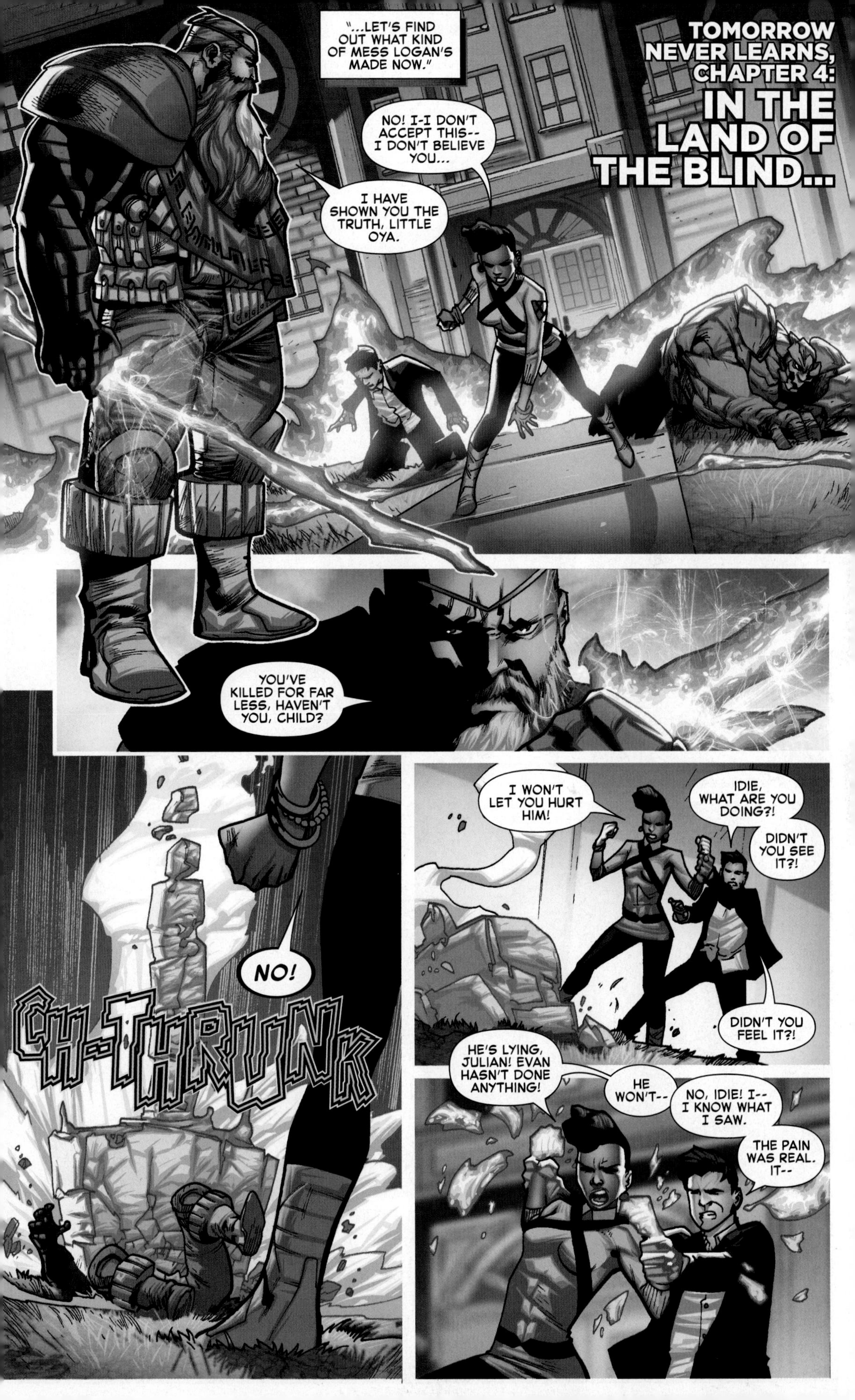
"...LET'S FIND OUT WHAT KIND OF MESS LOGAN'S MADE NOW."
TOMORROW NEVER LEARNS, CHAPTER 4:
IN THE LAND OF THE BLIND...
NO! I-I DON'T ACCEPT THIS-- I DON'T BELIEVE YOU...
I HAVE SHOWN YOU THE TRUTH, LITTLE OYA.
YOU'VE KILLED FOR FAR LESS, HAVEN'T YOU, CHILD?
NO!
CH-THRUNK
I WON'T LET YOU HURT HIM!
IDIE, WHAT ARE YOU DOING?!
DIDN'T YOU SEE IT?!
DIDN'T YOU FEEL IT?!
HE'S LYING, JULIAN! EVAN HASN'T DONE ANYTHING!
HE WON'T--
NO, IDIE! I-- I KNOW WHAT I SAW.
THE PAIN WAS REAL. IT--

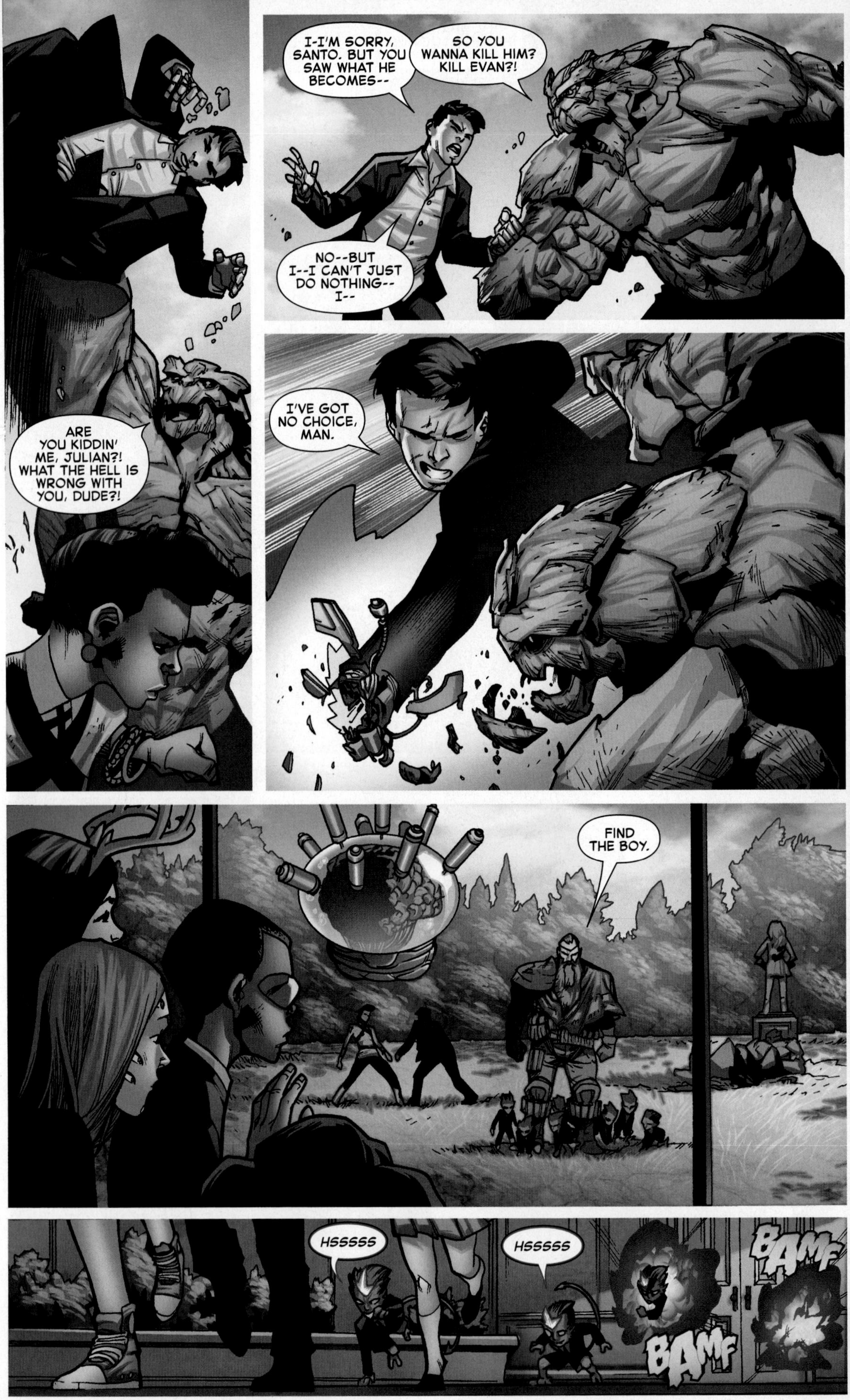

I-I'M SORRY, SANTO. BUT YOU SAW WHAT HE BECOMES--
SO YOU WANNA KILL HIM? KILL EVAN?!
NO--BUT I--I CAN'T JUST DO NOTHING-- I--
ARE YOU KIDDIN' ME, JULIAN?! WHAT THE HELL IS WRONG WITH YOU, DUDE?!
I'VE GOT NO CHOICE, MAN.
FIND THE BOY.
HSSSSS
HSSSSS
BAMF
BAMF

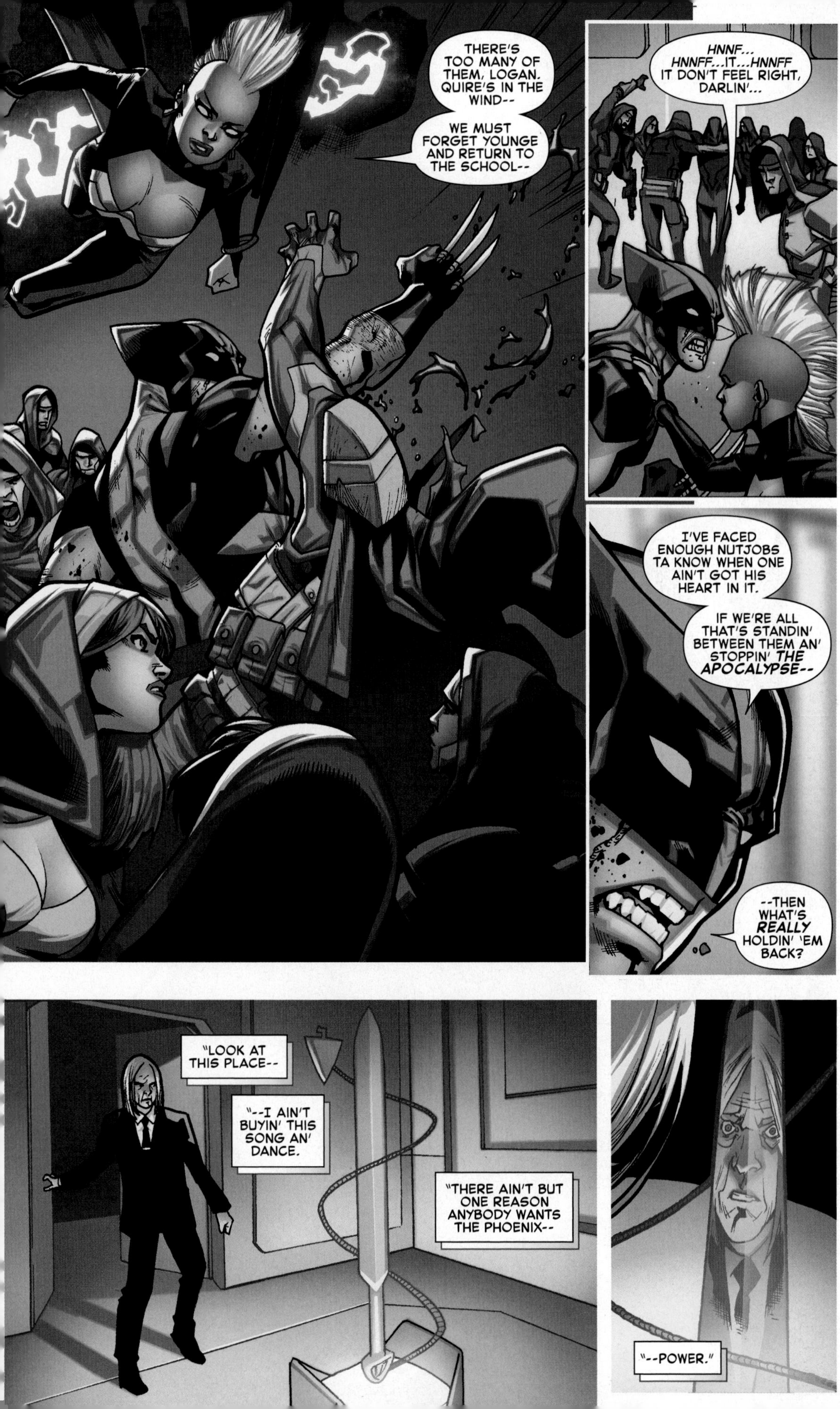
THERE'S TOO MANY OF THEM, LOGAN. QUIRE'S IN THE WIND--
WE MUST FORGET YOUNGE AND RETURN TO THE SCHOOL--
HNNF... HNNFF...IT...HNNFF IT DON'T FEEL RIGHT, DARLIN'...
I'VE FACED ENOUGH NUTJOBS TA KNOW WHEN ONE AIN'T GOT HIS HEART IN IT.
IF WE'RE ALL THAT'S STANDIN' BETWEEN THEM AN' STOPPIN' THE APOCALYPSE--
--THEN WHAT'S REALLY HOLDIN' 'EM BACK?
"LOOK AT THIS PLACE--
"--I AIN'T BUYIN' THIS SONG AN' DANCE.
"THERE AIN'T BUT ONE REASON ANYBODY WANTS THE PHOENIX--
"--POWER."

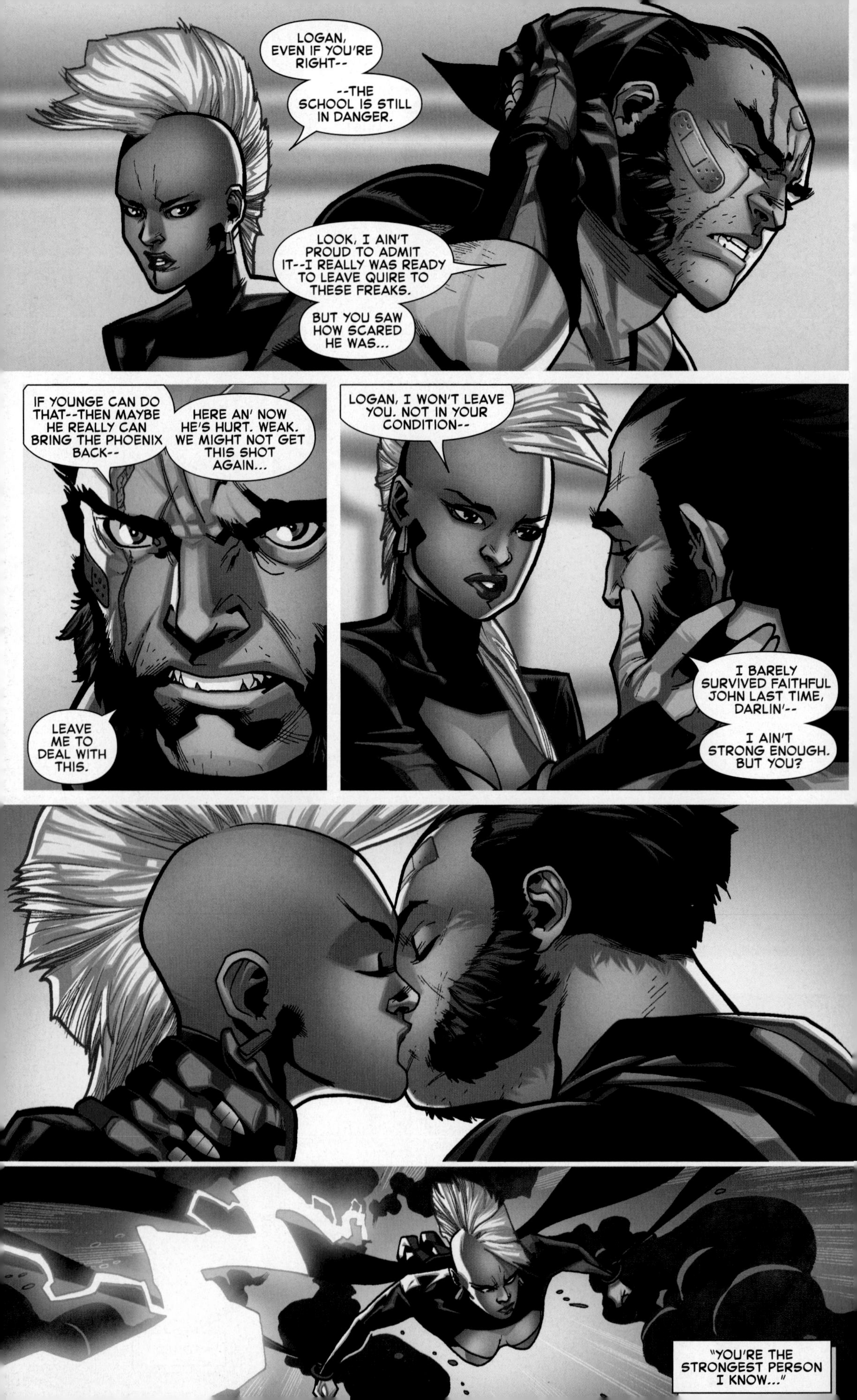
LOGAN, EVEN IF YOU'RE RIGHT--
--THE SCHOOL IS STILL IN DANGER.
LOOK, I AIN'T PROUD TO ADMIT IT--I REALLY WAS READY TO LEAVE QUIRE TO THESE FREAKS.
BUT YOU SAW HOW SCARED HE WAS...
IF YOUNGE CAN DO THAT--THEN MAYBE HE REALLY CAN BRING THE PHOENIX BACK--
HERE AN' NOW HE'S HURT. WEAK. WE MIGHT NOT GET THIS SHOT AGAIN...
LEAVE ME TO DEAL WITH THIS.
LOGAN, I WON'T LEAVE YOU. NOT IN YOUR CONDITION--
I BARELY SURVIVED FAITHFUL JOHN LAST TIME, DARLIN'--
I AIN'T STRONG ENOUGH. BUT YOU?
"YOU'RE THE STRONGEST PERSON I KNOW..."

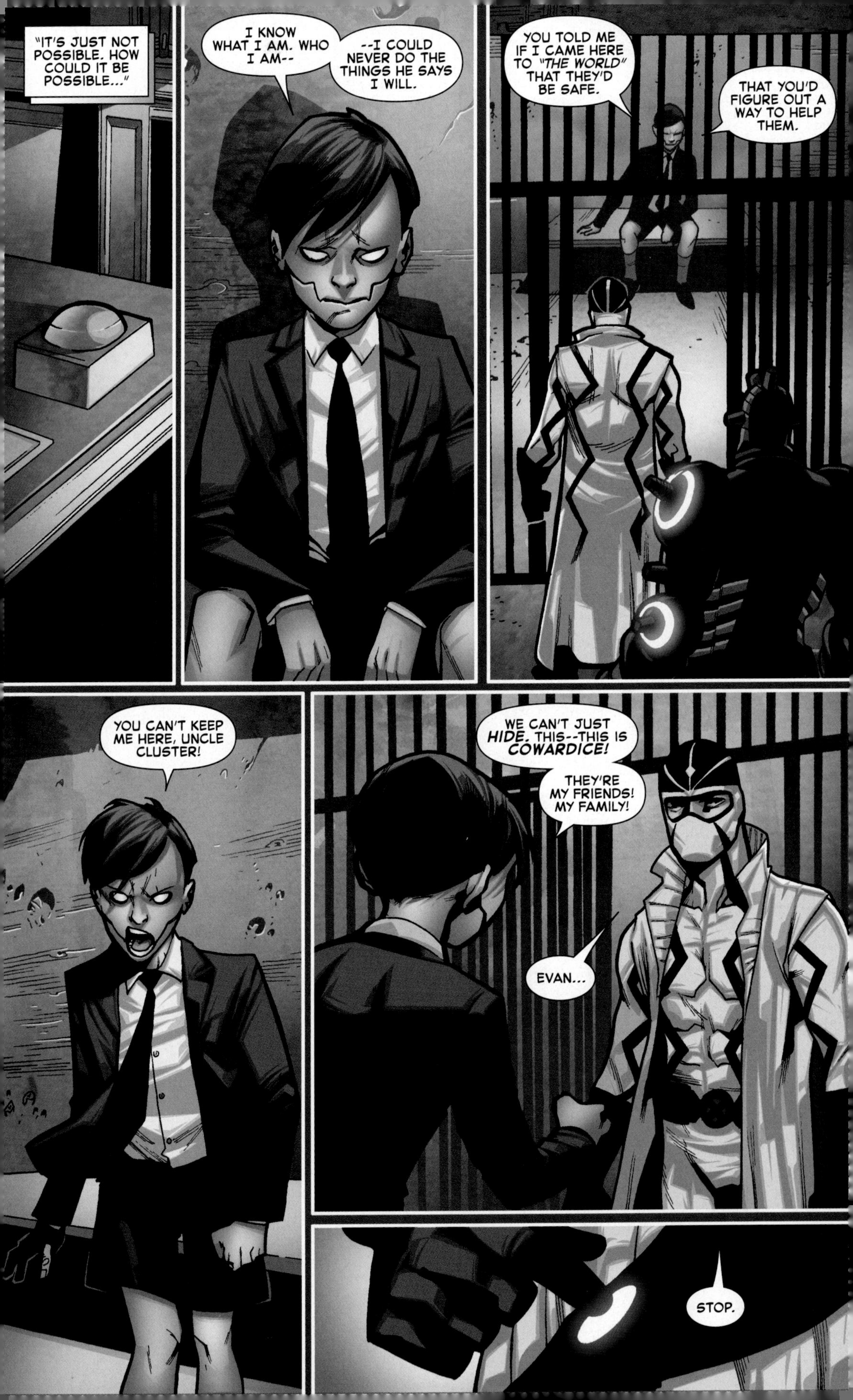
"IT'S JUST NOT POSSIBLE. HOW COULD IT BE POSSIBLE..."
I KNOW WHAT I AM. WHO I AM--
--I COULD NEVER DO THE THINGS HE SAYS I WILL.
YOU TOLD ME IF I CAME HERE TO "THE WORLD" THAT THEY'D BE SAFE.
THAT YOU'D FIGURE OUT A WAY TO HELP THEM.
YOU CAN'T KEEP ME HERE, UNCLE CLUSTER!
WE CAN'T JUST HIDE. THIS--THIS IS COWARDICE!
THEY'RE MY FRIENDS! MY FAMILY!
EVAN...
STOP.

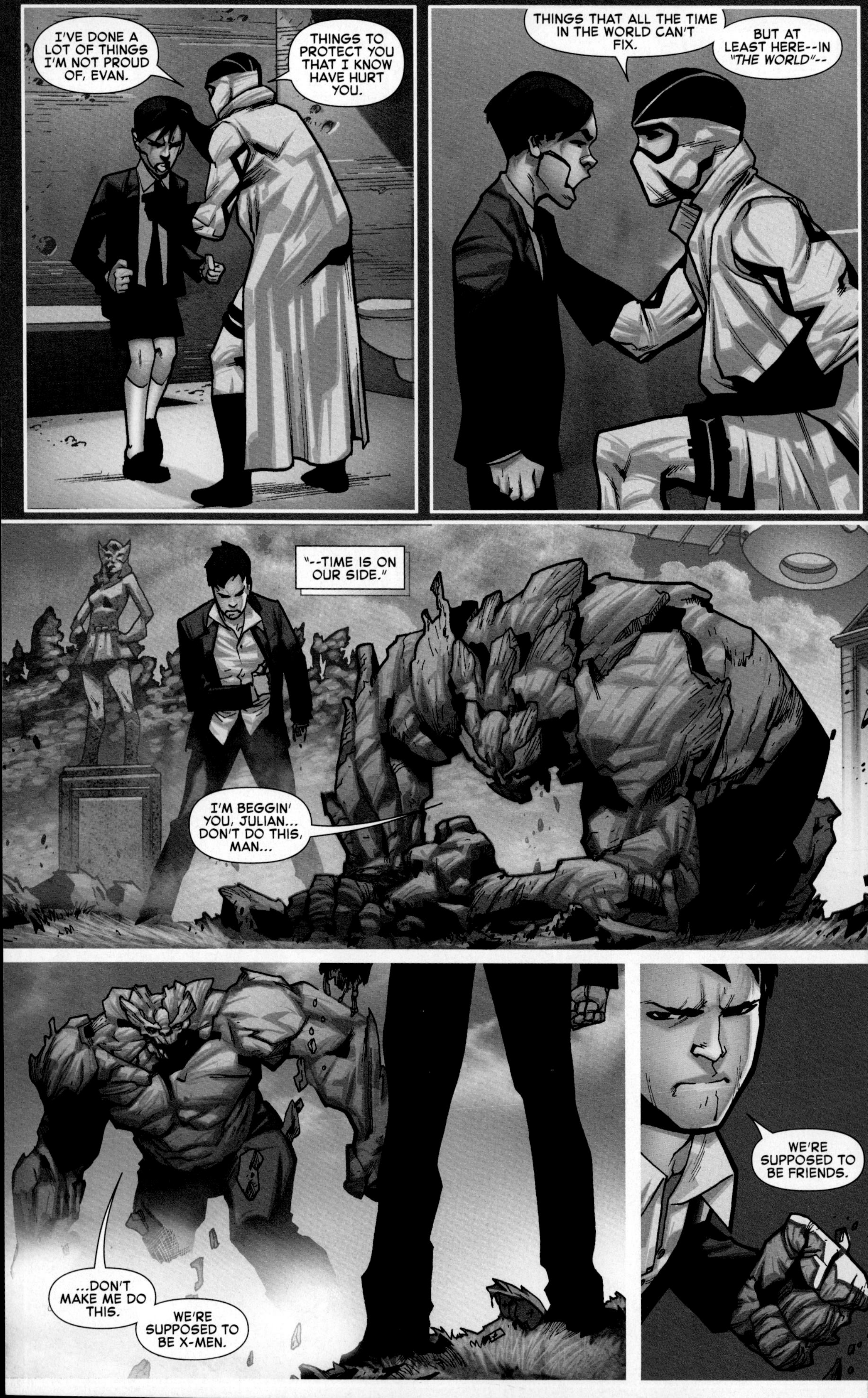
I'VE DONE A LOT OF THINGS I'M NOT PROUD OF, EVAN.
THINGS TO PROTECT YOU THAT I KNOW HAVE HURT YOU.
THINGS THAT ALL THE TIME IN THE WORLD CAN'T FIX.
BUT AT LEAST HERE--IN "THE WORLD"--
"--TIME IS ON OUR SIDE."
I'M BEGGIN' YOU, JULIAN... DON'T DO THIS, MAN...
...DON'T MAKE ME DO THIS.
WE'RE SUPPOSED TO BE X-MEN.
WE'RE SUPPOSED TO BE FRIENDS.

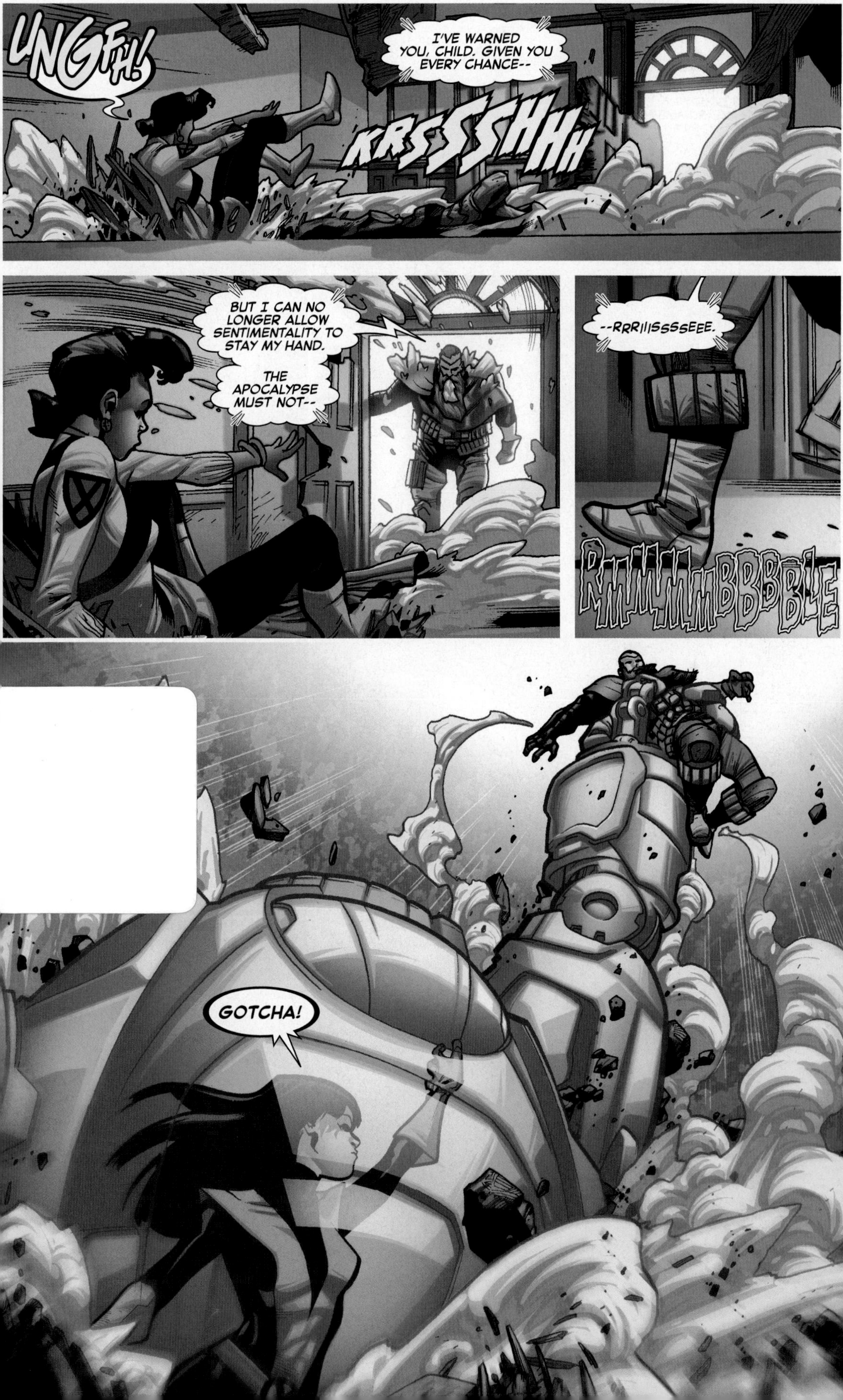
UNGFH!
I'VE WARNED YOU, CHILD. GIVEN YOU EVERY CHANCE--
KRSSSHHH
BUT I CAN NO LONGER ALLOW SENTIMENTALITY TO STAY MY HAND.
THE APOCALYPSE MUST NOT--
--RRRIIISSSSEEE.
RMMMMMBBBBLE
GOTCHA!

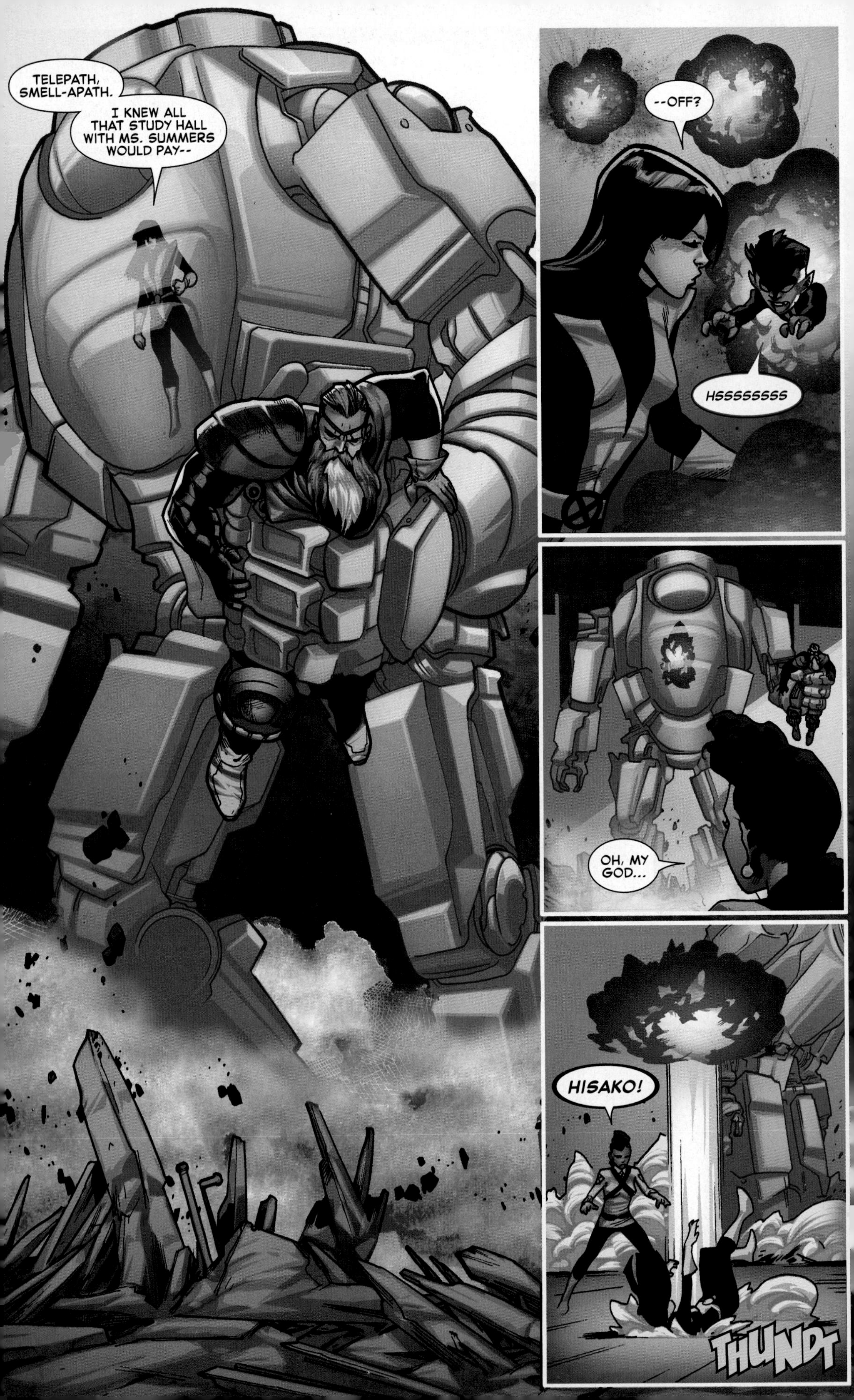
TELEPATH, SMELL-APATH.
I KNEW ALL THAT STUDY HALL WITH MS. SUMMERS WOULD PAY--
--OFF?
HSSSSSSSS
OH, MY GOD...
HISAKO!
THUNDT

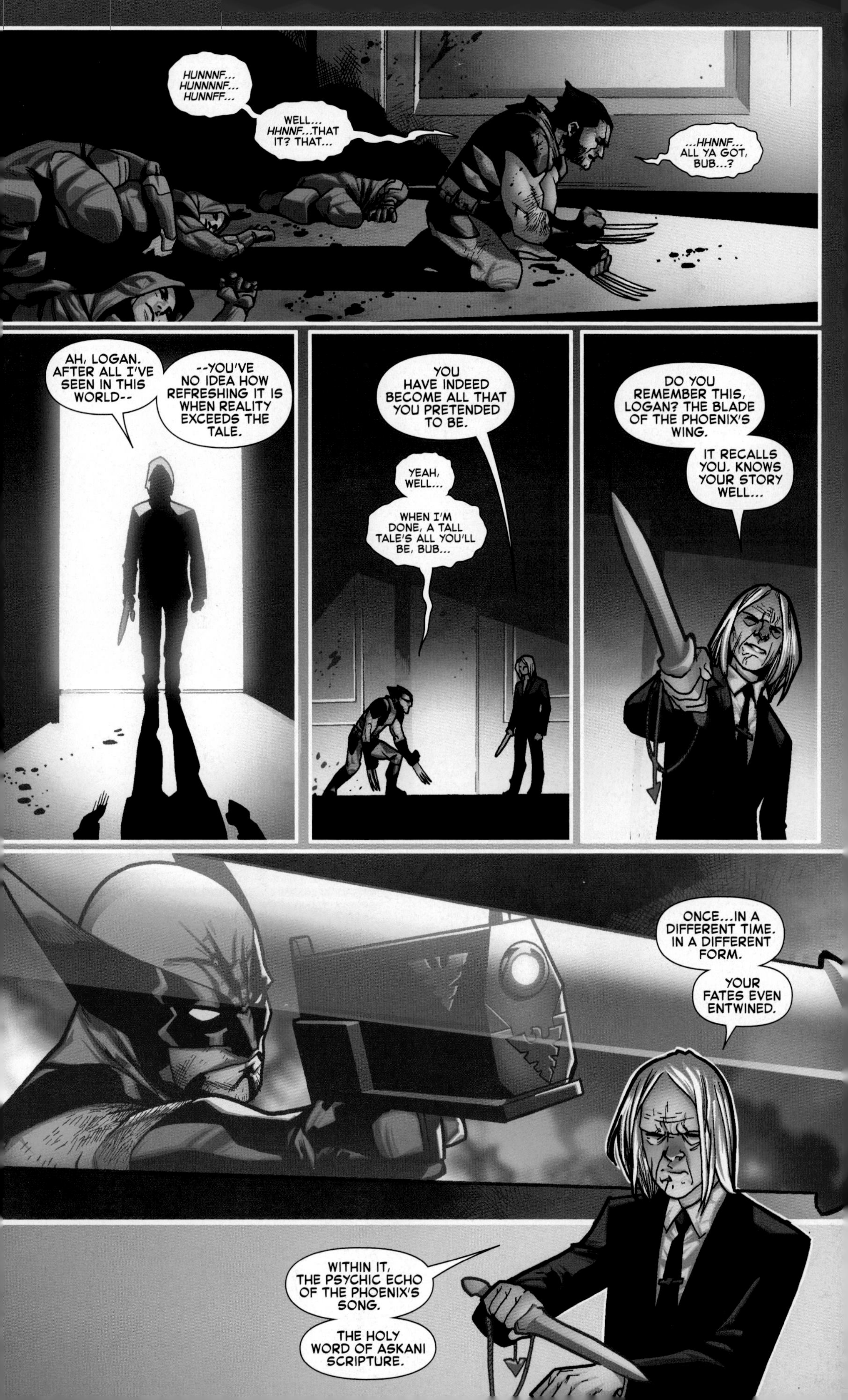
HUNNNF... HUNNNNF... HUNNFF...
WELL... HHNNF...THAT IT? THAT...
...HHNNF... ALL YA GOT, BUB...?
AH, LOGAN. AFTER ALL I'VE SEEN IN THIS WORLD--
--YOU'VE NO IDEA HOW REFRESHING IT IS WHEN REALITY EXCEEDS THE TALE.
YOU HAVE INDEED BECOME ALL THAT YOU PRETENDED TO BE.
YEAH, WELL...
WHEN I'M DONE, A TALL TALE'S ALL YOU'LL BE, BUB...
DO YOU REMEMBER THIS, LOGAN? THE BLADE OF THE PHOENIX'S WING.
IT RECALLS YOU. KNOWS YOUR STORY WELL...
ONCE...IN A DIFFERENT TIME. IN A DIFFERENT FORM.
YOUR FATES EVEN ENTWINED.
WITHIN IT, THE PSYCHIC ECHO OF THE PHOENIX'S SONG.
THE HOLY WORD OF ASKANI SCRIPTURE.

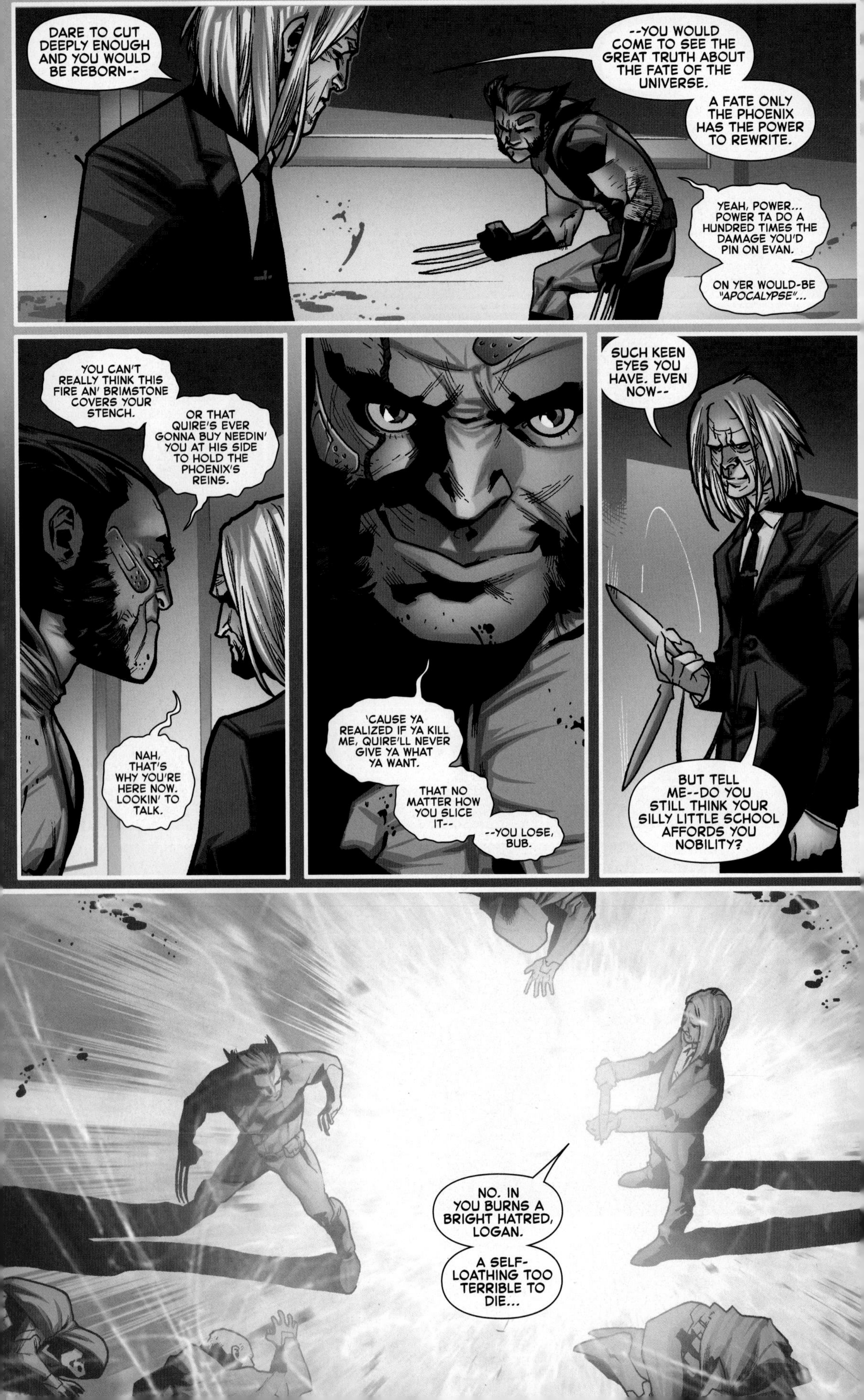
DARE TO CUT DEEPLY ENOUGH AND YOU WOULD BE REBORN--
--YOU WOULD COME TO SEE THE GREAT TRUTH ABOUT THE FATE OF THE UNIVERSE.
A FATE ONLY THE PHOENIX HAS THE POWER TO REWRITE.
YEAH, POWER... POWER TA DO A HUNDRED TIMES THE DAMAGE YOU'D PIN ON EVAN.
ON YER WOULD-BE "APOCALYPSE"...
YOU CAN'T REALLY THINK THIS FIRE AN' BRIMSTONE COVERS YOUR STENCH.
OR THAT QUIRE'S EVER GONNA BUY NEEDIN' YOU AT HIS SIDE TO HOLD THE PHOENIX'S REINS.
NAH, THAT'S WHY YOU'RE HERE NOW. LOOKIN' TO TALK.
'CAUSE YA REALIZED IF YA KILL ME, QUIRE'LL NEVER GIVE YA WHAT YA WANT.
THAT NO MATTER HOW YOU SLICE IT--
--YOU LOSE, BUB.
SUCH KEEN EYES YOU HAVE. EVEN NOW--
BUT TELL ME--DO YOU STILL THINK YOUR SILLY LITTLE SCHOOL AFFORDS YOU NOBILITY?
NO. IN YOU BURNS A BRIGHT HATRED, LOGAN.
A SELF-LOATHING TOO TERRIBLE TO DIE...

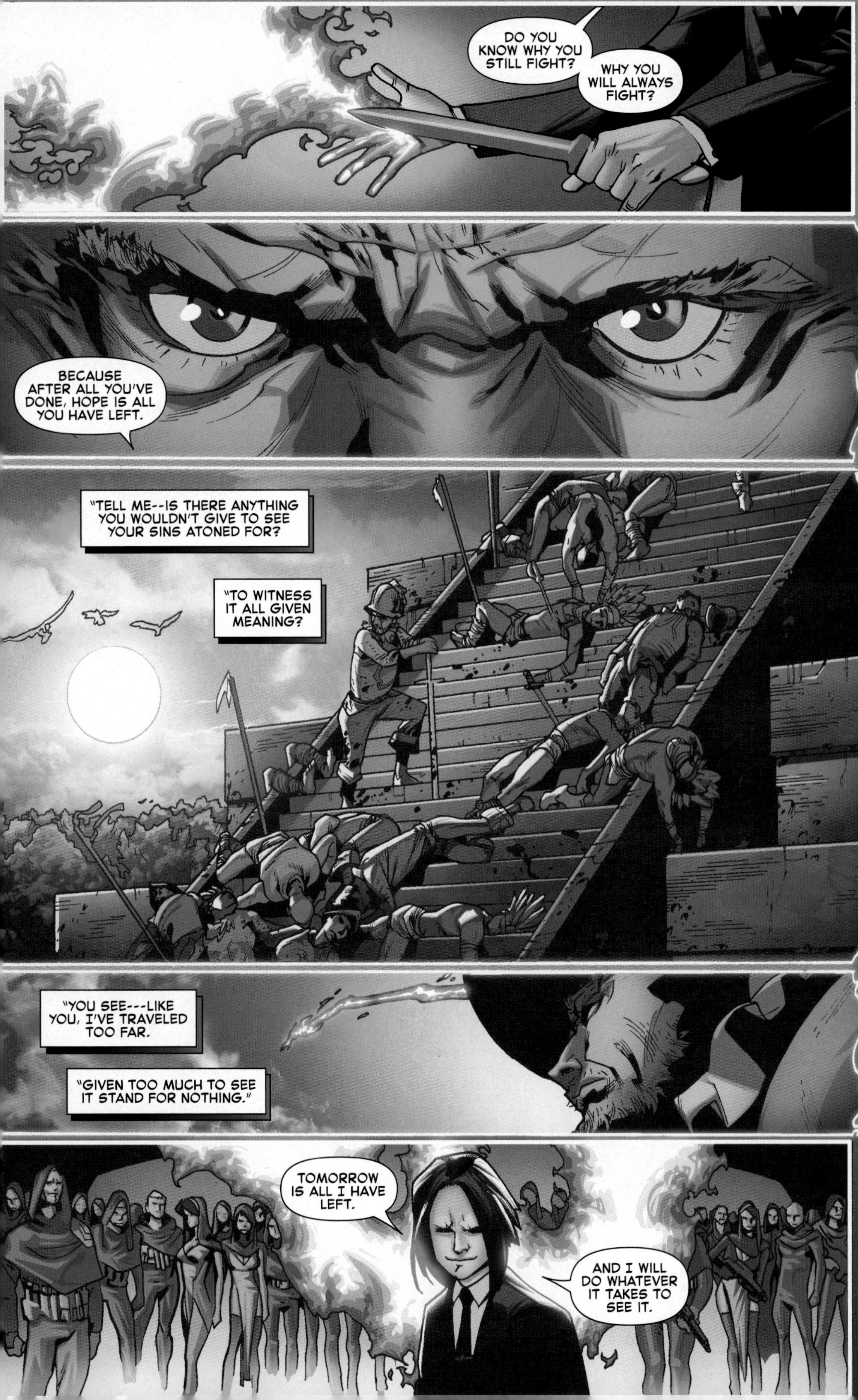
DO YOU KNOW WHY YOU STILL FIGHT?
WHY YOU WILL ALWAYS FIGHT?
BECAUSE AFTER ALL YOU'VE DONE, HOPE IS ALL YOU HAVE LEFT.
"TELL ME--IS THERE ANYTHING YOU WOULDN'T GIVE TO SEE YOUR SINS ATONED FOR?
"TO WITNESS IT ALL GIVEN MEANING?
"YOU SEE---LIKE YOU, I'VE TRAVELED TOO FAR.
"GIVEN TOO MUCH TO SEE IT STAND FOR NOTHING."
TOMORROW IS ALL I HAVE LEFT.
AND I WILL DO WHATEVER IT TAKES TO SEE IT.

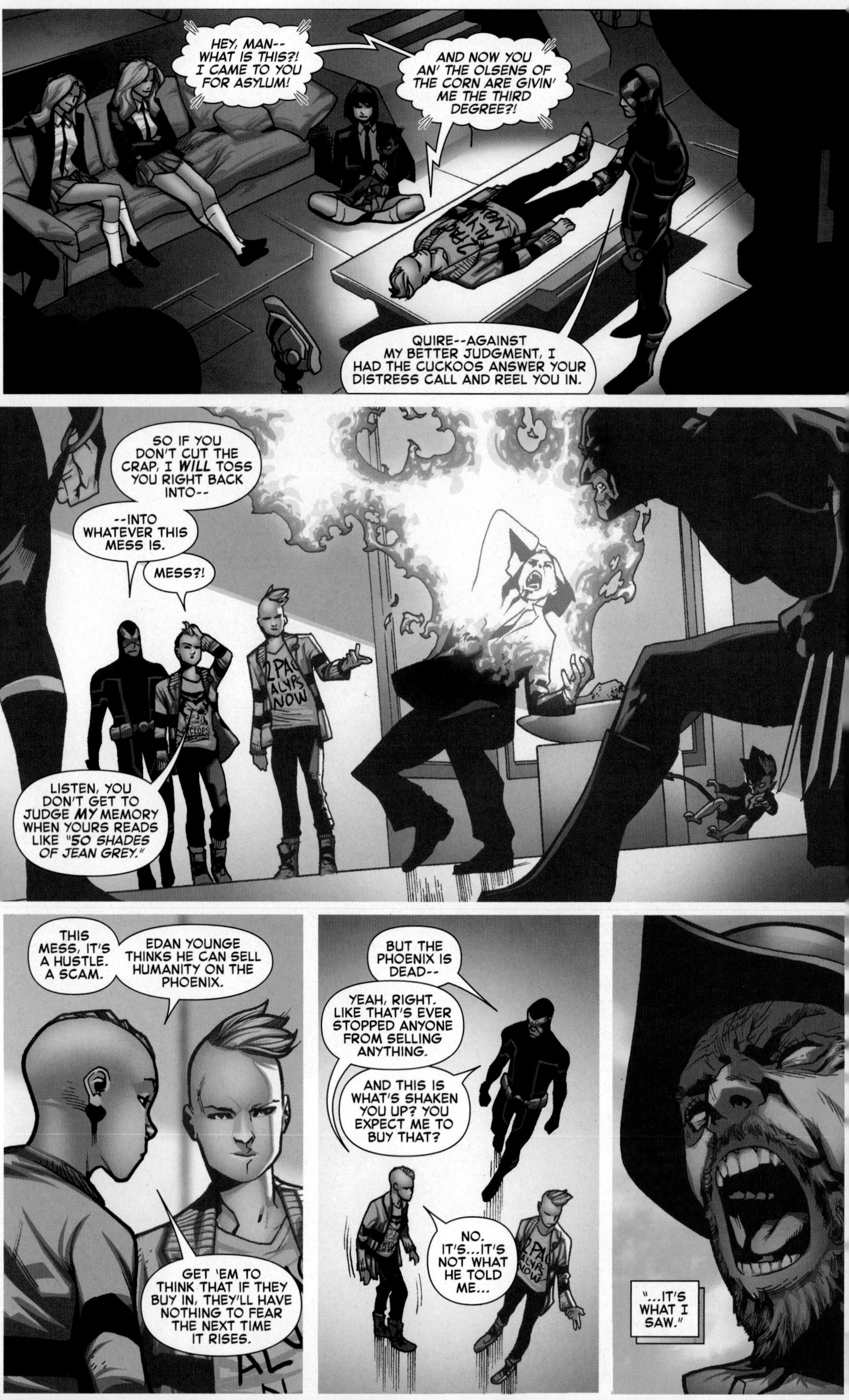
HEY, MAN--
WHAT IS THIS?!
I CAME TO YOU
FOR ASYLUM!
AND NOW YOU
AN' THE OLSENS OF
THE CORN ARE GIVIN'
ME THE THIRD
DEGREE?!
QUIRE--AGAINST
MY BETTER JUDGMENT, I
HAD THE CUCKOOS ANSWER YOUR
DISTRESS CALL AND REEL YOU IN.
SO IF YOU
DON'T CUT THE
CRAP, I WILL TOSS
YOU RIGHT BACK
INTO--
--INTO
WHATEVER THIS
MESS IS.
MESS?!
LISTEN, YOU
DON'T GET TO
JUDGE MY MEMORY
WHEN YOURS READS
LIKE "50 SHADES
OF JEAN GREY."
THIS
MESS, IT'S
A HUSTLE.
A SCAM.
EDAN YOUNGE
THINKS HE CAN SELL
HUMANITY ON THE
PHOENIX.
GET 'EM TO
THINK THAT IF THEY
BUY IN, THEY'LL HAVE
NOTHING TO FEAR
THE NEXT TIME
IT RISES.
BUT THE
PHOENIX IS
DEAD--
YEAH, RIGHT.
LIKE THAT'S EVER
STOPPED ANYONE
FROM SELLING
ANYTHING.
AND THIS IS
WHAT'S SHAKEN
YOU UP? YOU
EXPECT ME TO
BUY THAT?
NO.
IT'S...IT'S
NOT WHAT
HE TOLD
ME...
"...IT'S
WHAT I
SAW."

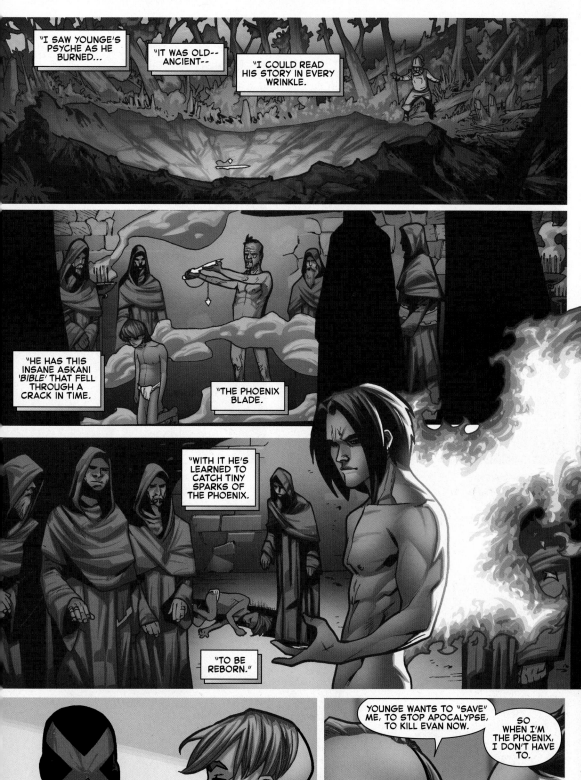

"I SAW YOUNGE'S PSYCHE AS HE BURNED...

"IT WAS OLD-- ANCIENT--

"I COULD READ HIS STORY IN EVERY WRINKLE.

"HE HAS THIS INSANE ASKANI *'BIBLE'* THAT FELL THROUGH A CRACK IN TIME.

"THE PHOENIX BLADE.

"WITH IT HE'S LEARNED TO CATCH TINY SPARKS OF THE PHOENIX.

"TO BE REBORN."

I THOUGHT THE FUTURE QUIRE WAS JUST TRYING TO SCARE ME.

BUT YOUNGE, THE PHOENIX CORP., IT'S ALL HAPPENING JUST LIKE HE SAID.

YOUNGE WANTS TO "SAVE" ME, TO STOP APOCALYPSE, TO KILL EVAN NOW.

SO WHEN I'M THE PHOENIX, I DON'T HAVE TO.

BUT HOW CAN I TRUST HIM? HE NEEDS THE PHOENIX ALIVE.

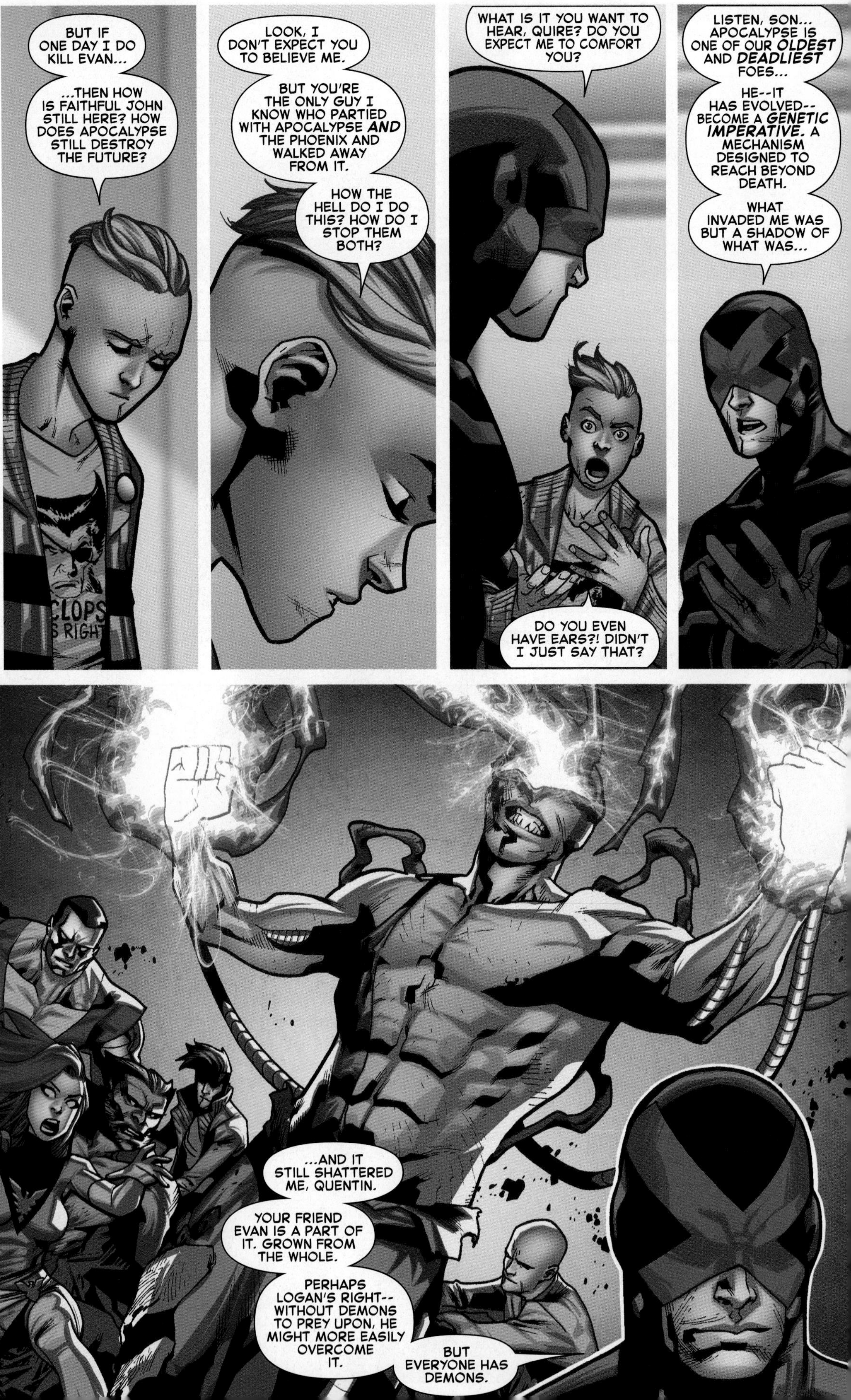

BUT IF ONE DAY I DO KILL EVAN...
...THEN HOW IS FAITHFUL JOHN STILL HERE? HOW DOES APOCALYPSE STILL DESTROY THE FUTURE?
LOOK, I DON'T EXPECT YOU TO BELIEVE ME.
BUT YOU'RE THE ONLY GUY I KNOW WHO PARTIED WITH APOCALYPSE *AND* THE PHOENIX AND WALKED AWAY FROM IT.
HOW THE HELL DO I DO THIS? HOW DO I STOP THEM BOTH?
WHAT IS IT YOU WANT TO HEAR, QUIRE? DO YOU EXPECT ME TO COMFORT YOU?
DO YOU EVEN HAVE EARS?! DIDN'T I JUST SAY THAT?
LISTEN, SON... APOCALYPSE IS ONE OF OUR *OLDEST* AND *DEADLIEST* FOES...
HE--IT HAS EVOLVED--BECOME A *GENETIC IMPERATIVE.* A MECHANISM DESIGNED TO REACH BEYOND DEATH.
WHAT INVADED ME WAS BUT A SHADOW OF WHAT WAS...
...AND IT STILL SHATTERED ME, QUENTIN.
YOUR FRIEND EVAN IS A PART OF IT. GROWN FROM THE WHOLE.
PERHAPS LOGAN'S RIGHT--WITHOUT DEMONS TO PREY UPON, HE MIGHT MORE EASILY OVERCOME IT.
BUT EVERYONE HAS DEMONS.

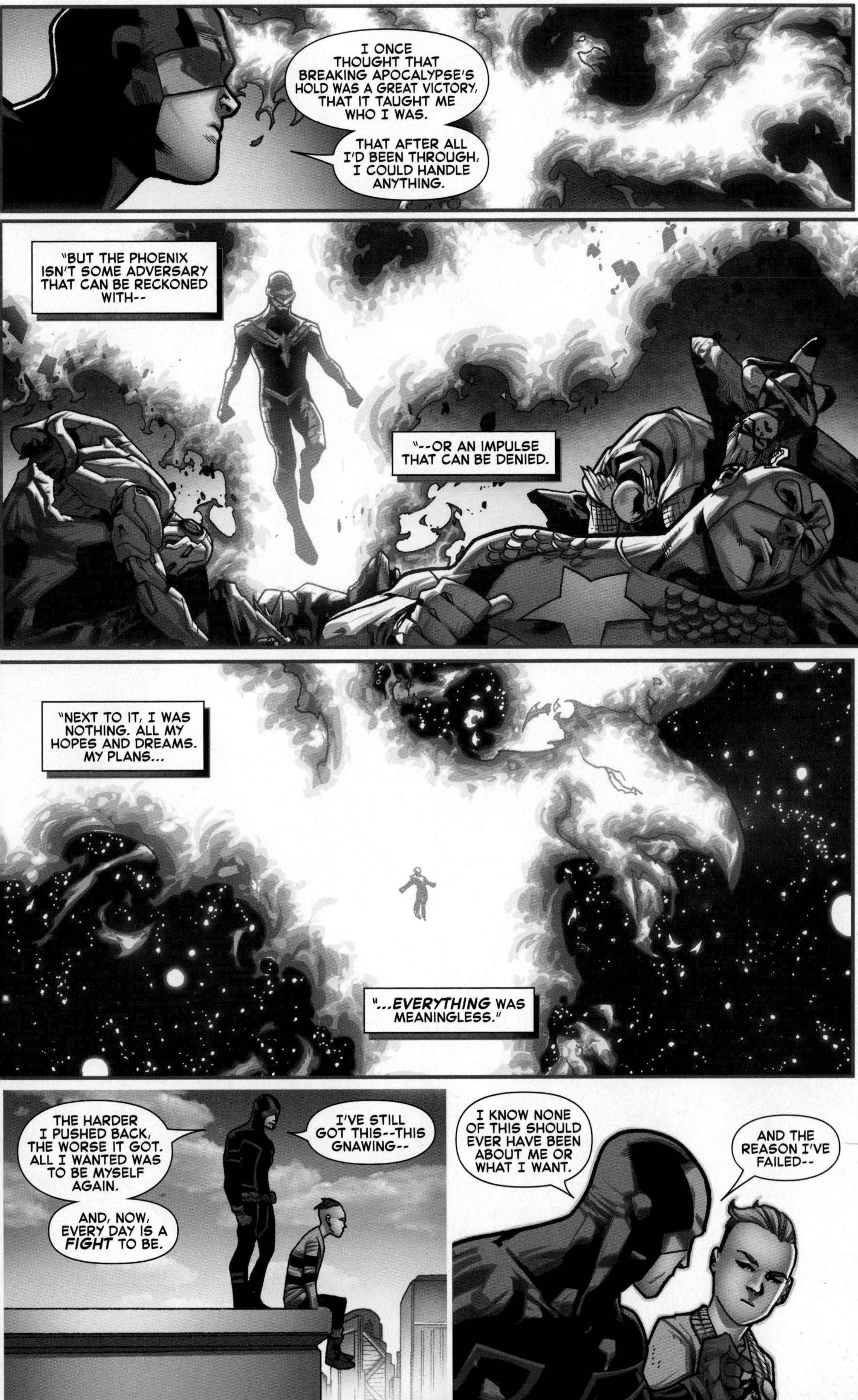
I ONCE THOUGHT THAT BREAKING APOCALYPSE'S HOLD WAS A GREAT VICTORY, THAT IT TAUGHT ME WHO I WAS.
THAT AFTER ALL I'D BEEN THROUGH, I COULD HANDLE ANYTHING.
"BUT THE PHOENIX ISN'T SOME ADVERSARY THAT CAN BE RECKONED WITH--
"--OR AN IMPULSE THAT CAN BE DENIED.
"NEXT TO IT, I WAS NOTHING. ALL MY HOPES AND DREAMS. MY PLANS...
"...*EVERYTHING* WAS MEANINGLESS."
THE HARDER I PUSHED BACK, THE WORSE IT GOT. ALL I WANTED WAS TO BE MYSELF AGAIN.
AND, NOW, EVERY DAY IS A ***FIGHT*** TO BE.
I'VE STILL GOT THIS--THIS GNAWING--
I KNOW NONE OF THIS SHOULD EVER HAVE BEEN ABOUT ME OR WHAT I WANT.
AND THE REASON I'VE FAILED--

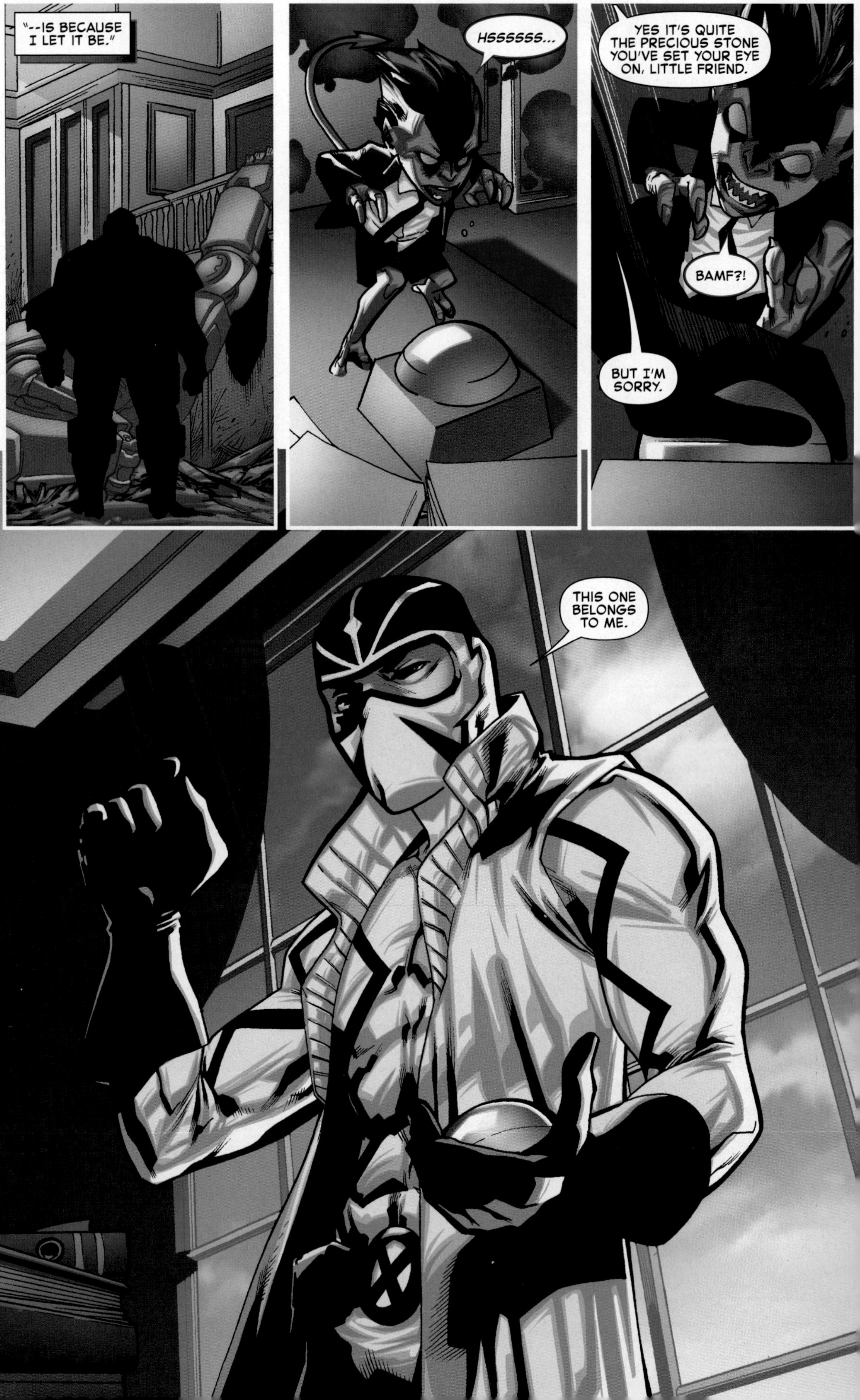
"--IS BECAUSE I LET IT BE."
HSSSSSS...
YES IT'S QUITE THE PRECIOUS STONE YOU'VE SET YOUR EYE ON, LITTLE FRIEND.
BAMF?!
BUT I'M SORRY.
THIS ONE BELONGS TO ME.

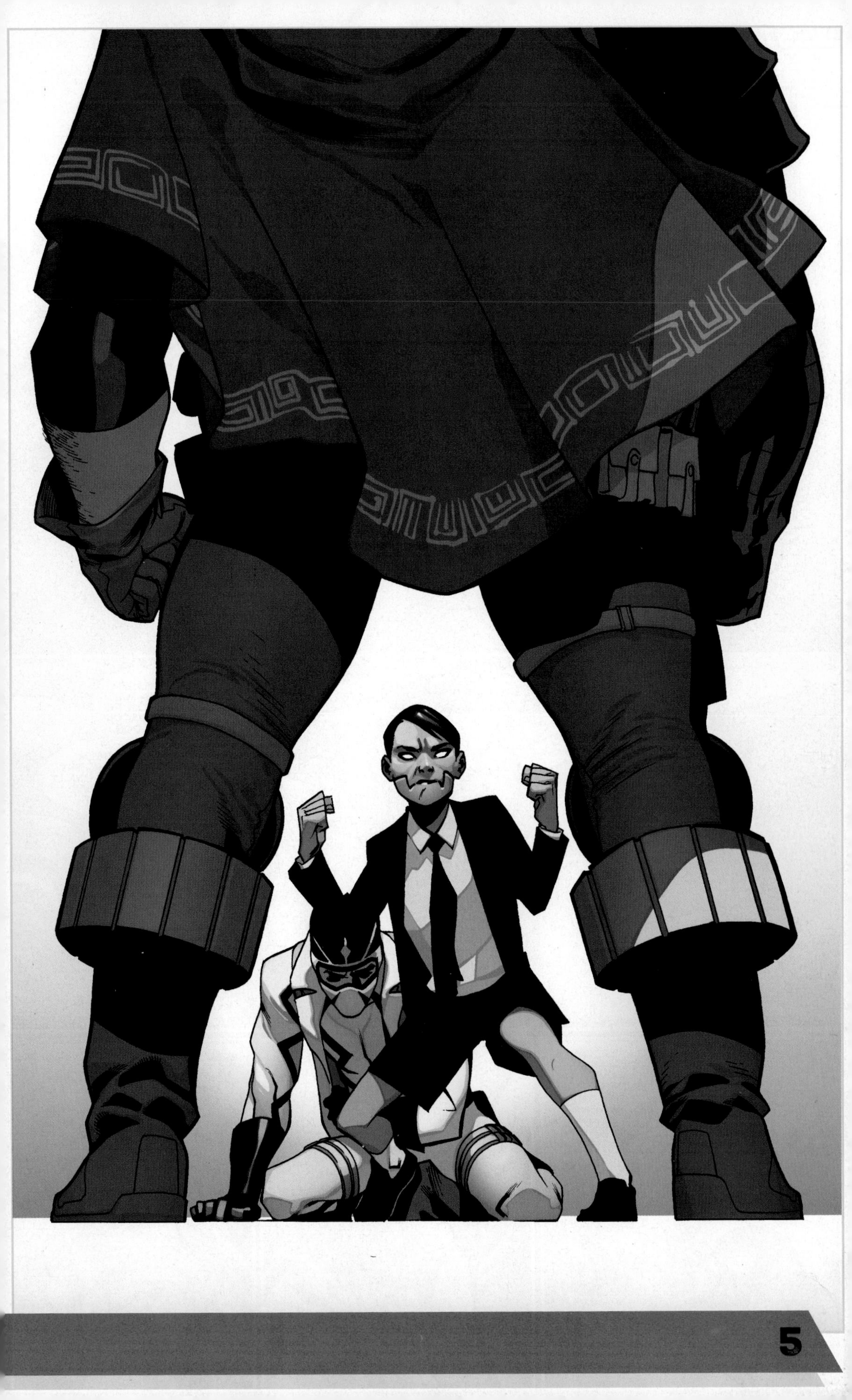

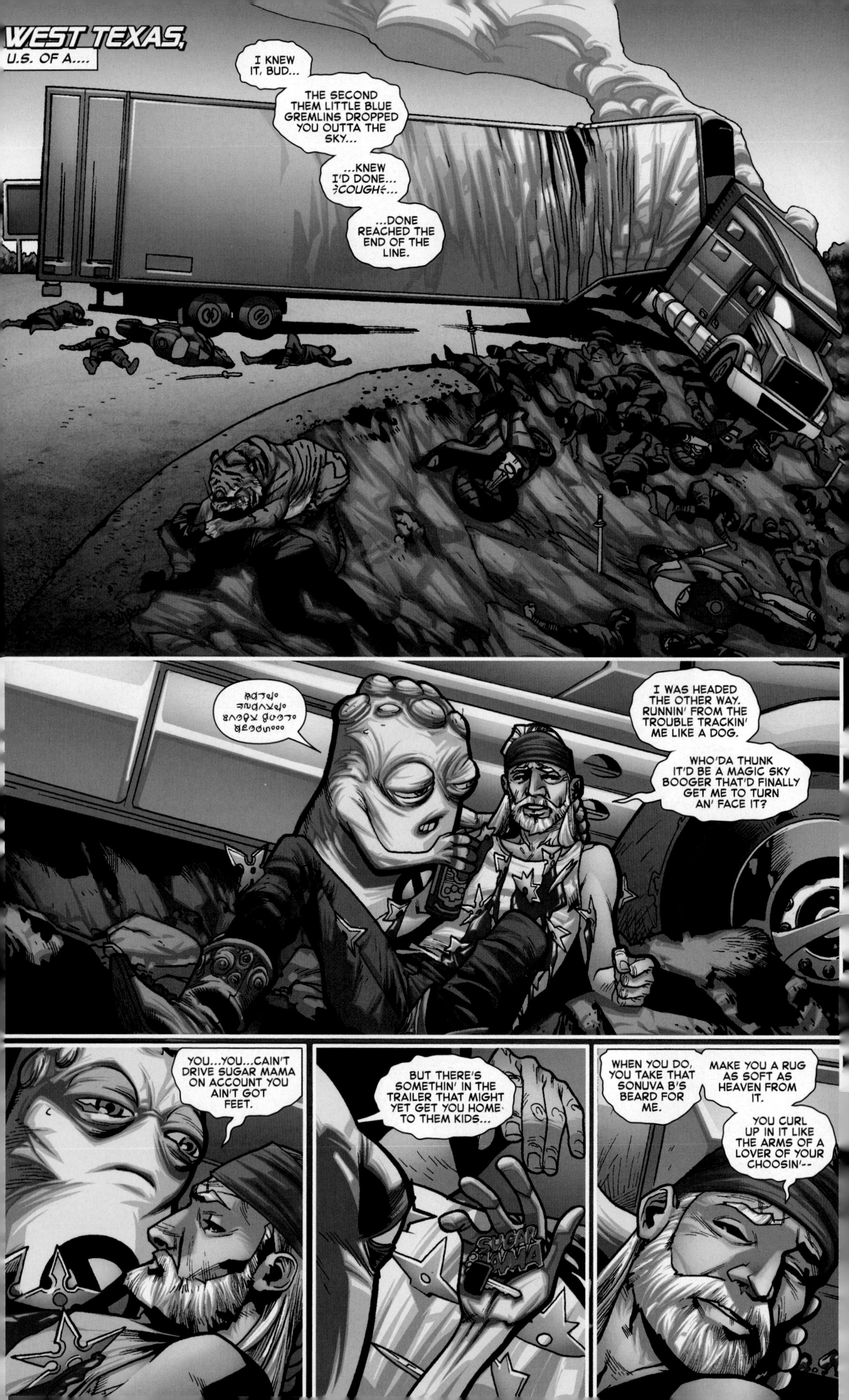
WEST TEXAS, U.S. OF A....
I KNEW IT, BUD...
THE SECOND THEM LITTLE BLUE GREMLINS DROPPED YOU OUTTA THE SKY...
...KNEW I'D DONE... *COUGH*...
...DONE REACHED THE END OF THE LINE.
I WAS HEADED THE OTHER WAY. RUNNIN' FROM THE TROUBLE TRACKIN' ME LIKE A DOG.
WHO'DA THUNK IT'D BE A MAGIC SKY BOOGER THAT'D FINALLY GET ME TO TURN AN' FACE IT?
YOU...YOU...CAIN'T DRIVE SUGAR MAMA ON ACCOUNT YOU AIN'T GOT FEET.
BUT THERE'S SOMETHIN' IN THE TRAILER THAT MIGHT YET GET YOU HOME TO THEM KIDS...
SUGAR MAMA
WHEN YOU DO, YOU TAKE THAT SONUVA B'S BEARD FOR ME.
MAKE YOU A RUG AS SOFT AS HEAVEN FROM IT.
YOU CURL UP IN IT LIKE THE ARMS OF A LOVER OF YOUR CHOOSIN'--

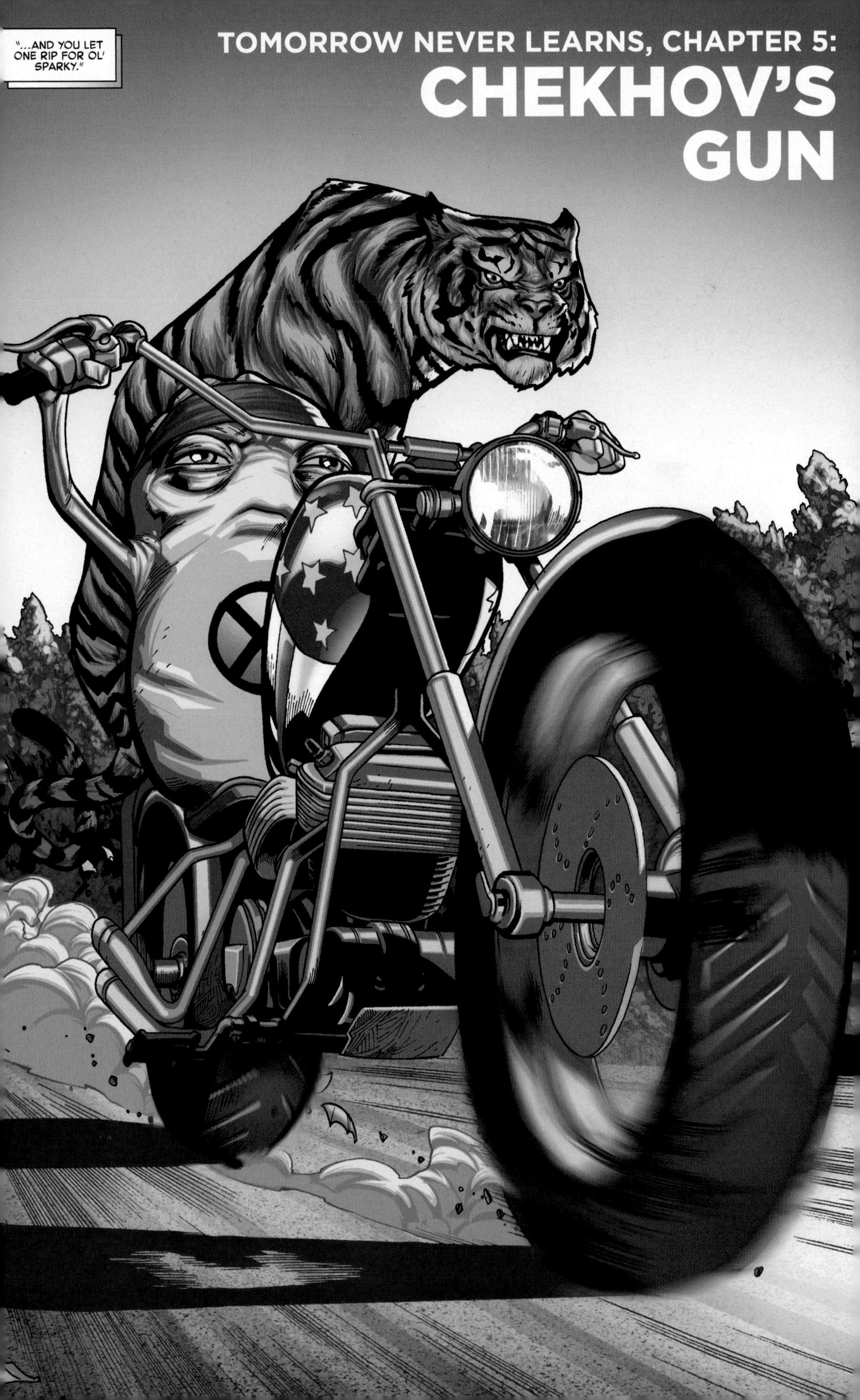
"...AND YOU LET ONE RIP FOR OL' SPARKY."
TOMORROW NEVER LEARNS, CHAPTER 5:
CHEKHOV'S GUN

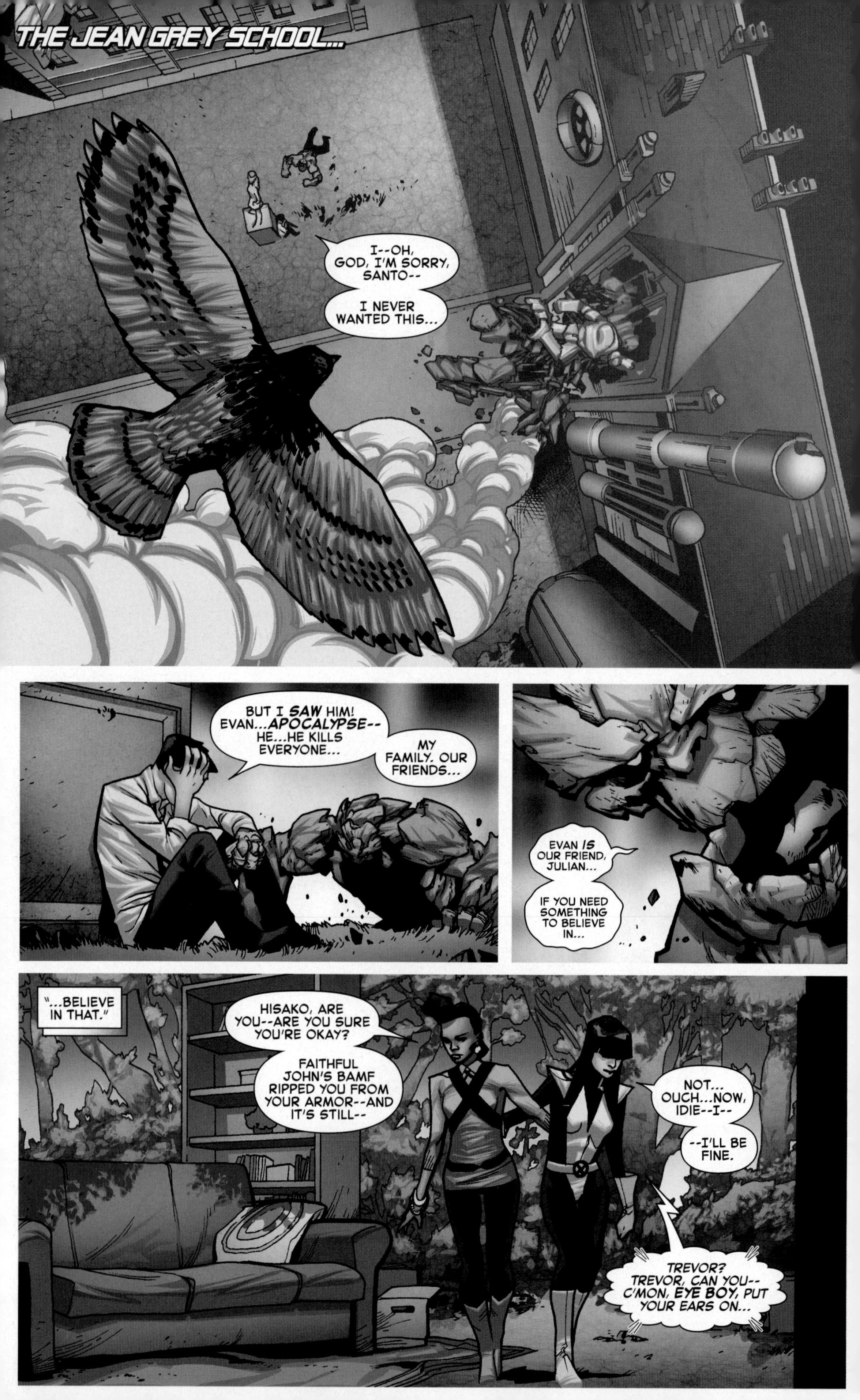
THE JEAN GREY SCHOOL...
I--OH, GOD, I'M SORRY, SANTO--
I NEVER WANTED THIS...
BUT I SAW HIM! EVAN...APOCALYPSE-- HE...HE KILLS EVERYONE...
MY FAMILY. OUR FRIENDS...
EVAN IS OUR FRIEND, JULIAN...
IF YOU NEED SOMETHING TO BELIEVE IN...
"...BELIEVE IN THAT."
HISAKO, ARE YOU--ARE YOU SURE YOU'RE OKAY?
FAITHFUL JOHN'S BAMF RIPPED YOU FROM YOUR ARMOR--AND IT'S STILL--
NOT... OUCH...NOW, IDIE--I--
--I'LL BE FINE.
TREVOR? TREVOR, CAN YOU-- C'MON, EYE BOY, PUT YOUR EARS ON...

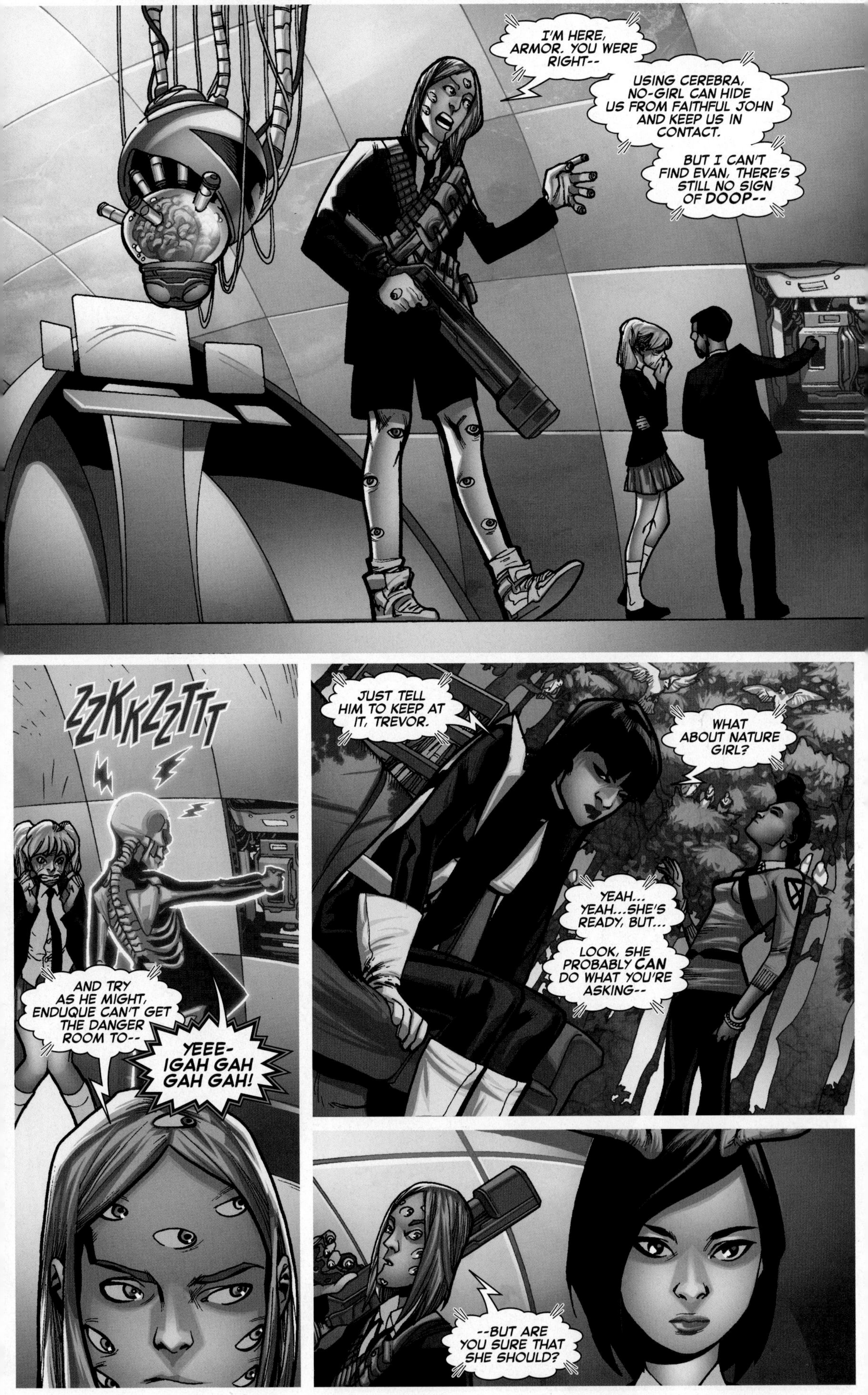
I'M HERE, ARMOR. YOU WERE RIGHT--
USING CEREBRA, NO-GIRL CAN HIDE US FROM FAITHFUL JOHN AND KEEP US IN CONTACT.
BUT I CAN'T FIND EVAN, THERE'S STILL NO SIGN OF DOOP--
ZZKKZZTTT
AND TRY AS HE MIGHT, ENDUQUE CAN'T GET THE DANGER ROOM TO--
YEEE-IGAH GAH GAH GAH!
JUST TELL HIM TO KEEP AT IT, TREVOR.
WHAT ABOUT NATURE GIRL?
YEAH... YEAH...SHE'S READY, BUT...
LOOK, SHE PROBABLY CAN DO WHAT YOU'RE ASKING--
--BUT ARE YOU SURE THAT SHE SHOULD?

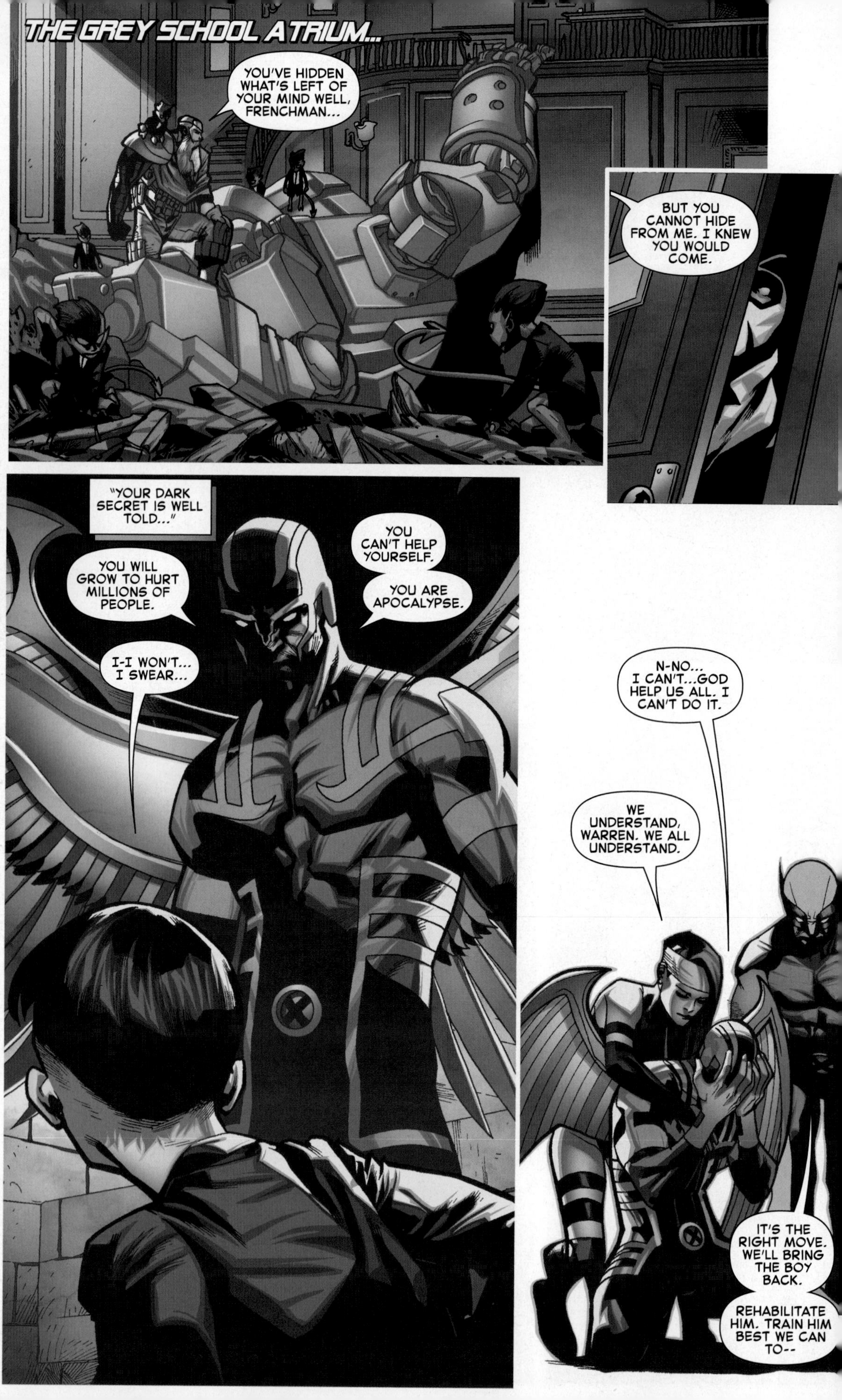
THE GREY SCHOOL ATRIUM...
YOU'VE HIDDEN WHAT'S LEFT OF YOUR MIND WELL, FRENCHMAN...
BUT YOU CANNOT HIDE FROM ME. I KNEW YOU WOULD COME.
"YOUR DARK SECRET IS WELL TOLD..."
YOU WILL GROW TO HURT MILLIONS OF PEOPLE.
YOU CAN'T HELP YOURSELF.
YOU ARE APOCALYPSE.
I-I WON'T... I SWEAR...
N-NO... I CAN'T...GOD HELP US ALL. I CAN'T DO IT.
WE UNDERSTAND, WARREN. WE ALL UNDERSTAND.
IT'S THE RIGHT MOVE. WE'LL BRING THE BOY BACK.
REHABILITATE HIM. TRAIN HIM BEST WE CAN TO--

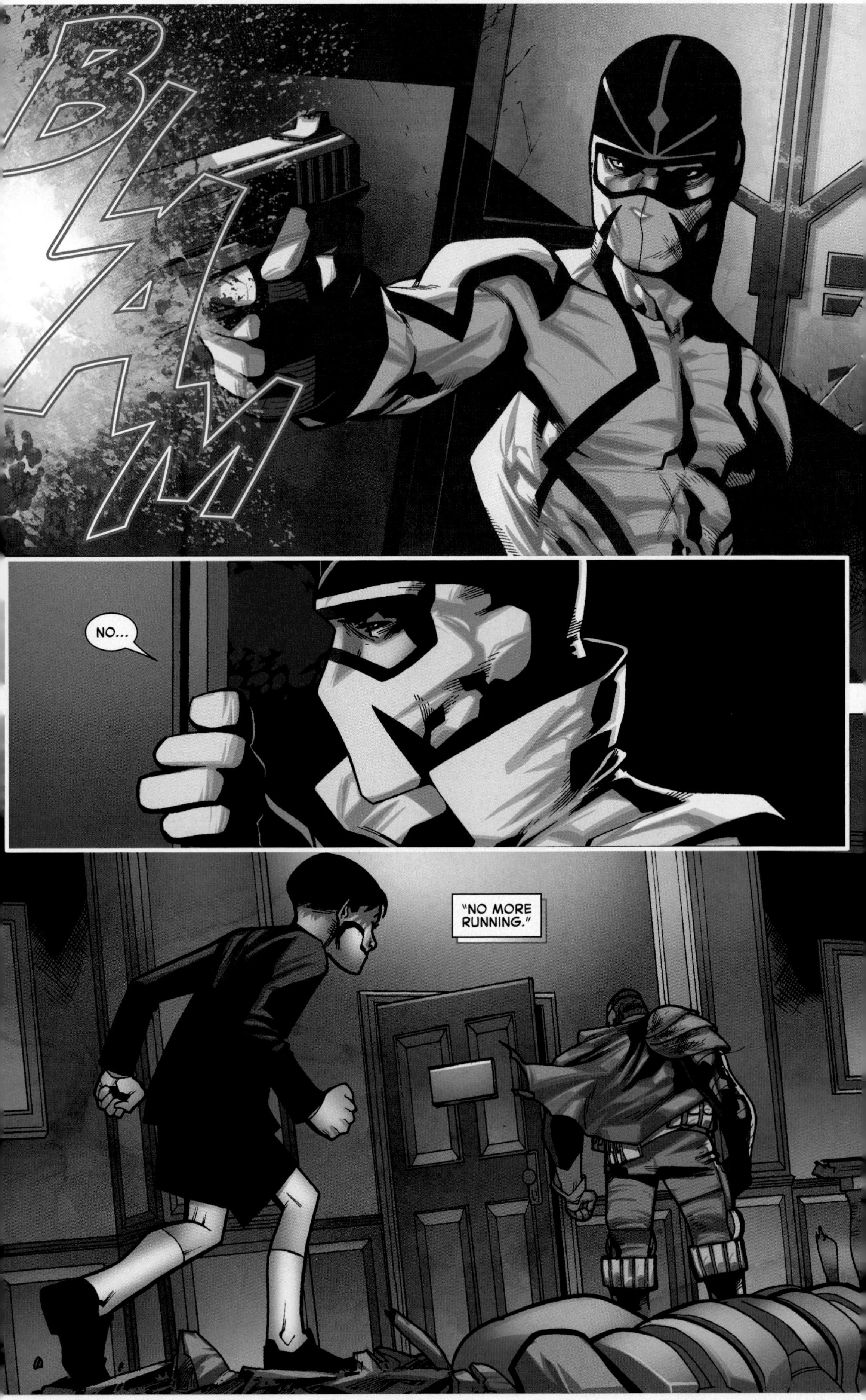
BLAM
NO...
"NO MORE RUNNING."

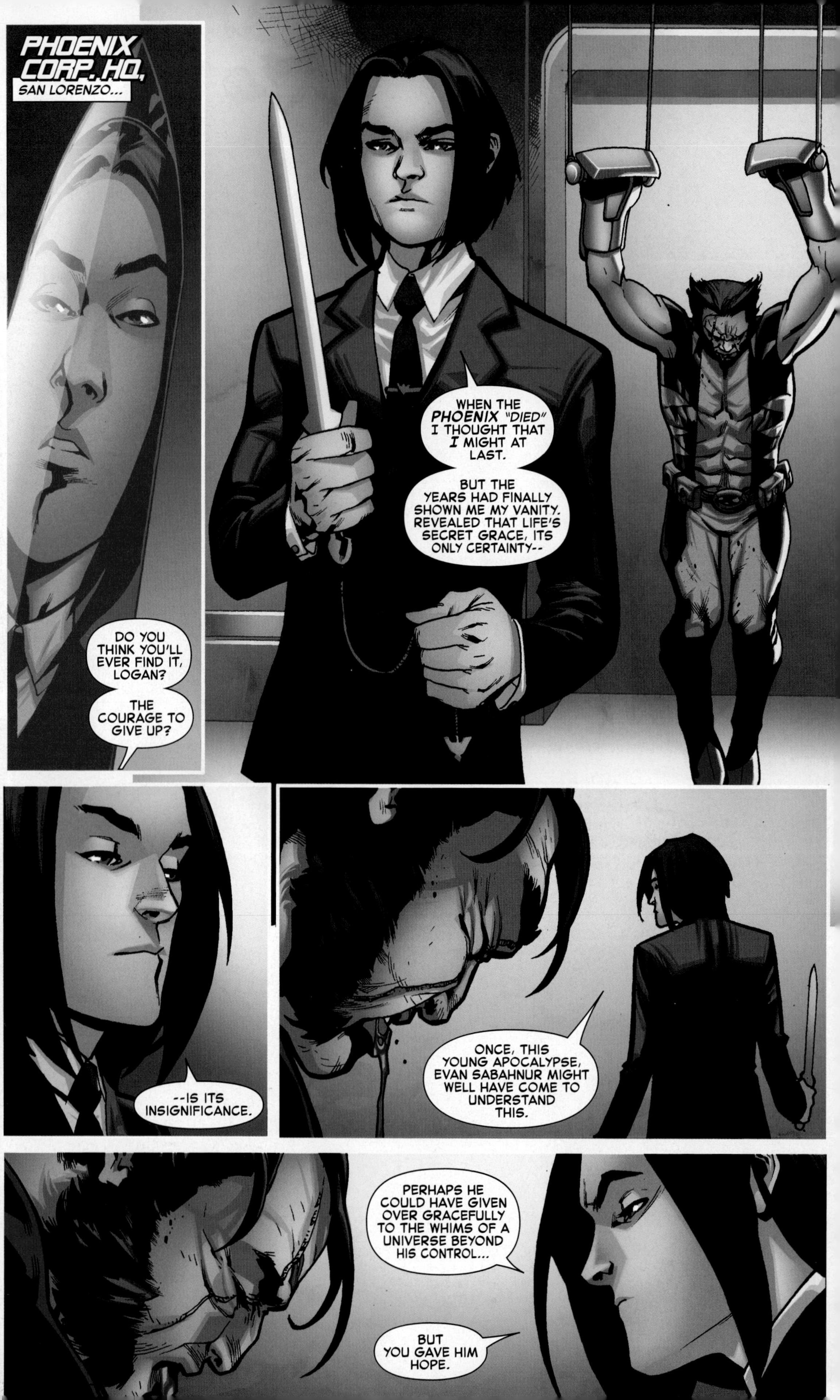
PHOENIX CORP. HQ, SAN LORENZO...
WHEN THE PHOENIX "DIED" I THOUGHT THAT I MIGHT AT LAST.
BUT THE YEARS HAD FINALLY SHOWN ME MY VANITY. REVEALED THAT LIFE'S SECRET GRACE, ITS ONLY CERTAINTY--
DO YOU THINK YOU'LL EVER FIND IT, LOGAN?
THE COURAGE TO GIVE UP?
--IS ITS INSIGNIFICANCE.
ONCE, THIS YOUNG APOCALYPSE, EVAN SABAHNUR MIGHT WELL HAVE COME TO UNDERSTAND THIS.
PERHAPS HE COULD HAVE GIVEN OVER GRACEFULLY TO THE WHIMS OF A UNIVERSE BEYOND HIS CONTROL...
BUT YOU GAVE HIM HOPE.

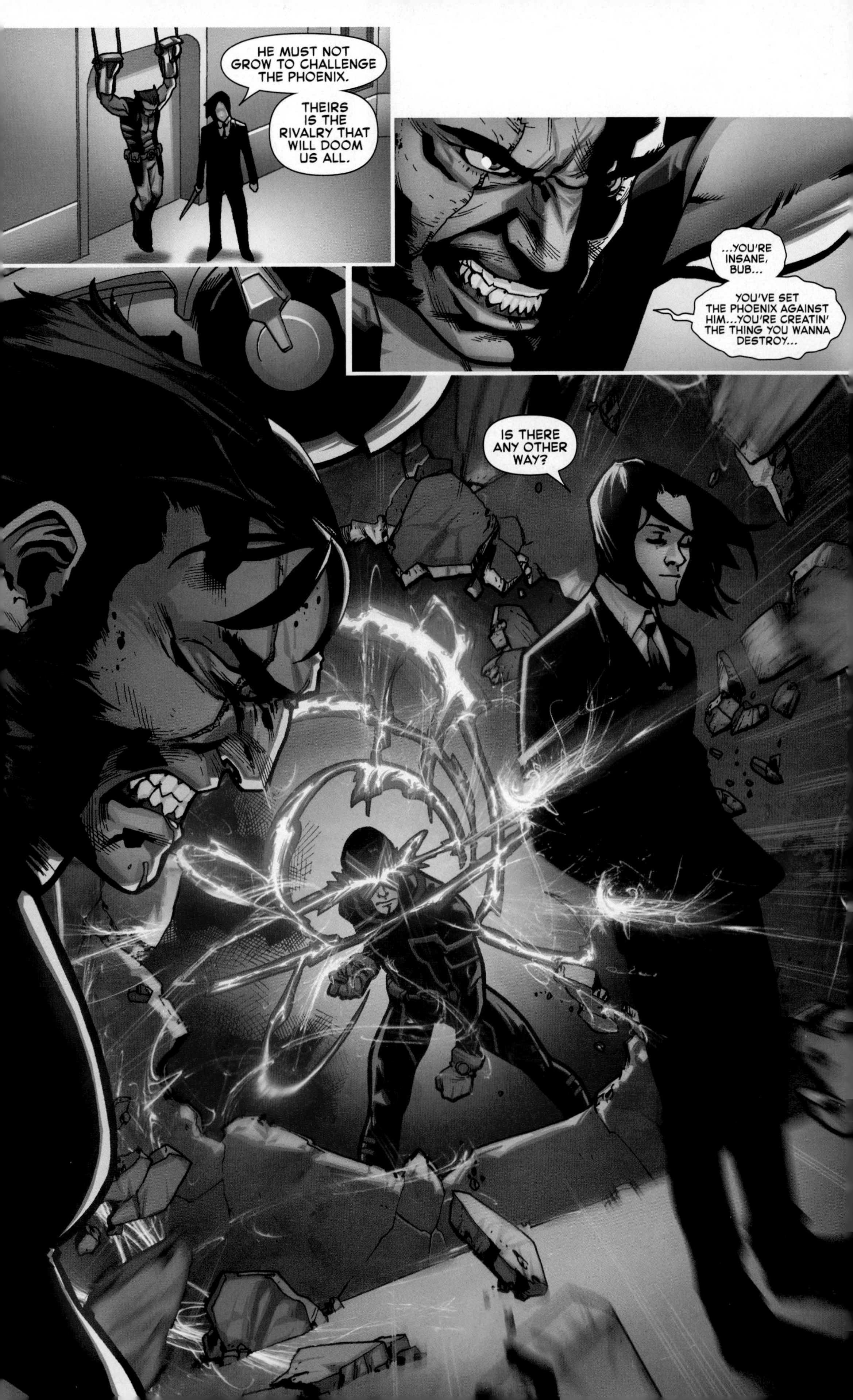
HE MUST NOT GROW TO CHALLENGE THE PHOENIX.
THEIRS IS THE RIVALRY THAT WILL DOOM US ALL.
...YOU'RE INSANE, BUB...
YOU'VE SET THE PHOENIX AGAINST HIM...YOU'RE CREATIN' THE THING YOU WANNA DESTROY...
IS THERE ANY OTHER WAY?

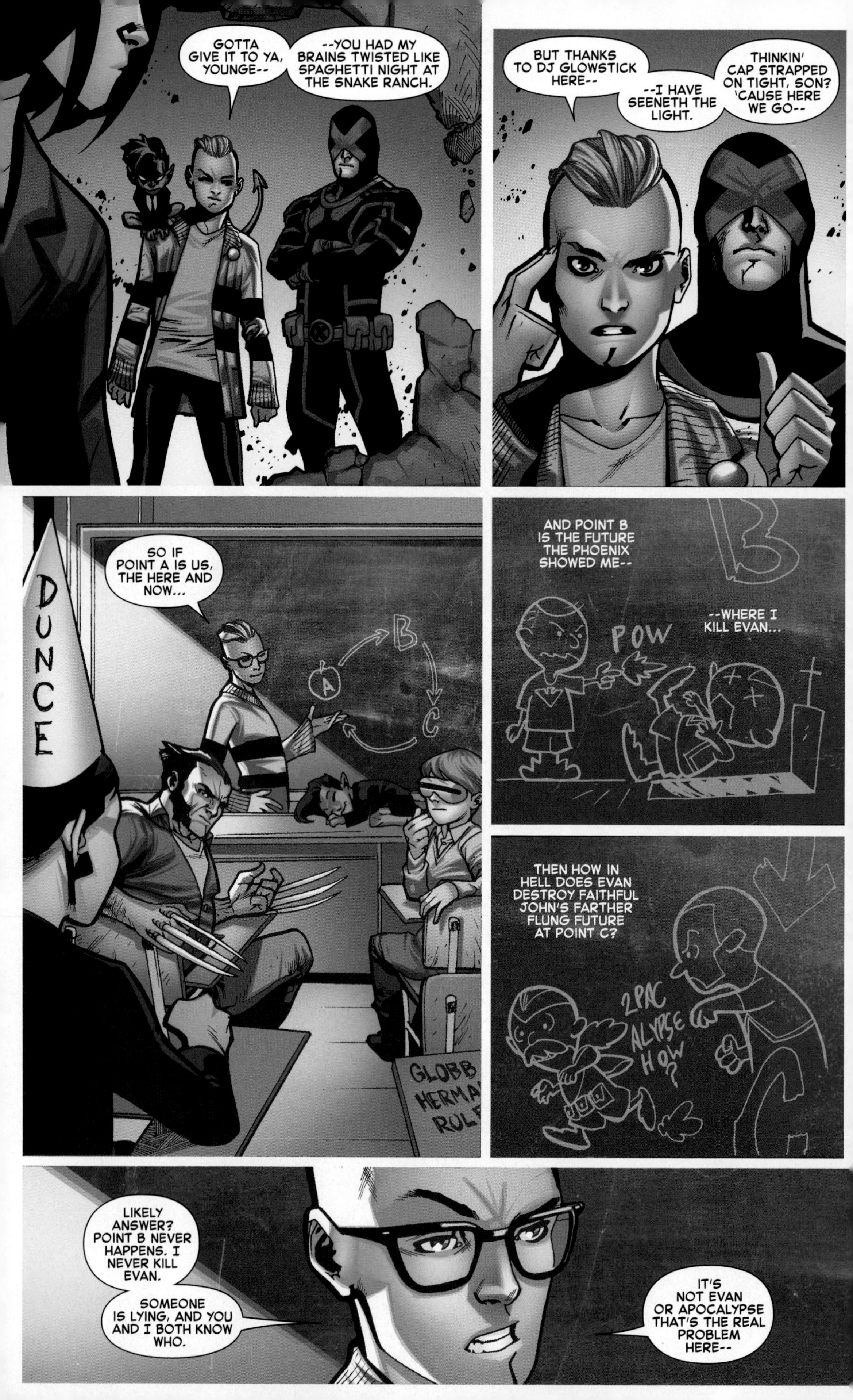
GOTTA GIVE IT TO YA, YOUNGE--
--YOU HAD MY BRAINS TWISTED LIKE SPAGHETTI NIGHT AT THE SNAKE RANCH.
BUT THANKS TO DJ GLOWSTICK HERE--
--I HAVE SEENETH THE LIGHT.
THINKIN' CAP STRAPPED ON TIGHT, SON? 'CAUSE HERE WE GO--
DUNCE
SO IF POINT A IS US, THE HERE AND NOW...
A
B
C
AND POINT B IS THE FUTURE THE PHOENIX SHOWED ME--
POW
--WHERE I KILL EVAN...
THEN HOW IN HELL DOES EVAN DESTROY FAITHFUL JOHN'S FARTHER FLUNG FUTURE AT POINT C?
2PAC ALYPSE HOW ?
LIKELY ANSWER? POINT B NEVER HAPPENS. I NEVER KILL EVAN.
SOMEONE IS LYING, AND YOU AND I BOTH KNOW WHO.
IT'S NOT EVAN OR APOCALYPSE THAT'S THE REAL PROBLEM HERE--

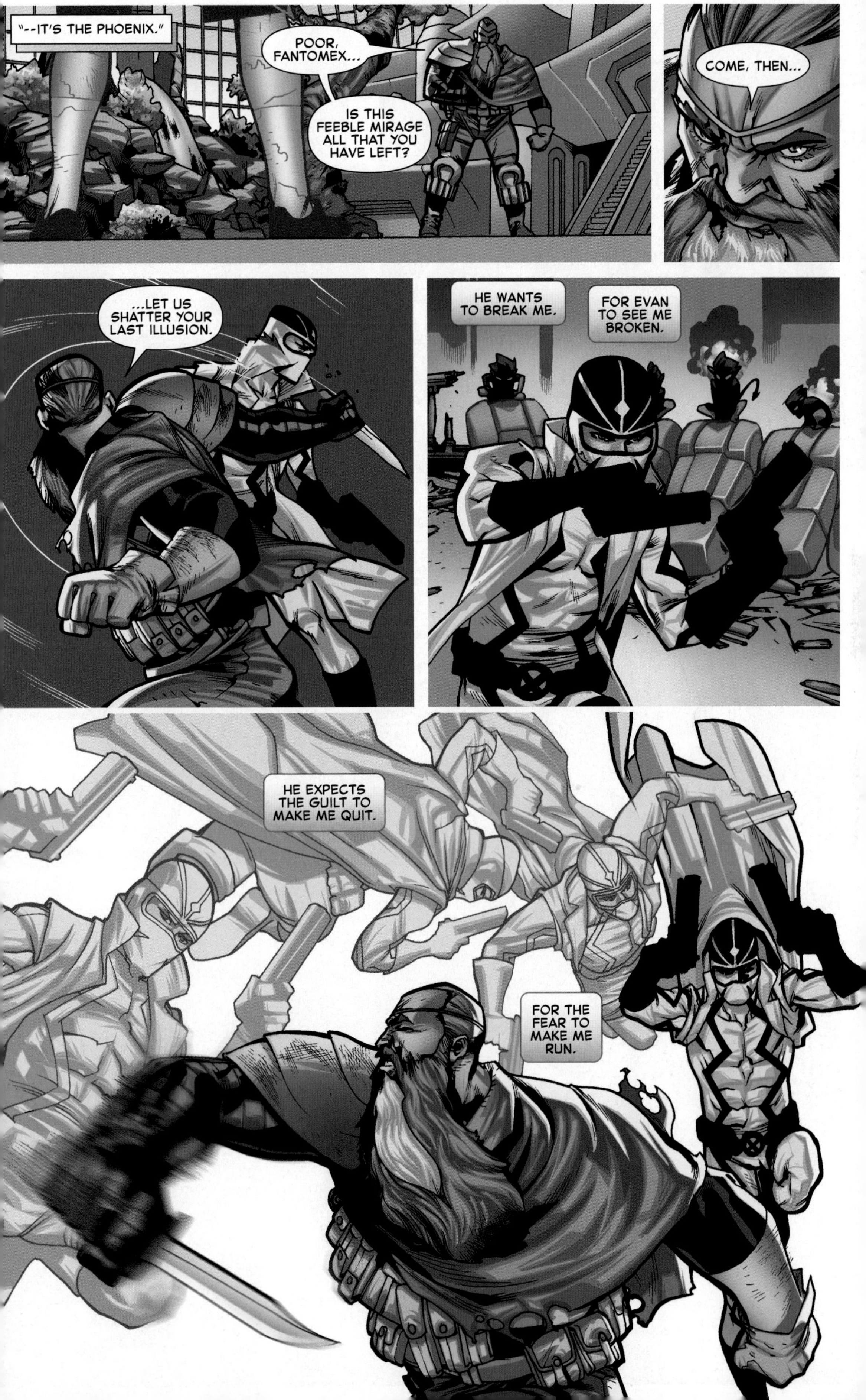
"--IT'S THE PHOENIX."
POOR, FANTOMEX...
IS THIS FEEBLE MIRAGE ALL THAT YOU HAVE LEFT?
COME, THEN...
...LET US SHATTER YOUR LAST ILLUSION.
HE WANTS TO BREAK ME.
FOR EVAN TO SEE ME BROKEN.
HE EXPECTS THE GUILT TO MAKE ME QUIT.
FOR THE FEAR TO MAKE ME RUN.

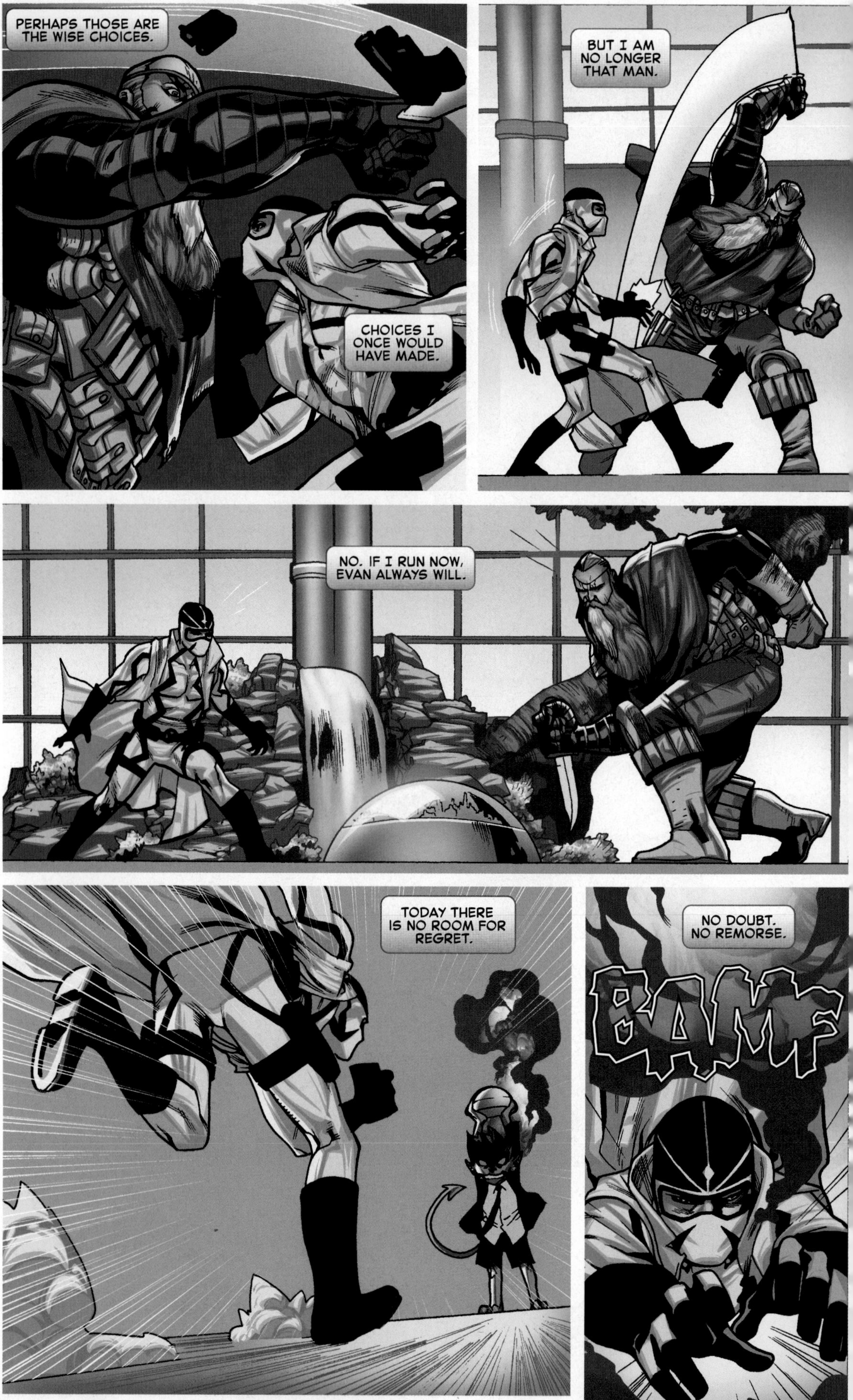
PERHAPS THOSE ARE THE WISE CHOICES.
CHOICES I ONCE WOULD HAVE MADE.
BUT I AM NO LONGER THAT MAN.
NO. IF I RUN NOW, EVAN ALWAYS WILL.
TODAY THERE IS NO ROOM FOR REGRET.
NO DOUBT. NO REMORSE.
BAMF

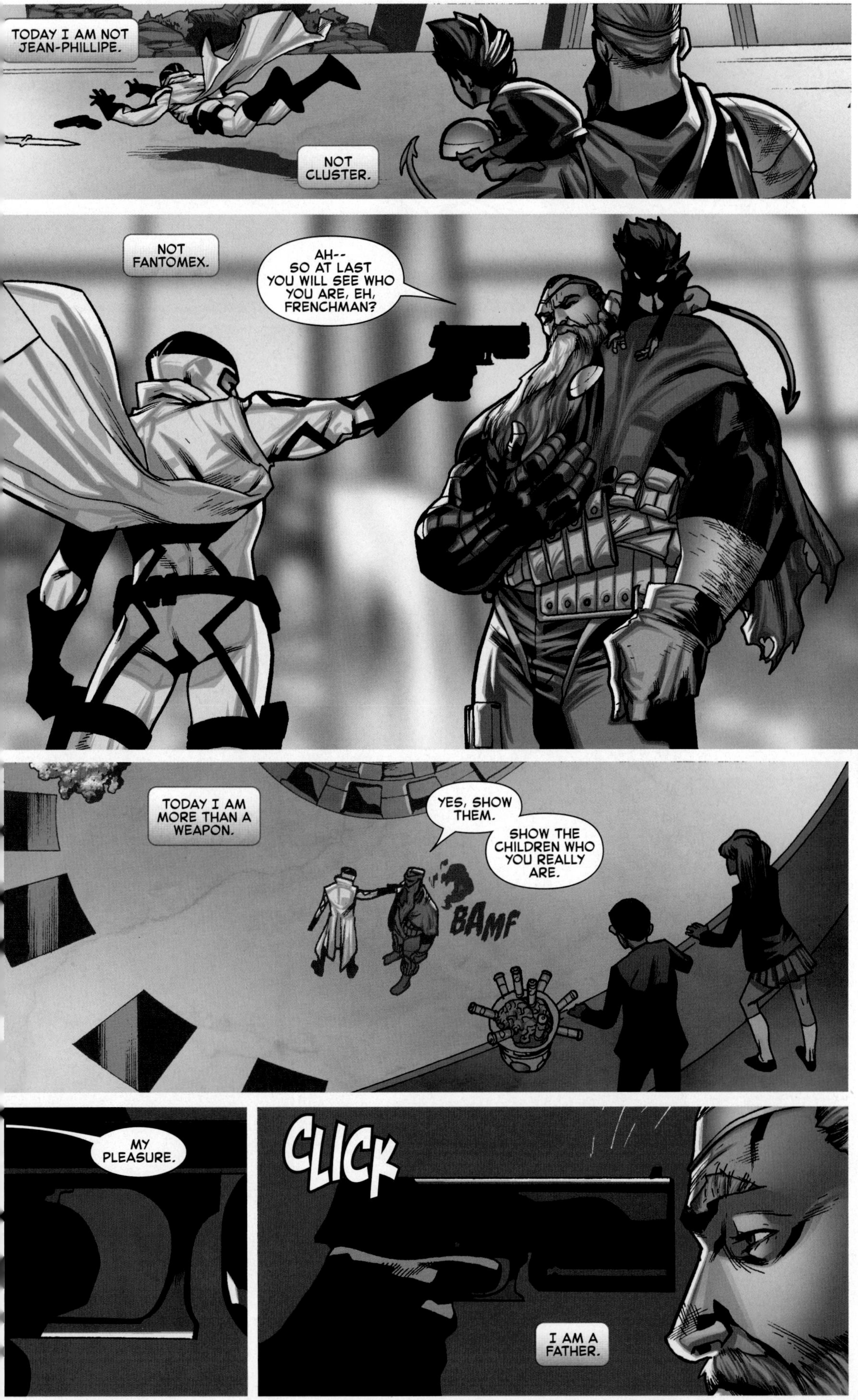

TODAY I AM NOT JEAN-PHILLIPE.
NOT CLUSTER.
NOT FANTOMEX.
AH-- SO AT LAST YOU WILL SEE WHO YOU ARE, EH, FRENCHMAN?
TODAY I AM MORE THAN A WEAPON.
YES, SHOW THEM.
SHOW THE CHILDREN WHO YOU REALLY ARE.
BAMF
MY PLEASURE.
CLICK
I AM A FATHER.

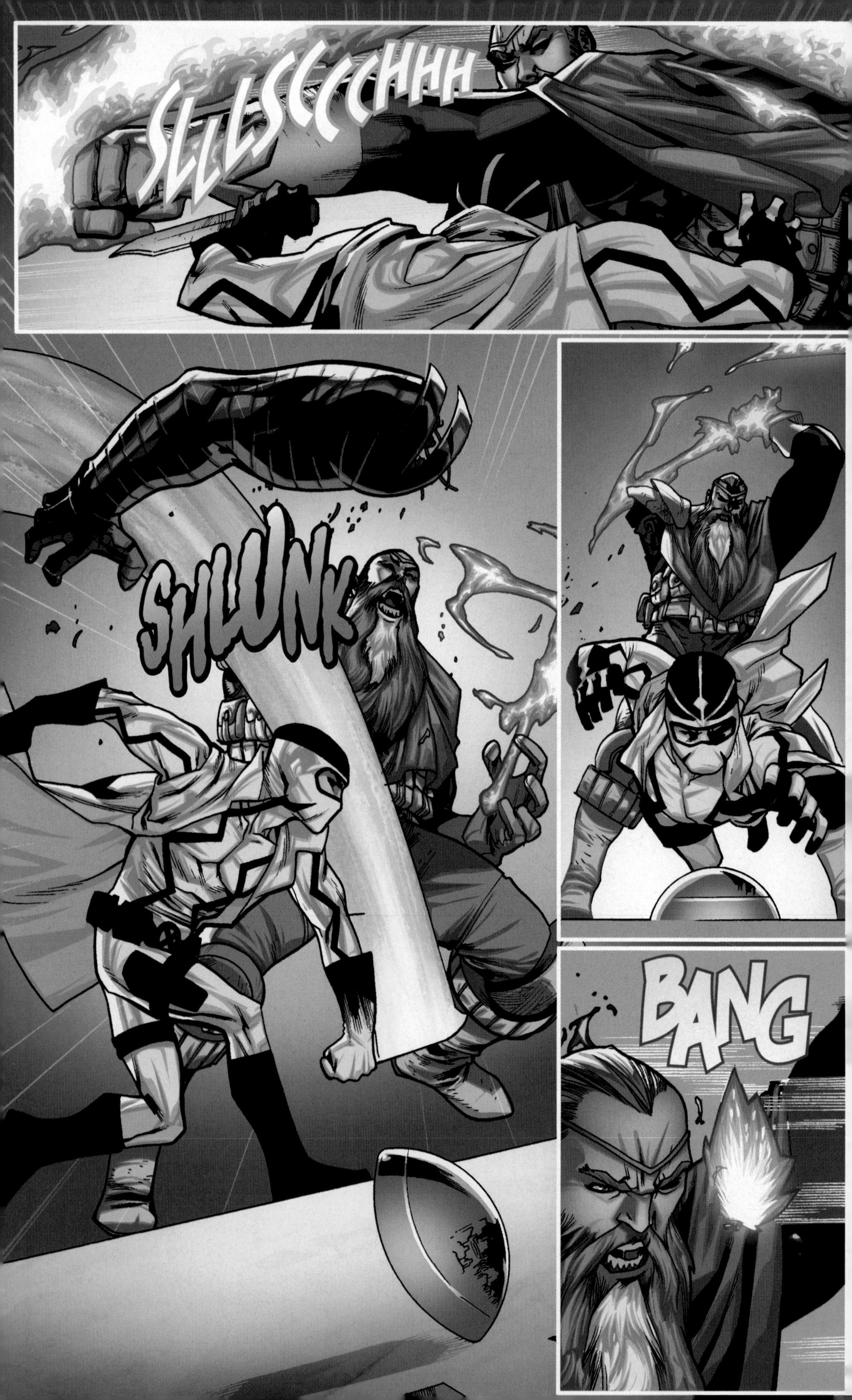
SLLLSCCCHHH
SHLUNK
BANG

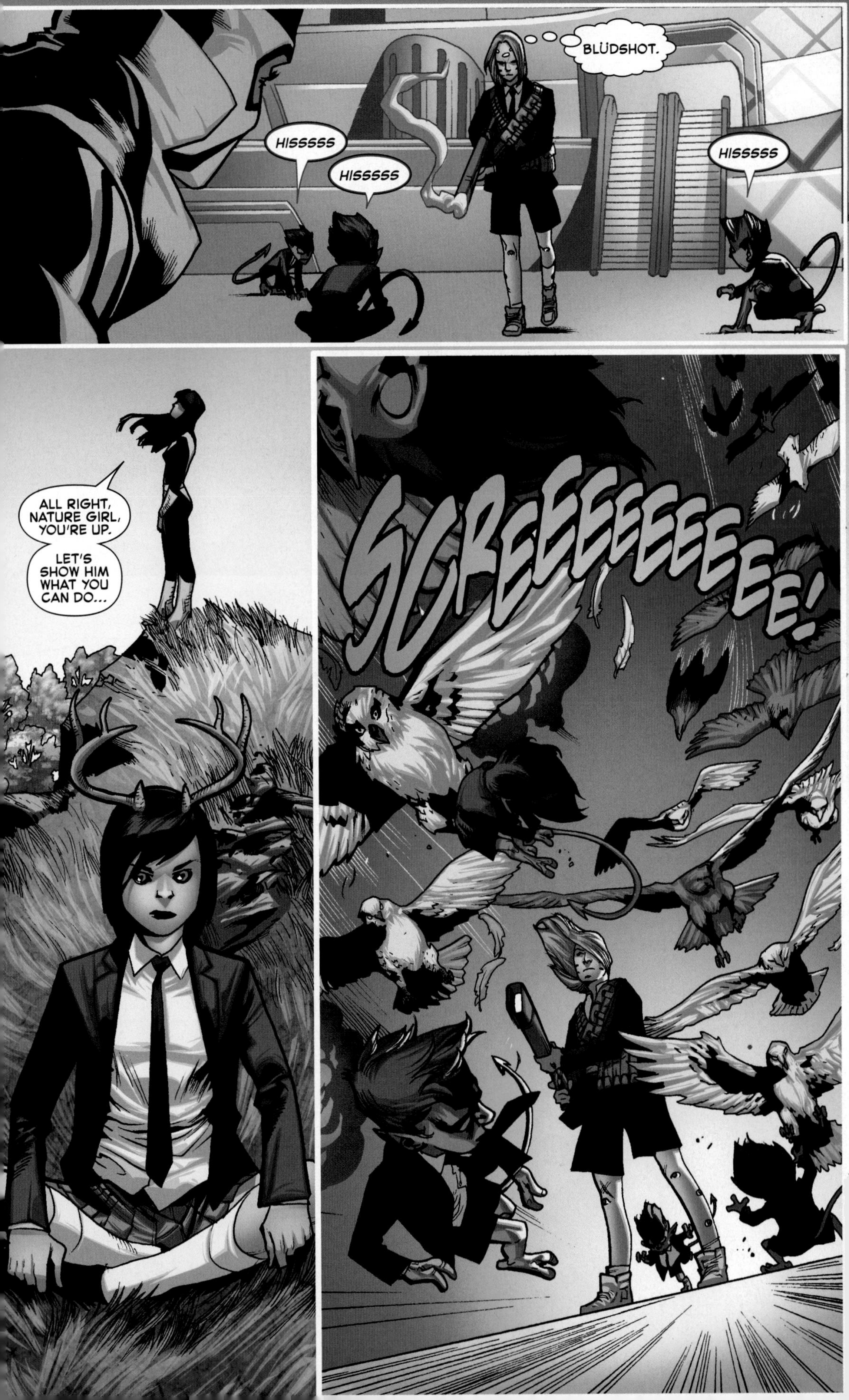
BLÜDSHOT.
HISSSSS
HISSSSS
HISSSSS
ALL RIGHT, NATURE GIRL, YOU'RE UP.
LET'S SHOW HIM WHAT YOU CAN DO...
SCREEEEEEEEEE!

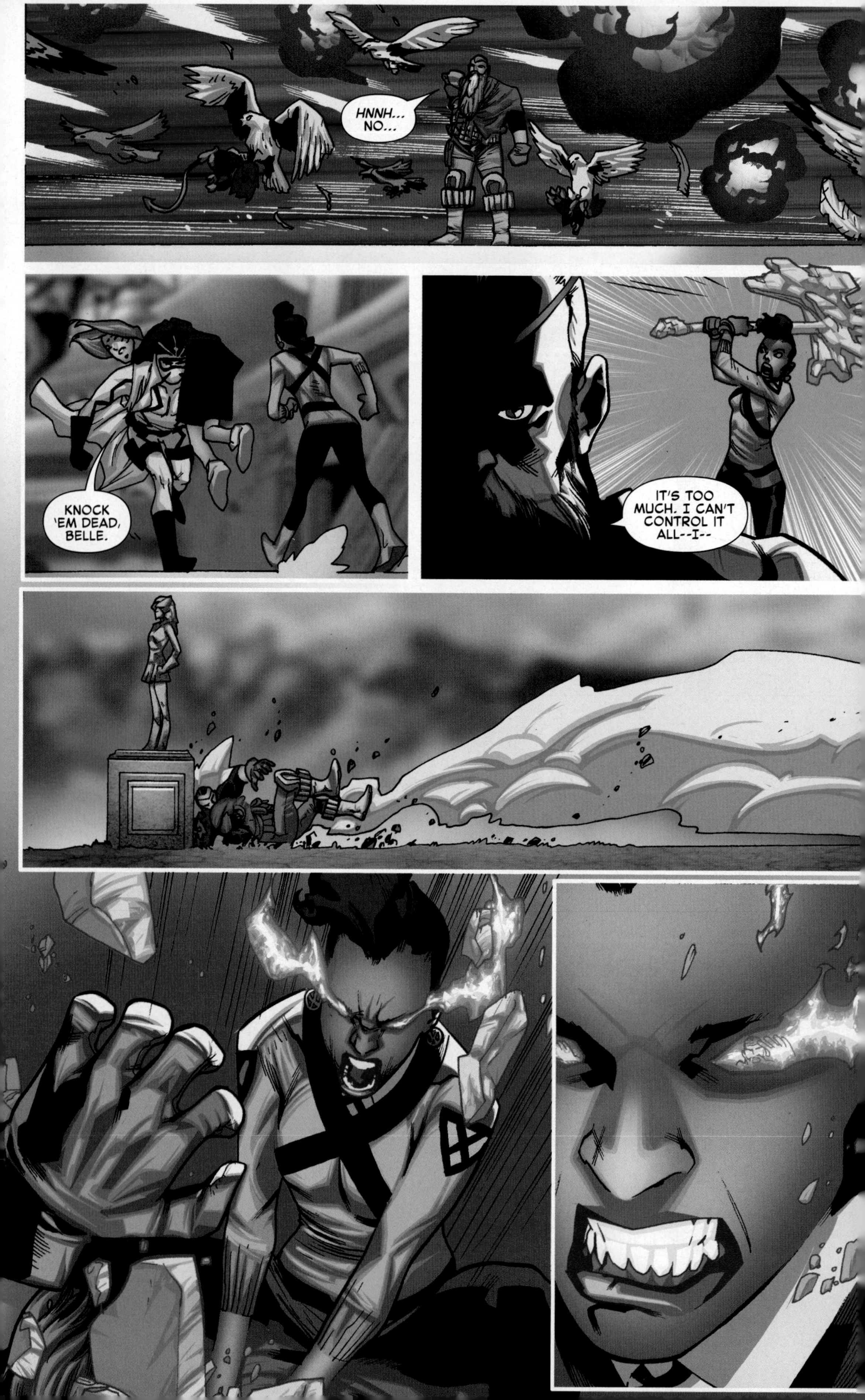
HNNH... NO...
KNOCK 'EM DEAD, BELLE.
IT'S TOO MUCH. I CAN'T CONTROL IT ALL--I--

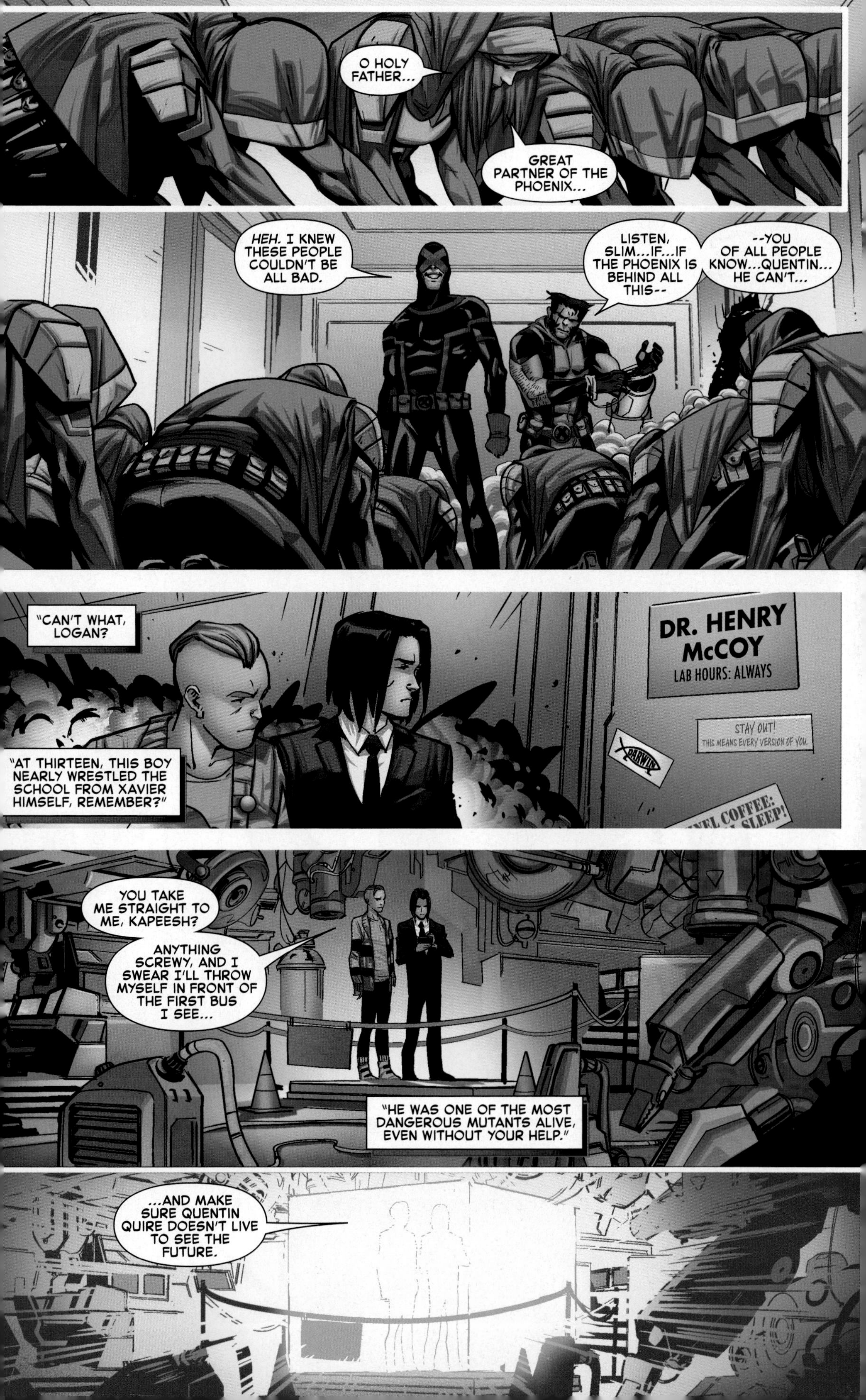
O HOLY FATHER...
GREAT PARTNER OF THE PHOENIX...
HEH. I KNEW THESE PEOPLE COULDN'T BE ALL BAD.
LISTEN, SLIM...IF...IF THE PHOENIX IS BEHIND ALL THIS--
--YOU OF ALL PEOPLE KNOW...QUENTIN... HE CAN'T...
"CAN'T WHAT, LOGAN?
DR. HENRY McCOY
LAB HOURS: ALWAYS
STAY OUT!
THIS MEANS EVERY VERSION OF YOU.
DARWIN
"AT THIRTEEN, THIS BOY NEARLY WRESTLED THE SCHOOL FROM XAVIER HIMSELF, REMEMBER?"
YOU TAKE ME STRAIGHT TO ME, KAPEESH?
ANYTHING SCREWY, AND I SWEAR I'LL THROW MYSELF IN FRONT OF THE FIRST BUS I SEE...
"HE WAS ONE OF THE MOST DANGEROUS MUTANTS ALIVE, EVEN WITHOUT YOUR HELP."
...AND MAKE SURE QUENTIN QUIRE DOESN'T LIVE TO SEE THE FUTURE.

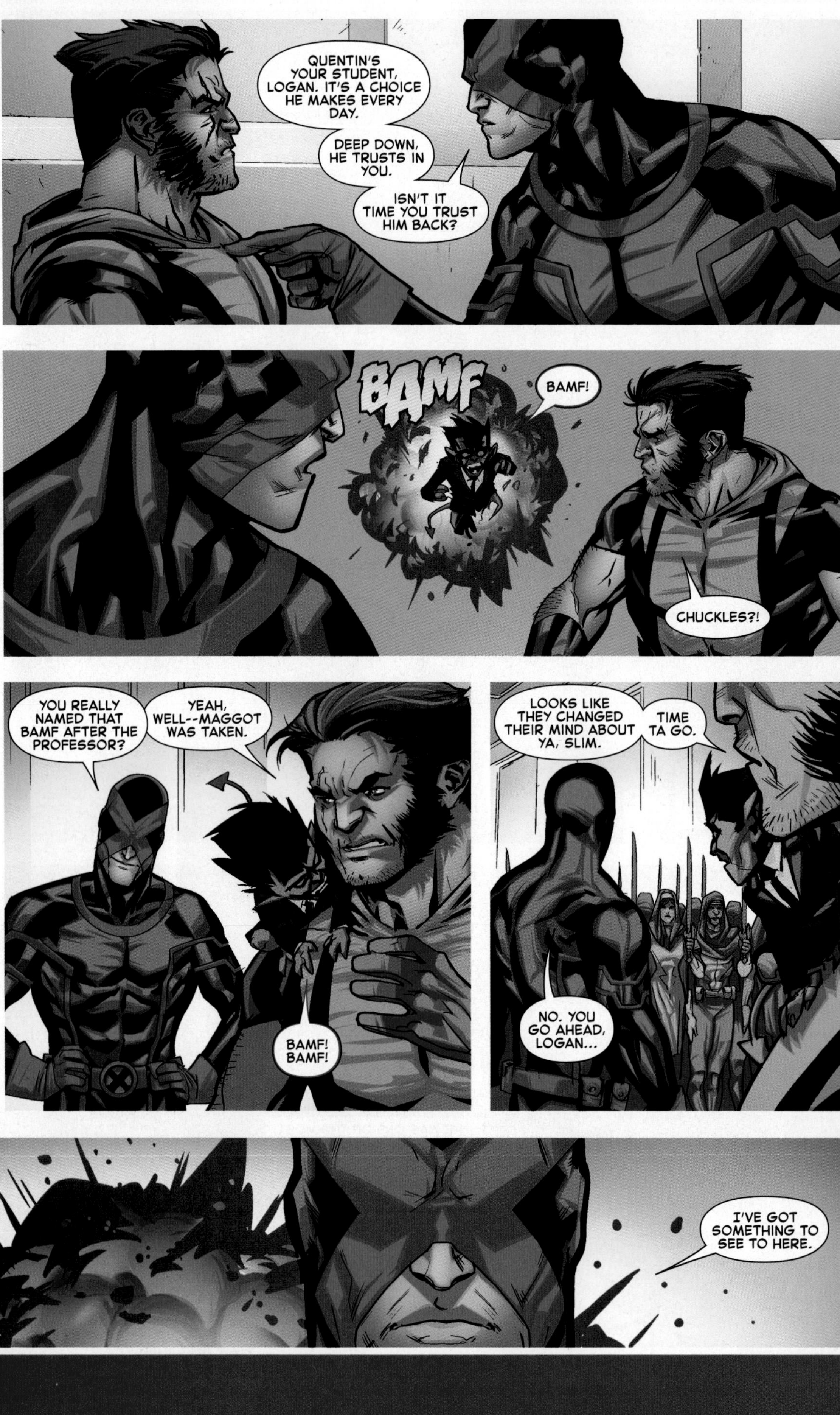
QUENTIN'S YOUR STUDENT, LOGAN. IT'S A CHOICE HE MAKES EVERY DAY.
DEEP DOWN, HE TRUSTS IN YOU.
ISN'T IT TIME YOU TRUST HIM BACK?
BAMF
BAMF!
CHUCKLES?!
YOU REALLY NAMED THAT BAMF AFTER THE PROFESSOR?
YEAH, WELL--MAGGOT WAS TAKEN.
BAMF! BAMF!
LOOKS LIKE THEY CHANGED THEIR MIND ABOUT YA, SLIM.
TIME TA GO.
NO. YOU GO AHEAD, LOGAN...
I'VE GOT SOMETHING TO SEE TO HERE.

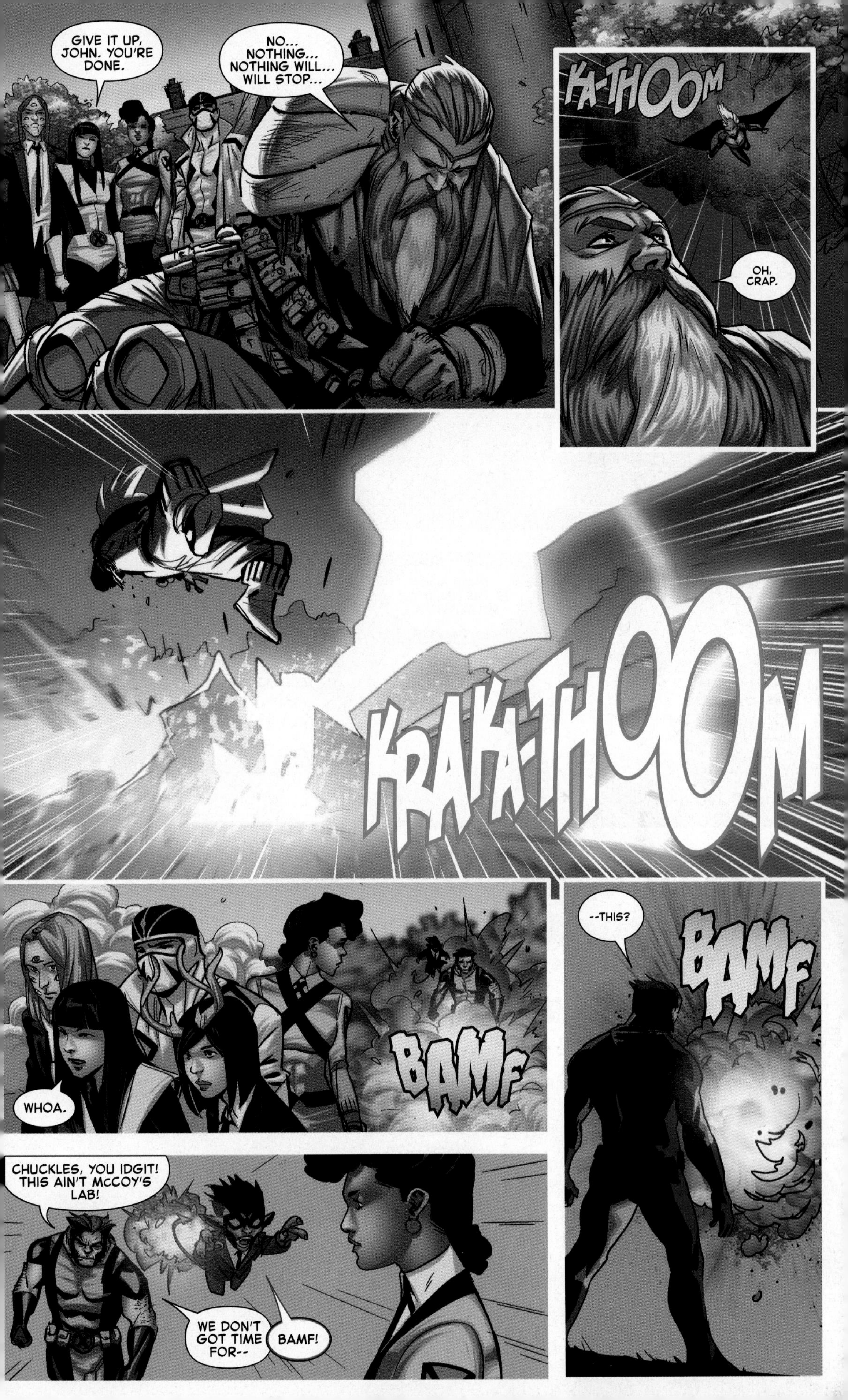
GIVE IT UP, JOHN. YOU'RE DONE.
NO... NOTHING... NOTHING WILL... WILL STOP...
KA-THOOM
OH, CRAP.
KRAKA-THOOOM
WHOA.
BAMF
--THIS?
BAMF
CHUCKLES, YOU IDGIT! THIS AIN'T MCCOY'S LAB!
WE DON'T GOT TIME FOR--
BAMF!

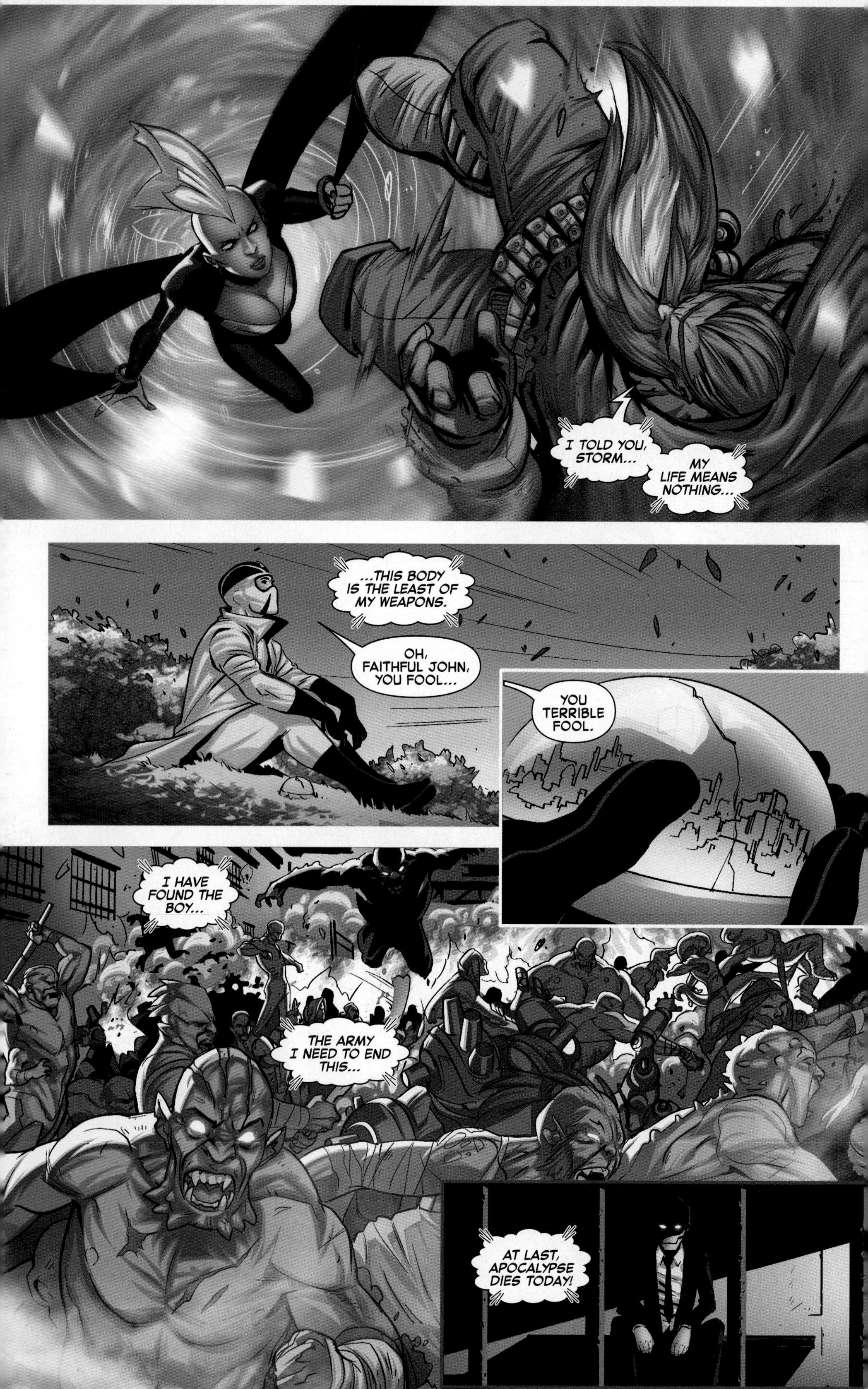
I TOLD YOU, STORM...
MY LIFE MEANS NOTHING...
...THIS BODY IS THE LEAST OF MY WEAPONS.
OH, FAITHFUL JOHN, YOU FOOL...
YOU TERRIBLE FOOL.
I HAVE FOUND THE BOY...
THE ARMY I NEED TO END THIS...
AT LAST, APOCALYPSE DIES TODAY!

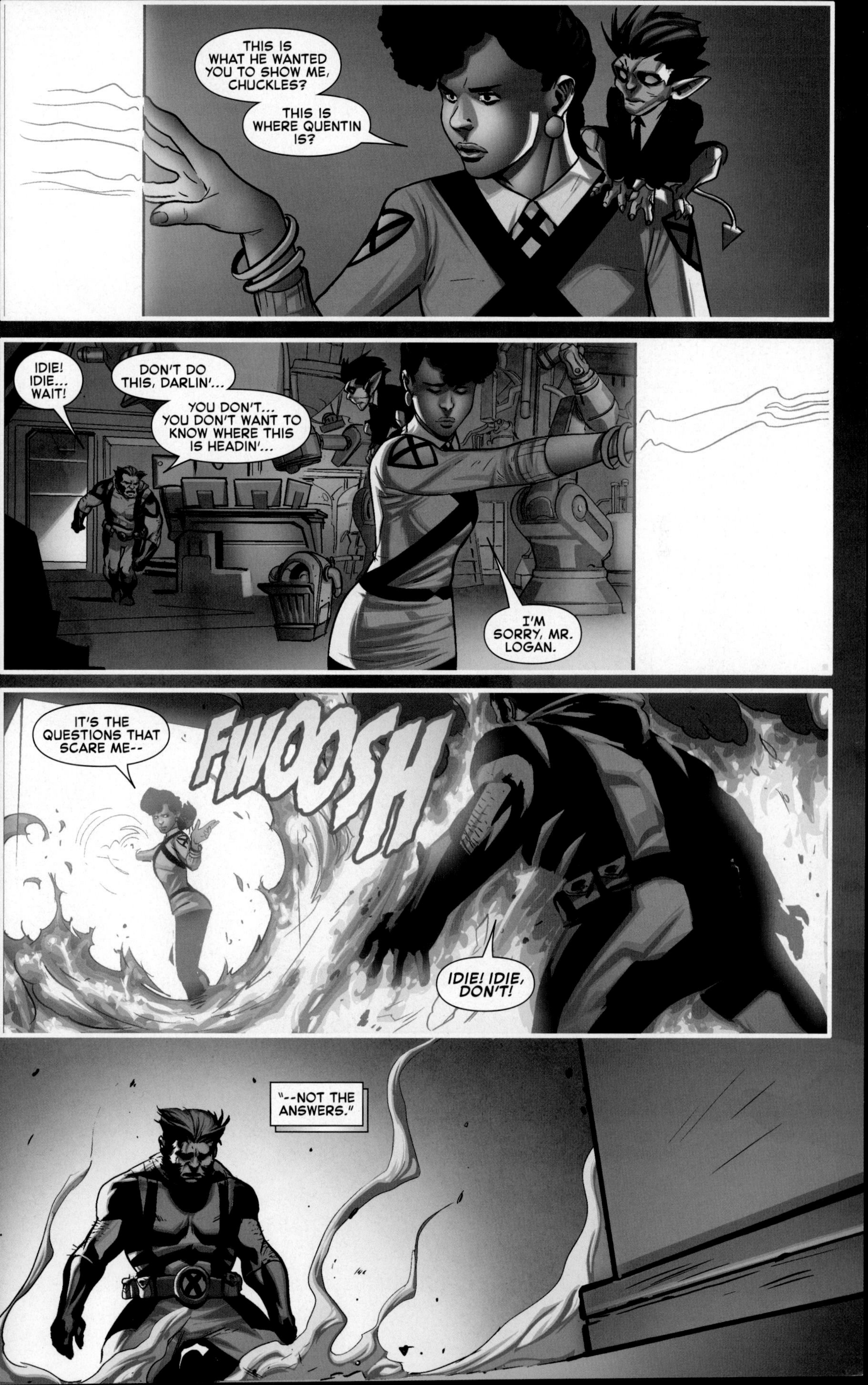
THIS IS WHAT HE WANTED YOU TO SHOW ME, CHUCKLES?
THIS IS WHERE QUENTIN IS?
IDIE! IDIE... WAIT!
DON'T DO THIS, DARLIN'...
YOU DON'T... YOU DON'T WANT TO KNOW WHERE THIS IS HEADIN'...
I'M SORRY, MR. LOGAN.
IT'S THE QUESTIONS THAT SCARE ME--
FWOOSH
IDIE! IDIE, DON'T!
"--NOT THE ANSWERS."

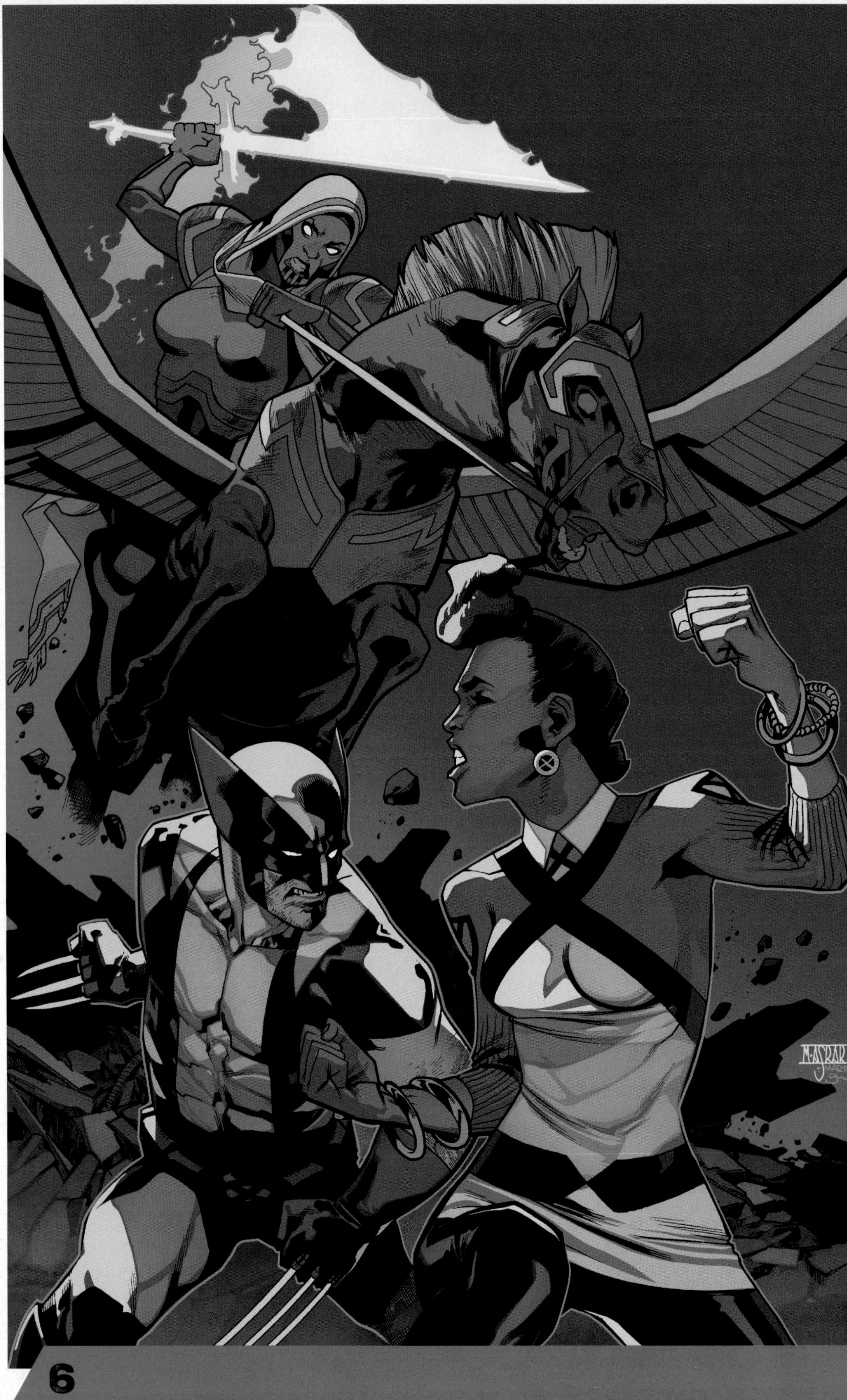

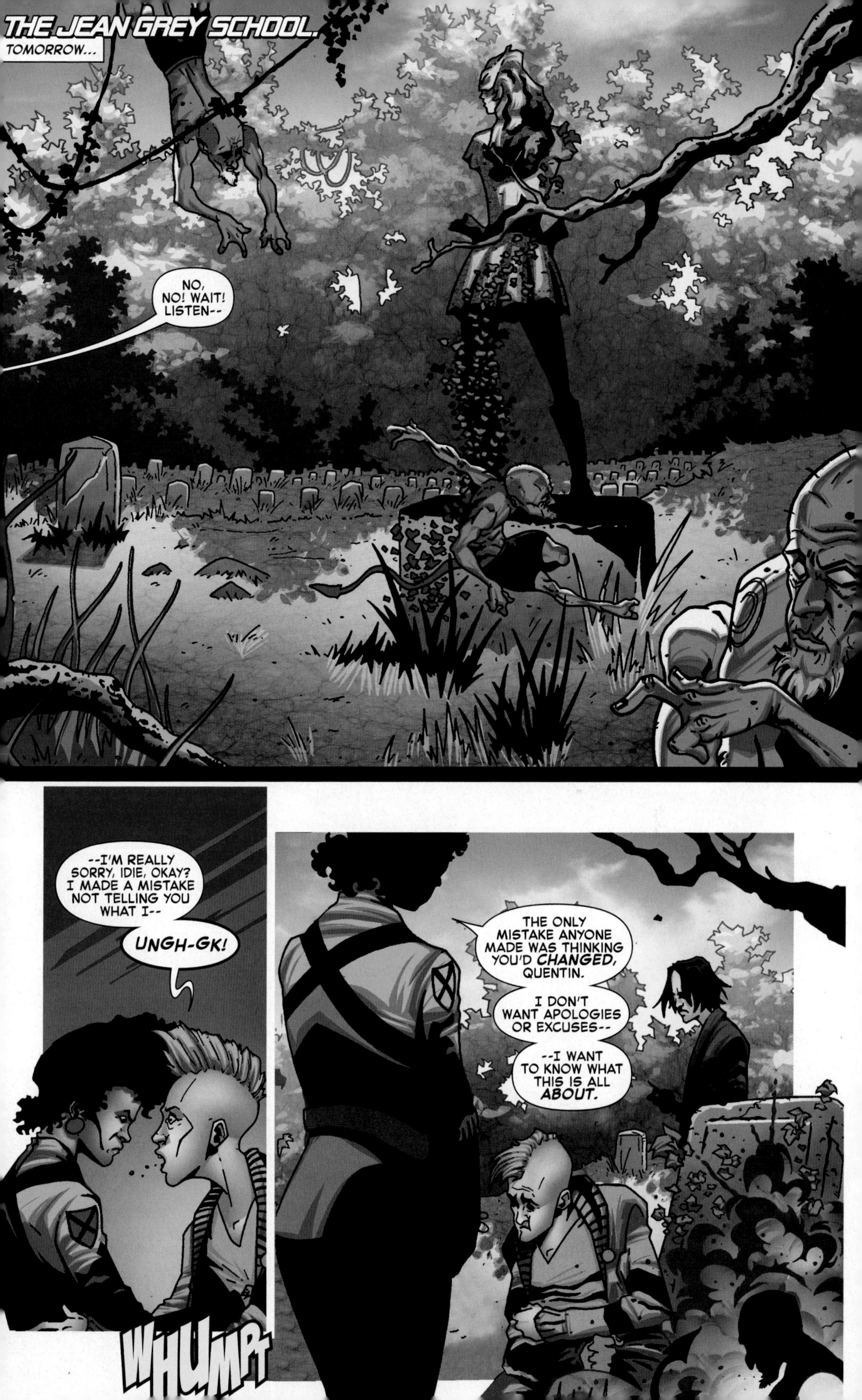
THE JEAN GREY SCHOOL.
TOMORROW...
NO, NO! WAIT! LISTEN--
--I'M REALLY SORRY, IDIE, OKAY? I MADE A MISTAKE NOT TELLING YOU WHAT I--
UNGH-GK!
WHUMPT
THE ONLY MISTAKE ANYONE MADE WAS THINKING YOU'D CHANGED, QUENTIN.
I DON'T WANT APOLOGIES OR EXCUSES--
--I WANT TO KNOW WHAT THIS IS ALL ABOUT.

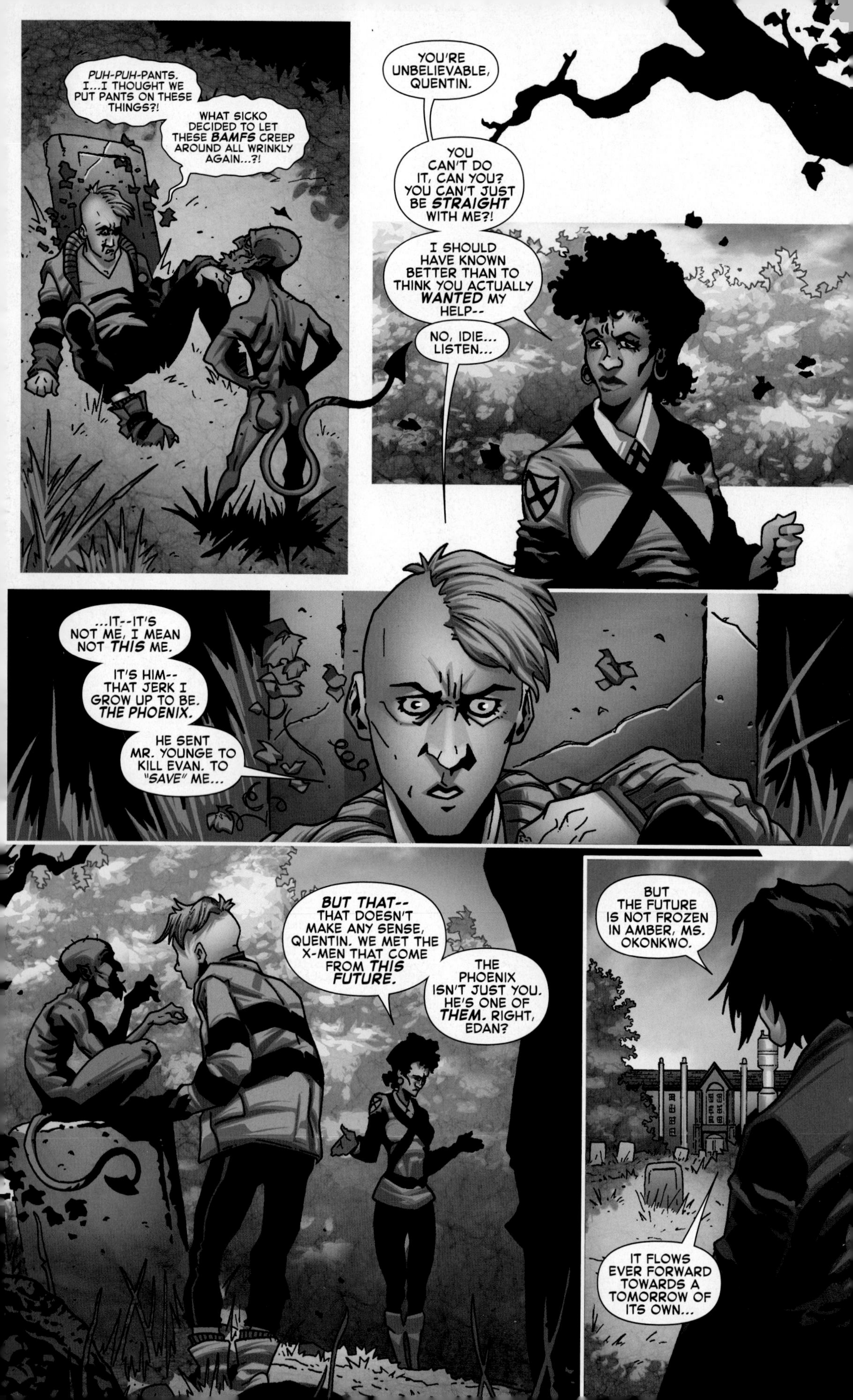
PUH-PUH-PANTS. I...I THOUGHT WE PUT PANTS ON THESE THINGS?!
WHAT SICKO DECIDED TO LET THESE BAMFS CREEP AROUND ALL WRINKLY AGAIN...?!
YOU'RE UNBELIEVABLE, QUENTIN.
YOU CAN'T DO IT, CAN YOU? YOU CAN'T JUST BE STRAIGHT WITH ME?!
I SHOULD HAVE KNOWN BETTER THAN TO THINK YOU ACTUALLY WANTED MY HELP--
NO, IDIE... LISTEN...
...IT--IT'S NOT ME, I MEAN NOT THIS ME.
IT'S HIM-- THAT JERK I GROW UP TO BE. THE PHOENIX.
HE SENT MR. YOUNGE TO KILL EVAN. TO "SAVE" ME...
BUT THAT-- THAT DOESN'T MAKE ANY SENSE, QUENTIN. WE MET THE X-MEN THAT COME FROM THIS FUTURE.
THE PHOENIX ISN'T JUST YOU. HE'S ONE OF THEM. RIGHT, EDAN?
BUT THE FUTURE IS NOT FROZEN IN AMBER, MS. OKONKWO.
IT FLOWS EVER FORWARD TOWARDS A TOMORROW OF ITS OWN...

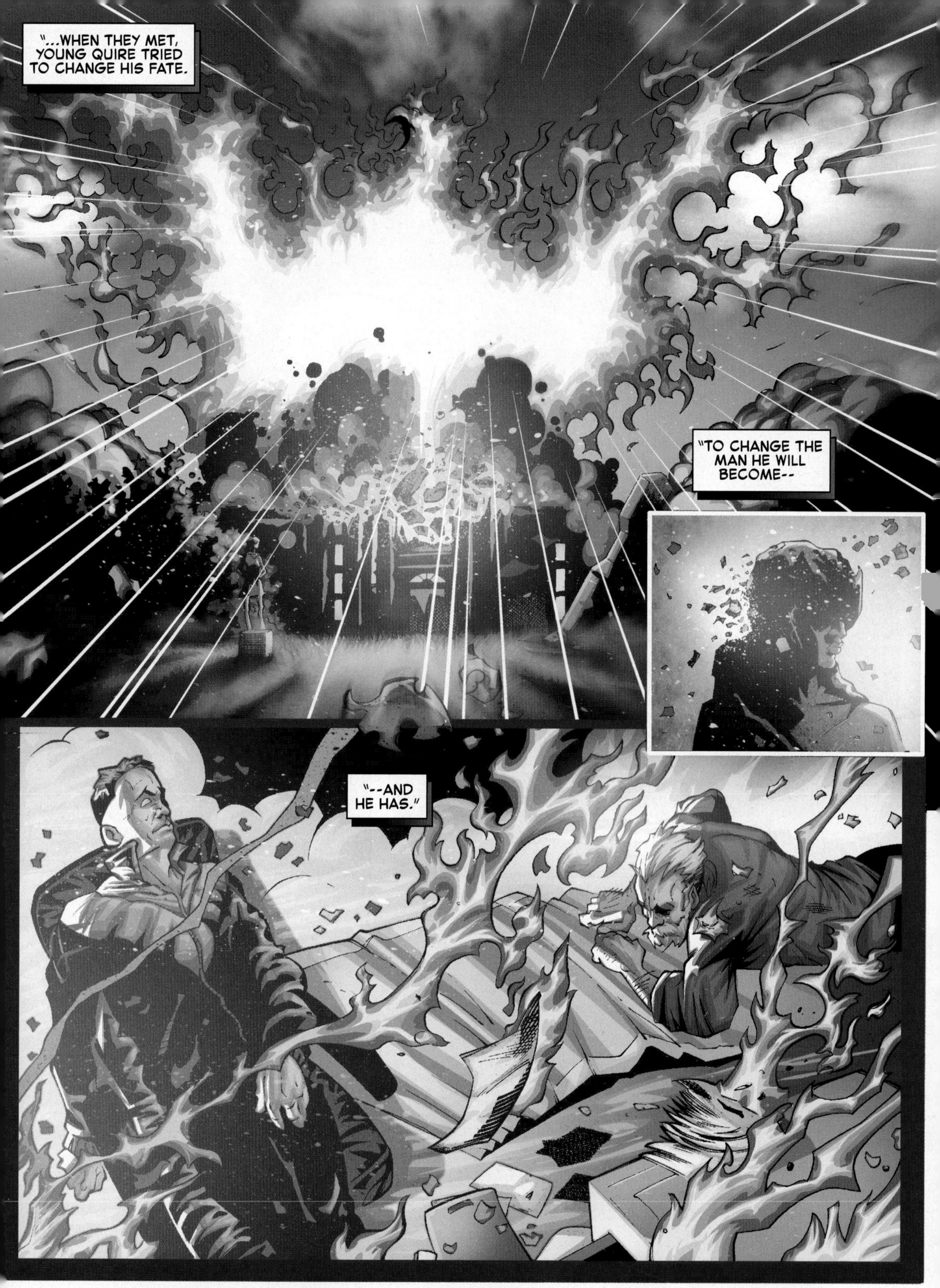
"...WHEN THEY MET, YOUNG QUIRE TRIED TO CHANGE HIS FATE.
"TO CHANGE THE MAN HE WILL BECOME--
"--AND HE HAS."

TOMORROW NEVER LEARNS CHAPTER 6:

A FATE FAR WORSE

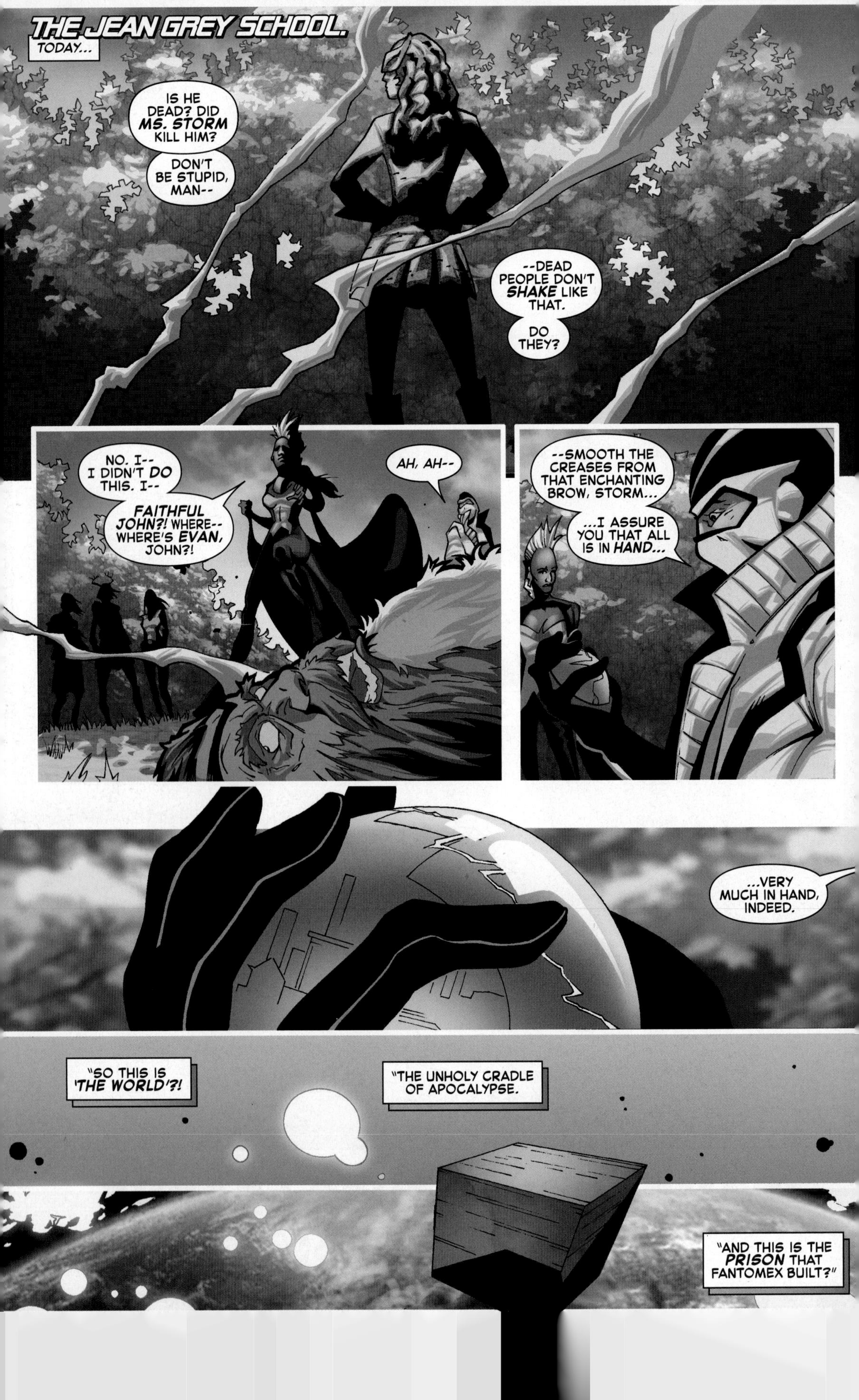
THE JEAN GREY SCHOOL.
TODAY...
IS HE DEAD? DID MS. STORM KILL HIM?
DON'T BE STUPID, MAN--
--DEAD PEOPLE DON'T SHAKE LIKE THAT.
DO THEY?
NO. I-- I DIDN'T DO THIS. I--
FAITHFUL JOHN?! WHERE-- WHERE'S EVAN, JOHN?!
AH, AH--
--SMOOTH THE CREASES FROM THAT ENCHANTING BROW, STORM...
...I ASSURE YOU THAT ALL IS IN HAND...
...VERY MUCH IN HAND, INDEED.
"SO THIS IS 'THE WORLD'?!
"THE UNHOLY CRADLE OF APOCALYPSE.
"AND THIS IS THE PRISON THAT FANTOMEX BUILT?"

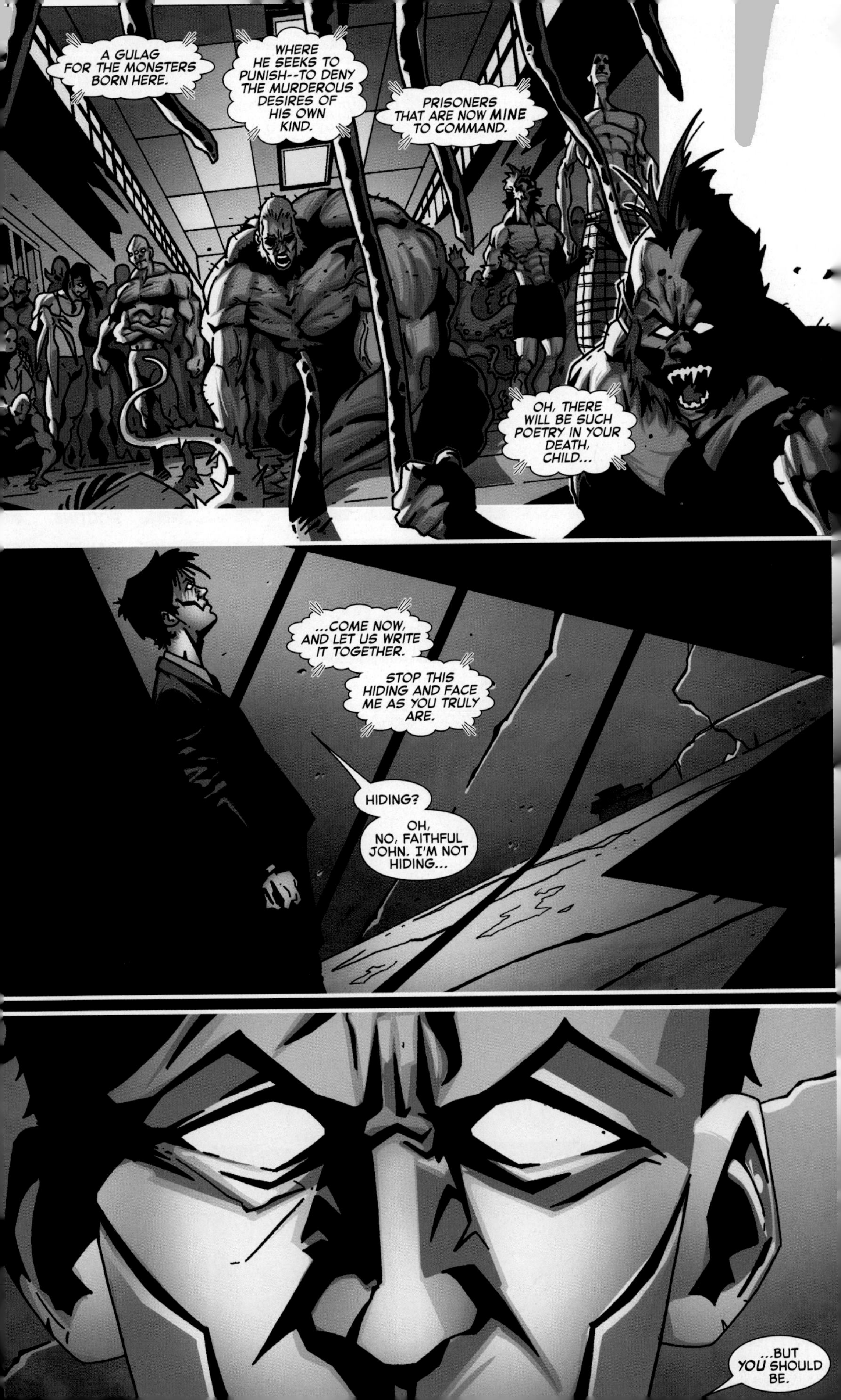

A GULAG FOR THE MONSTERS BORN HERE.
WHERE HE SEEKS TO PUNISH--TO DENY THE MURDEROUS DESIRES OF HIS OWN KIND.
PRISONERS THAT ARE NOW MINE TO COMMAND.
OH, THERE WILL BE SUCH POETRY IN YOUR DEATH, CHILD...
...COME NOW, AND LET US WRITE IT TOGETHER.
STOP THIS HIDING AND FACE ME AS YOU TRULY ARE.
HIDING?
OH, NO, FAITHFUL JOHN. I'M NOT HIDING...
...BUT YOU SHOULD BE.

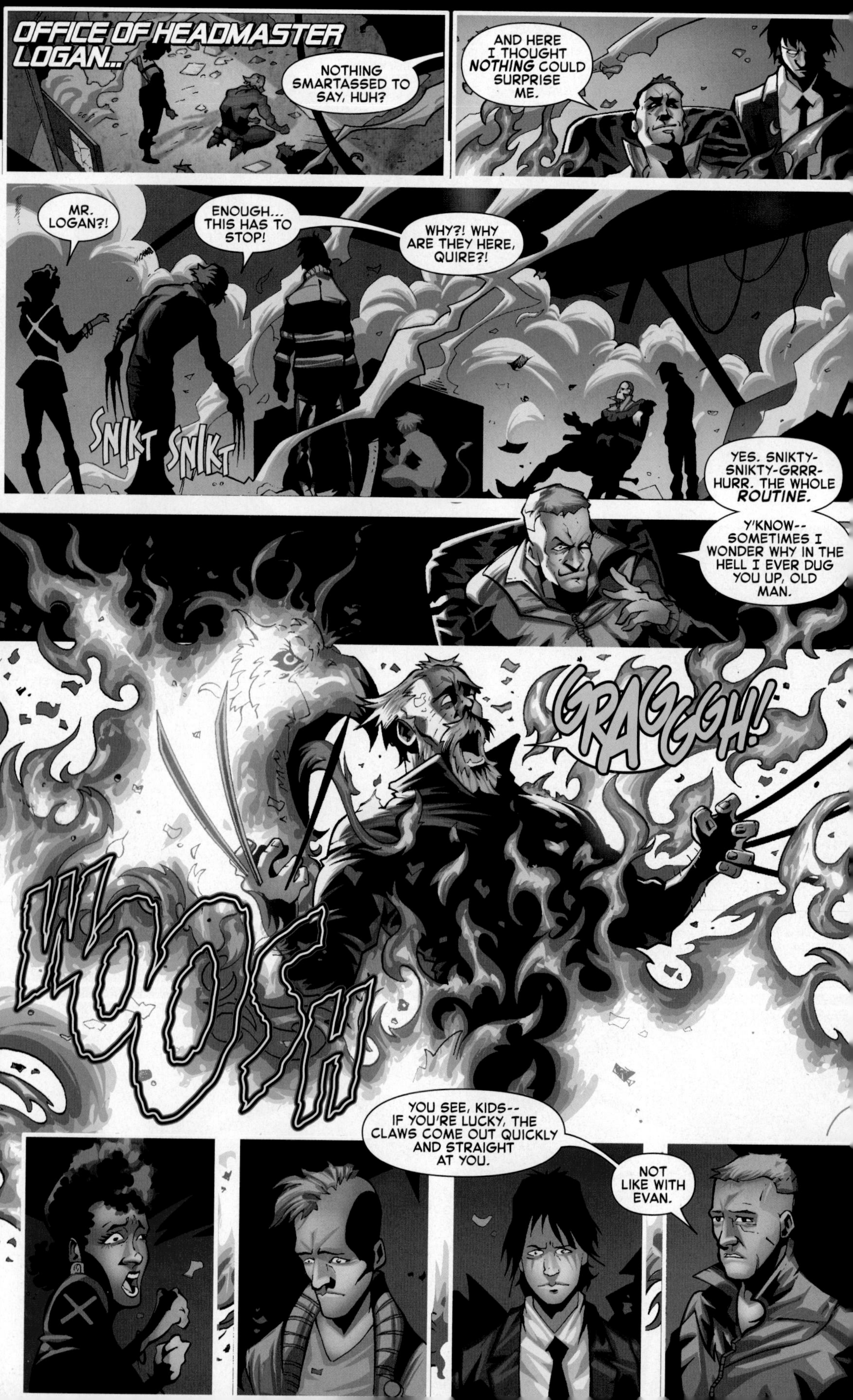
OFFICE OF HEADMASTER LOGAN...
NOTHING SMARTASSED TO SAY, HUH?
AND HERE I THOUGHT NOTHING COULD SURPRISE ME.
MR. LOGAN?!
ENOUGH... THIS HAS TO STOP!
WHY?! WHY ARE THEY HERE, QUIRE?!
SNIKT SNIKT
YES. SNIKTY-SNIKTY-GRRR-HURR. THE WHOLE ROUTINE.
Y'KNOW-- SOMETIMES I WONDER WHY IN THE HELL I EVER DUG YOU UP, OLD MAN.
GRAGGGH!
WHOOSH
YOU SEE, KIDS-- IF YOU'RE LUCKY, THE CLAWS COME OUT QUICKLY AND STRAIGHT AT YOU.
NOT LIKE WITH EVAN.

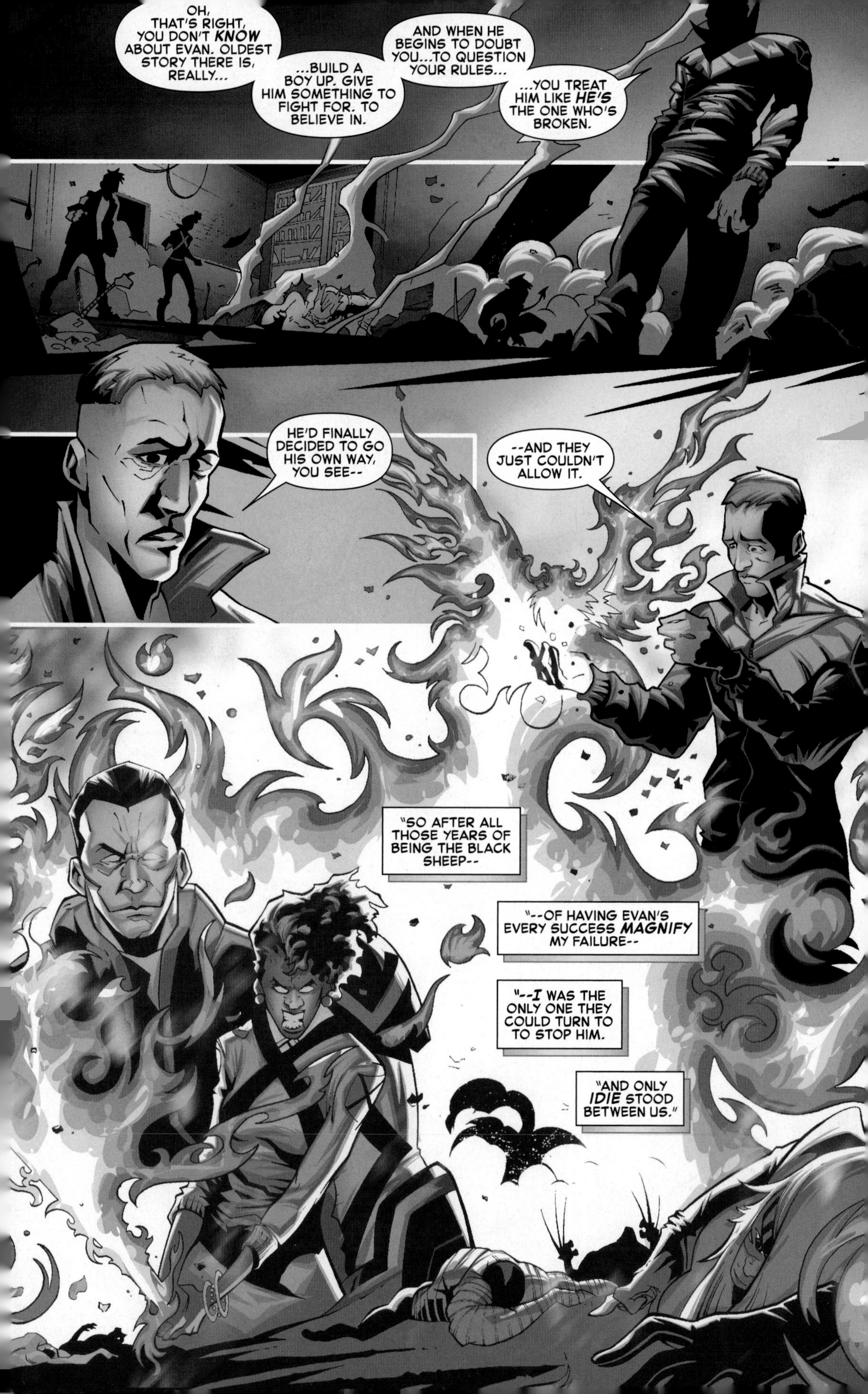
OH, THAT'S RIGHT, YOU DON'T KNOW ABOUT EVAN. OLDEST STORY THERE IS, REALLY...
...BUILD A BOY UP. GIVE HIM SOMETHING TO FIGHT FOR. TO BELIEVE IN.
AND WHEN HE BEGINS TO DOUBT YOU...TO QUESTION YOUR RULES...
...YOU TREAT HIM LIKE HE'S THE ONE WHO'S BROKEN.
HE'D FINALLY DECIDED TO GO HIS OWN WAY, YOU SEE--
--AND THEY JUST COULDN'T ALLOW IT.
"SO AFTER ALL THOSE YEARS OF BEING THE BLACK SHEEP--
"--OF HAVING EVAN'S EVERY SUCCESS MAGNIFY MY FAILURE--
"--I WAS THE ONLY ONE THEY COULD TURN TO TO STOP HIM.
"AND ONLY IDIE STOOD BETWEEN US."

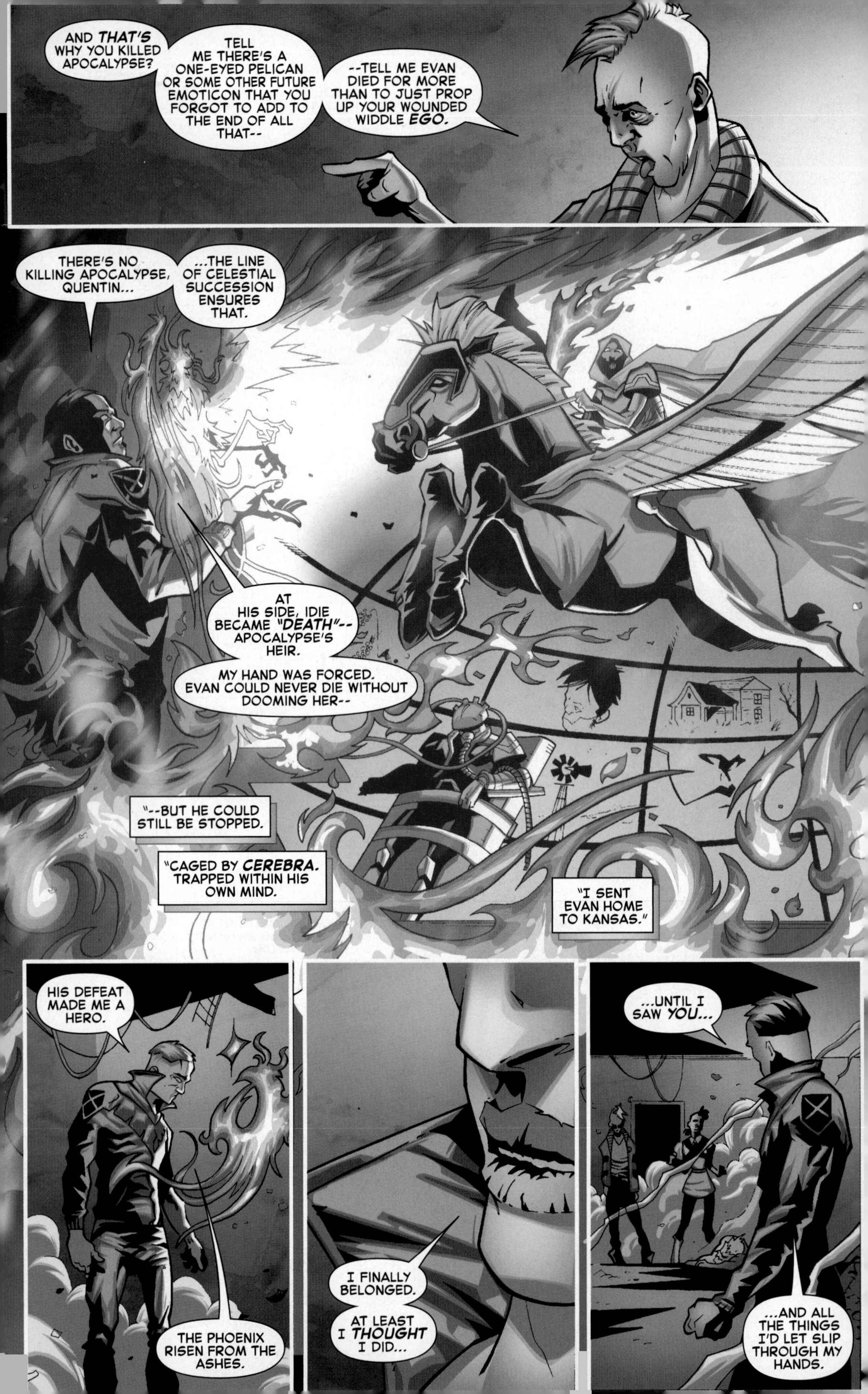

AND THAT'S WHY YOU KILLED APOCALYPSE?
TELL ME THERE'S A ONE-EYED PELICAN OR SOME OTHER FUTURE EMOTICON THAT YOU FORGOT TO ADD TO THE END OF ALL THAT--
--TELL ME EVAN DIED FOR MORE THAN TO JUST PROP UP YOUR WOUNDED WIDDLE EGO.
THERE'S NO KILLING APOCALYPSE, QUENTIN...
...THE LINE OF CELESTIAL SUCCESSION ENSURES THAT.
AT HIS SIDE, IDIE BECAME "DEATH"--APOCALYPSE'S HEIR.
MY HAND WAS FORCED. EVAN COULD NEVER DIE WITHOUT DOOMING HER--
"--BUT HE COULD STILL BE STOPPED.
"CAGED BY CEREBRA. TRAPPED WITHIN HIS OWN MIND.
"I SENT EVAN HOME TO KANSAS."
HIS DEFEAT MADE ME A HERO.
THE PHOENIX RISEN FROM THE ASHES.
I FINALLY BELONGED.
AT LEAST I THOUGHT I DID...
...UNTIL I SAW YOU...
...AND ALL THE THINGS I'D LET SLIP THROUGH MY HANDS.

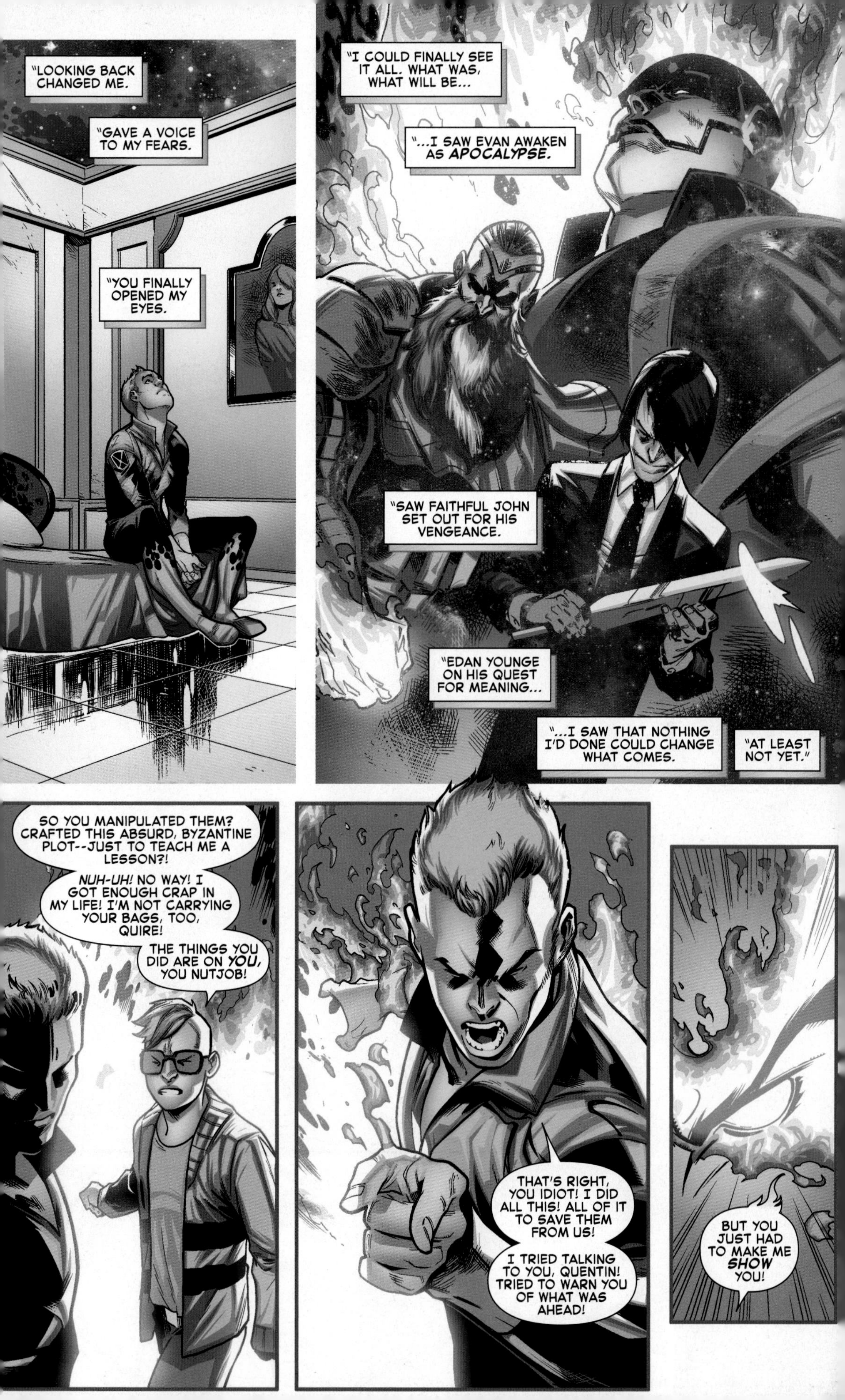

"LOOKING BACK CHANGED ME.
"GAVE A VOICE TO MY FEARS.
"YOU FINALLY OPENED MY EYES.
"I COULD FINALLY SEE IT ALL. WHAT WAS, WHAT WILL BE...
"...I SAW EVAN AWAKEN AS *APOCALYPSE.*
"SAW FAITHFUL JOHN SET OUT FOR HIS VENGEANCE.
"EDAN YOUNGE ON HIS QUEST FOR MEANING...
"...I SAW THAT NOTHING I'D DONE COULD CHANGE WHAT COMES.
"AT LEAST NOT YET."
SO YOU MANIPULATED THEM? CRAFTED THIS ABSURD, BYZANTINE PLOT--JUST TO TEACH ME A LESSON?!
NUH-UH! NO WAY! I GOT ENOUGH CRAP IN MY LIFE! I'M NOT CARRYING YOUR BAGS, TOO, QUIRE!
THE THINGS YOU DID ARE ON *YOU,* YOU NUTJOB!
THAT'S RIGHT, YOU IDIOT! I DID ALL THIS! ALL OF IT TO SAVE THEM FROM US!
I TRIED TALKING TO YOU, QUENTIN! TRIED TO WARN YOU OF WHAT WAS AHEAD!
BUT YOU JUST HAD TO MAKE ME *SHOW* YOU!

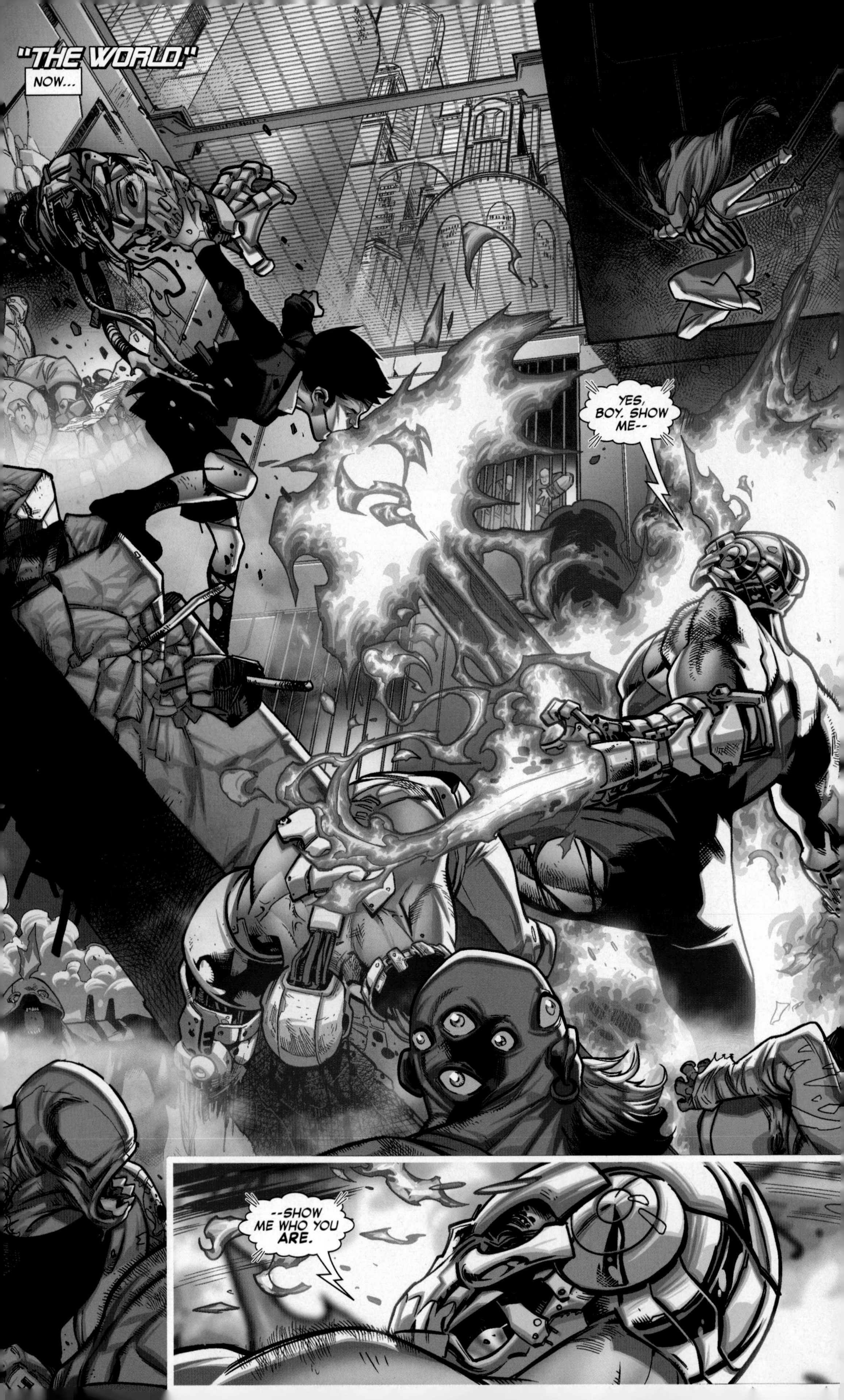
"THE WORLD."
NOW...
YES, BOY. SHOW ME--
--SHOW ME WHO YOU ARE.

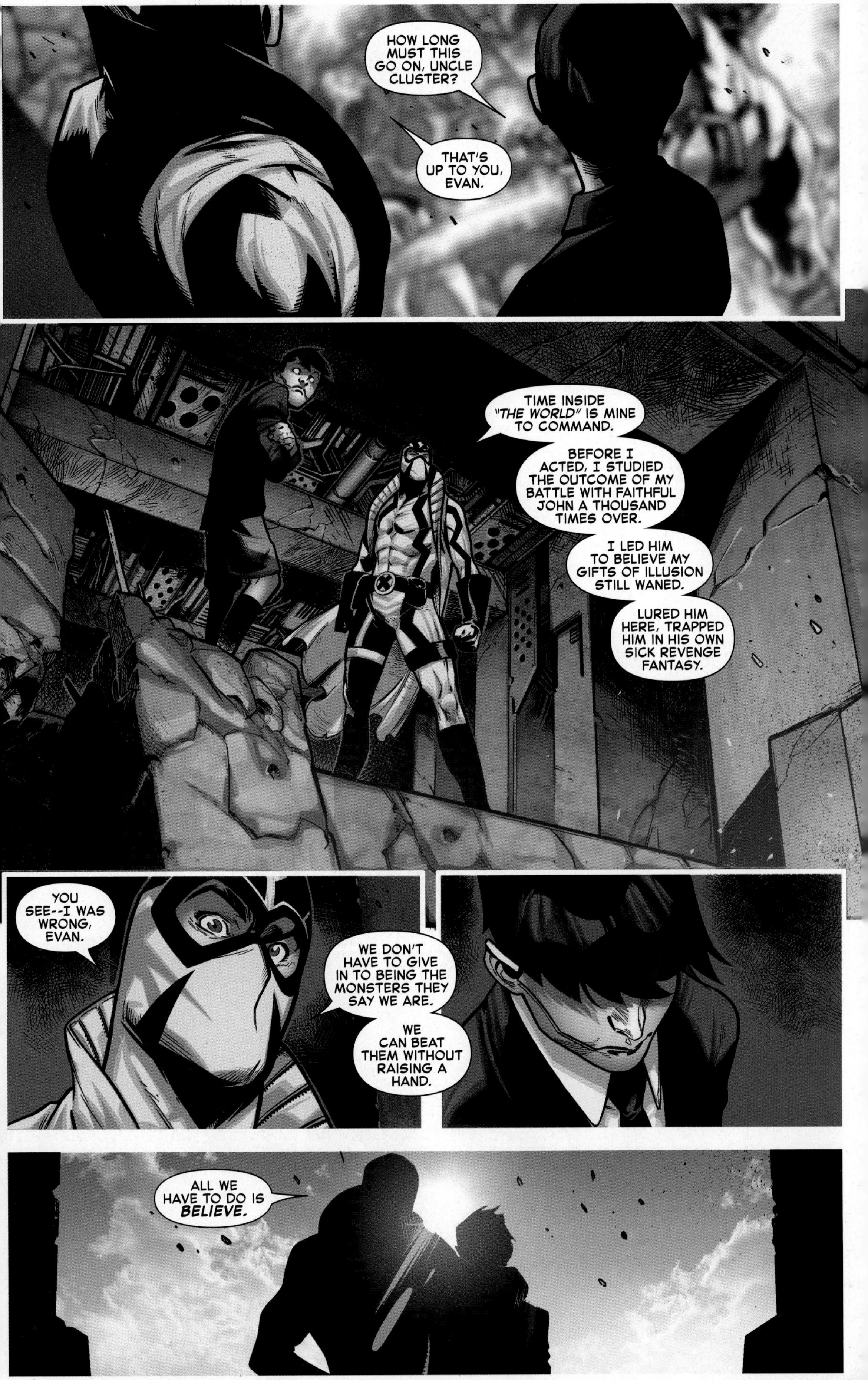
HOW LONG MUST THIS GO ON, UNCLE CLUSTER?
THAT'S UP TO YOU, EVAN.
TIME INSIDE "THE WORLD" IS MINE TO COMMAND.
BEFORE I ACTED, I STUDIED THE OUTCOME OF MY BATTLE WITH FAITHFUL JOHN A THOUSAND TIMES OVER.
I LED HIM TO BELIEVE MY GIFTS OF ILLUSION STILL WANED.
LURED HIM HERE, TRAPPED HIM IN HIS OWN SICK REVENGE FANTASY.
YOU SEE--I WAS WRONG, EVAN.
WE DON'T HAVE TO GIVE IN TO BEING THE MONSTERS THEY SAY WE ARE.
WE CAN BEAT THEM WITHOUT RAISING A HAND.
ALL WE HAVE TO DO IS BELIEVE.

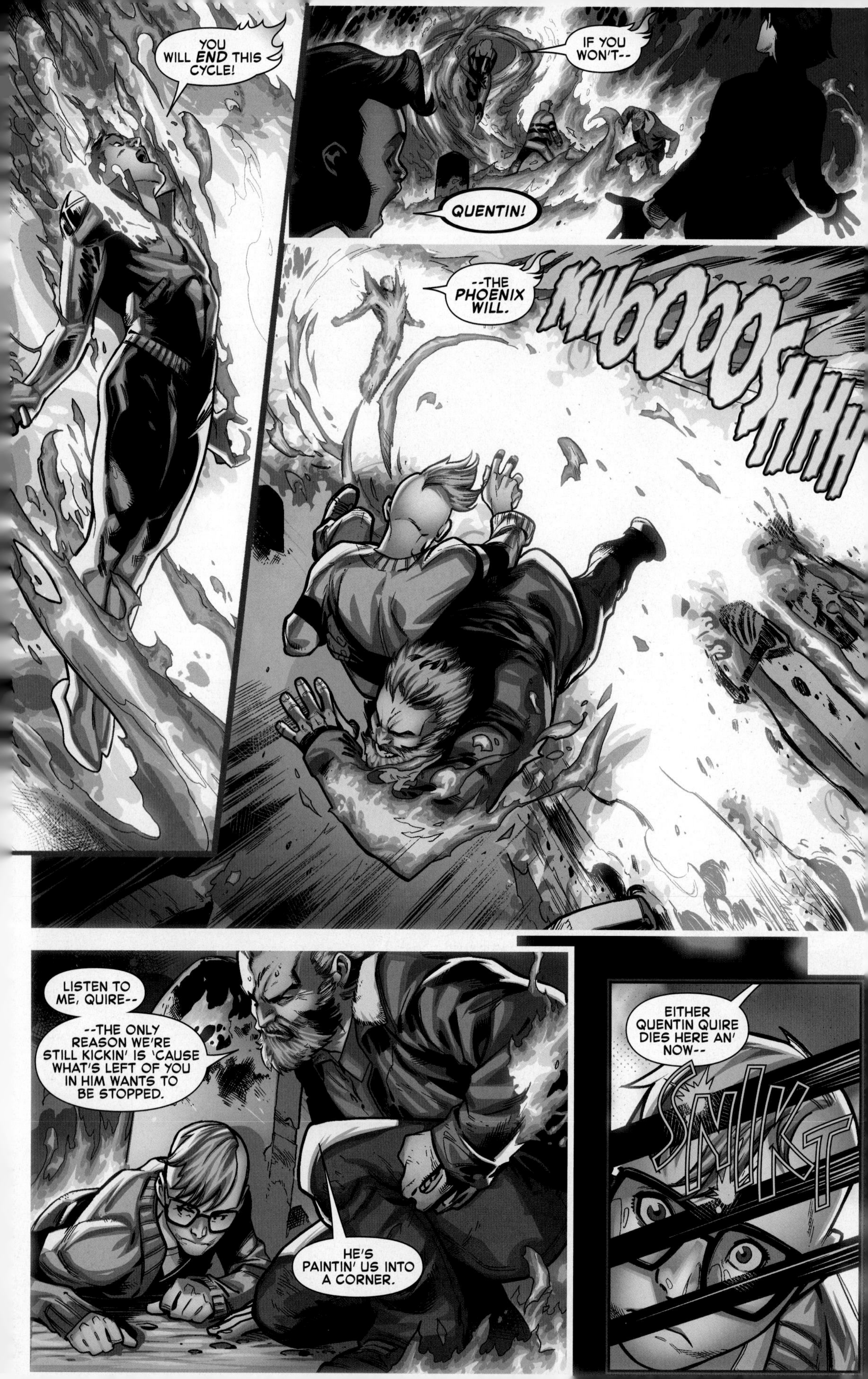
YOU WILL END THIS CYCLE!
IF YOU WON'T--
QUENTIN!
--THE PHOENIX WILL.
KWOOOOSHHH
LISTEN TO ME, QUIRE--
--THE ONLY REASON WE'RE STILL KICKIN' IS 'CAUSE WHAT'S LEFT OF YOU IN HIM WANTS TO BE STOPPED.
HE'S PAINTIN' US INTO A CORNER.
EITHER QUENTIN QUIRE DIES HERE AN' NOW--
SNIKT

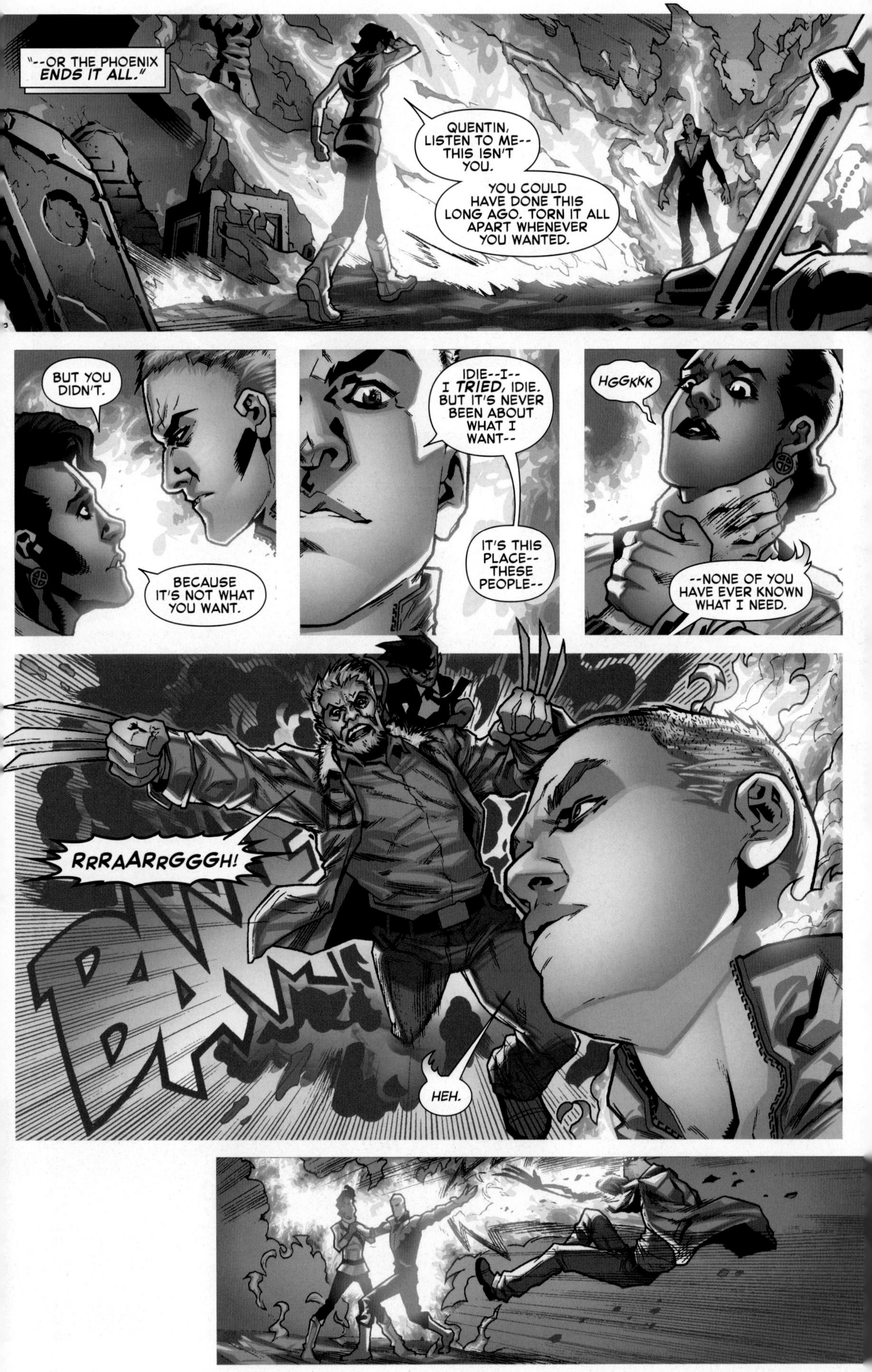
"--OR THE PHOENIX ENDS IT ALL."
QUENTIN, LISTEN TO ME-- THIS ISN'T YOU.
YOU COULD HAVE DONE THIS LONG AGO. TORN IT ALL APART WHENEVER YOU WANTED.
BUT YOU DIDN'T.
BECAUSE IT'S NOT WHAT YOU WANT.
IDIE--I-- I TRIED, IDIE. BUT IT'S NEVER BEEN ABOUT WHAT I WANT--
IT'S THIS PLACE-- THESE PEOPLE--
HGGKKK
--NONE OF YOU HAVE EVER KNOWN WHAT I NEED.
RRRAARRGGGH!
BAMF
HEH.

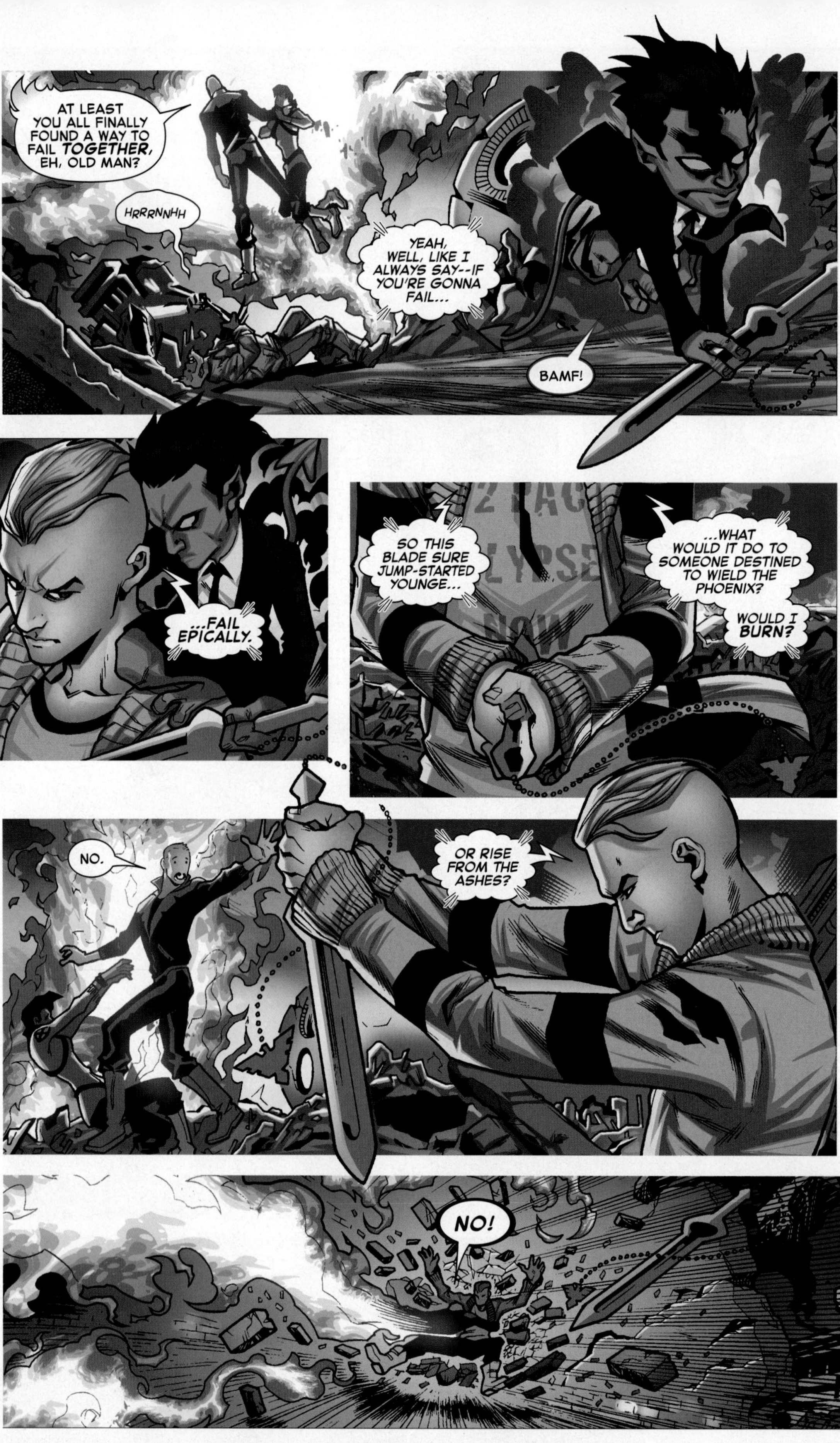
AT LEAST YOU ALL FINALLY FOUND A WAY TO FAIL TOGETHER, EH, OLD MAN?
HRRRNNHH
YEAH, WELL, LIKE I ALWAYS SAY--IF YOU'RE GONNA FAIL...
BAMF!
...FAIL EPICALLY.
SO THIS BLADE SURE JUMP-STARTED YOUNGE...
...WHAT WOULD IT DO TO SOMEONE DESTINED TO WIELD THE PHOENIX?
WOULD I BURN?
NO.
OR RISE FROM THE ASHES?
NO!

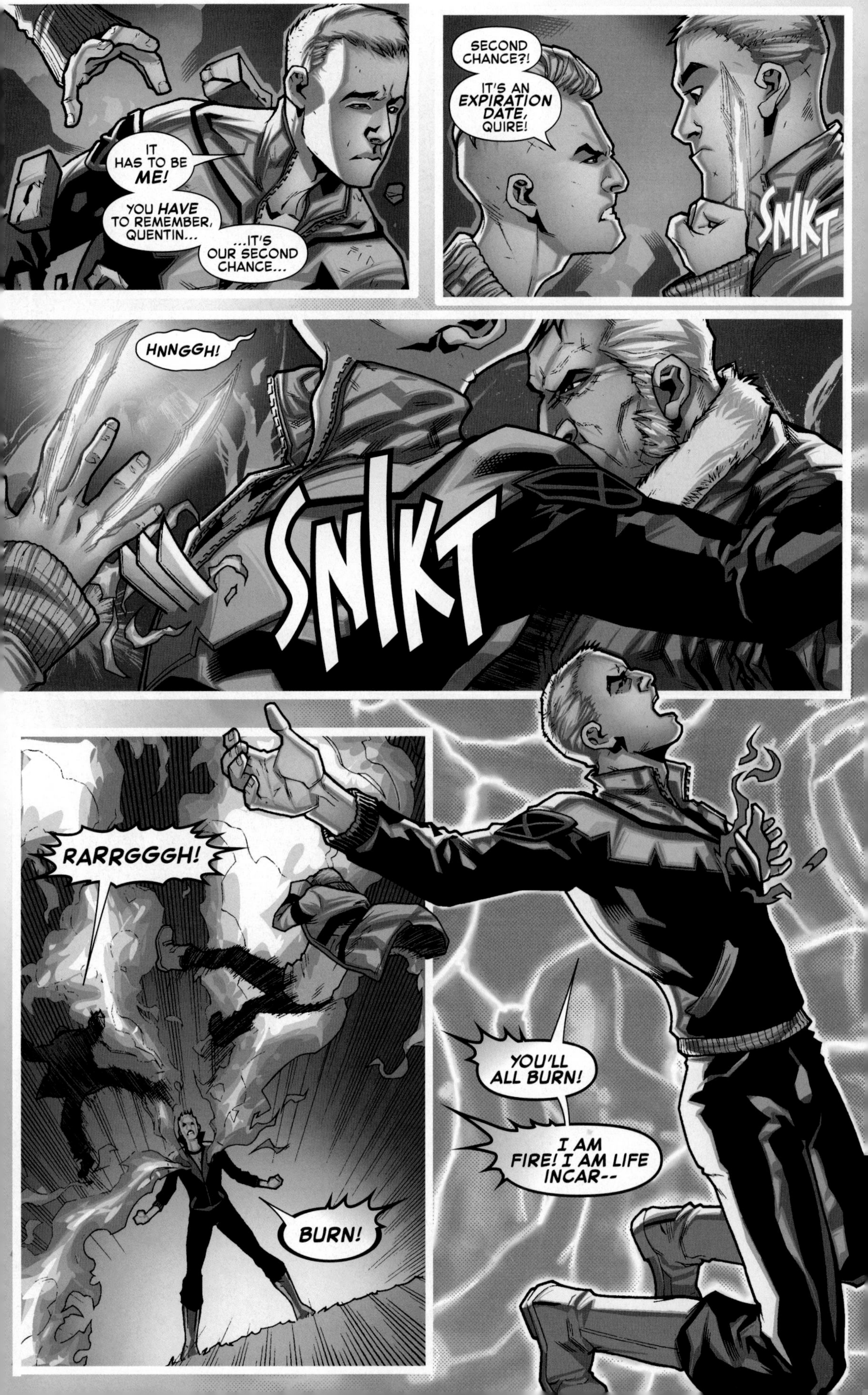

IT HAS TO BE ME!
YOU HAVE TO REMEMBER, QUENTIN...
...IT'S OUR SECOND CHANCE...
SECOND CHANCE?!
IT'S AN EXPIRATION DATE, QUIRE!
SNIKT
HNNGGH!
SNIKT
RARRGGGH!
BURN!
YOU'LL ALL BURN!
I AM FIRE! I AM LIFE INCAR--

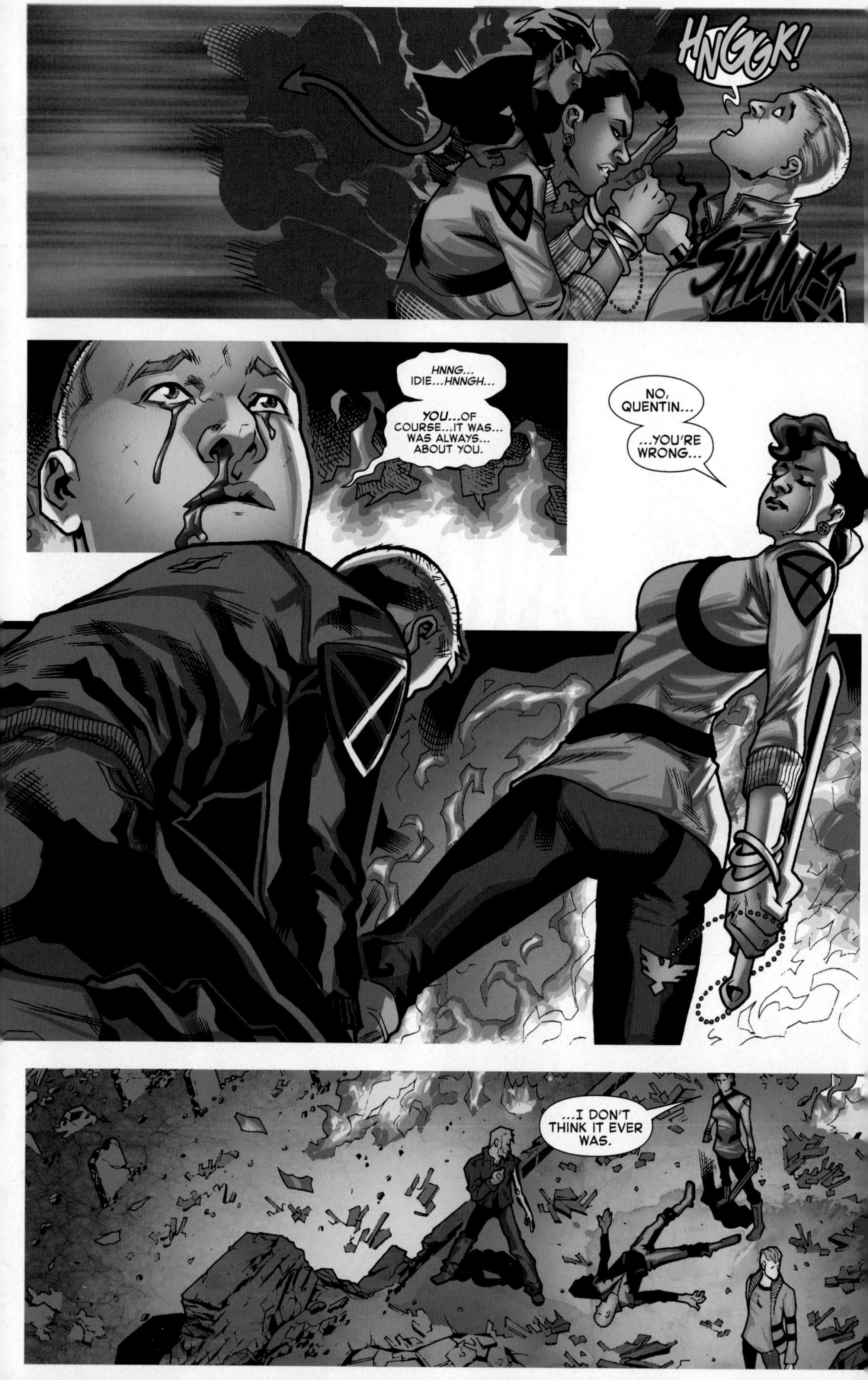
HNGGK!
SHUNK!
HNNG... IDIE...HNNGH...
YOU...OF COURSE...IT WAS... WAS ALWAYS... ABOUT YOU.
NO, QUENTIN...
...YOU'RE WRONG...
...I DON'T THINK IT EVER WAS.

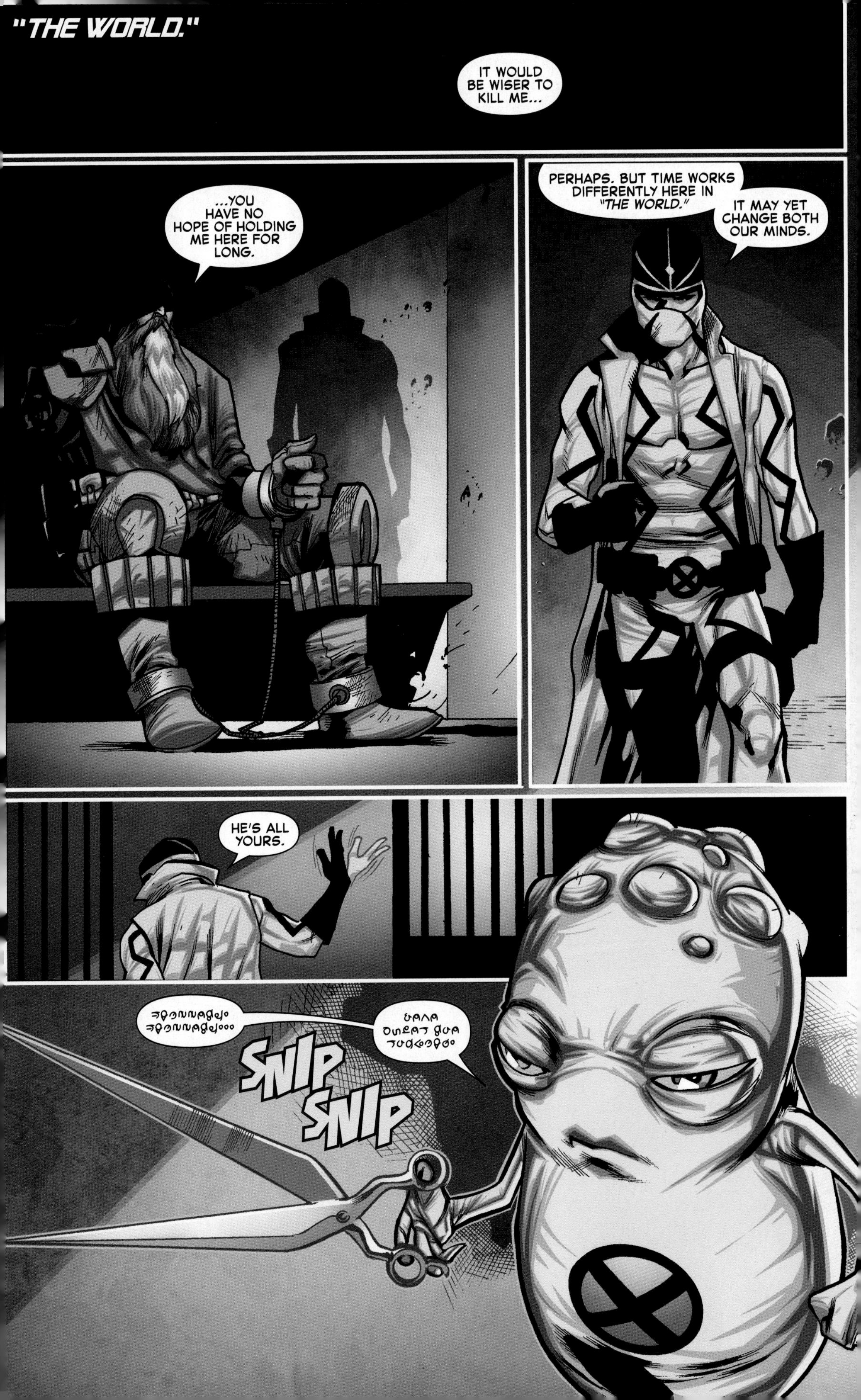
"THE WORLD."
IT WOULD BE WISER TO KILL ME...
...YOU HAVE NO HOPE OF HOLDING ME HERE FOR LONG.
PERHAPS. BUT TIME WORKS DIFFERENTLY HERE IN "THE WORLD."
IT MAY YET CHANGE BOTH OUR MINDS.
HE'S ALL YOURS.
SNIP SNIP

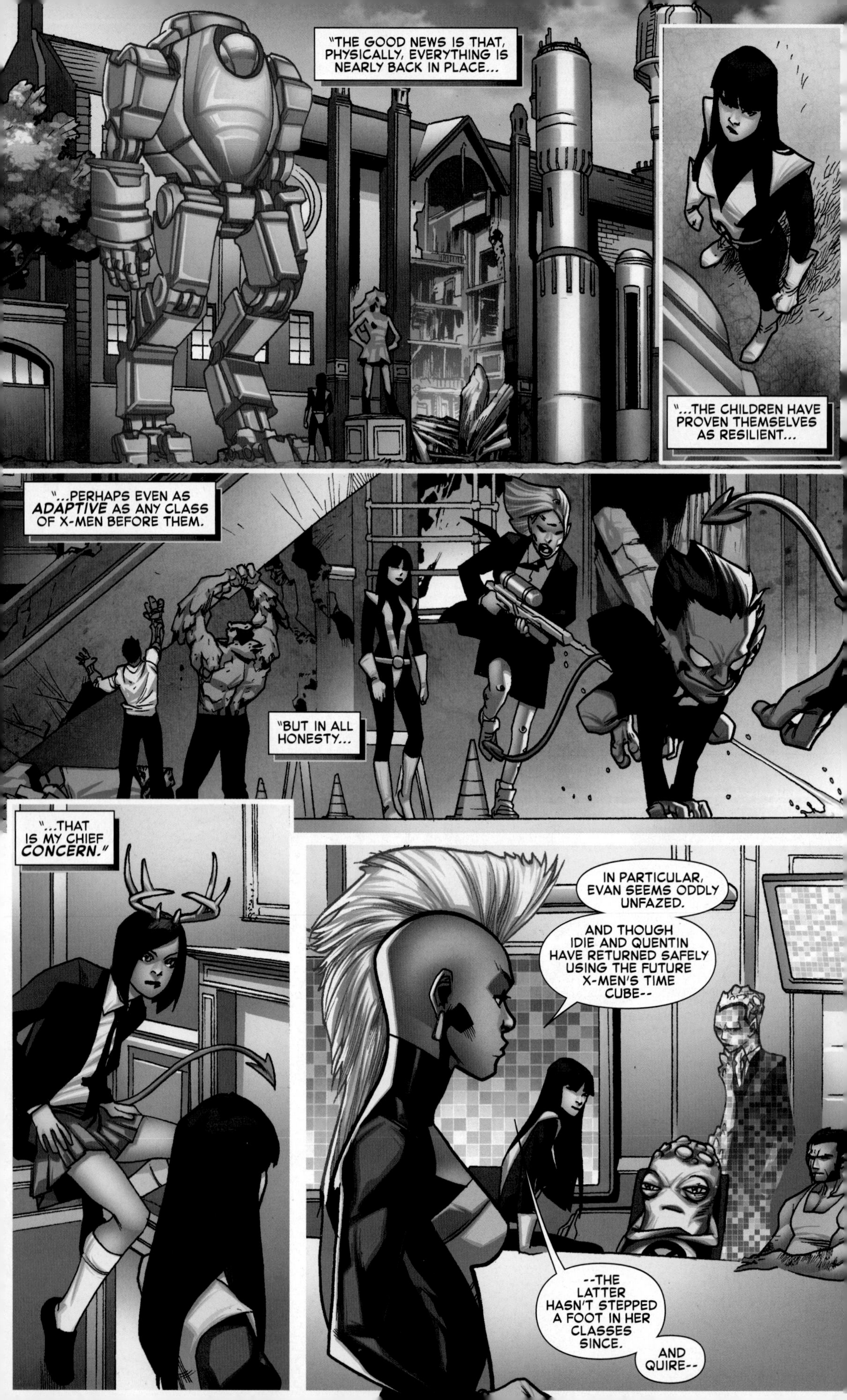
"THE GOOD NEWS IS THAT, PHYSICALLY, EVERYTHING IS NEARLY BACK IN PLACE...
"...THE CHILDREN HAVE PROVEN THEMSELVES AS RESILIENT...
"...PERHAPS EVEN AS ADAPTIVE AS ANY CLASS OF X-MEN BEFORE THEM.
"BUT IN ALL HONESTY...
"...THAT IS MY CHIEF CONCERN."
IN PARTICULAR, EVAN SEEMS ODDLY UNFAZED.
AND THOUGH IDIE AND QUENTIN HAVE RETURNED SAFELY USING THE FUTURE X-MEN'S TIME CUBE--
--THE LATTER HASN'T STEPPED A FOOT IN HER CLASSES SINCE.
AND QUIRE--

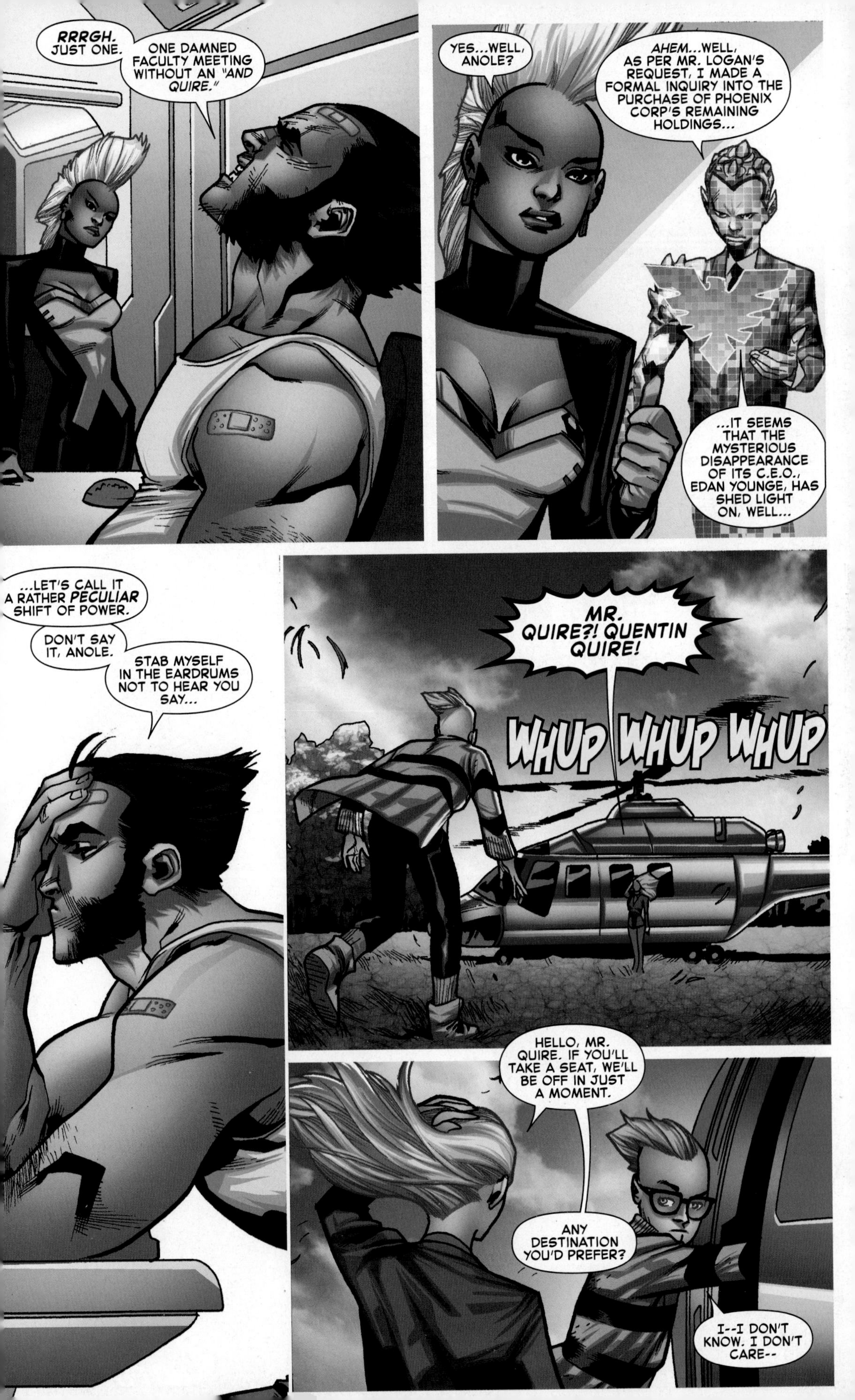
RRRGH. JUST ONE.
ONE DAMNED FACULTY MEETING WITHOUT AN "AND QUIRE."
YES...WELL, ANOLE?
AHEM...WELL, AS PER MR. LOGAN'S REQUEST, I MADE A FORMAL INQUIRY INTO THE PURCHASE OF PHOENIX CORP'S REMAINING HOLDINGS...
...IT SEEMS THAT THE MYSTERIOUS DISAPPEARANCE OF ITS C.E.O., EDAN YOUNGE, HAS SHED LIGHT ON, WELL...
...LET'S CALL IT A RATHER PECULIAR SHIFT OF POWER.
DON'T SAY IT, ANOLE.
STAB MYSELF IN THE EARDRUMS NOT TO HEAR YOU SAY...
MR. QUIRE?! QUENTIN QUIRE!
WHUP WHUP WHUP
HELLO, MR. QUIRE. IF YOU'LL TAKE A SEAT, WE'LL BE OFF IN JUST A MOMENT.
ANY DESTINATION YOU'D PREFER?
I--I DON'T KNOW. I DON'T CARE--

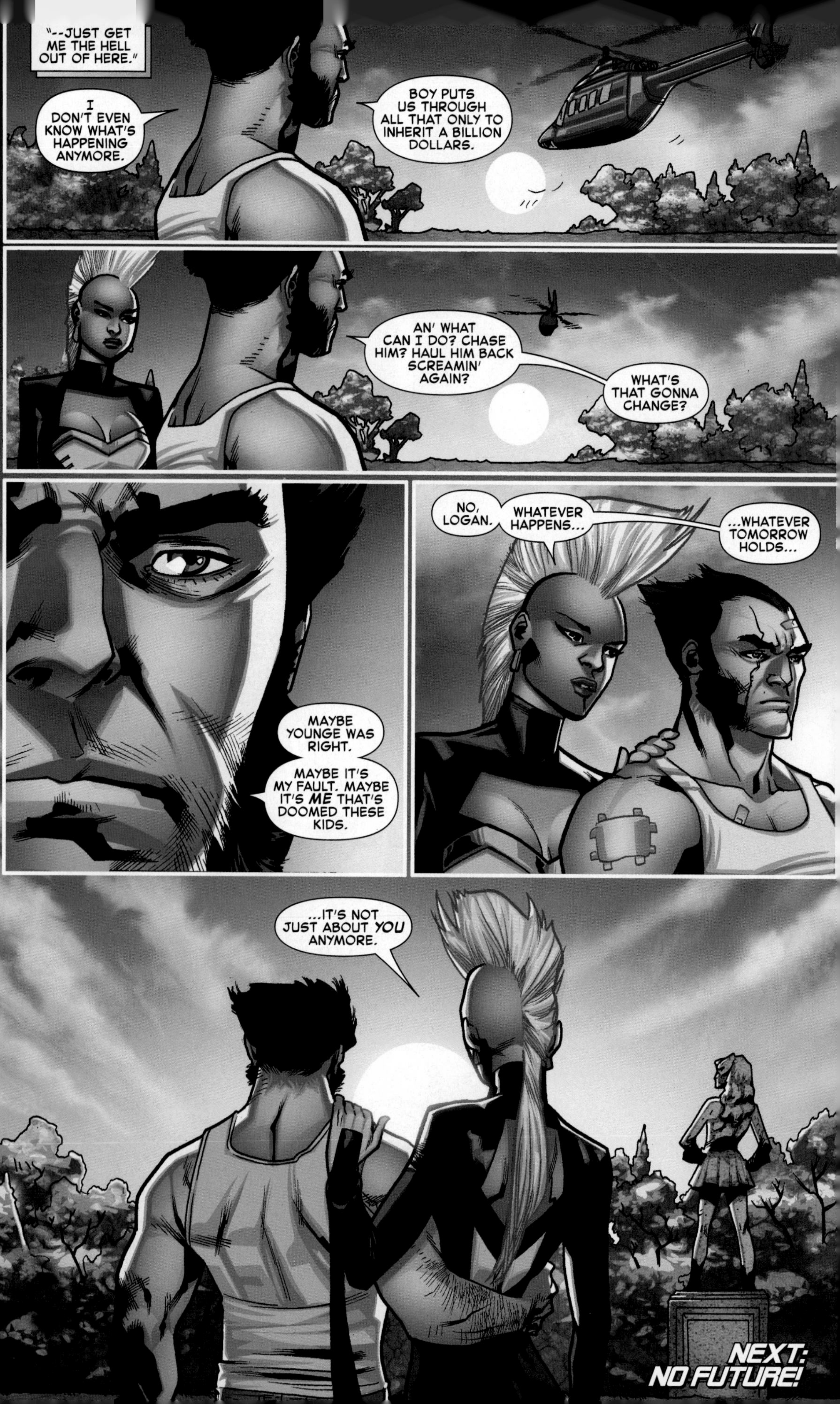
"--JUST GET ME THE HELL OUT OF HERE."
I DON'T EVEN KNOW WHAT'S HAPPENING ANYMORE.
BOY PUTS US THROUGH ALL THAT ONLY TO INHERIT A BILLION DOLLARS.
AN' WHAT CAN I DO? CHASE HIM? HAUL HIM BACK SCREAMIN' AGAIN?
WHAT'S THAT GONNA CHANGE?
MAYBE YOUNGE WAS RIGHT.
MAYBE IT'S MY FAULT. MAYBE IT'S ME THAT'S DOOMED THESE KIDS.
NO, LOGAN.
WHATEVER HAPPENS...
...WHATEVER TOMORROW HOLDS...
...IT'S NOT JUST ABOUT YOU ANYMORE.
NEXT: NO FUTURE!

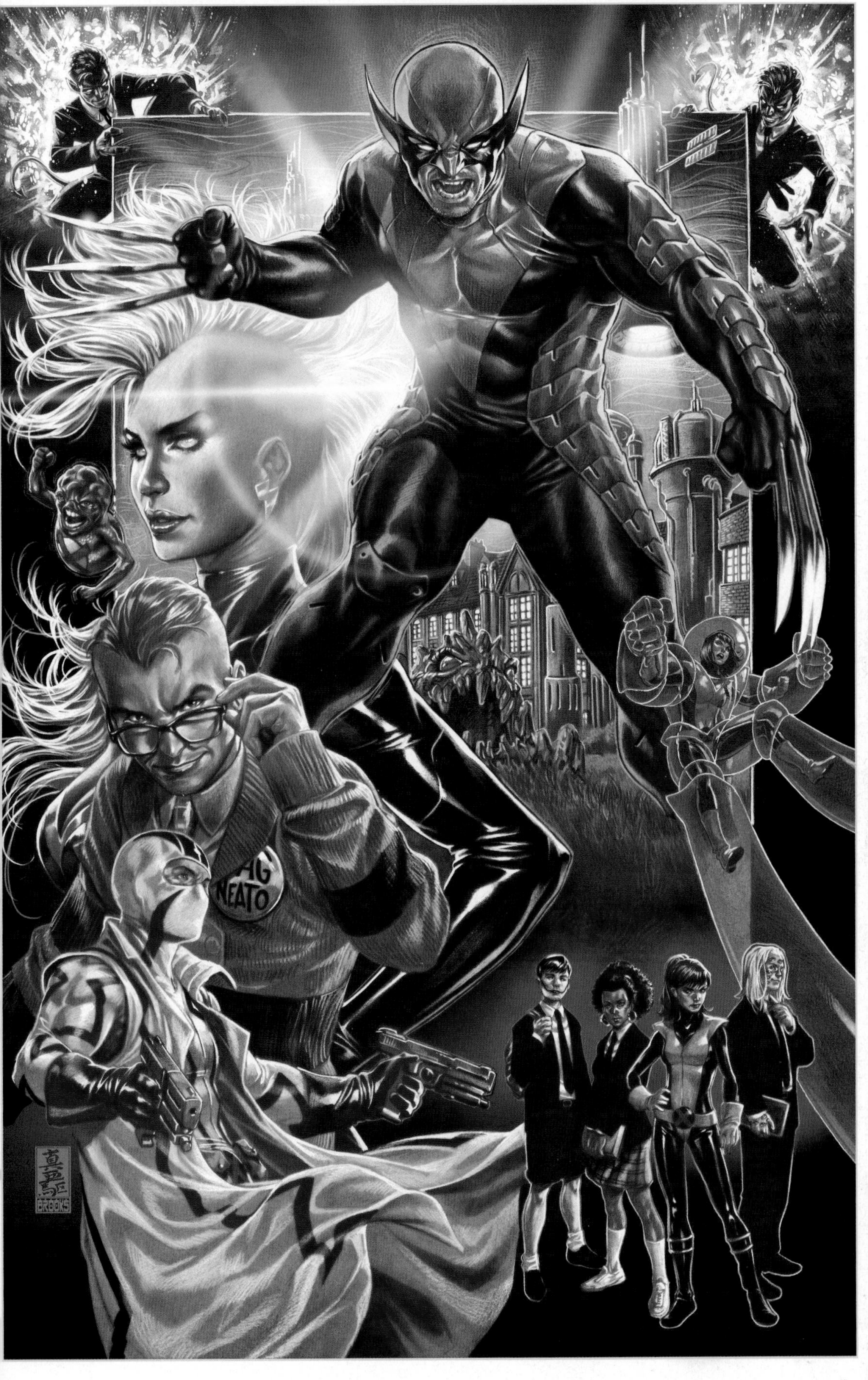
NEATO
BROOKS

#1 VARIANT BY MARK BROOKS

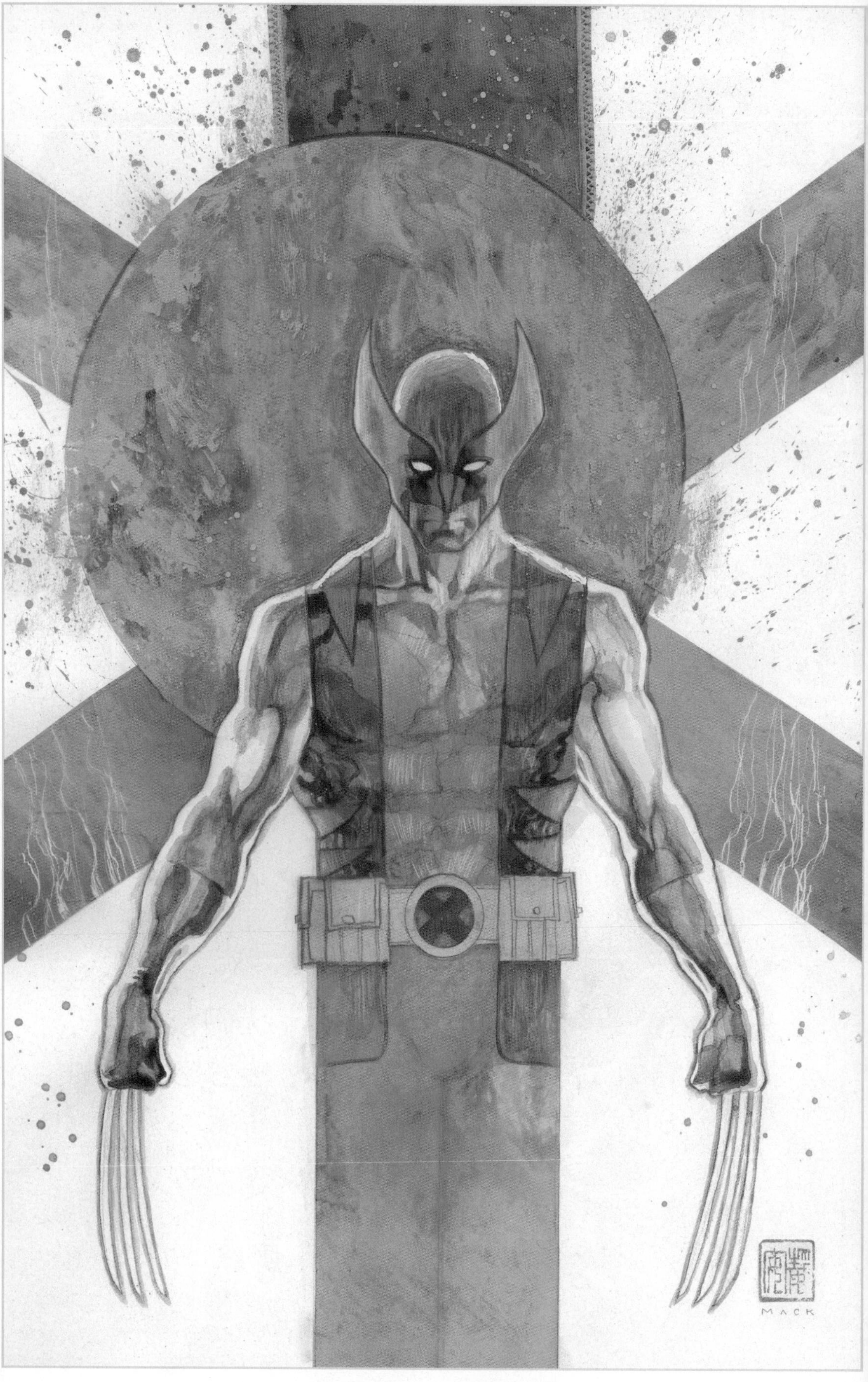
MACK

#1 VARIANT BY DAVID MACK

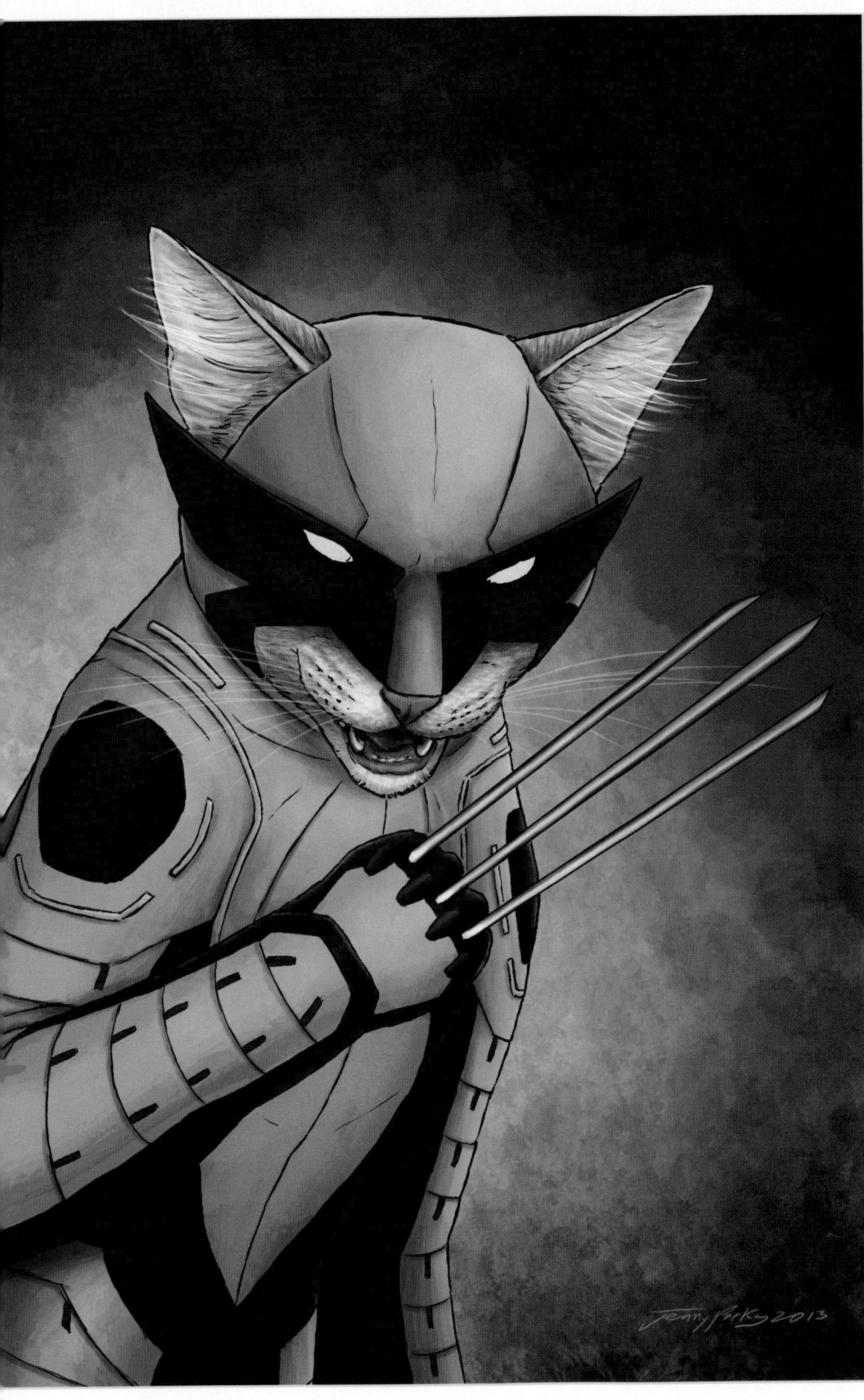
Jenny Parks 2013

#1 ANIMAL VARIANT BY JENNY PARKS

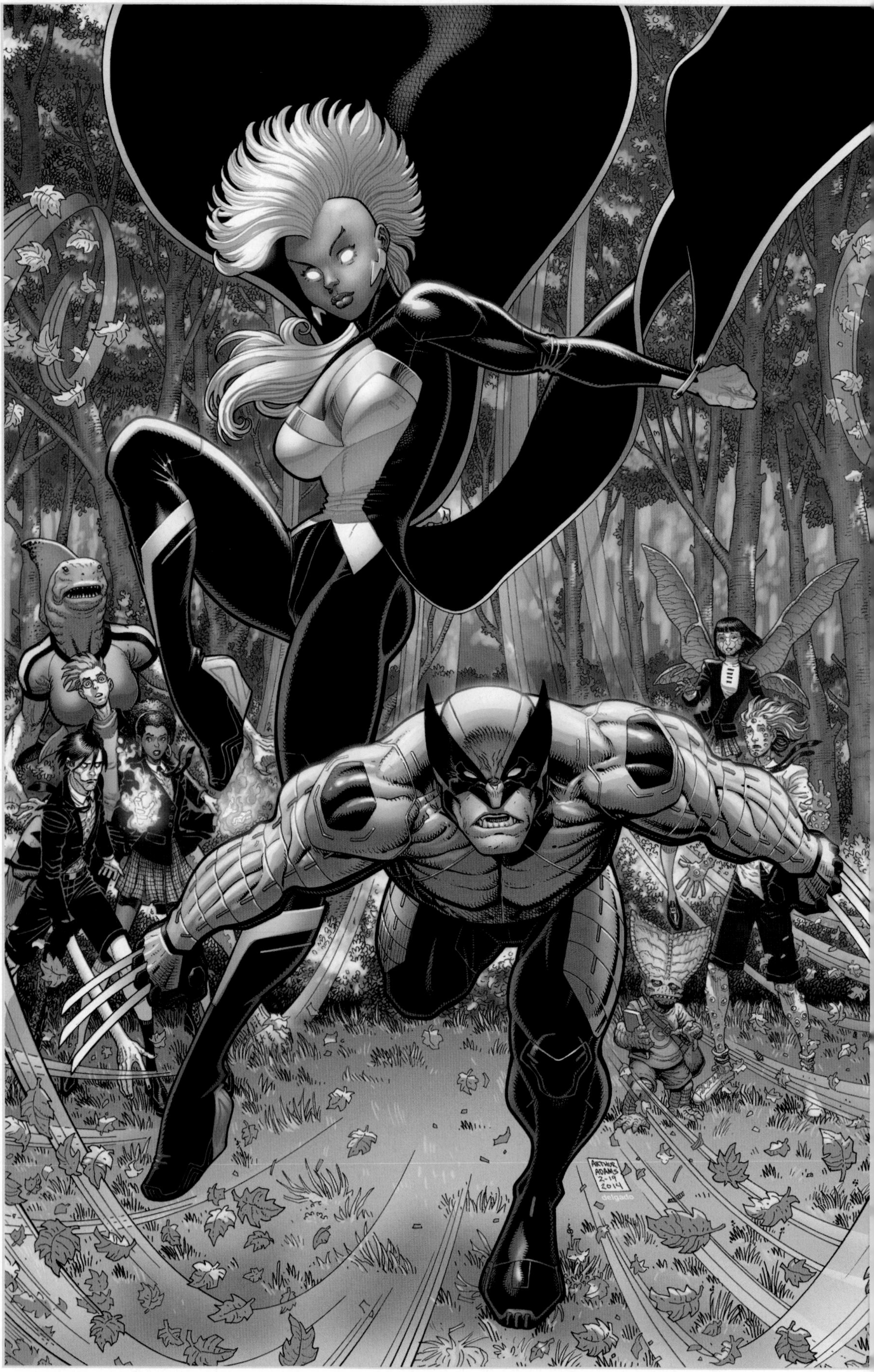
ARTHUR ADAMS 2-19 2014
delgado

#2 VARIANT BY ARTHUR ADAMS & EDGAR DELGADO

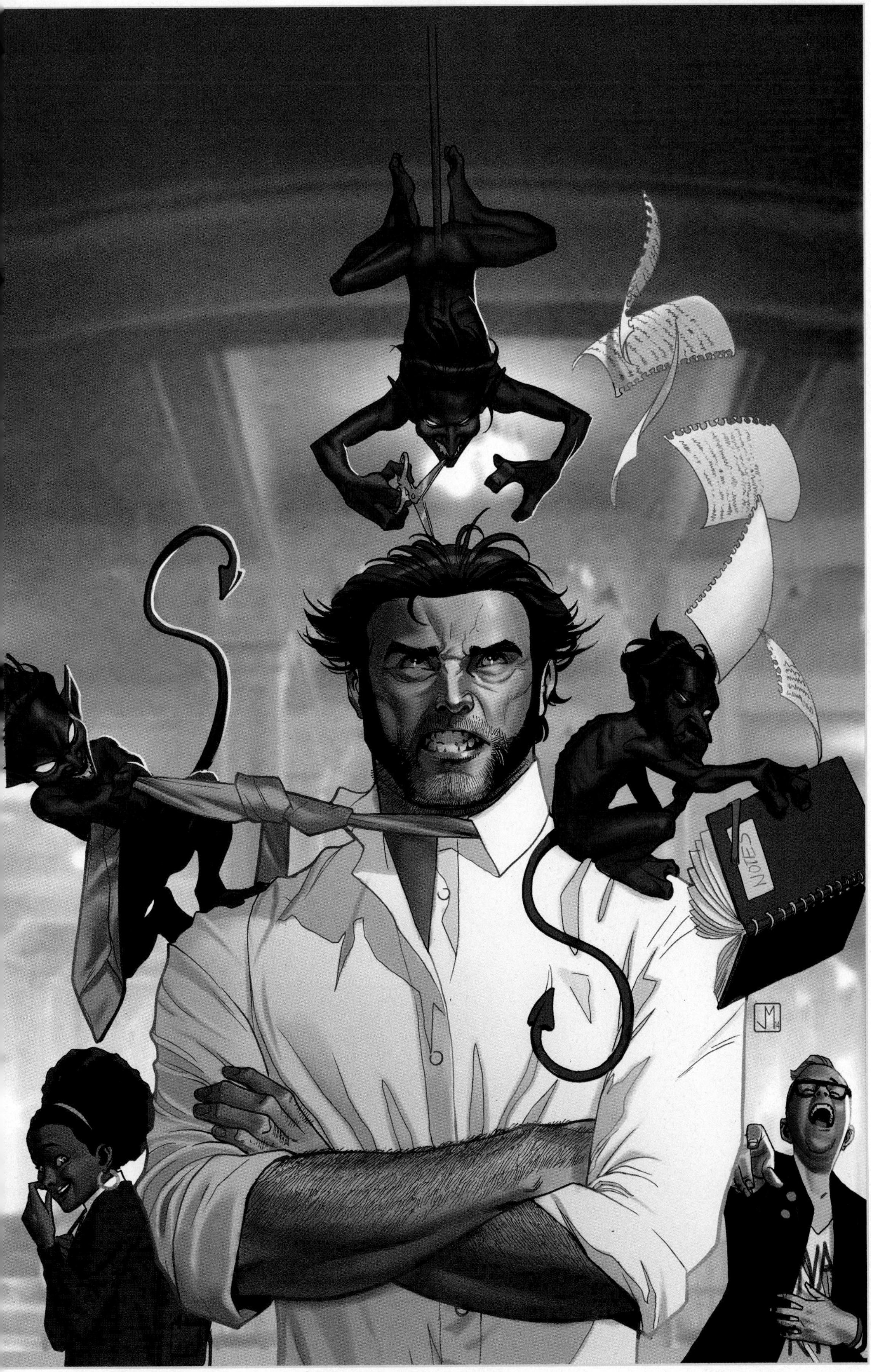
NOTES

#3 VARIANT BY JORGE MOLINA

PREVIEW OF THINGS TO COME

BY JASON LATOUR

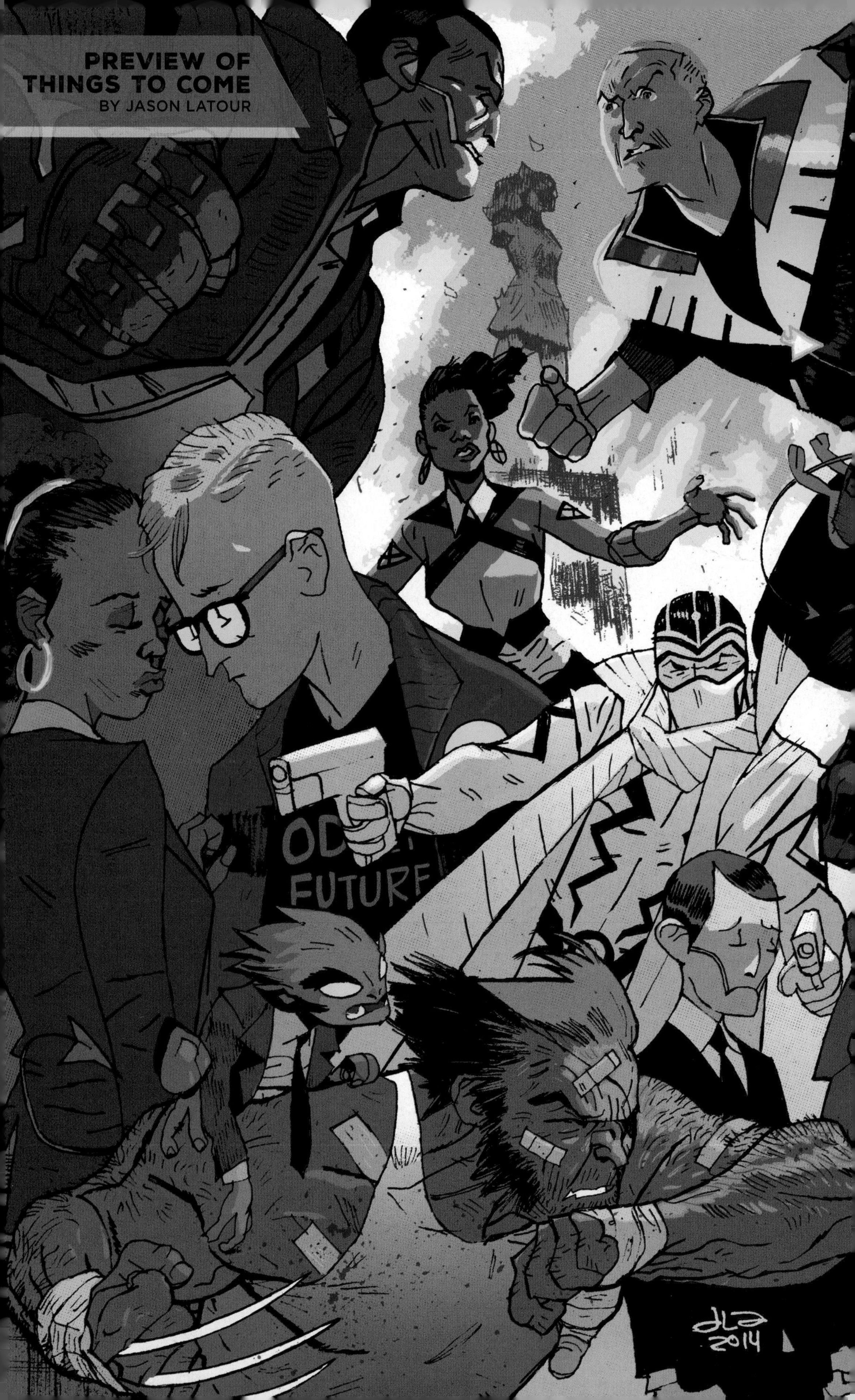
FUTURE
2014

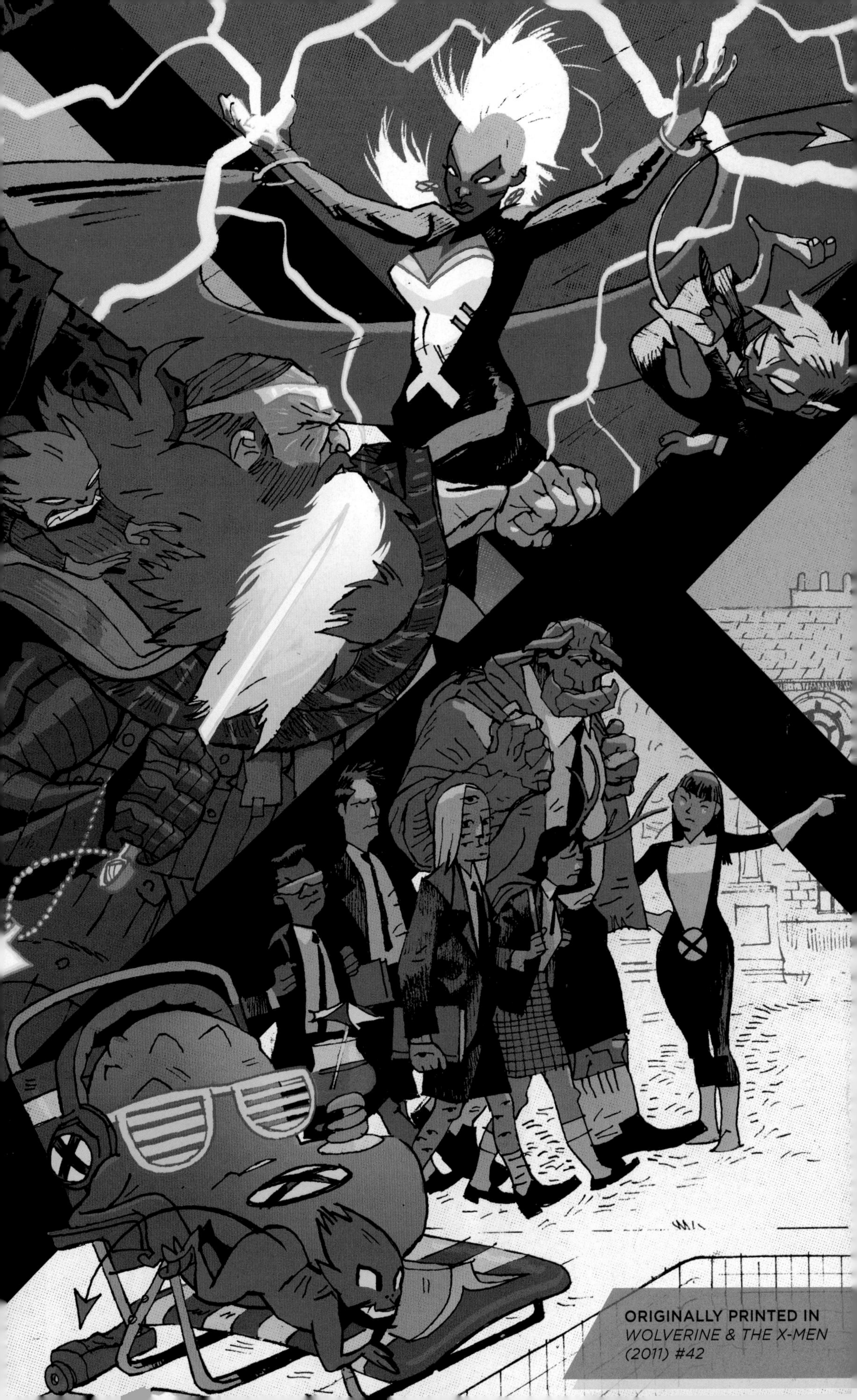

ORIGINALLY PRINTED IN
WOLVERINE & THE X-MEN
(2011) #42

CHARACTER DESIGNS
BY JASON LATOUR

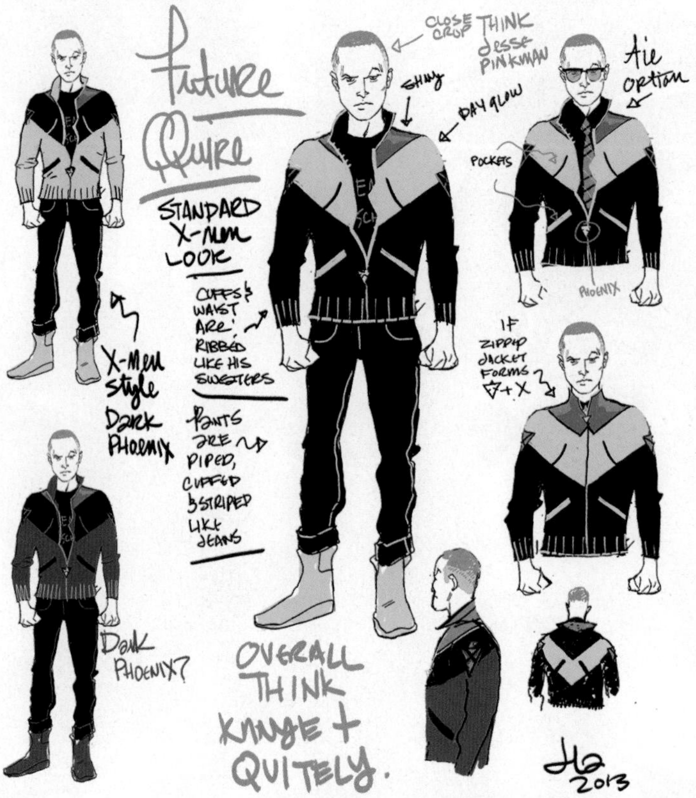

Future Quire
CLOSE CROP
THINK Jesse PINKMAN
SHINY
DAY GLOW
Tie option
POCKETS
PHOENIX
STANDARD X-MEN LOOK
CUFFS & WAIST ARE RIBBED LIKE HIS SWEATERS
X-Men style Dark PHOENIX
PANTS ARE PIPED, CUFFED & STRIPED LIKE JEANS
IF ZIPPED JACKET FORMS ▽+X
Dark PHOENIX?
OVERALL THINK
QUITELY.
JLA 2013

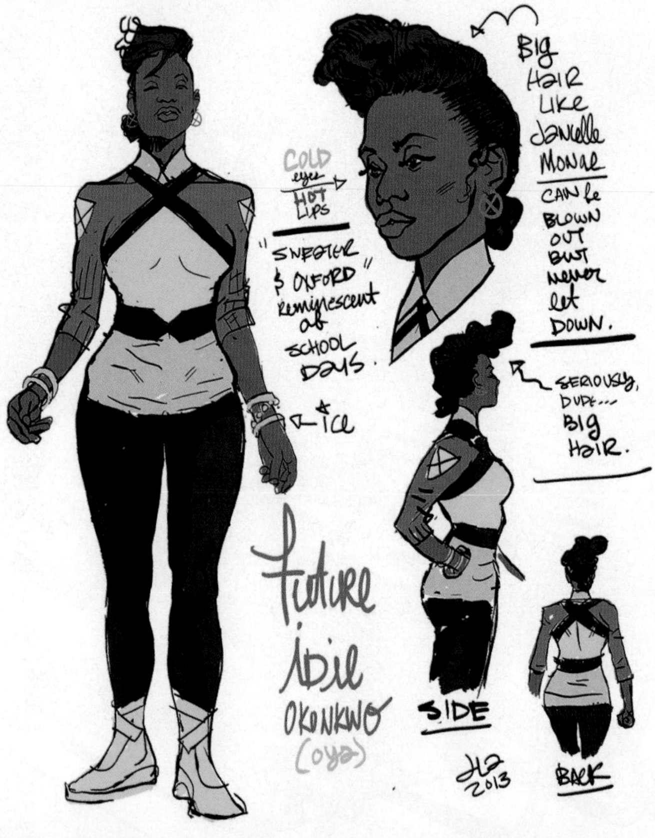

Big Hair Like Janelle Monae
CAN be BLOWN OUT BUT never let DOWN.
COLD eyes
HOT LIPS
"SWEATER & OXFORD" reminiscent of SCHOOL Days.
ICE
SERIOUSLY, DUDE--- BIG Hair.
Future Idie OKONKWO
(oya)
SIDE
BACK
JLA 2013

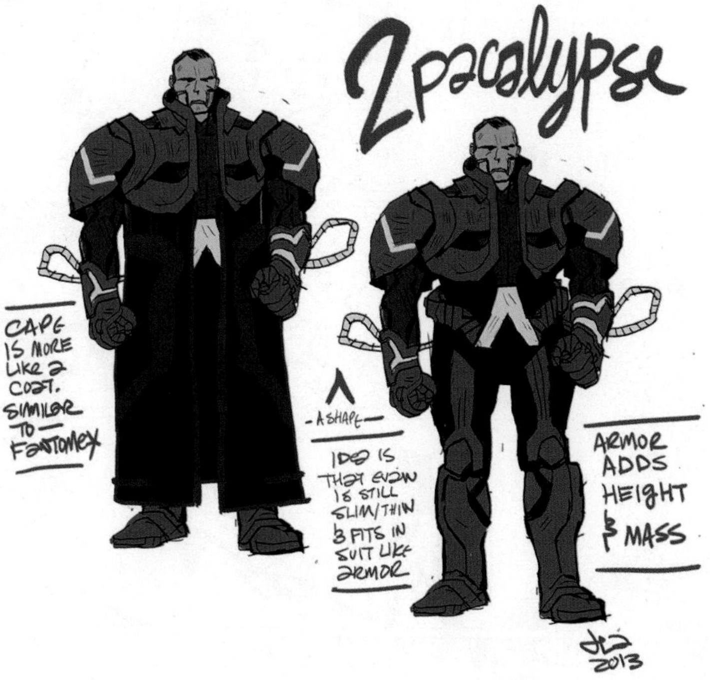
2pacalypse
CAPE IS MORE LIKE A COAT. SIMILAR TO FANTOMEX
A SHAPE
IDEA IS THAT EVAN IS STILL SLIM/THIN & FITS IN SUIT LIKE ARMOR
ARMOR ADDS HEIGHT & MASS
JLA 2013

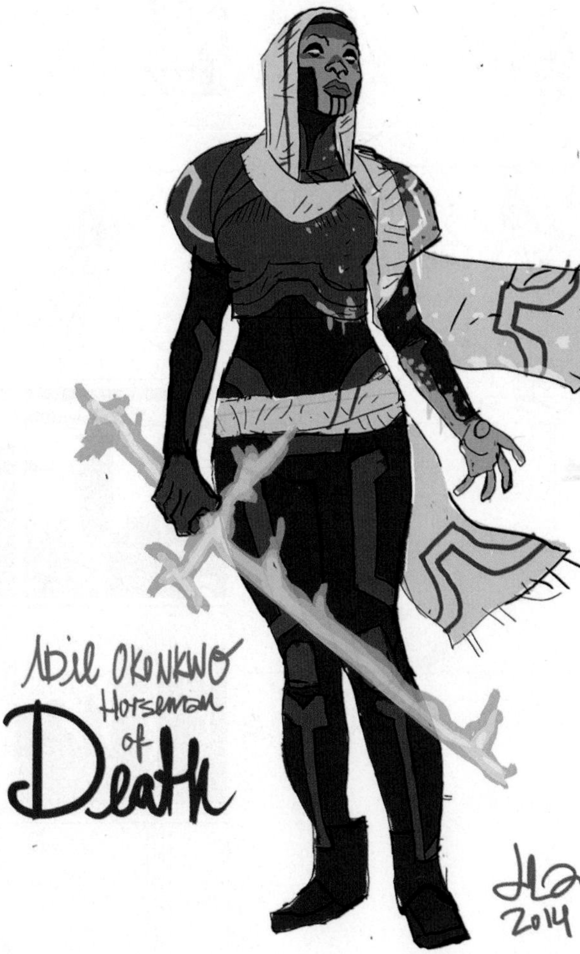
ADIL OKONKWO
Horseman of Death
JLA 2014

LAYOUTS & INKS
BY MAHMUD ASRAR

#2, PAGE 1

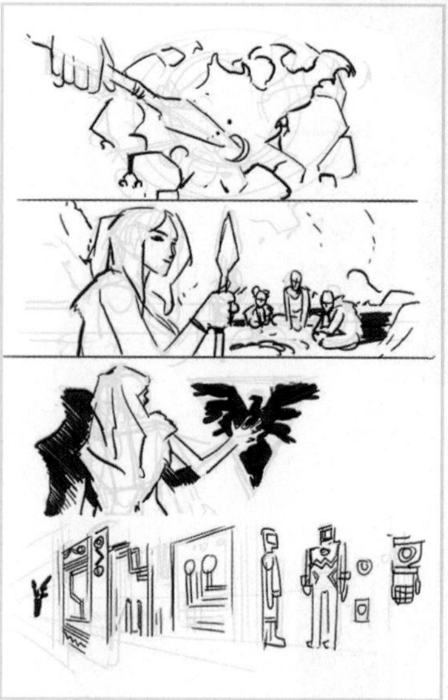

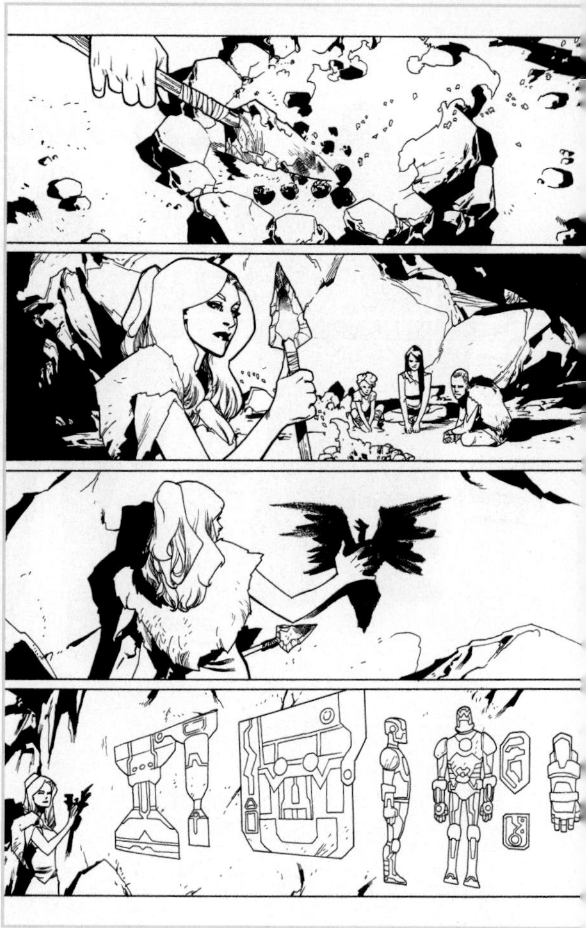

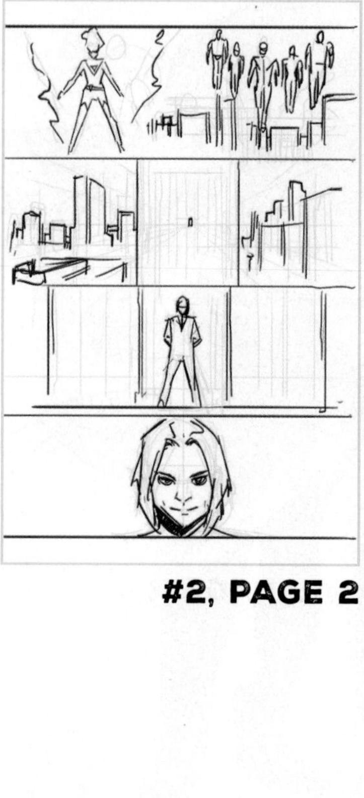

#2, PAGE 2

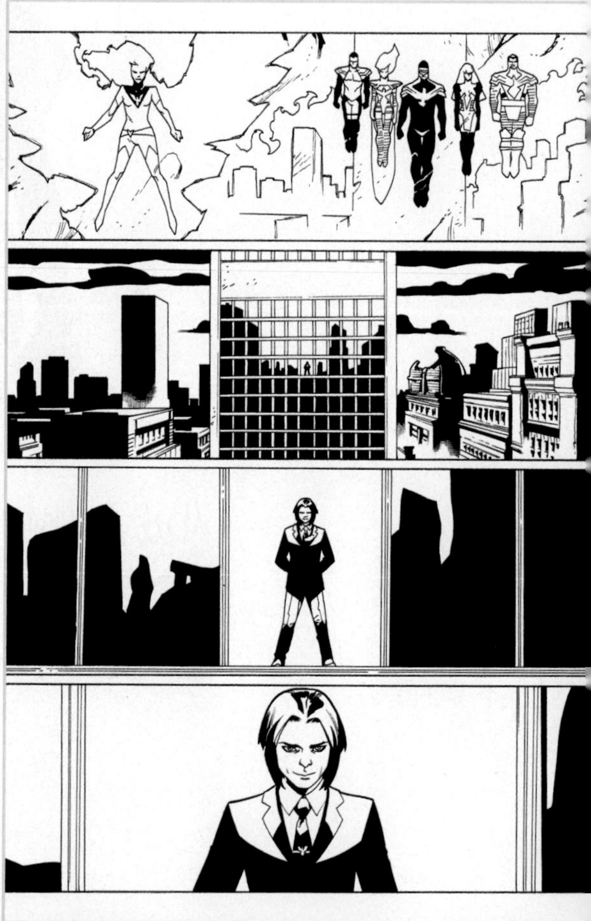

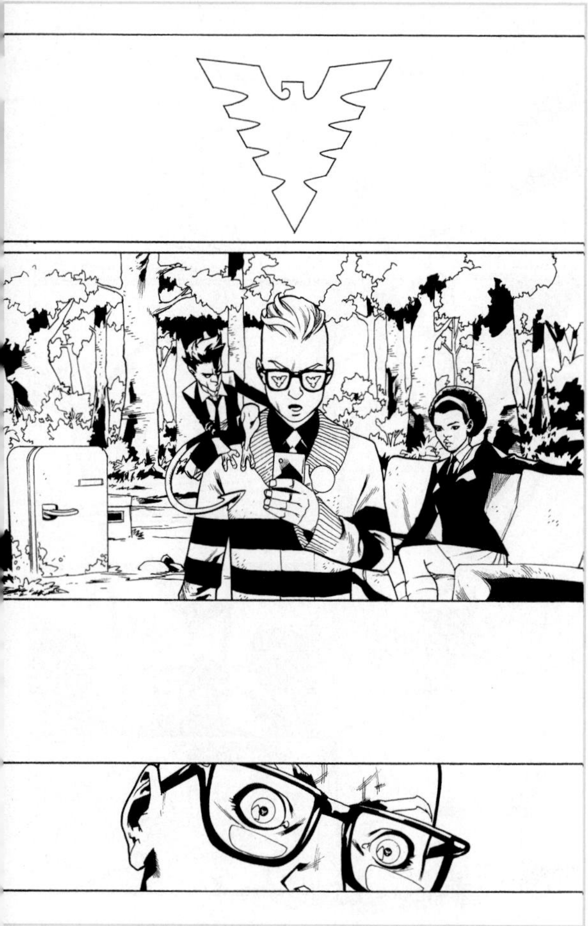

#2, PAGE 3

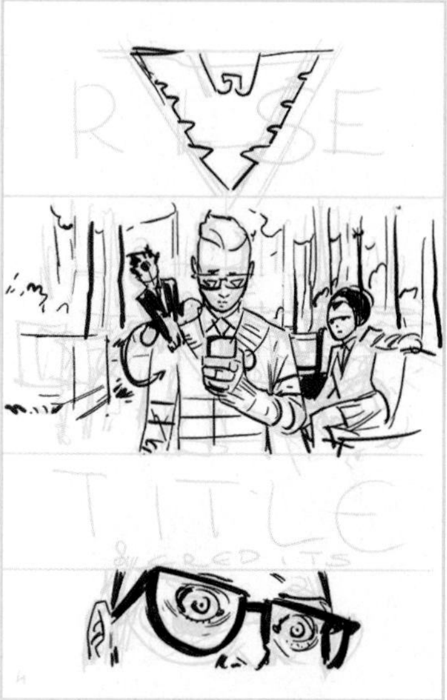

TITLE
& CREDITS

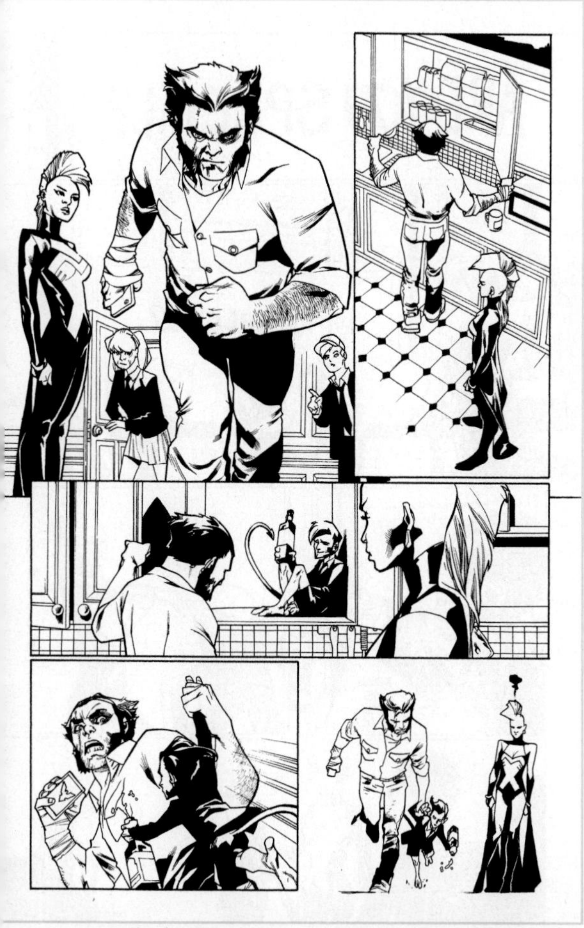

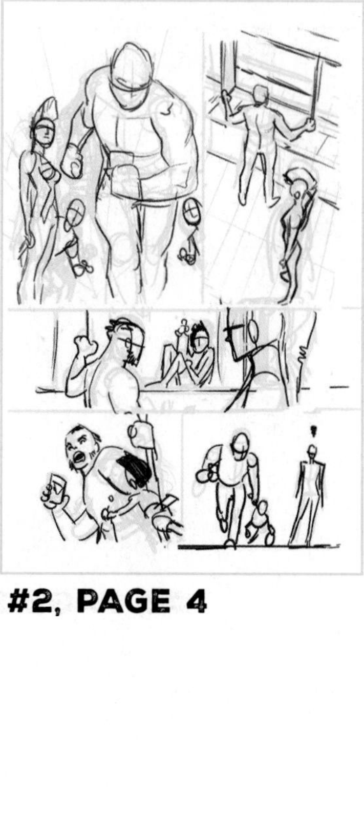

#2, PAGE 4

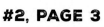

LAYOUTS & INKS
BY MAHMUD ASRAR

#2, PAGE 5

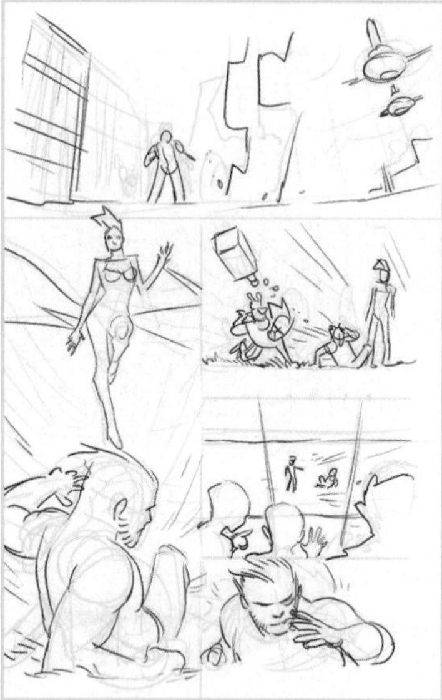

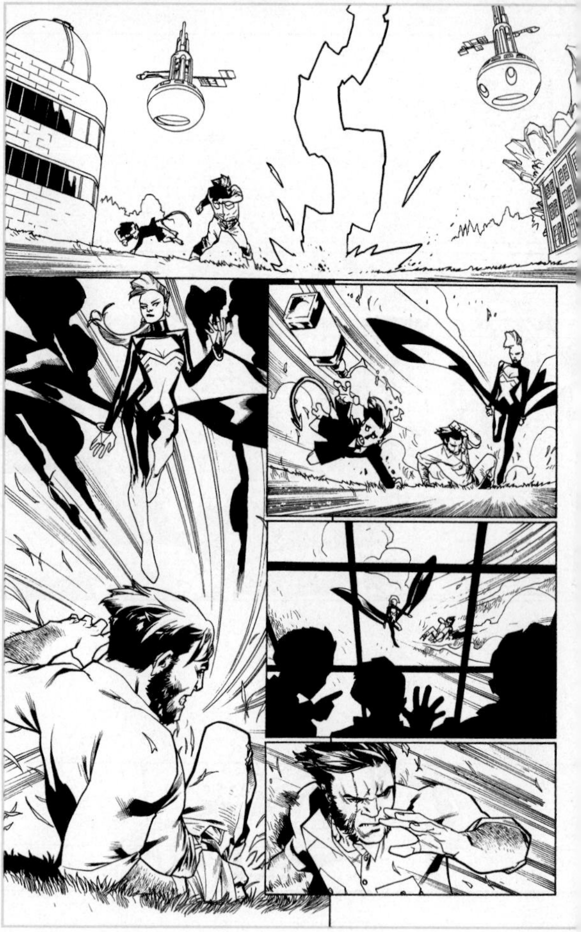

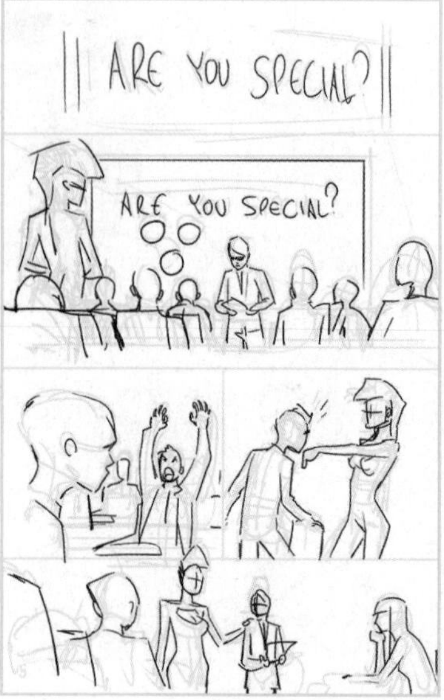
ARE YOU SPECIAL?
ARE YOU SPECIAL?

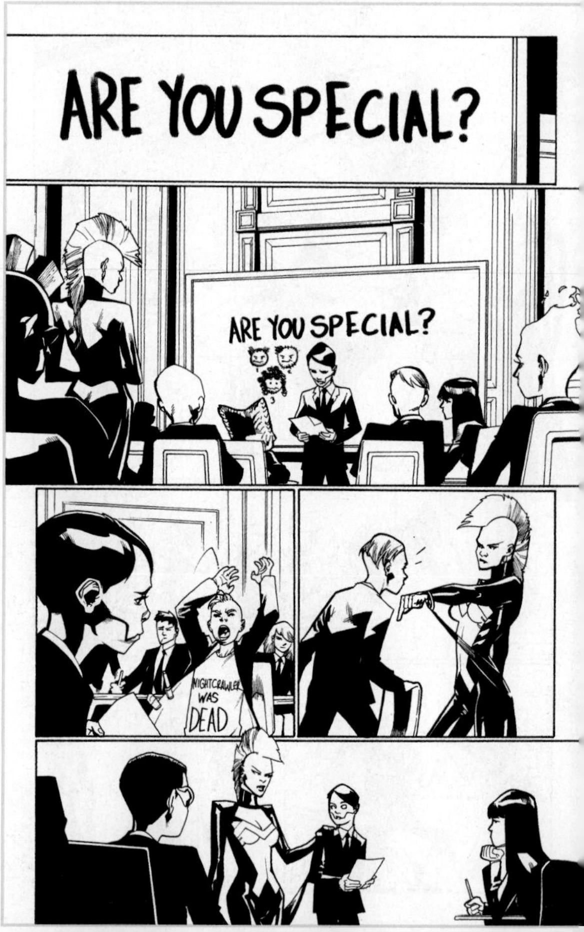
ARE YOU SPECIAL?
ARE YOU SPECIAL?
NIGHTCRAWLER WAS DEAD

#3, PAGE 1

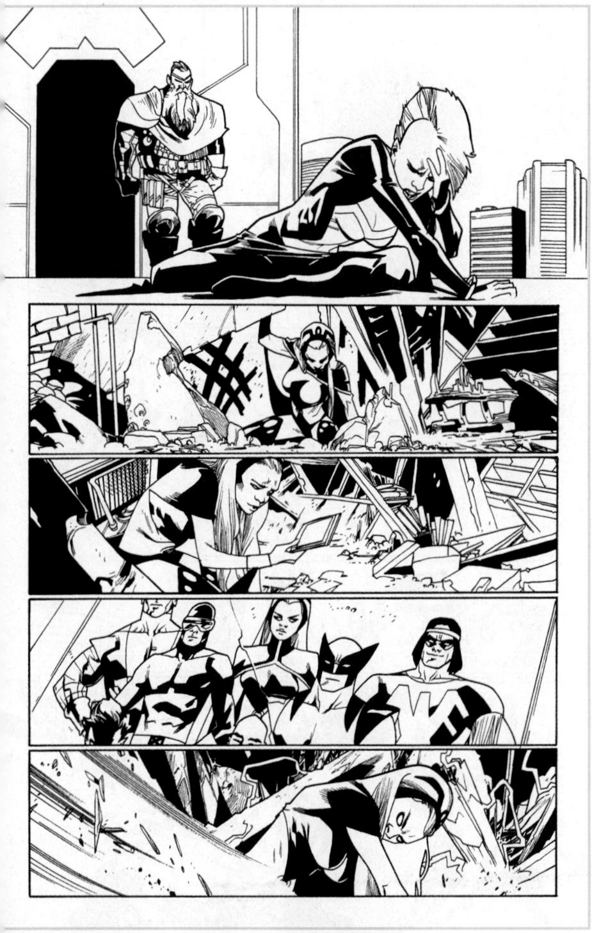

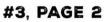

#3, PAGE 2

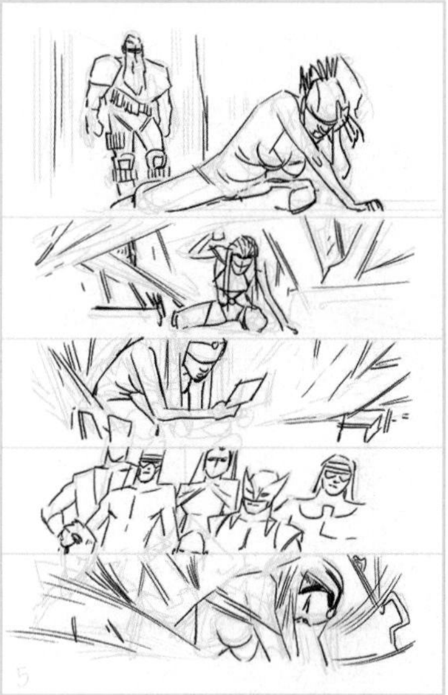

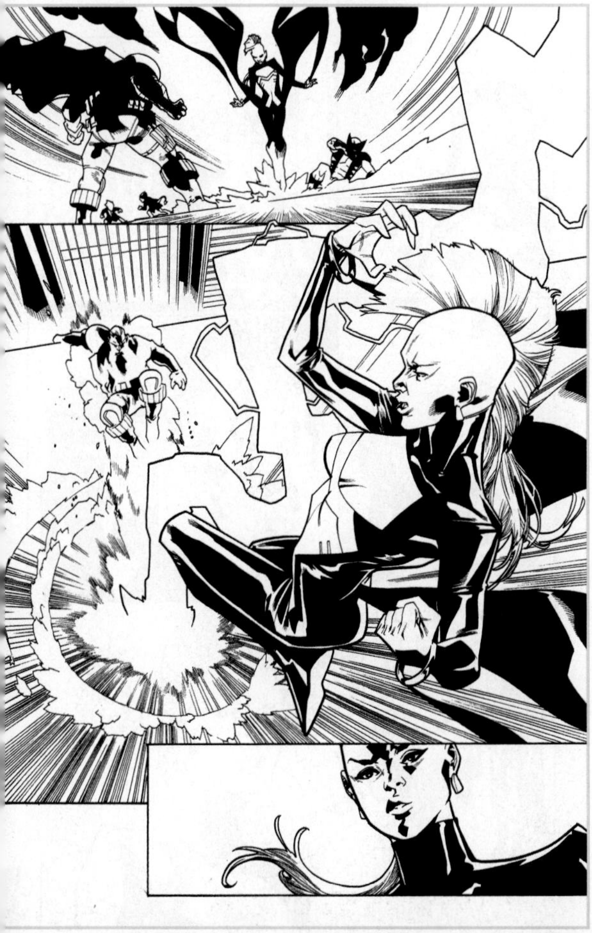

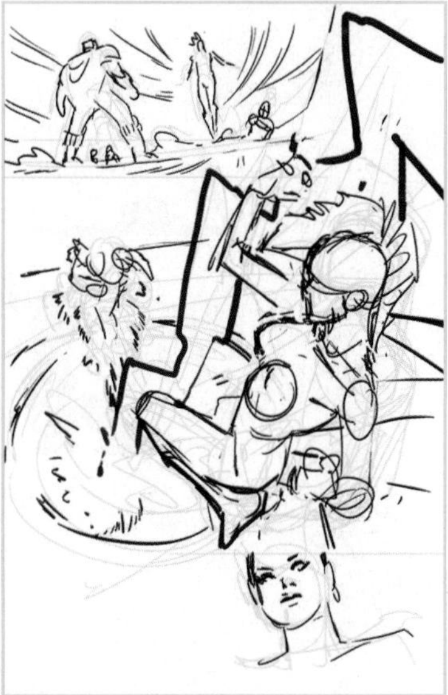

#3, PAGE 3

LAYOUTS & INKS

BY MAHMUD ASRAR

#3, PAGE 4

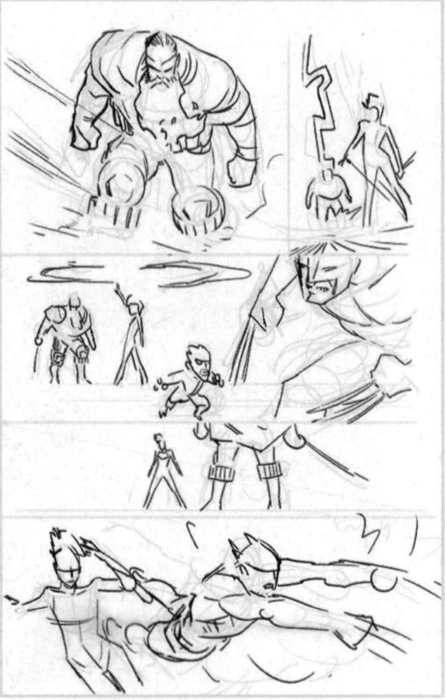

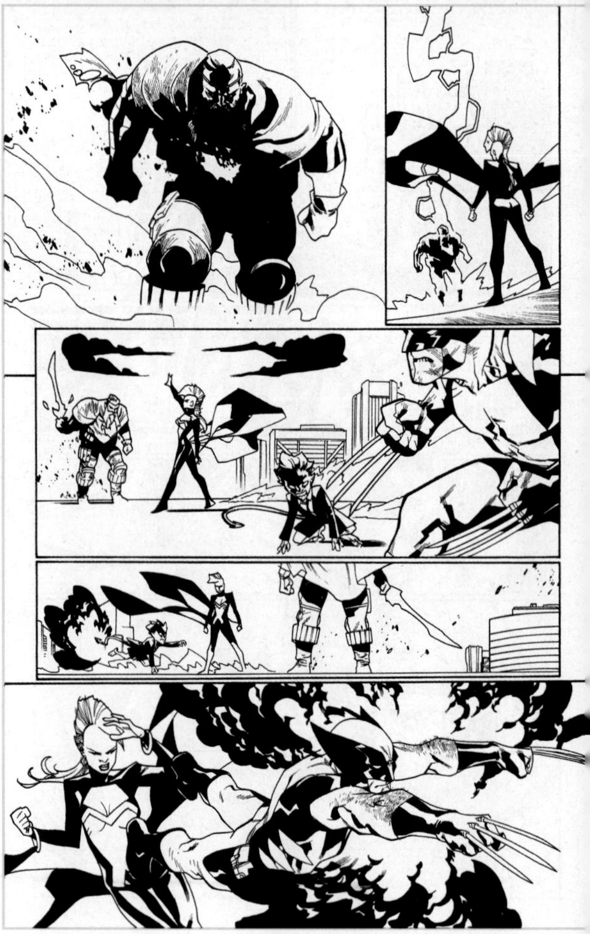

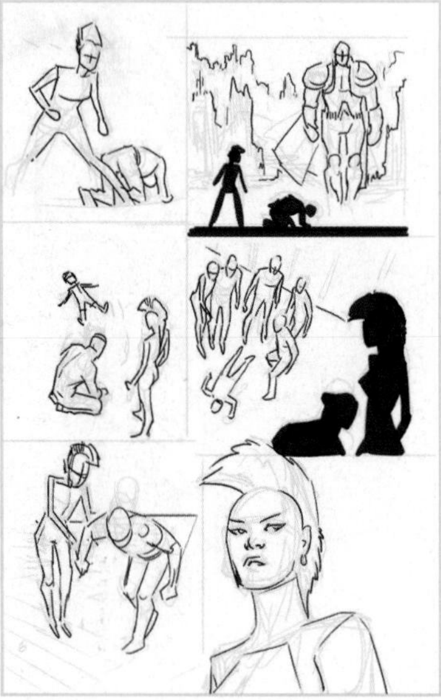

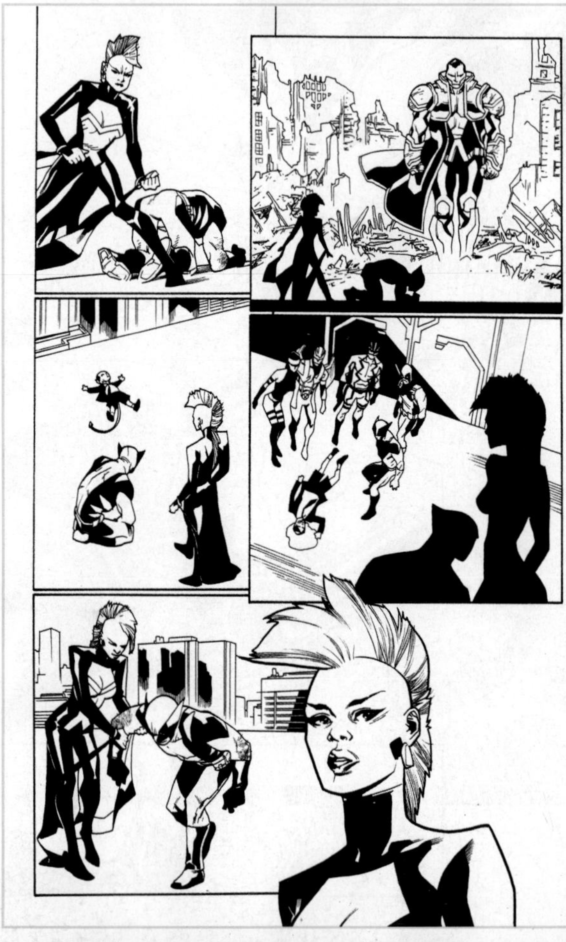

#3, PAGE 5